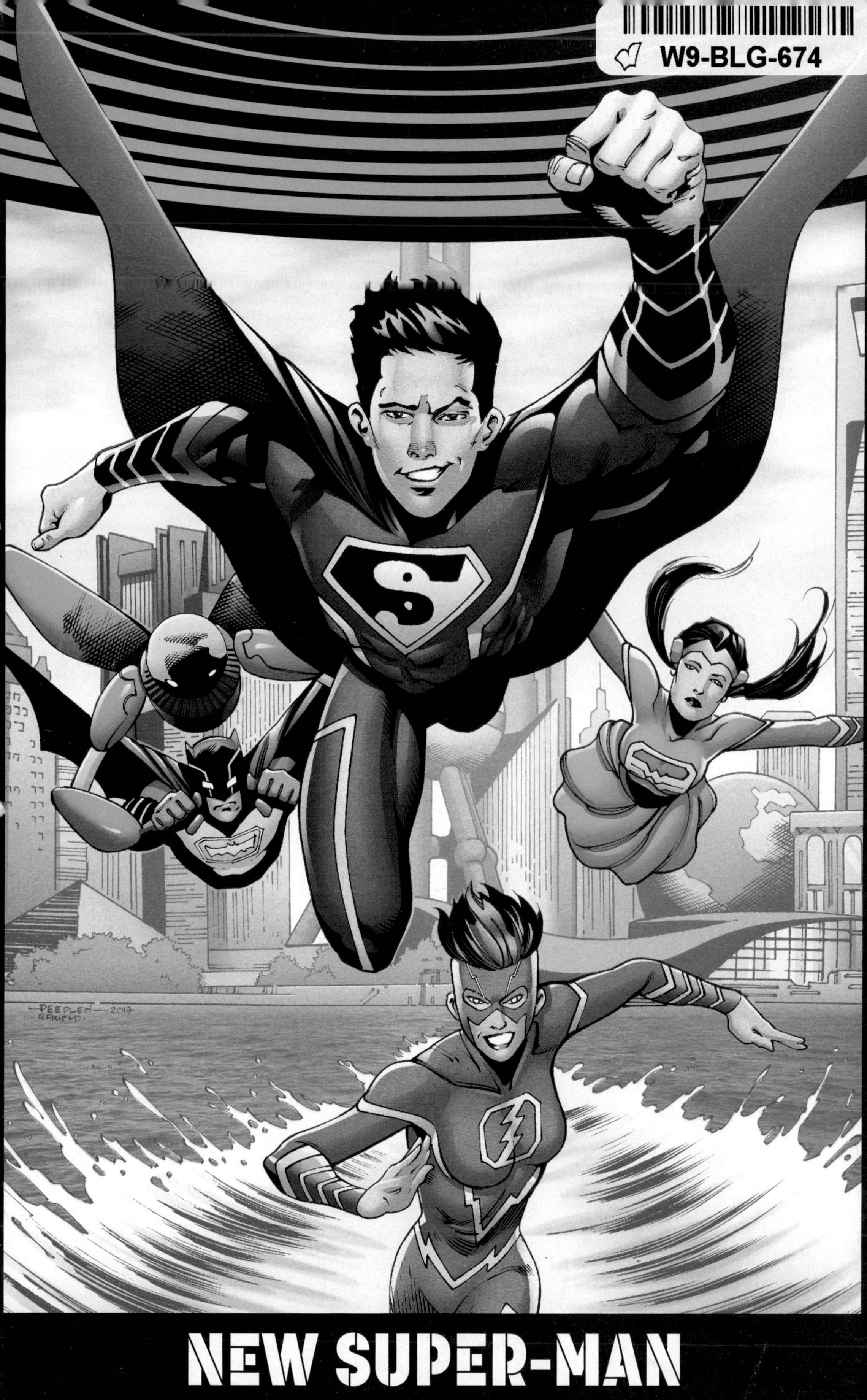

NEW SUPER-MAN

VOL.3 EQUILIBRIUM

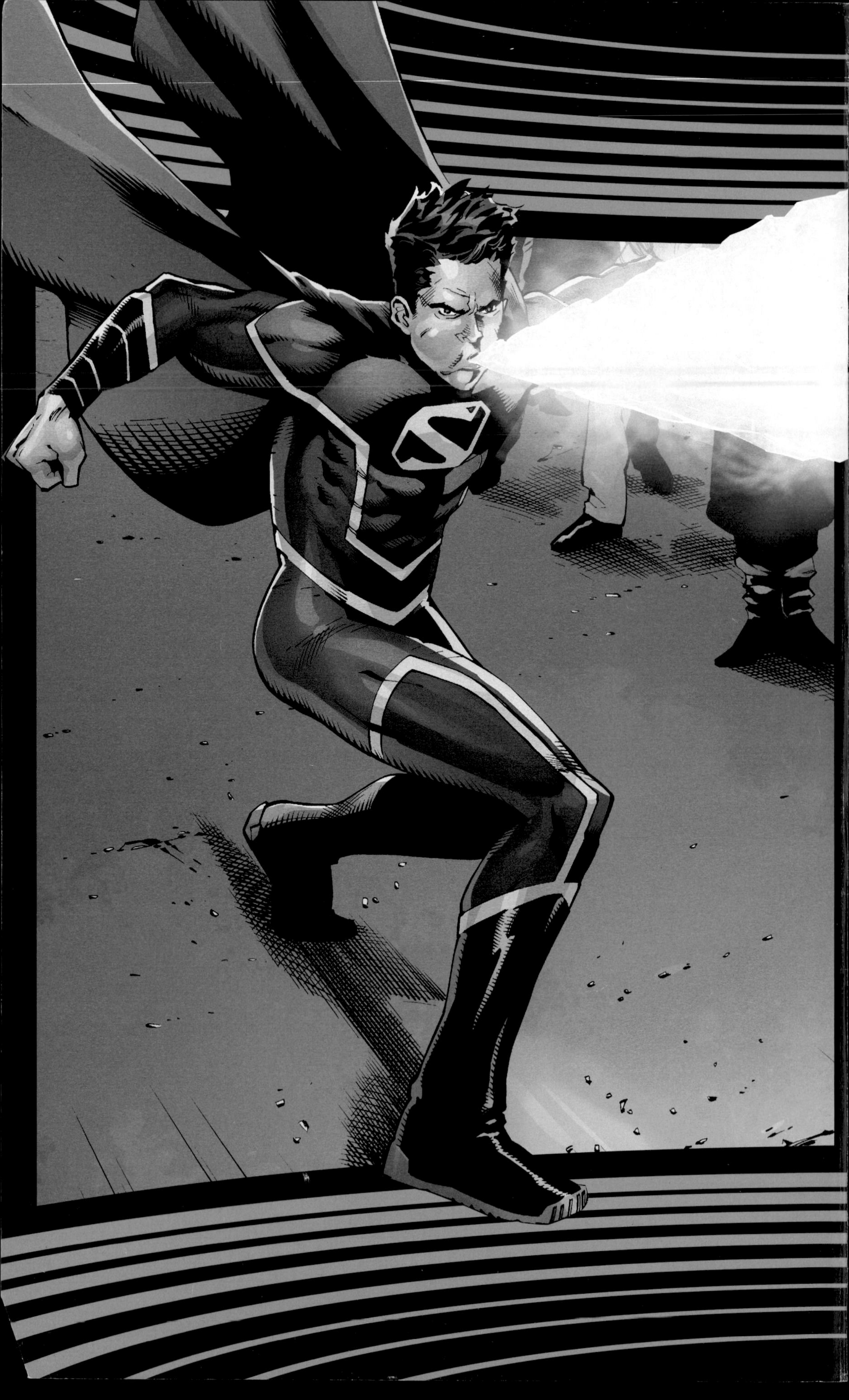

NEW SUPER-MAN
VOL.3 EQUILIBRIUM

GENE LUEN YANG
MARIKO TAMAKI
writers

BRENT PEEPLES
BILLY TAN
JOE LALICH
pencillers

RICHARD FRIEND
HAINING
KARO
SCOTT HANNA
inkers

HI-FI
GADSON
colorists

DAVE SHARPE
TOM NAPOLITANO
letterers

BERNARD CHANG
collection cover artist

SUPERMAN created by **JERRY SIEGEL** and **JOE SHUSTER**
By special arrangement with the Jerry Siegel family

PAUL KAMINSKI Editor - Original Series ✳ JESSICA CHEN Associate Editor - Original Series
JEB WOODARD Group Editor - Collected Editions ✳ ALEX GALER Editor - Collected Edition
STEVE COOK Design Director - Books ✳ SHANNON STEWART Publication Design

BOB HARRAS Senior VP - Editor-in-Chief, DC Comics
PAT McCALLUM Executive Editor, DC Comics

DIANE NELSON President ✳ DAN DiDIO Publisher ✳ JIM LEE Publisher ✳ GEOFF JOHNS President & Chief Creative Officer
AMIT DESAI Executive VP - Business & Marketing Strategy, Direct to Consumer & Global Franchise Management
SAM ADES Senior VP & General Manager, Digital Services ✳ BOBBIE CHASE VP & Executive Editor, Young Reader & Talent Development
MARK CHIARELLO Senior VP - Art, Design & Collected Editions ✳ JOHN CUNNINGHAM Senior VP - Sales & Trade Marketing
ANNE DePIES Senior VP - Business Strategy, Finance & Administration ✳ DON FALLETTI VP - Manufacturing Operations
LAWRENCE GANEM VP - Editorial Administration & Talent Relations ✳ ALISON GILL Senior VP - Manufacturing & Operations
HANK KANALZ Senior VP - Editorial Strategy & Administration ✳ JAY KOGAN VP - Legal Affairs
JACK MAHAN VP - Business Affairs ✳ NICK J. NAPOLITANO VP - Manufacturing Administration ✳ EDDIE SCANNELL VP - Consumer Marketing
COURTNEY SIMMONS Senior VP - Publicity & Communications ✳ JIM (SKI) SOKOLOWSKI VP - Comic Book Specialty Sales & Trade Marketing
NANCY SPEARS VP - Mass, Book, Digital Sales & Trade Marketing ✳ MICHELE R. WELLS VP - Content Strategy

NEW SUPER-MAN VOL. 3: EQUILIBRIUM

DC Comics, 2900 West Alameda Ave., Burbank, CA 91505
Printed by LSC Communications, Kendallville, IN, USA. 5/11/18. First Printing.
ISBN: 978-1-4012-8044-4

Library of Congress Cataloging-in-Publication Data is available.

PEFC Certified

Printed on paper from
sustainably managed
forests, controlled
sources

PEFC/29-31-337   www.pefc.org

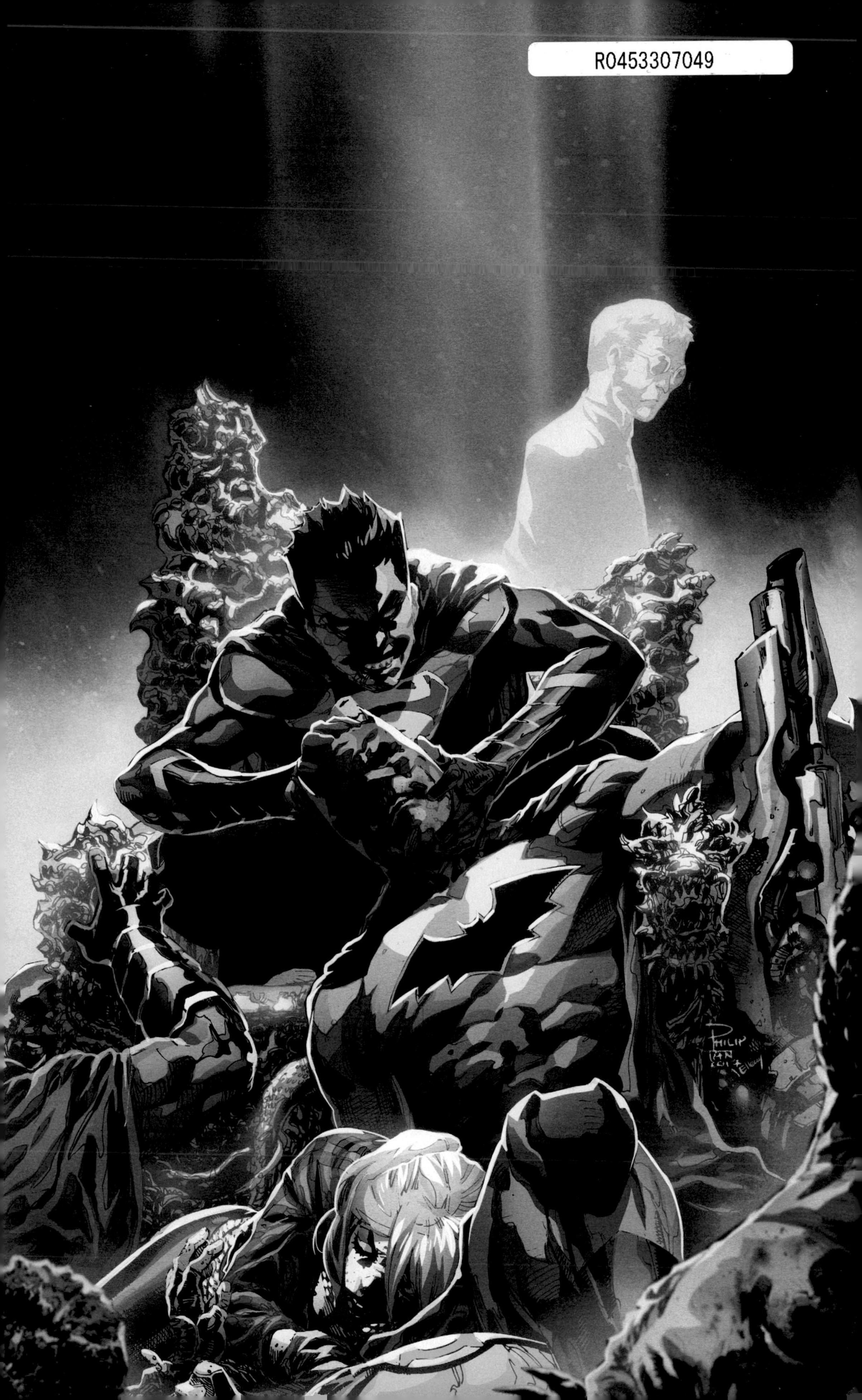

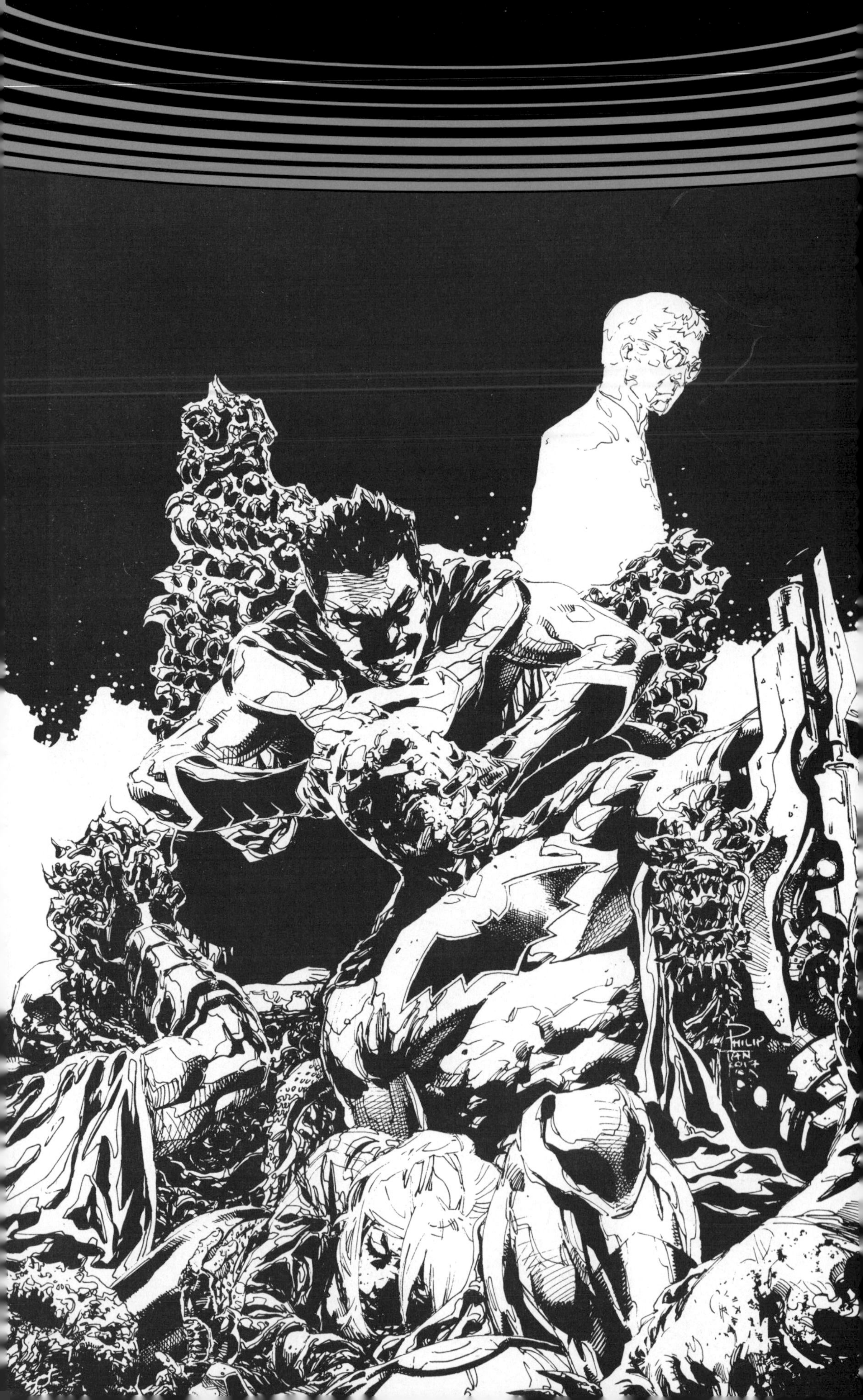
PHILIP TAN 2017

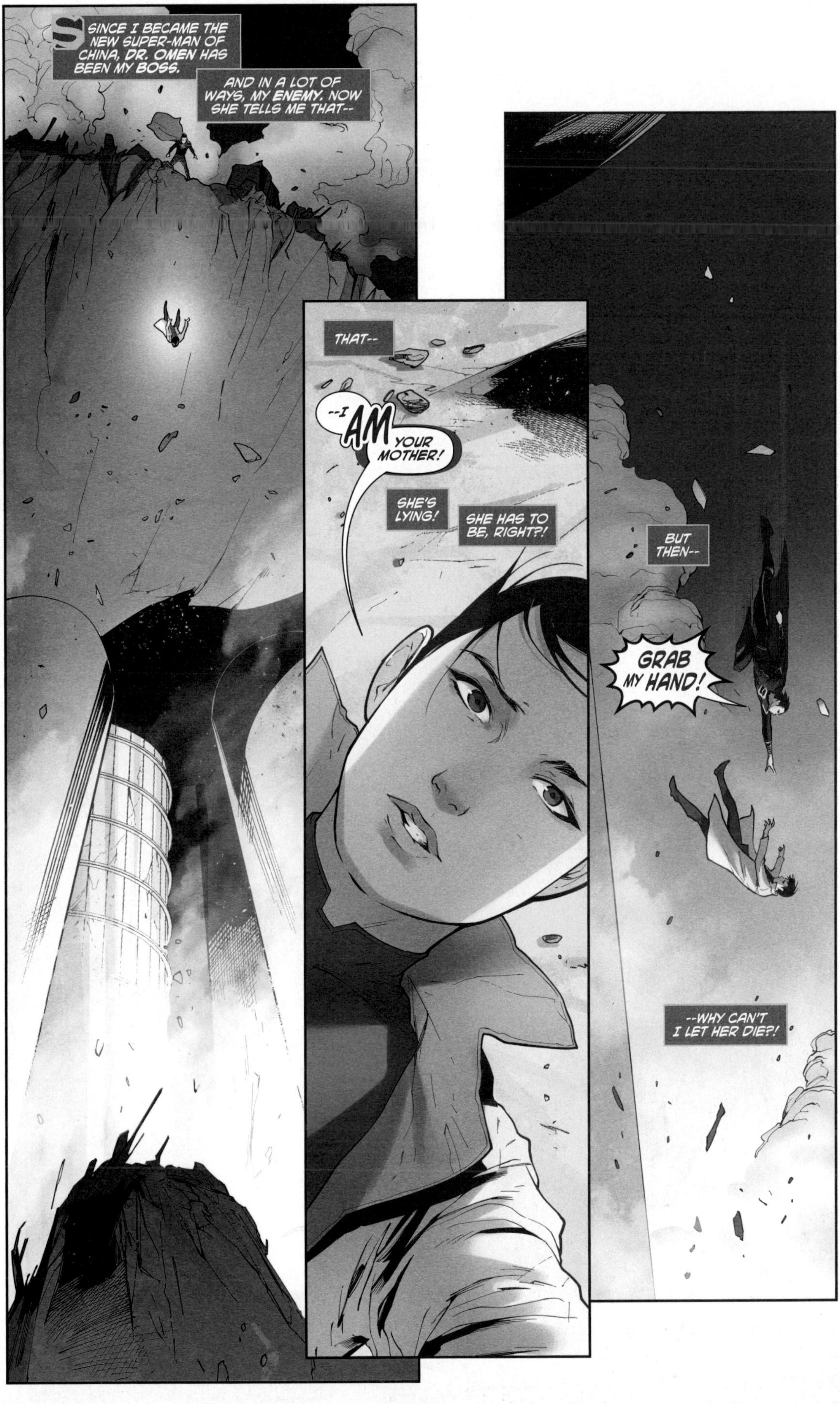
SINCE I BECAME THE NEW SUPER-MAN OF CHINA, DR. OMEN HAS BEEN MY BOSS.
AND IN A LOT OF WAYS, MY ENEMY. NOW SHE TELLS ME THAT--
THAT--
--I AM YOUR MOTHER!
SHE'S LYING!
SHE HAS TO BE, RIGHT?!
BUT THEN--
GRAB MY HAND!
--WHY CAN'T I LET HER DIE?!

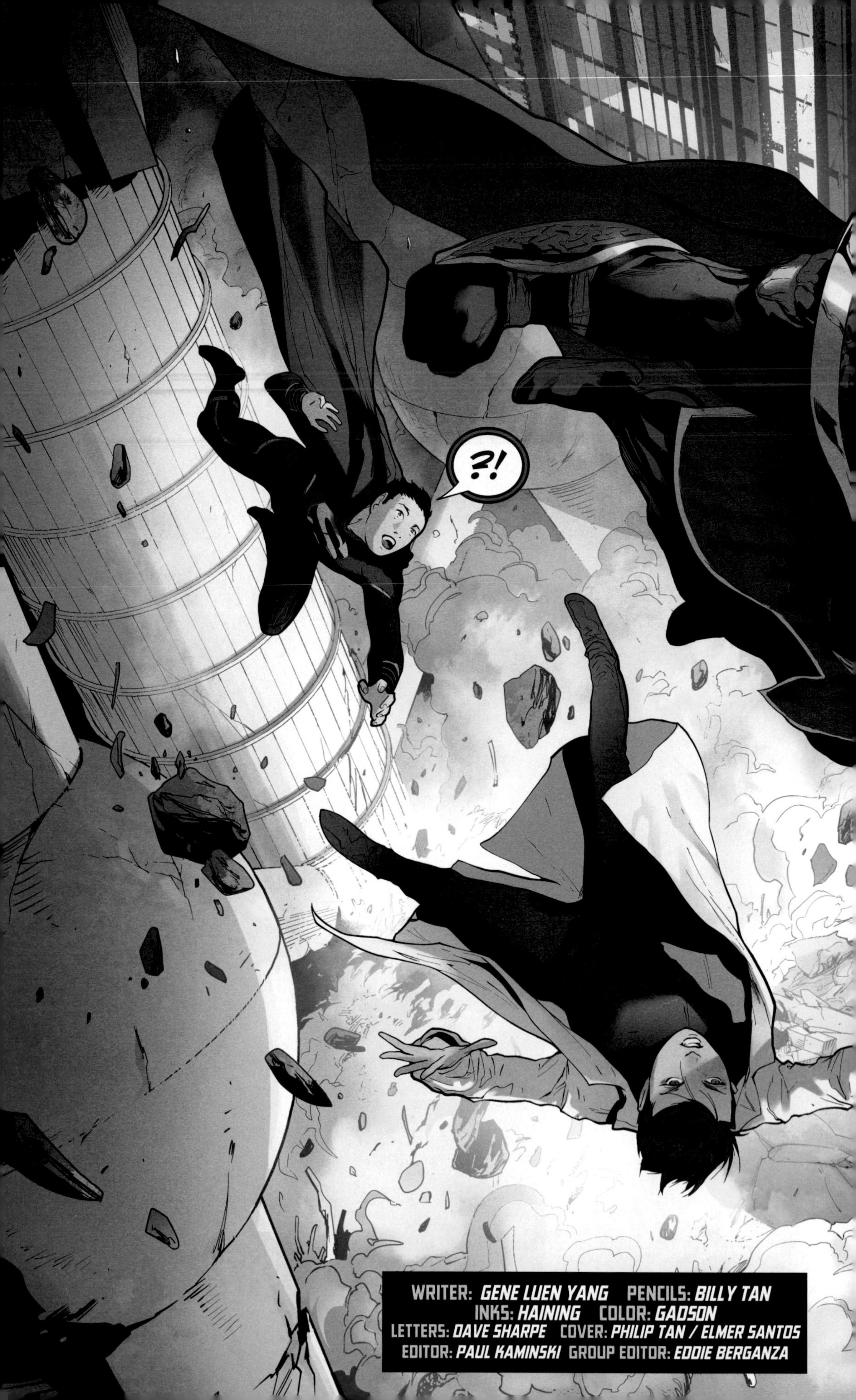
?!
WRITER: GENE LUEN YANG PENCILS: BILLY TAN
INKS: HAINING COLOR: GADSON
LETTERS: DAVE SHARPE COVER: PHILIP TAN / ELMER SANTOS
EDITOR: PAUL KAMINSKI GROUP EDITOR: EDDIE BERGANZA

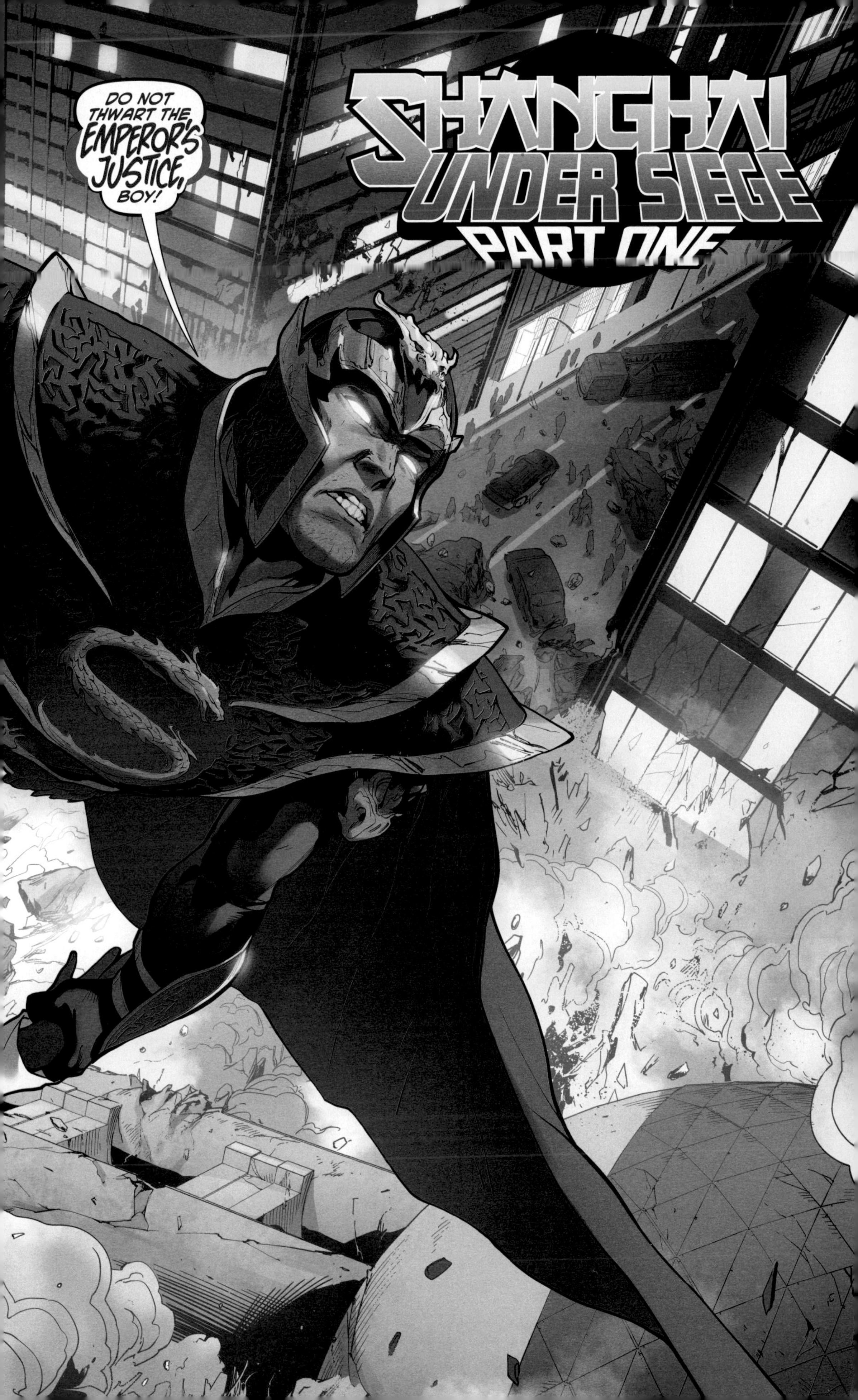
DO NOT THWART THE EMPEROR'S JUSTICE, BOY!
SHANGHAI UNDER SIEGE
PART ONE

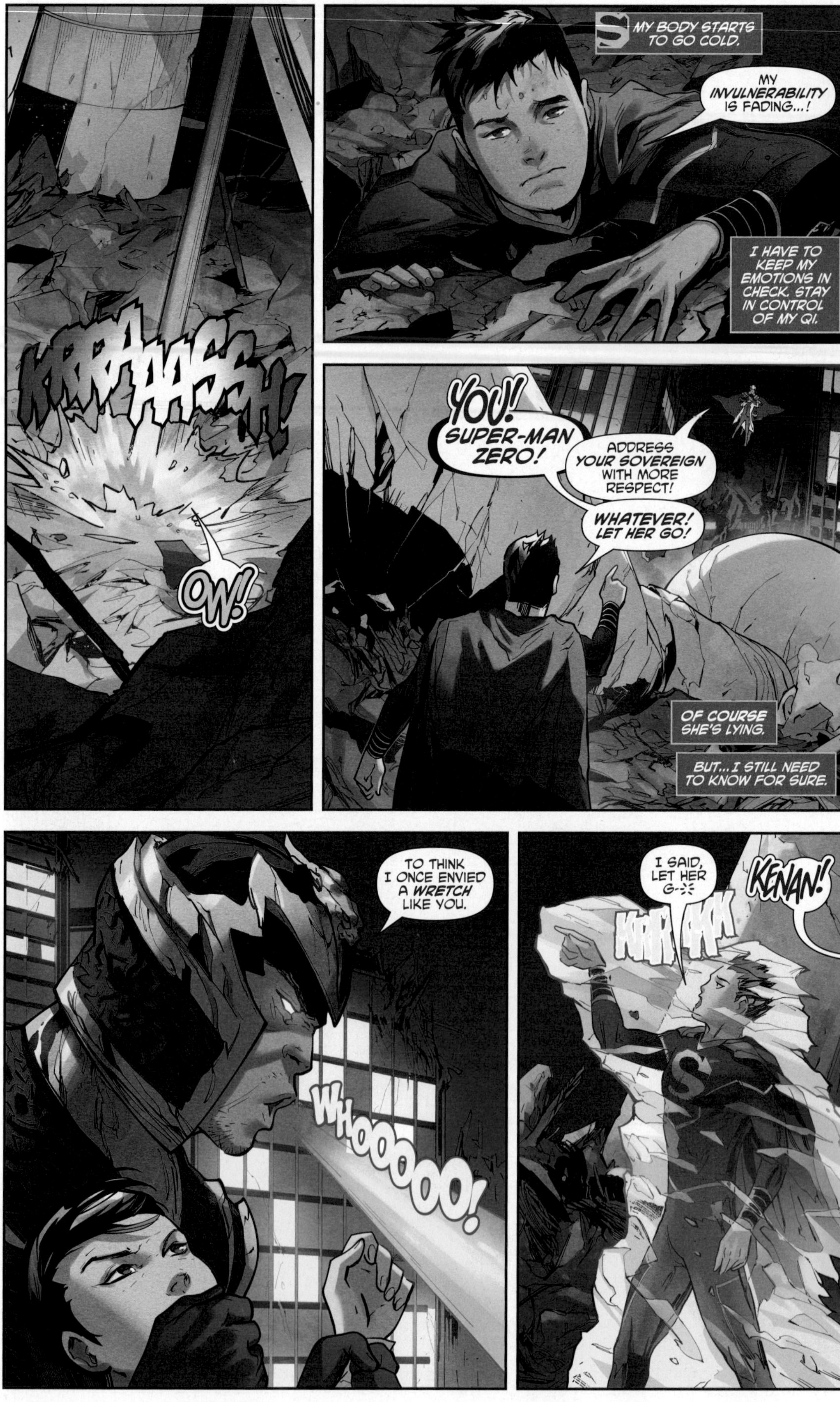

KRRAASSH!
OW!
MY BODY STARTS TO GO COLD.
MY INVULNERABILITY IS FADING...!
I HAVE TO KEEP MY EMOTIONS IN CHECK. STAY IN CONTROL OF MY QI.
YOU! SUPER-MAN ZERO!
ADDRESS YOUR SOVEREIGN WITH MORE RESPECT!
WHATEVER! LET HER GO!
OF COURSE SHE'S LYING.
BUT... I STILL NEED TO KNOW FOR SURE.
TO THINK I ONCE ENVIED A WRETCH LIKE YOU.
WHOOOOOO!
I SAID, LET HER G--
KENAN!

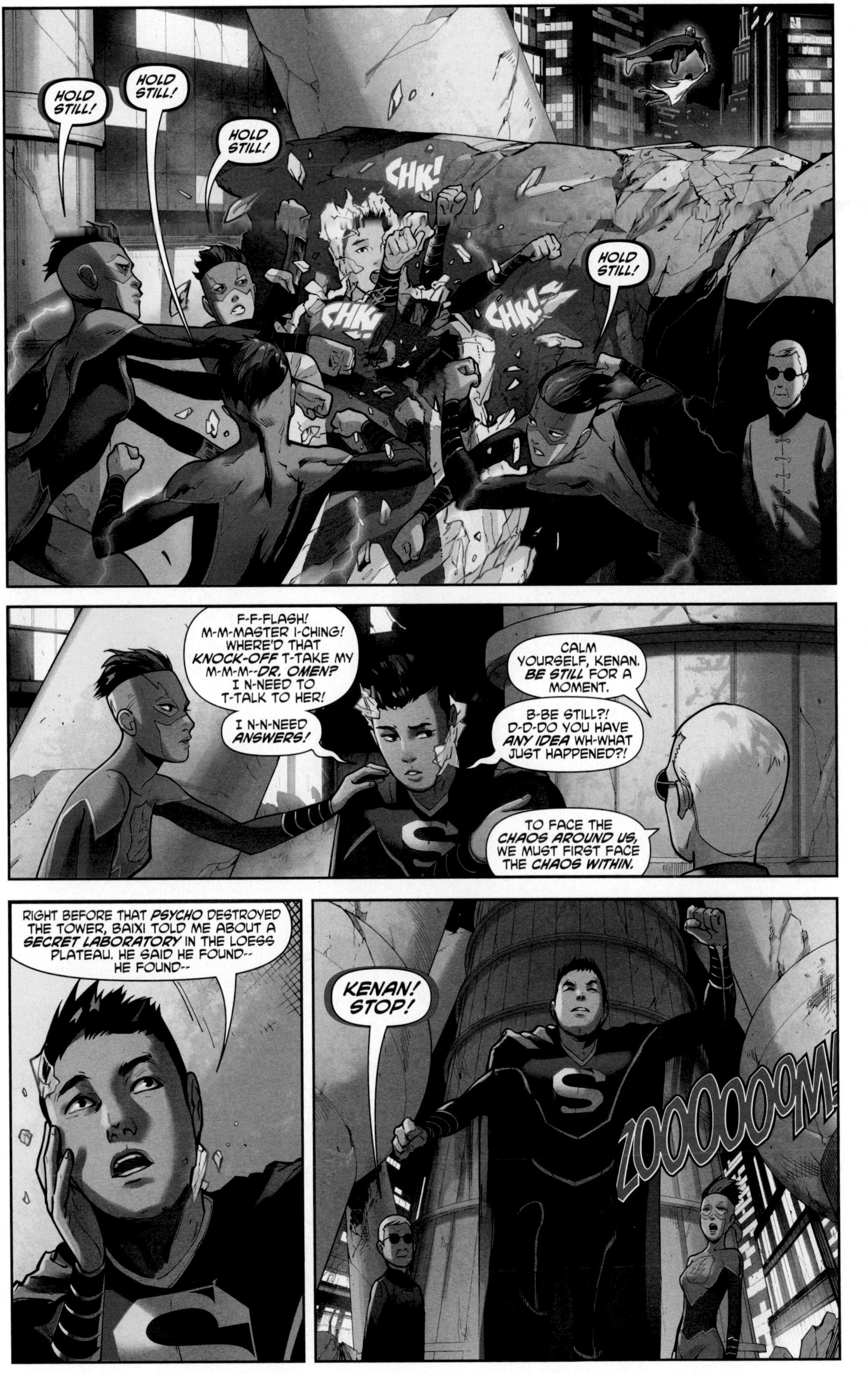
HOLD STILL!
HOLD STILL!
HOLD STILL!
CHK!
CHK!
CHK!
HOLD STILL!
F-F-FLASH! M-M-MASTER I-CHING! WHERE'D THAT KNOCK-OFF T-TAKE MY M-M-M--DR. OMEN? I N-NEED TO T-TALK TO HER!
I N-N-NEED ANSWERS!
CALM YOURSELF, KENAN. BE STILL FOR A MOMENT.
B-BE STILL?! D-D-DO YOU HAVE ANY IDEA WH-WHAT JUST HAPPENED?!
TO FACE THE CHAOS AROUND US, WE MUST FIRST FACE THE CHAOS WITHIN.
RIGHT BEFORE THAT PSYCHO DESTROYED THE TOWER, BAIXI TOLD ME ABOUT A SECRET LABORATORY IN THE LOESS PLATEAU. HE SAID HE FOUND-- HE FOUND--
KENAN! STOP!
ZOOOOOOM!

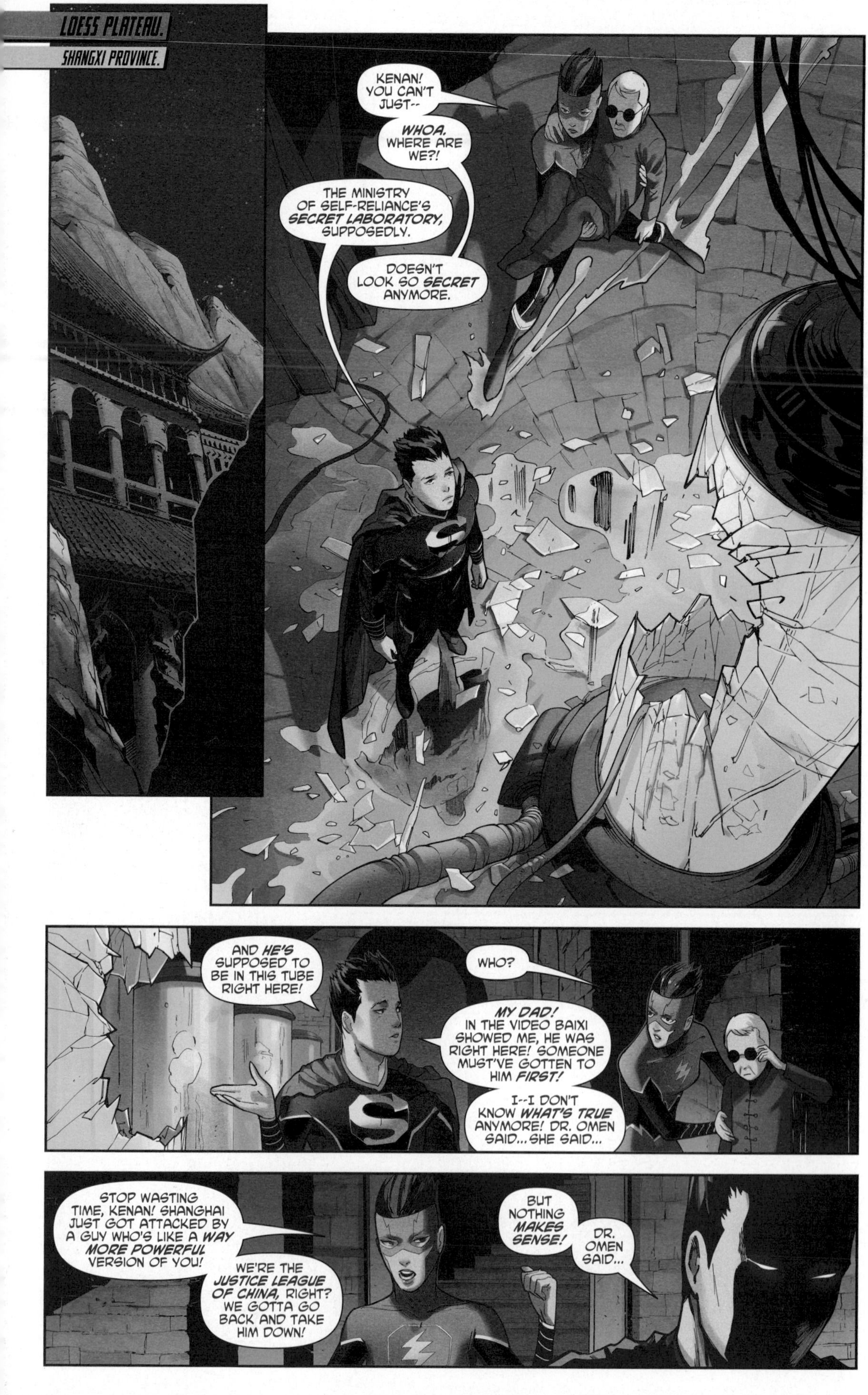
LOESS PLATEAU.
SHANGXI PROVINCE.
KENAN! YOU CAN'T JUST--
WHOA. WHERE ARE WE?!
THE MINISTRY OF SELF-RELIANCE'S SECRET LABORATORY, SUPPOSEDLY.
DOESN'T LOOK SO SECRET ANYMORE.
AND HE'S SUPPOSED TO BE IN THIS TUBE RIGHT HERE!
WHO?
MY DAD! IN THE VIDEO BAIXI SHOWED ME, HE WAS RIGHT HERE! SOMEONE MUST'VE GOTTEN TO HIM FIRST!
I--I DON'T KNOW WHAT'S TRUE ANYMORE! DR. OMEN SAID... SHE SAID...
STOP WASTING TIME, KENAN! SHANGHAI JUST GOT ATTACKED BY A GUY WHO'S LIKE A WAY MORE POWERFUL VERSION OF YOU!
WE'RE THE JUSTICE LEAGUE OF CHINA, RIGHT? WE GOTTA GO BACK AND TAKE HIM DOWN!
BUT NOTHING MAKES SENSE!
DR. OMEN SAID...

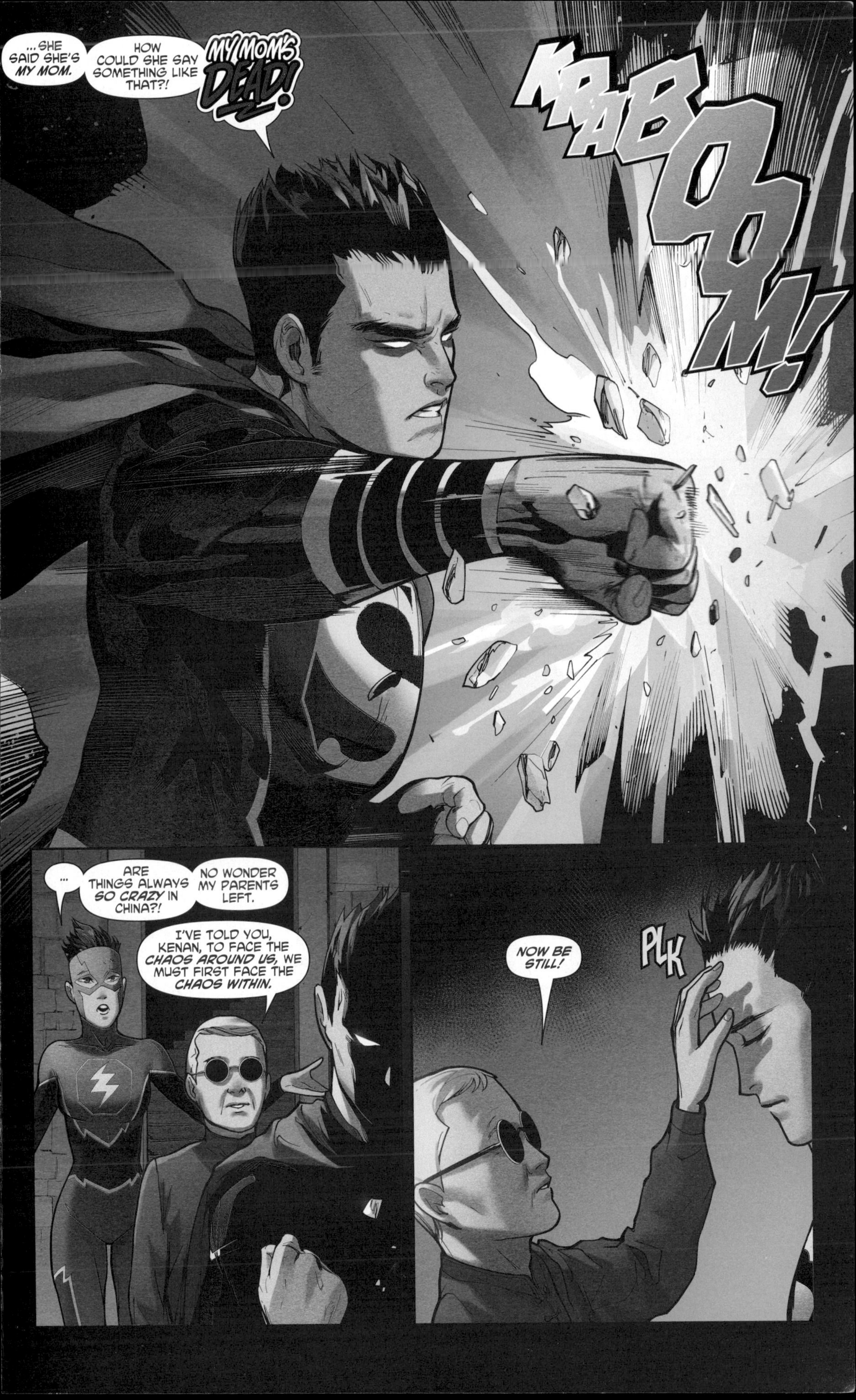
...SHE SAID SHE'S MY MOM.
HOW COULD SHE SAY SOMETHING LIKE THAT?!
MY MOM'S DEAD!
KRABOOM!
...
ARE THINGS ALWAYS SO CRAZY IN CHINA?!
NO WONDER MY PARENTS LEFT.
I'VE TOLD YOU, KENAN, TO FACE THE CHAOS AROUND US, WE MUST FIRST FACE THE CHAOS WITHIN.
NOW BE STILL!
PLK

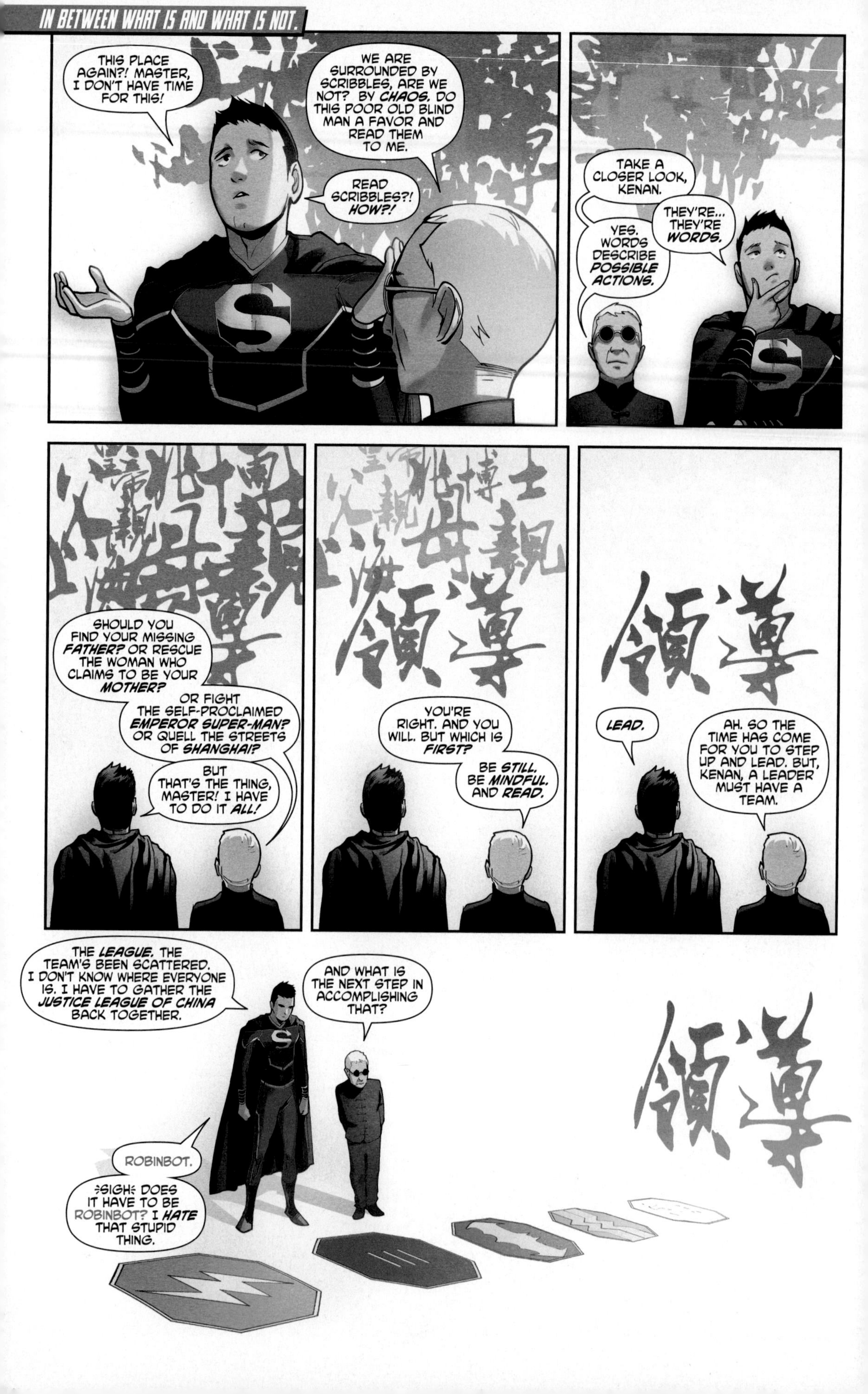
IN BETWEEN WHAT IS AND WHAT IS NOT.
THIS PLACE AGAIN?! MASTER, I DON'T HAVE TIME FOR THIS!
WE ARE SURROUNDED BY SCRIBBLES, ARE WE NOT? BY CHAOS. DO THIS POOR OLD BLIND MAN A FAVOR AND READ THEM TO ME.
READ SCRIBBLES?! HOW?!
TAKE A CLOSER LOOK, KENAN.
THEY'RE... THEY'RE WORDS.
YES. WORDS DESCRIBE POSSIBLE ACTIONS.
SHOULD YOU FIND YOUR MISSING FATHER? OR RESCUE THE WOMAN WHO CLAIMS TO BE YOUR MOTHER?
OR FIGHT THE SELF-PROCLAIMED EMPEROR SUPER-MAN? OR QUELL THE STREETS OF SHANGHAI?
BUT THAT'S THE THING, MASTER! I HAVE TO DO IT ALL!
YOU'RE RIGHT. AND YOU WILL. BUT WHICH IS FIRST?
BE STILL. BE MINDFUL. AND READ.
領導
LEAD.
AH. SO THE TIME HAS COME FOR YOU TO STEP UP AND LEAD. BUT, KENAN, A LEADER MUST HAVE A TEAM.
THE LEAGUE. THE TEAM'S BEEN SCATTERED. I DON'T KNOW WHERE EVERYONE IS. I HAVE TO GATHER THE JUSTICE LEAGUE OF CHINA BACK TOGETHER.
AND WHAT IS THE NEXT STEP IN ACCOMPLISHING THAT?
領導
ROBINBOT.
⩤SIGH⩥ DOES IT HAVE TO BE ROBINBOT? I HATE THAT STUPID THING.

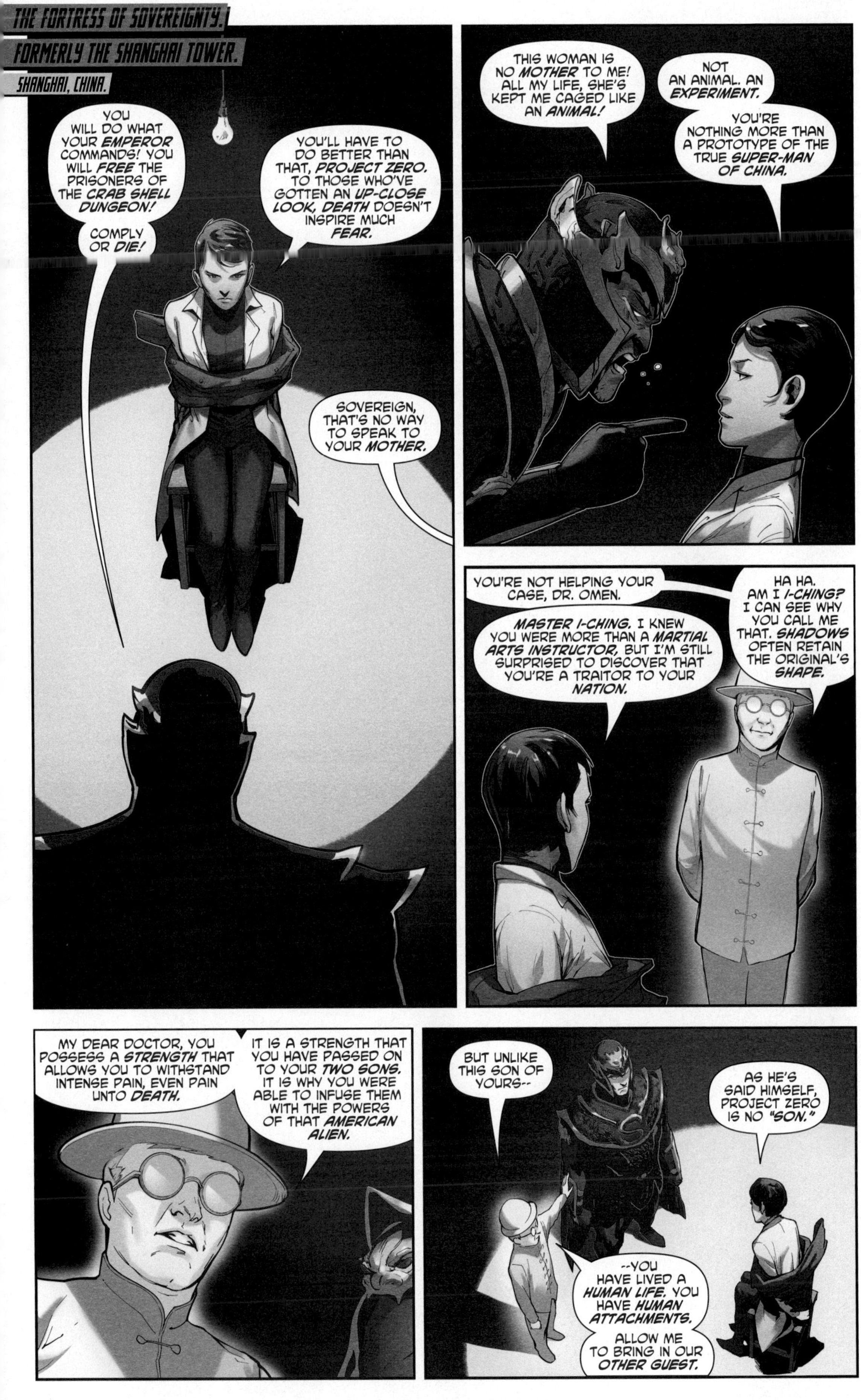
THE FORTRESS OF SOVEREIGNTY.
FORMERLY THE SHANGHAI TOWER.
SHANGHAI, CHINA.
YOU WILL DO WHAT YOUR EMPEROR COMMANDS! YOU WILL FREE THE PRISONERS OF THE CRAB SHELL DUNGEON!
COMPLY OR DIE!
YOU'LL HAVE TO DO BETTER THAN THAT, PROJECT ZERO. TO THOSE WHO'VE GOTTEN AN UP-CLOSE LOOK, DEATH DOESN'T INSPIRE MUCH FEAR.
SOVEREIGN, THAT'S NO WAY TO SPEAK TO YOUR MOTHER.
THIS WOMAN IS NO MOTHER TO ME! ALL MY LIFE, SHE'S KEPT ME CAGED LIKE AN ANIMAL!
NOT AN ANIMAL. AN EXPERIMENT.
YOU'RE NOTHING MORE THAN A PROTOTYPE OF THE TRUE SUPER-MAN OF CHINA.
YOU'RE NOT HELPING YOUR CASE, DR. OMEN.
MASTER I-CHING. I KNEW YOU WERE MORE THAN A MARTIAL ARTS INSTRUCTOR, BUT I'M STILL SURPRISED TO DISCOVER THAT YOU'RE A TRAITOR TO YOUR NATION.
HA HA. AM I I-CHING? I CAN SEE WHY YOU CALL ME THAT. SHADOWS OFTEN RETAIN THE ORIGINAL'S SHAPE.
MY DEAR DOCTOR, YOU POSSESS A STRENGTH THAT ALLOWS YOU TO WITHSTAND INTENSE PAIN, EVEN PAIN UNTO DEATH.
IT IS A STRENGTH THAT YOU HAVE PASSED ON TO YOUR TWO SONS. IT IS WHY YOU WERE ABLE TO INFUSE THEM WITH THE POWERS OF THAT AMERICAN ALIEN.
BUT UNLIKE THIS SON OF YOURS--
AS HE'S SAID HIMSELF, PROJECT ZERO IS NO "SON."
--YOU HAVE LIVED A HUMAN LIFE. YOU HAVE HUMAN ATTACHMENTS.
ALLOW ME TO BRING IN OUR OTHER GUEST.

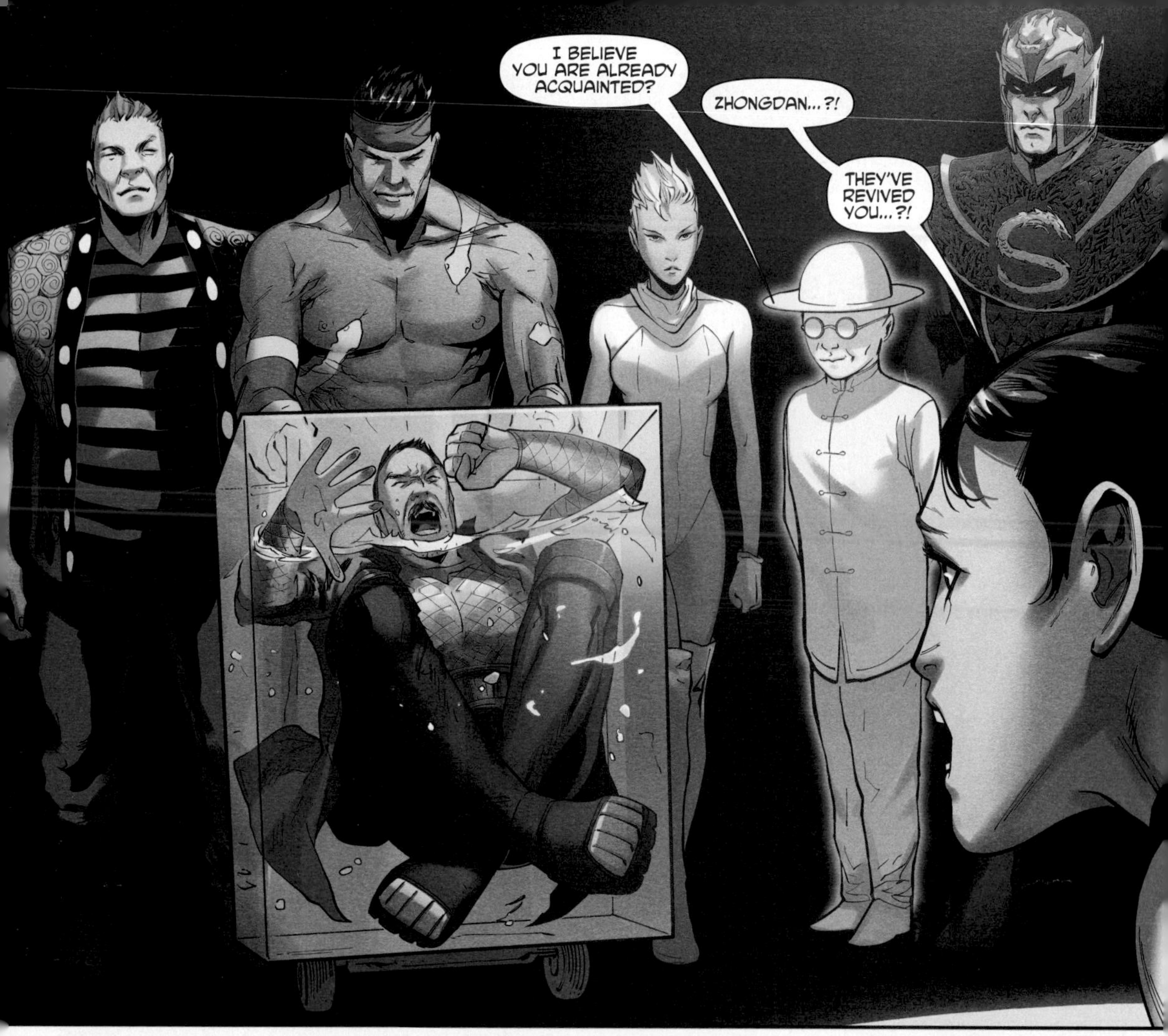
I BELIEVE YOU ARE ALREADY ACQUAINTED?
ZHONGDAN...?!
THEY'VE REVIVED YOU...?!

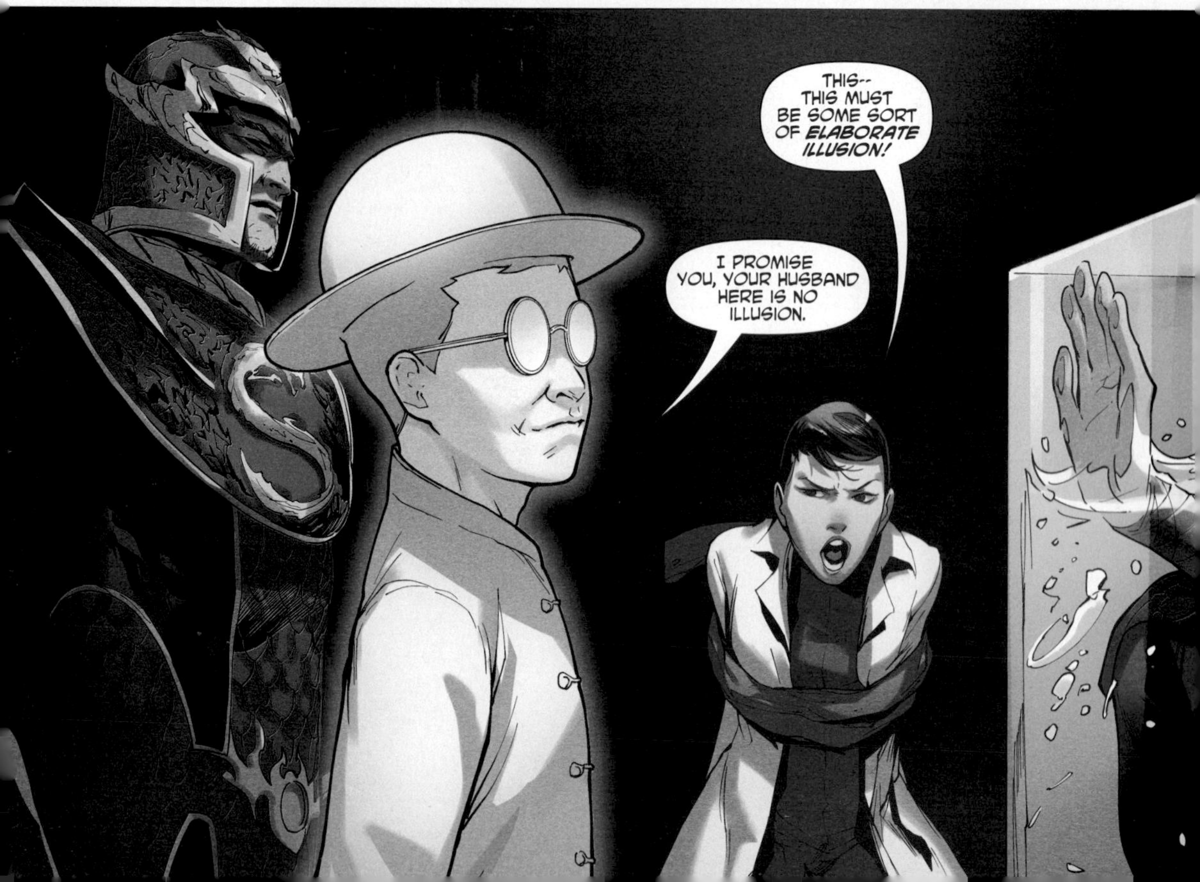
THIS-- THIS MUST BE SOME SORT OF *ELABORATE ILLUSION!*
I PROMISE YOU, YOUR HUSBAND HERE IS NO ILLUSION.

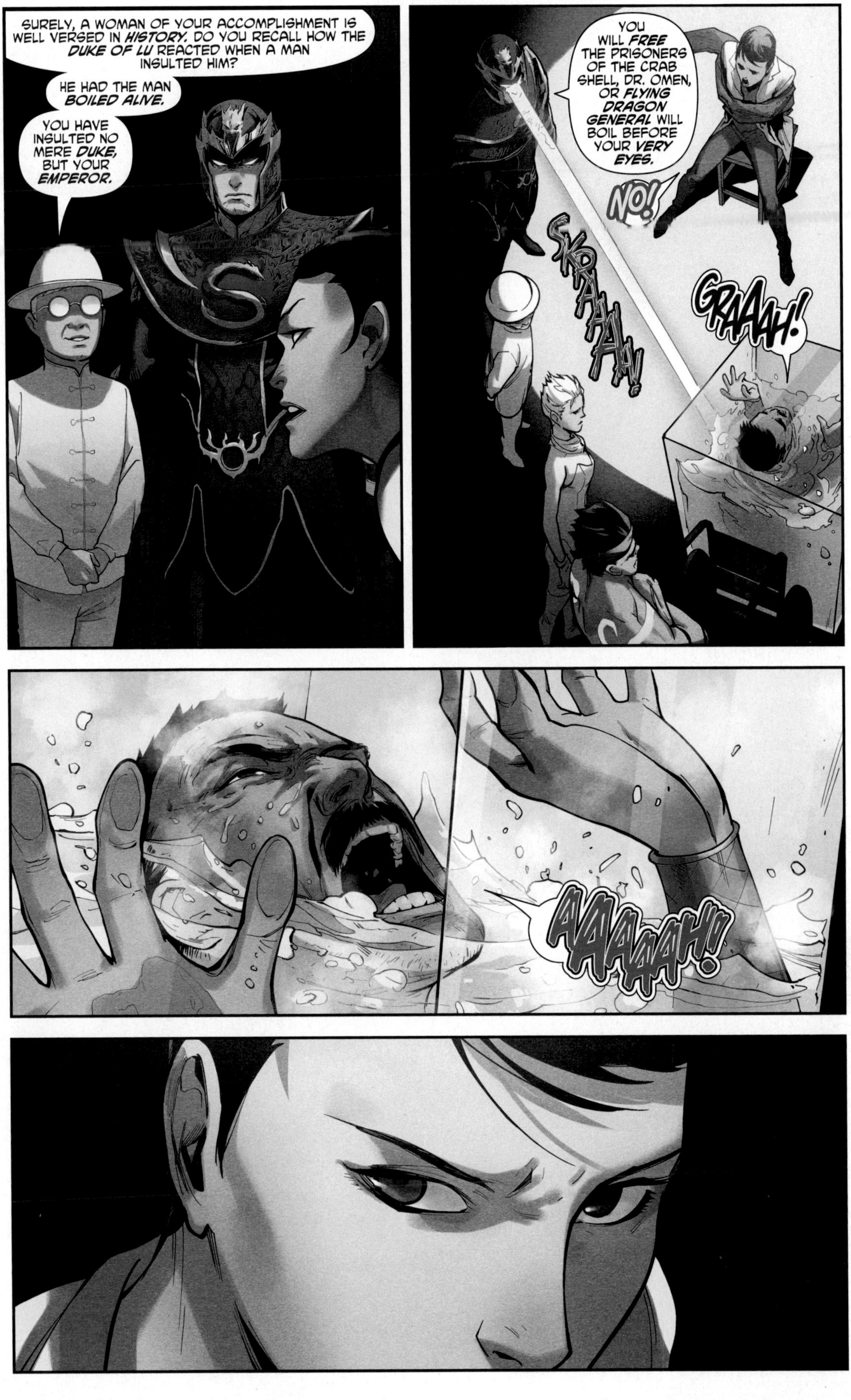
SURELY, A WOMAN OF YOUR ACCOMPLISHMENT IS WELL VERSED IN HISTORY. DO YOU RECALL HOW THE DUKE OF LU REACTED WHEN A MAN INSULTED HIM?
HE HAD THE MAN BOILED ALIVE.
YOU HAVE INSULTED NO MERE DUKE, BUT YOUR EMPEROR.
YOU WILL FREE THE PRISONERS OF THE CRAB SHELL, DR. OMEN, OR FLYING DRAGON GENERAL WILL BOIL BEFORE YOUR VERY EYES.
NO!
SKRAAAAAAW!
GRAAAH!
AAAAAAH!

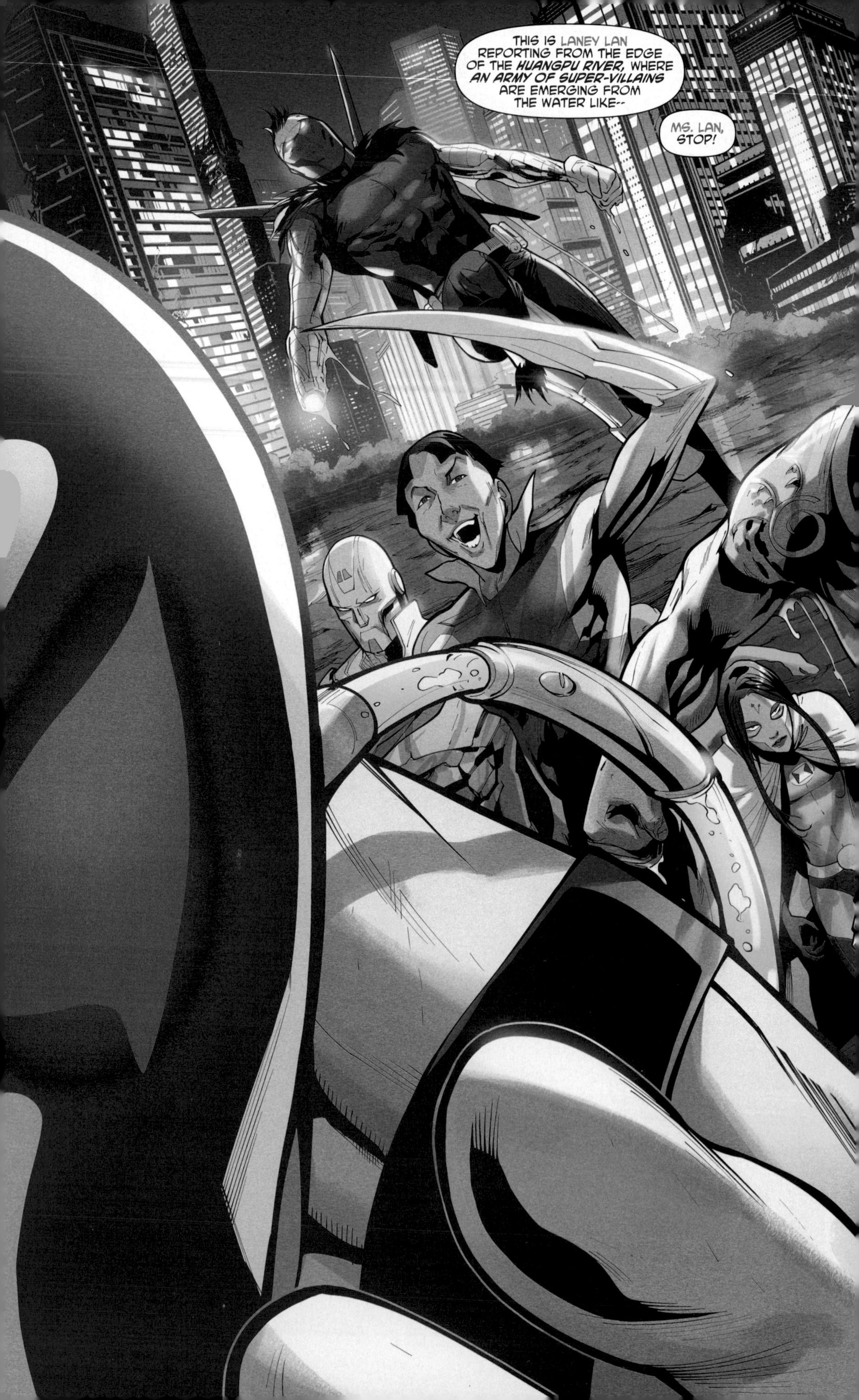
THIS IS LANEY LAN REPORTING FROM THE EDGE OF THE HUANGPU RIVER, WHERE AN ARMY OF SUPER-VILLAINS ARE EMERGING FROM THE WATER LIKE--
MS. LAN, STOP!

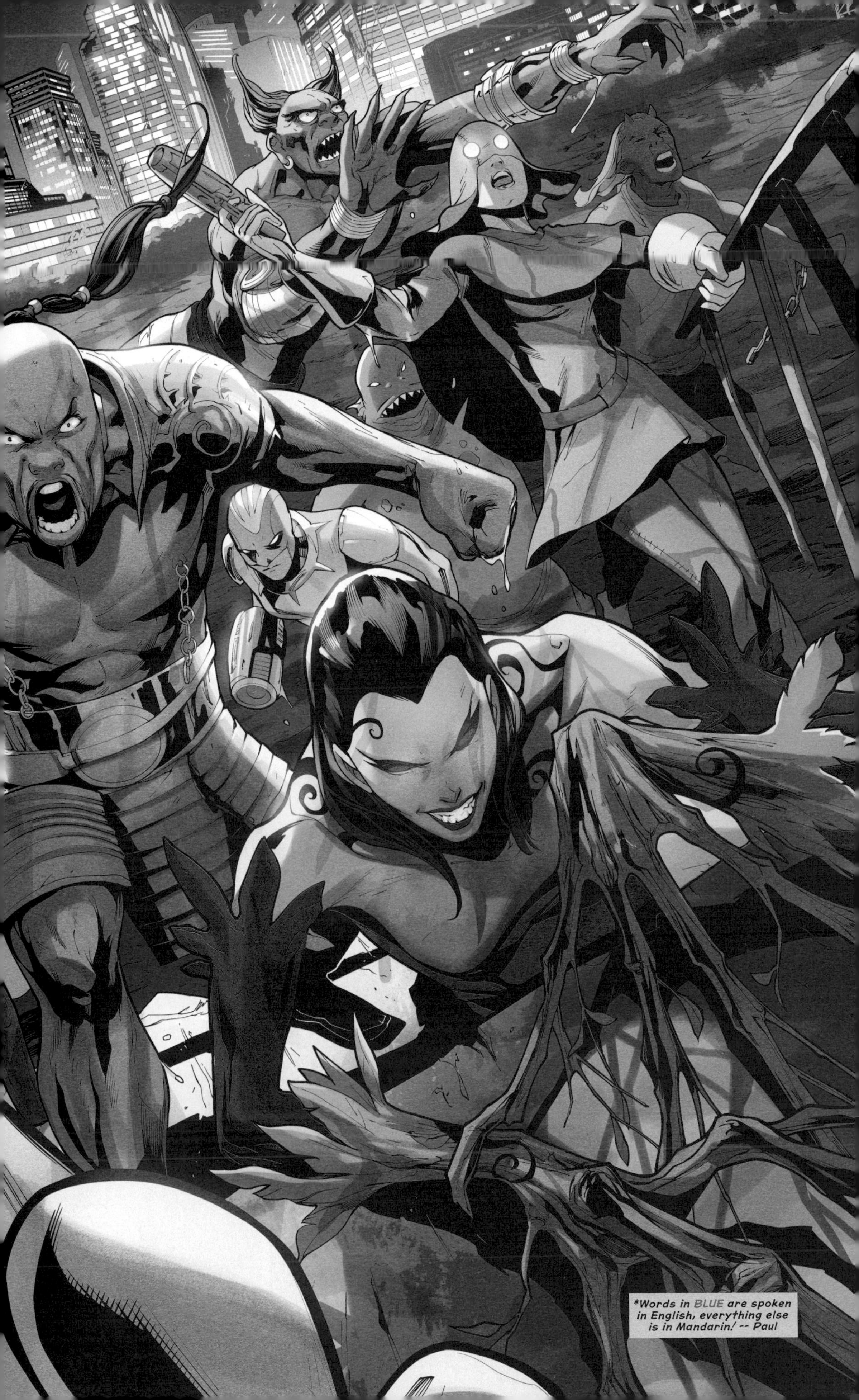
*Words in BLUE are spoken in English, everything else is in Mandarin! -- Paul

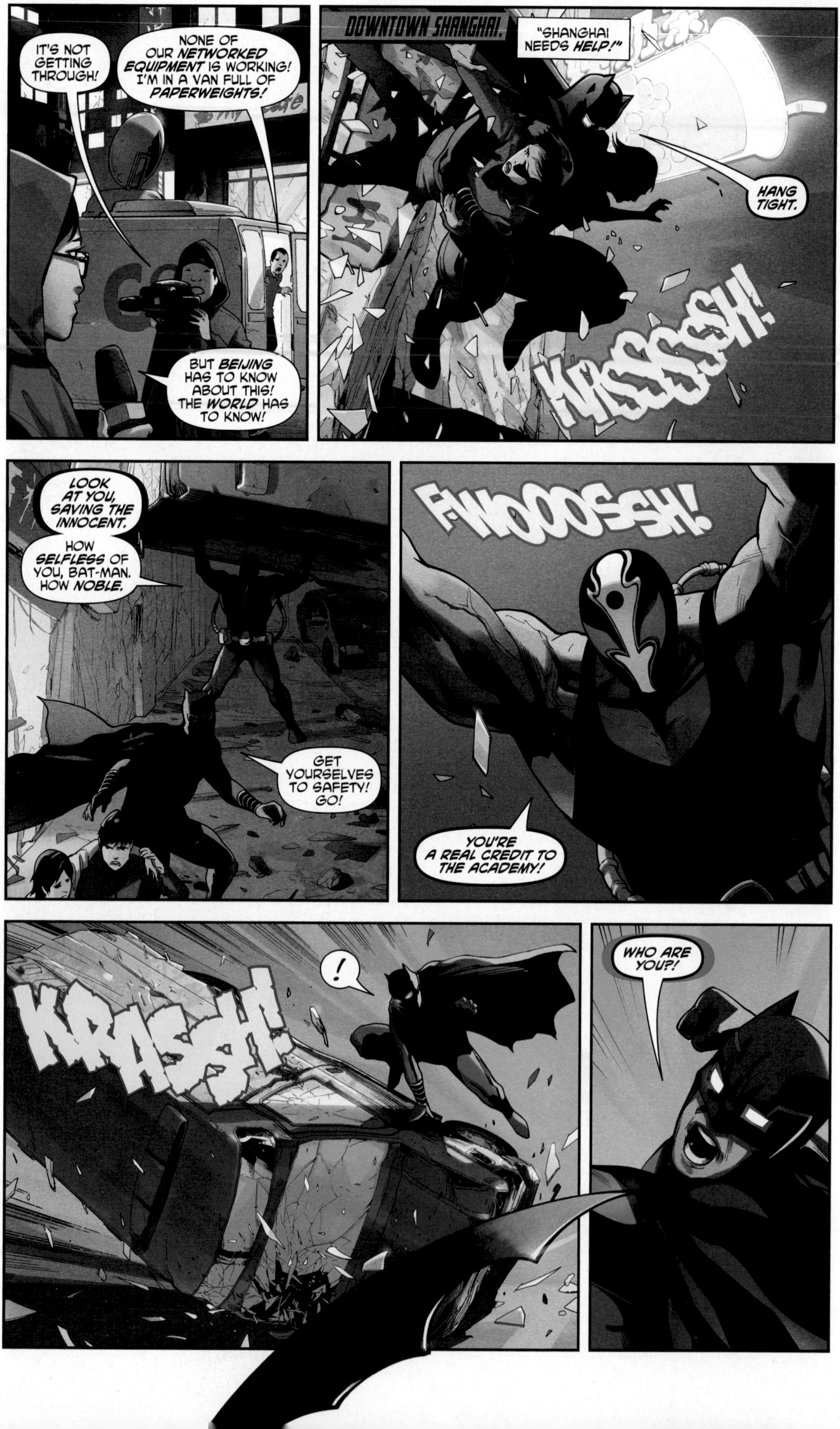
IT'S NOT GETTING THROUGH!
NONE OF OUR NETWORKED EQUIPMENT IS WORKING! I'M IN A VAN FULL OF PAPERWEIGHTS!
BUT BEIJING HAS TO KNOW ABOUT THIS! THE WORLD HAS TO KNOW!
DOWNTOWN SHANGHAI.
"SHANGHAI NEEDS HELP!"
HANG TIGHT.
KHSSSSH!
LOOK AT YOU, SAVING THE INNOCENT.
HOW SELFLESS OF YOU, BAT-MAN. HOW NOBLE.
GET YOURSELVES TO SAFETY! GO!
FWOOOSSH!
YOU'RE A REAL CREDIT TO THE ACADEMY!
KRASSH!
!
WHO ARE YOU?!

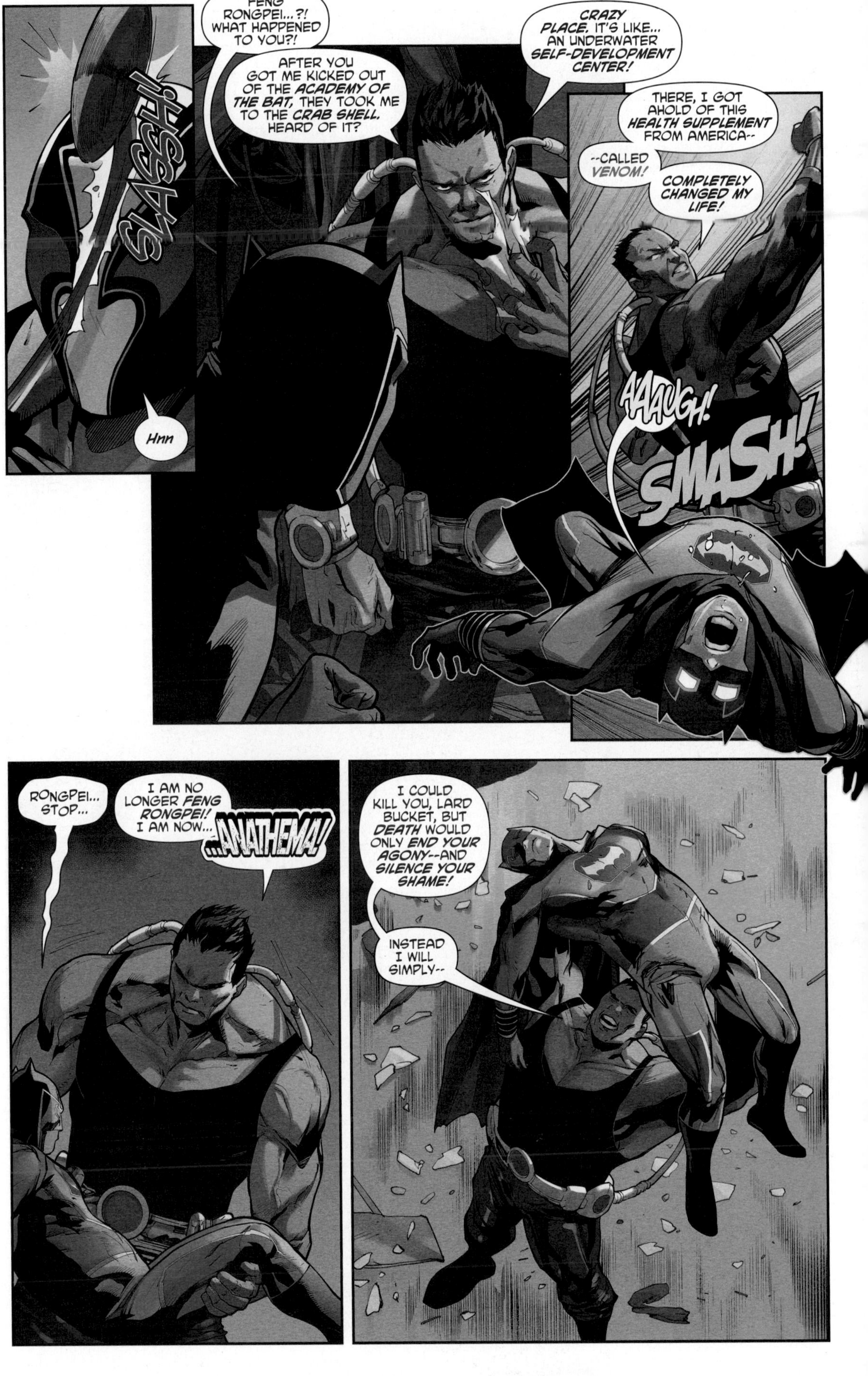
SMASH!
Hnn
FENG RONGPEI...?! WHAT HAPPENED TO YOU?!
AFTER YOU GOT ME KICKED OUT OF THE ACADEMY OF THE BAT, THEY TOOK ME TO THE CRAB SHELL. HEARD OF IT?
CRAZY PLACE. IT'S LIKE... AN UNDERWATER SELF-DEVELOPMENT CENTER!
THERE, I GOT AHOLD OF THIS HEALTH SUPPLEMENT FROM AMERICA--
--CALLED VENOM!
COMPLETELY CHANGED MY LIFE!
AAAUGH!
SMASH!
RONGPEI... STOP...
I AM NO LONGER FENG RONGPEI! I AM NOW...
...ANATHEMA!
I COULD KILL YOU, LARD BUCKET, BUT DEATH WOULD ONLY END YOUR AGONY--AND SILENCE YOUR SHAME!
INSTEAD I WILL SIMPLY--

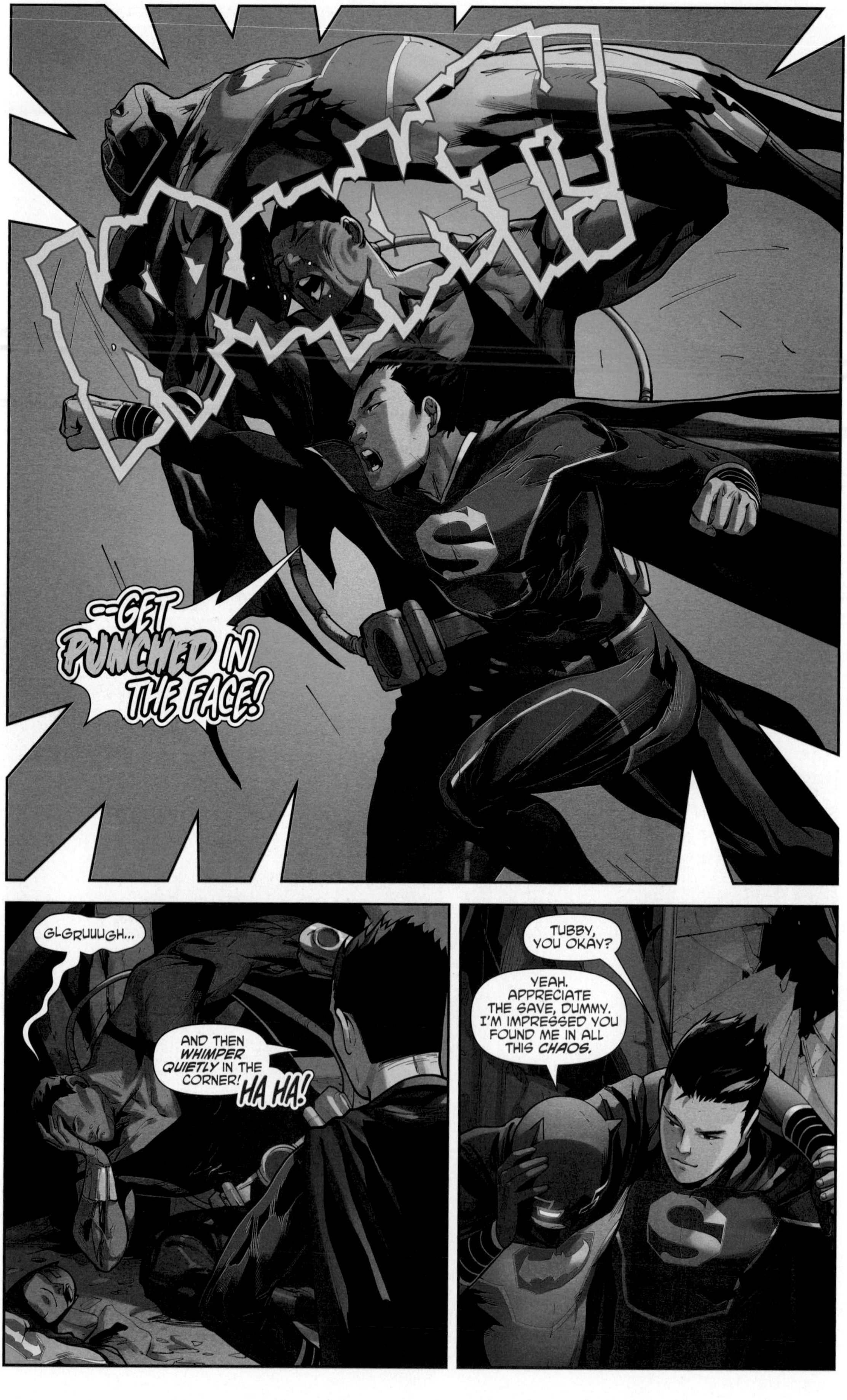
--GET PUNCHED IN THE FACE!
GLGRUUUGH...
AND THEN WHIMPER QUIETLY IN THE CORNER! HA HA!
TUBBY, YOU OKAY?
YEAH. APPRECIATE THE SAVE, DUMMY. I'M IMPRESSED YOU FOUND ME IN ALL THIS CHAOS.

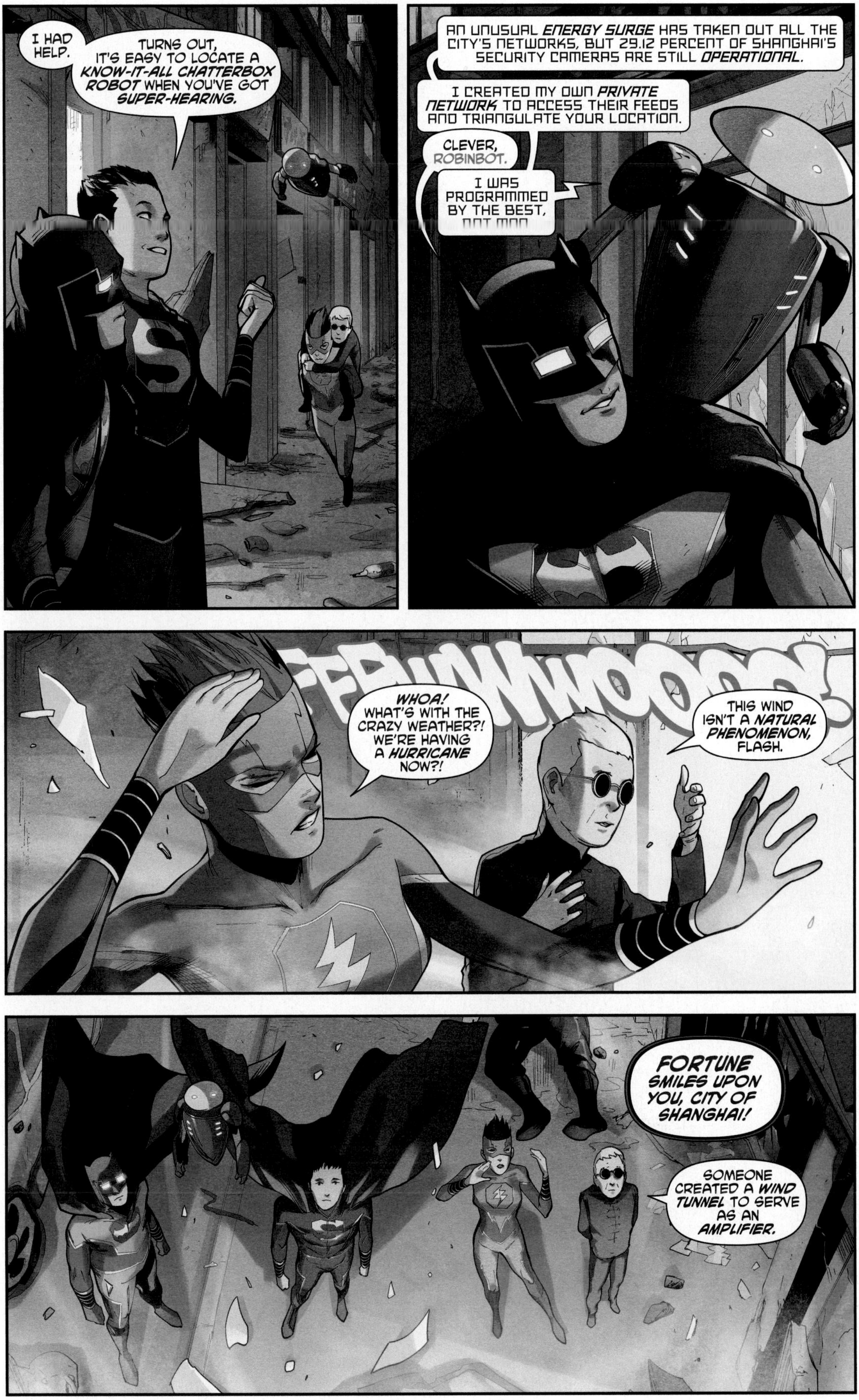
I HAD HELP.
TURNS OUT, IT'S EASY TO LOCATE A *KNOW-IT-ALL CHATTERBOX ROBOT* WHEN YOU'VE GOT *SUPER-HEARING.*
AN UNUSUAL *ENERGY SURGE* HAS TAKEN OUT ALL THE CITY'S NETWORKS, BUT 29.12 PERCENT OF SHANGHAI'S SECURITY CAMERAS ARE STILL *OPERATIONAL.*
I CREATED MY OWN *PRIVATE NETWORK* TO ACCESS THEIR FEEDS AND TRIANGULATE YOUR LOCATION.
CLEVER, ROBINBOT.
I WAS PROGRAMMED BY THE BEST,
WHOA! WHAT'S WITH THE CRAZY WEATHER?! WE'RE HAVING A *HURRICANE* NOW?!
THIS WIND ISN'T A *NATURAL PHENOMENON,* FLASH.
FORTUNE SMILES UPON YOU, CITY OF SHANGHAI!
SOMEONE CREATED A *WIND TUNNEL* TO SERVE AS AN *AMPLIFIER.*

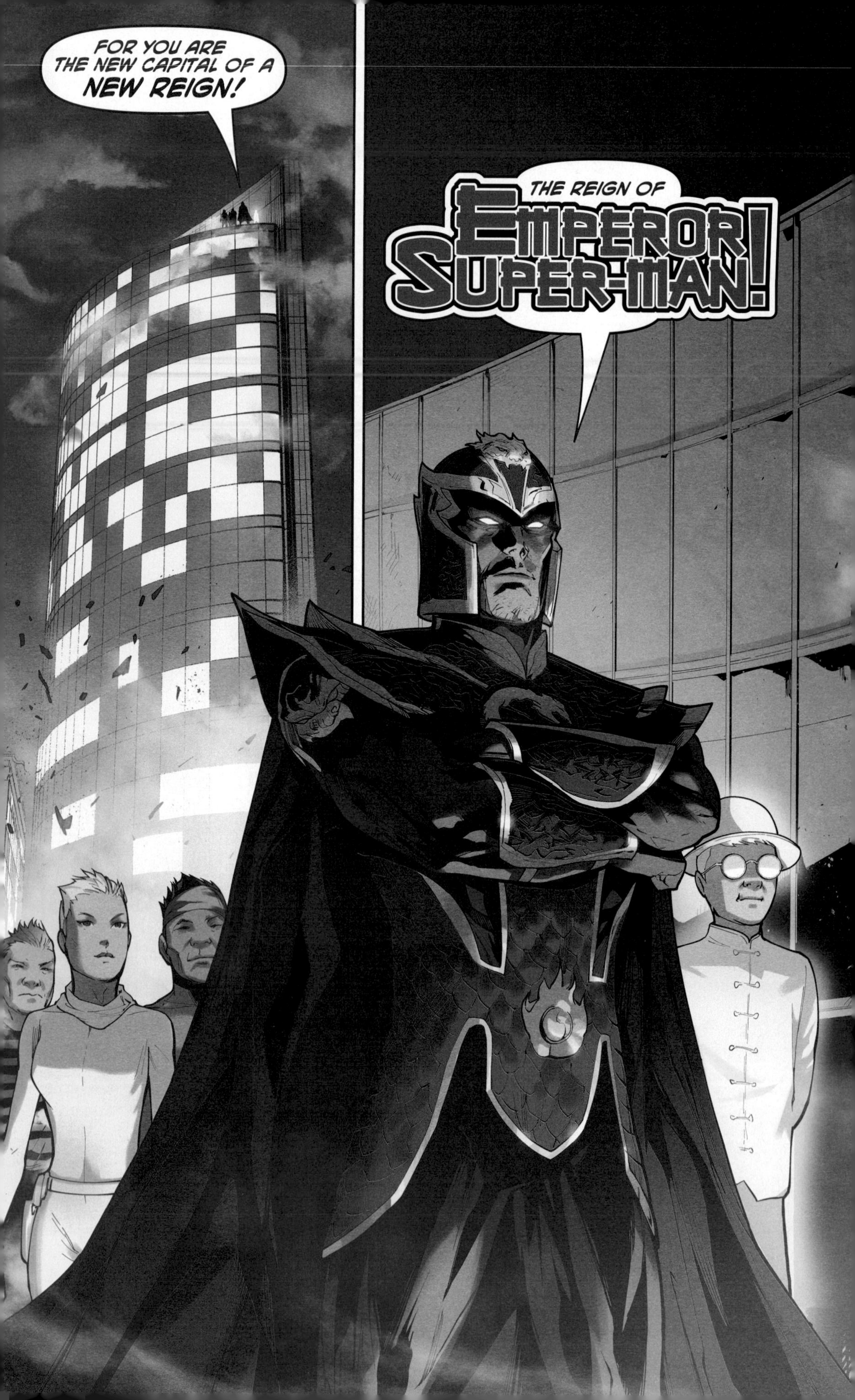
FOR YOU ARE THE NEW CAPITAL OF A NEW REIGN!
THE REIGN OF EMPEROR SUPER-MAN!

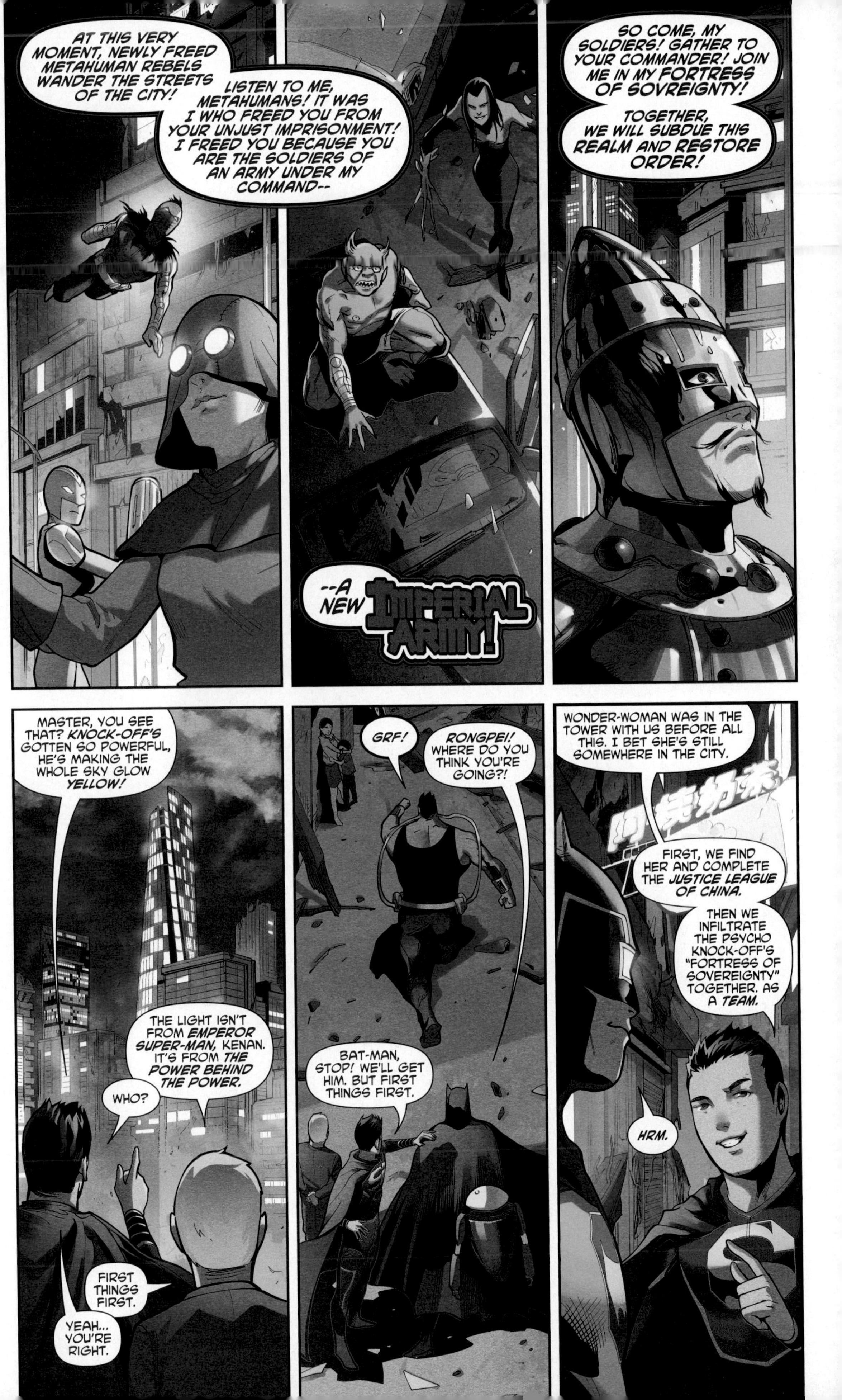

AT THIS VERY MOMENT, NEWLY FREED METAHUMAN REBELS WANDER THE STREETS OF THE CITY!
LISTEN TO ME, METAHUMANS! IT WAS I WHO FREED YOU FROM YOUR UNJUST IMPRISONMENT! I FREED YOU BECAUSE YOU ARE THE SOLDIERS OF AN ARMY UNDER MY COMMAND--
--A NEW IMPERIAL ARMY!
SO COME, MY SOLDIERS! GATHER TO YOUR COMMANDER! JOIN ME IN MY FORTRESS OF SOVEREIGNTY!
TOGETHER, WE WILL SUBDUE THIS REALM AND RESTORE ORDER!
MASTER, YOU SEE THAT? KNOCK-OFF'S GOTTEN SO POWERFUL, HE'S MAKING THE WHOLE SKY GLOW YELLOW!
THE LIGHT ISN'T FROM EMPEROR SUPER-MAN, KENAN. IT'S FROM THE POWER BEHIND THE POWER.
WHO?
FIRST THINGS FIRST.
YEAH... YOU'RE RIGHT.
GRF!
RONGPEI! WHERE DO YOU THINK YOU'RE GOING?!
BAT-MAN, STOP! WE'LL GET HIM. BUT FIRST THINGS FIRST.
WONDER-WOMAN WAS IN THE TOWER WITH US BEFORE ALL THIS. I BET SHE'S STILL SOMEWHERE IN THE CITY.
FIRST, WE FIND HER AND COMPLETE THE JUSTICE LEAGUE OF CHINA.
THEN WE INFILTRATE THE PSYCHO KNOCK-OFF'S "FORTRESS OF SOVEREIGNTY" TOGETHER. AS A TEAM.
HRM.

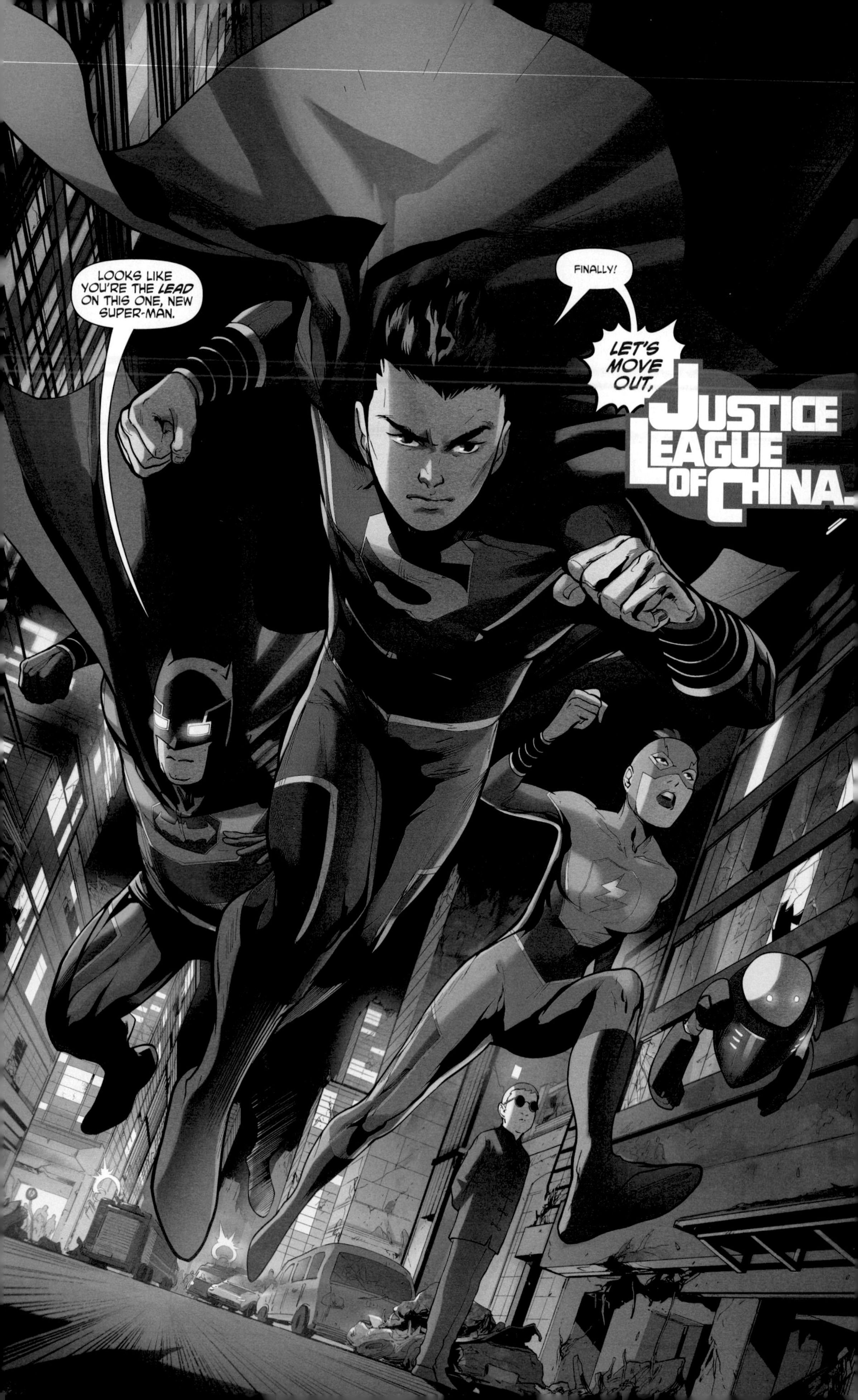
LOOKS LIKE YOU'RE THE *LEAD* ON THIS ONE, NEW SUPER-MAN.
FINALLY!
LET'S MOVE OUT,
JUSTICE LEAGUE OF CHINA.

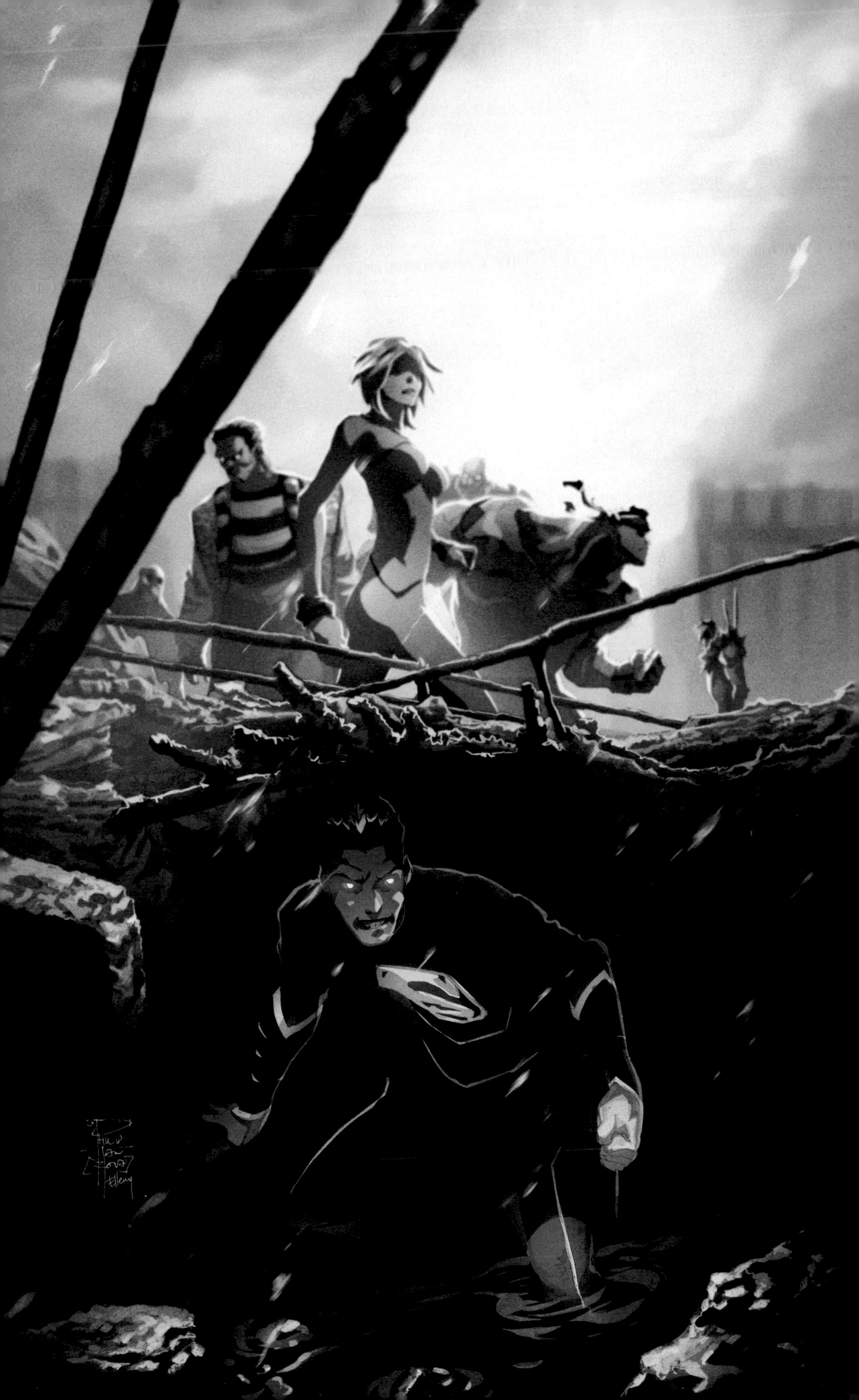

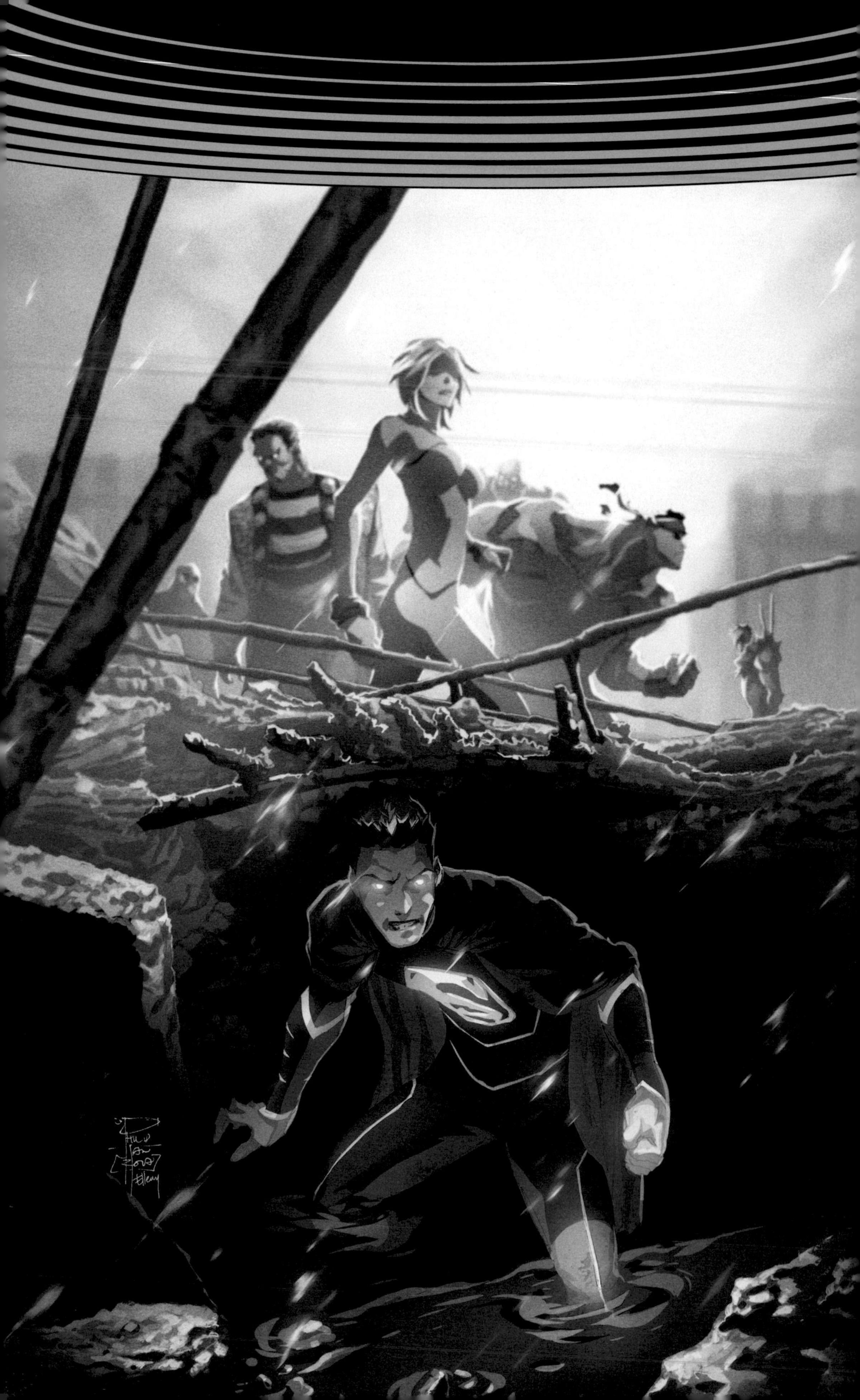

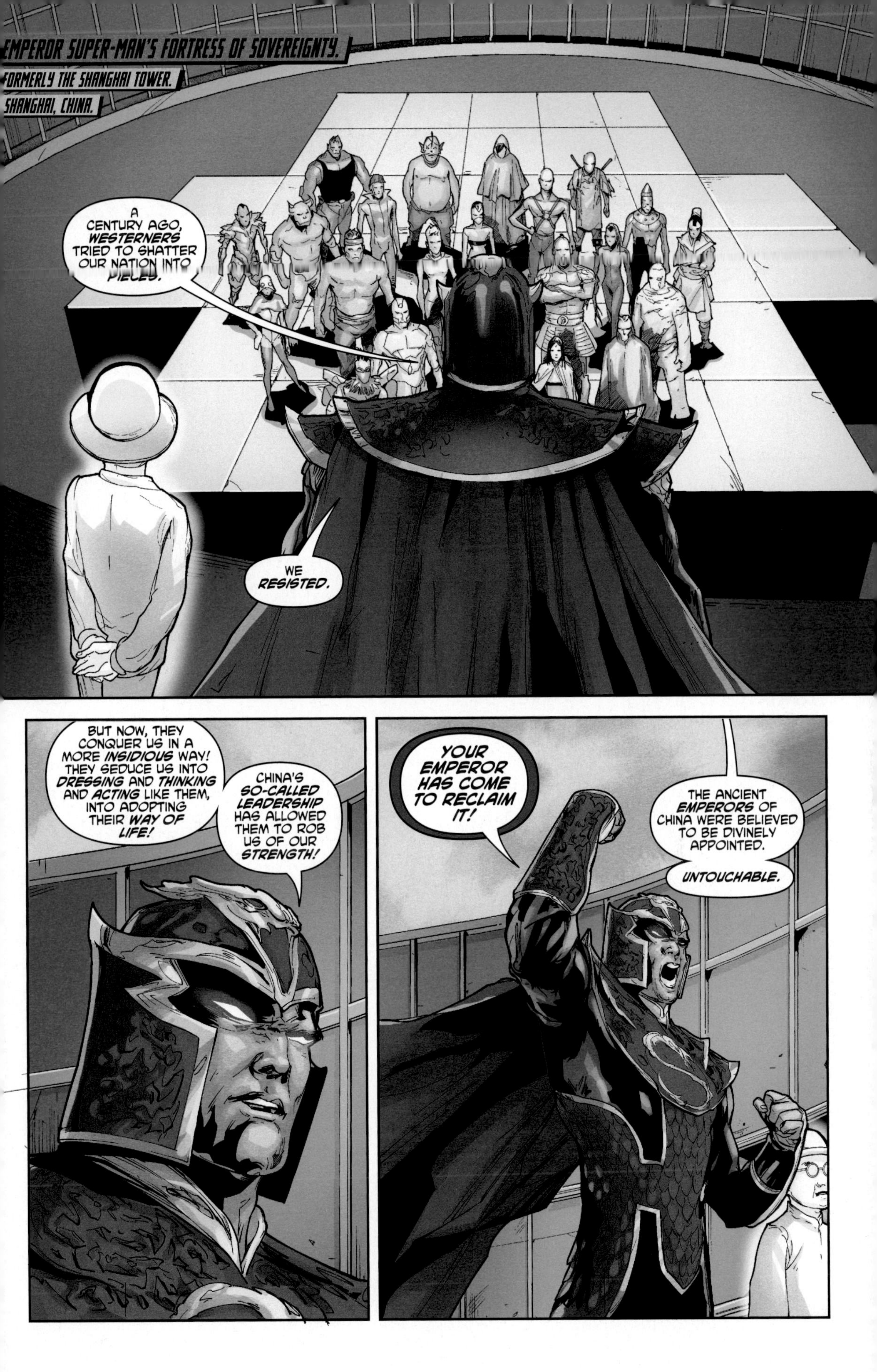
EMPEROR SUPER-MAN'S FORTRESS OF SOVEREIGNTY.
FORMERLY THE SHANGHAI TOWER.
SHANGHAI, CHINA.
A CENTURY AGO, WESTERNERS TRIED TO SHATTER OUR NATION INTO PIECES.
WE RESISTED.
BUT NOW, THEY CONQUER US IN A MORE INSIDIOUS WAY! THEY SEDUCE US INTO DRESSING AND THINKING AND ACTING LIKE THEM, INTO ADOPTING THEIR WAY OF LIFE!
CHINA'S SO-CALLED LEADERSHIP HAS ALLOWED THEM TO ROB US OF OUR STRENGTH!
YOUR EMPEROR HAS COME TO RECLAIM IT!
THE ANCIENT EMPERORS OF CHINA WERE BELIEVED TO BE DIVINELY APPOINTED.
UNTOUCHABLE.

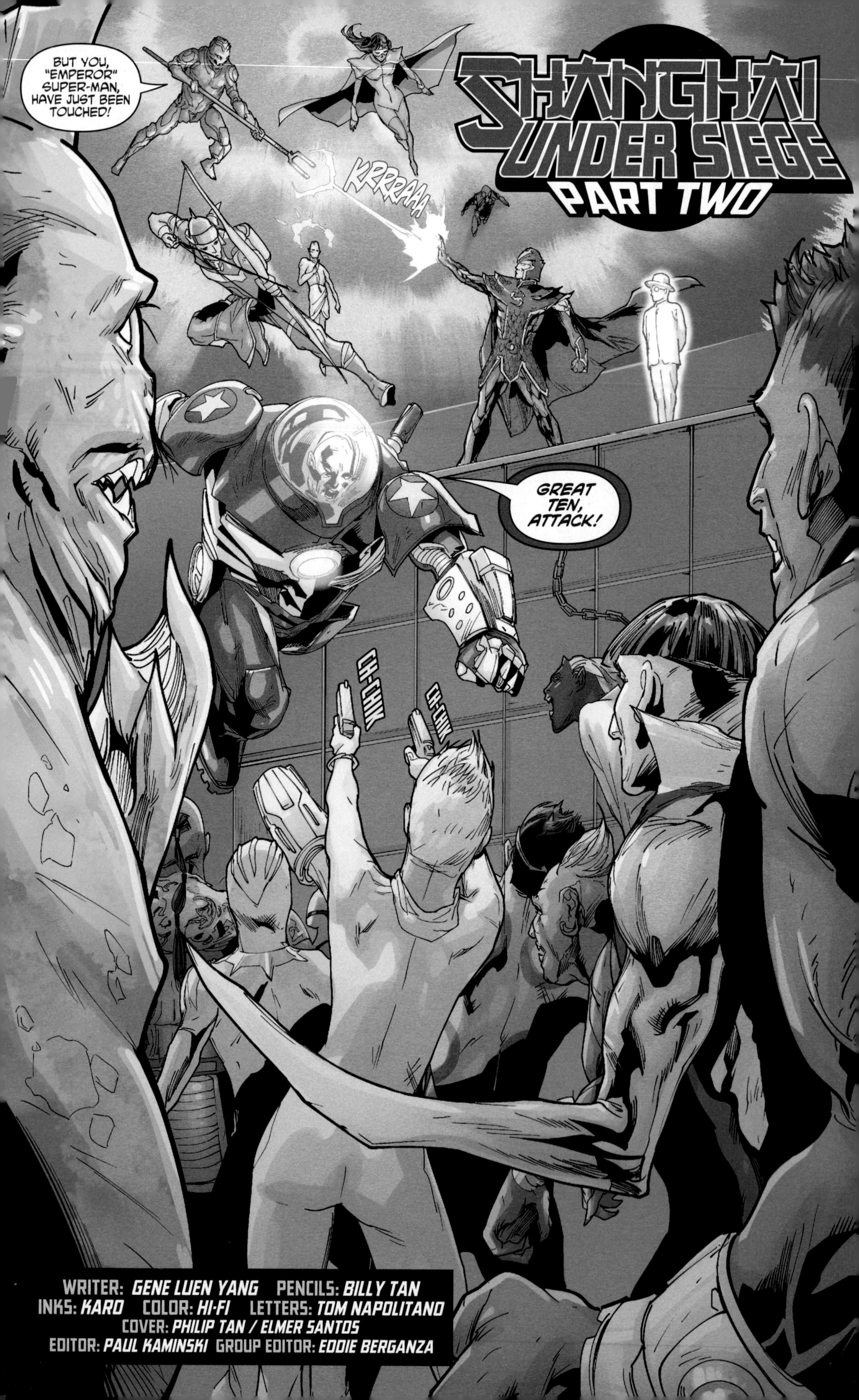
BUT YOU, "EMPEROR" SUPER-MAN, HAVE JUST BEEN TOUCHED!
SHANGHAI UNDER SIEGE
PART TWO
KRRRAAA
GREAT TEN, ATTACK!
CH-CHIK
CH-CHIK
WRITER: GENE LUEN YANG PENCILS: BILLY TAN
INKS: KARO COLOR: HI-FI LETTERS: TOM NAPOLITANO
COVER: PHILIP TAN / ELMER SANTOS
EDITOR: PAUL KAMINSKI GROUP EDITOR: EDDIE BERGANZA

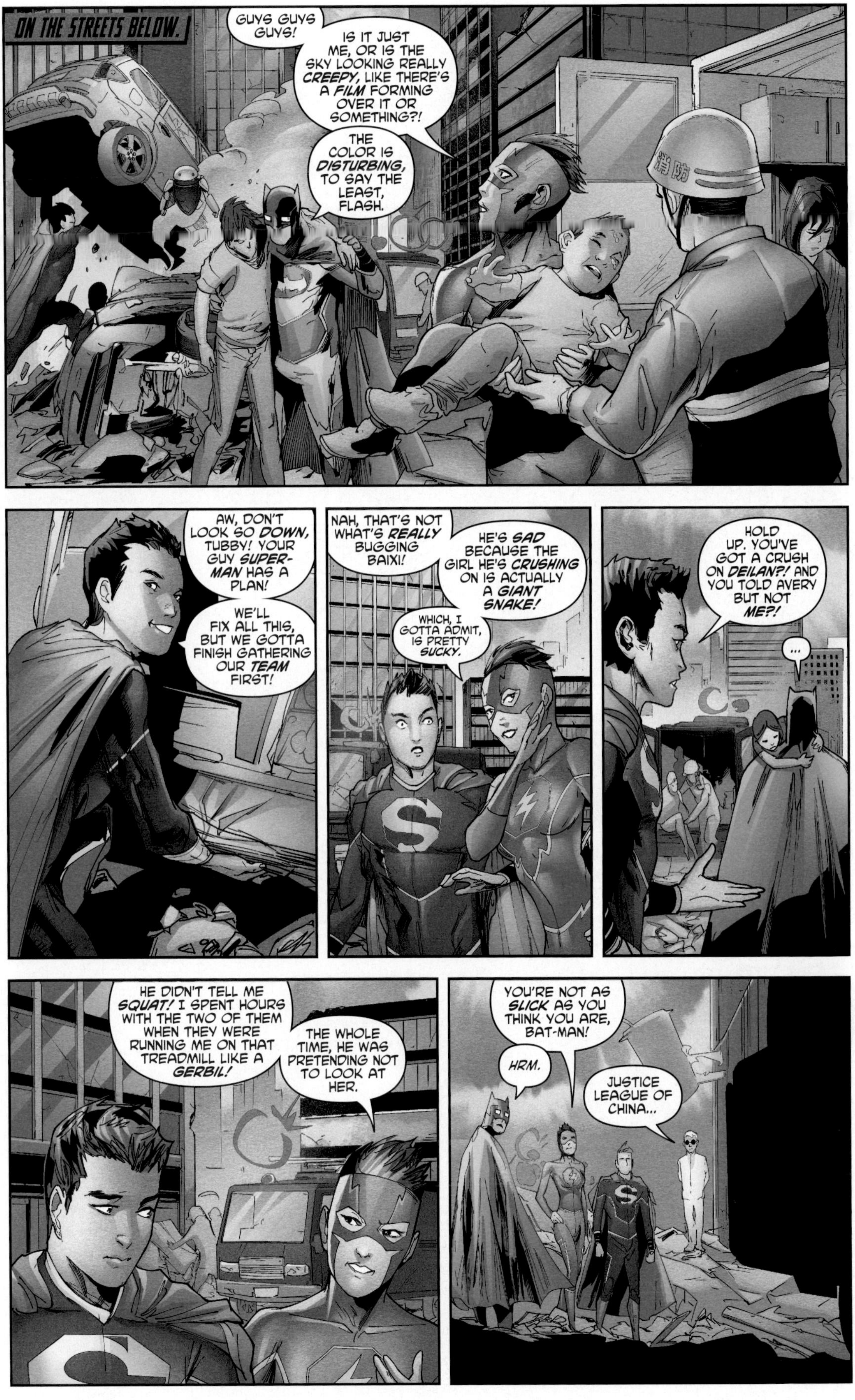

ON THE STREETS BELOW.
GUYS GUYS GUYS!
IS IT JUST ME, OR IS THE SKY LOOKING REALLY CREEPY, LIKE THERE'S A FILM FORMING OVER IT OR SOMETHING?!
THE COLOR IS DISTURBING, TO SAY THE LEAST, FLASH.
消防
AW, DON'T LOOK SO DOWN, TUBBY! YOUR GUY SUPER-MAN HAS A PLAN!
WE'LL FIX ALL THIS, BUT WE GOTTA FINISH GATHERING OUR TEAM FIRST!
NAH, THAT'S NOT WHAT'S REALLY BUGGING BAIXI!
HE'S SAD BECAUSE THE GIRL HE'S CRUSHING ON IS ACTUALLY A GIANT SNAKE!
WHICH, I GOTTA ADMIT, IS PRETTY SUCKY.
HOLD UP. YOU'VE GOT A CRUSH ON DEILAN?! AND YOU TOLD AVERY BUT NOT ME?!
...
HE DIDN'T TELL ME SQUAT! I SPENT HOURS WITH THE TWO OF THEM WHEN THEY WERE RUNNING ME ON THAT TREADMILL LIKE A GERBIL!
THE WHOLE TIME, HE WAS PRETENDING NOT TO LOOK AT HER.
YOU'RE NOT AS SLICK AS YOU THINK YOU ARE, BAT-MAN!
HRM.
JUSTICE LEAGUE OF CHINA...

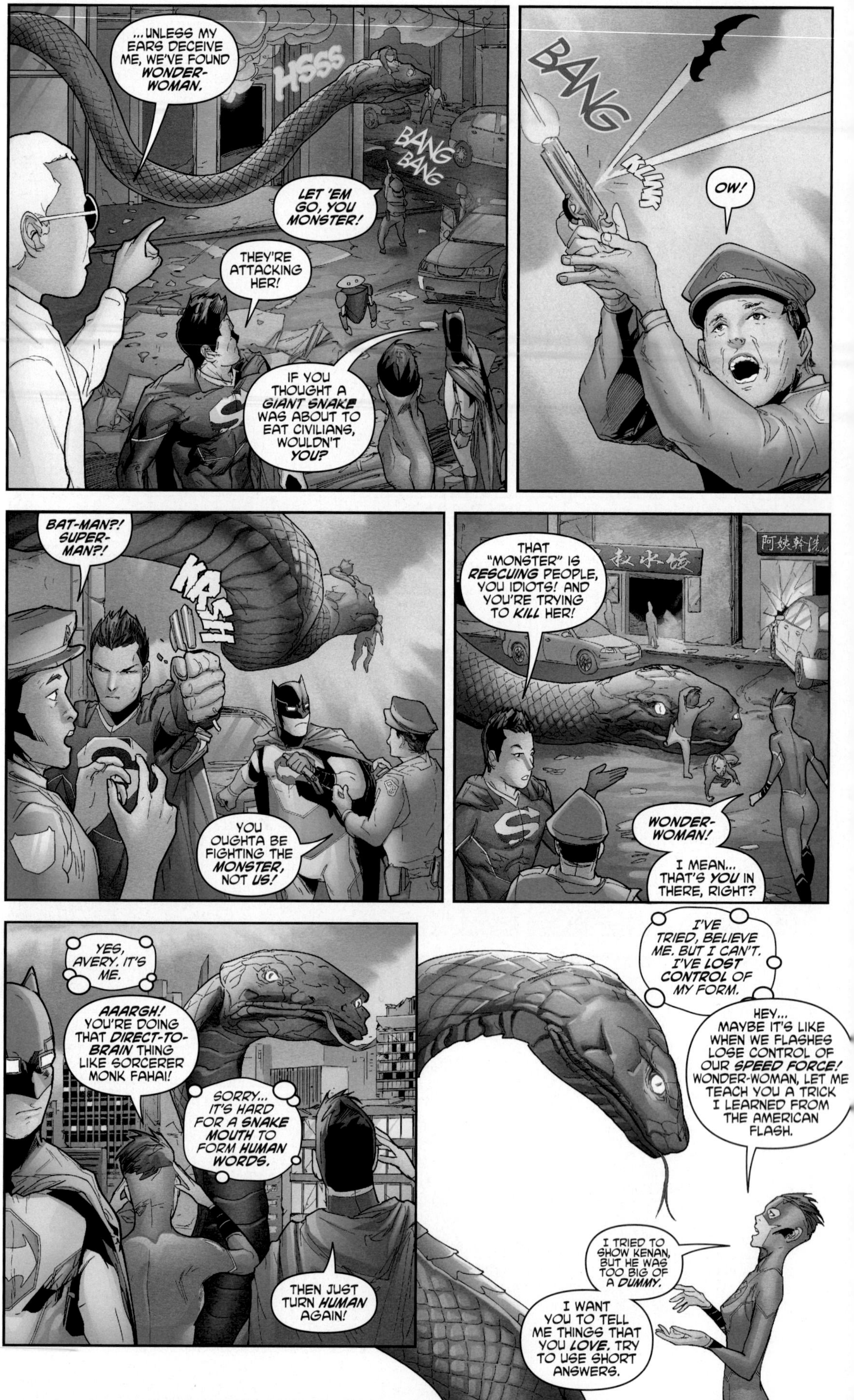
...UNLESS MY EARS DECEIVE ME, WE'VE FOUND WONDER-WOMAN.
HSSS
BANG BANG
LET 'EM GO, YOU MONSTER!
THEY'RE ATTACKING HER!
IF YOU THOUGHT A GIANT SNAKE WAS ABOUT TO EAT CIVILIANS, WOULDN'T YOU?
BANG
KLINK
OW!
BAT-MAN?! SUPER-MAN?!
KRASH
YOU OUGHTA BE FIGHTING THE MONSTER, NOT US!
THAT "MONSTER" IS RESCUING PEOPLE, YOU IDIOTS! AND YOU'RE TRYING TO KILL HER!
WONDER-WOMAN!
I MEAN... THAT'S YOU IN THERE, RIGHT?
YES, AVERY. IT'S ME.
AAARGH! YOU'RE DOING THAT DIRECT-TO-BRAIN THING LIKE SORCERER MONK FAHAI!
SORRY... IT'S HARD FOR A SNAKE MOUTH TO FORM HUMAN WORDS.
THEN JUST TURN HUMAN AGAIN!
I'VE TRIED, BELIEVE ME. BUT I CAN'T. I'VE LOST CONTROL OF MY FORM.
HEY... MAYBE IT'S LIKE WHEN WE FLASHES LOSE CONTROL OF OUR SPEED FORCE! WONDER-WOMAN, LET ME TEACH YOU A TRICK I LEARNED FROM THE AMERICAN FLASH.
I TRIED TO SHOW KENAN, BUT HE WAS TOO BIG OF A DUMMY.
I WANT YOU TO TELL ME THINGS THAT YOU LOVE. TRY TO USE SHORT ANSWERS.

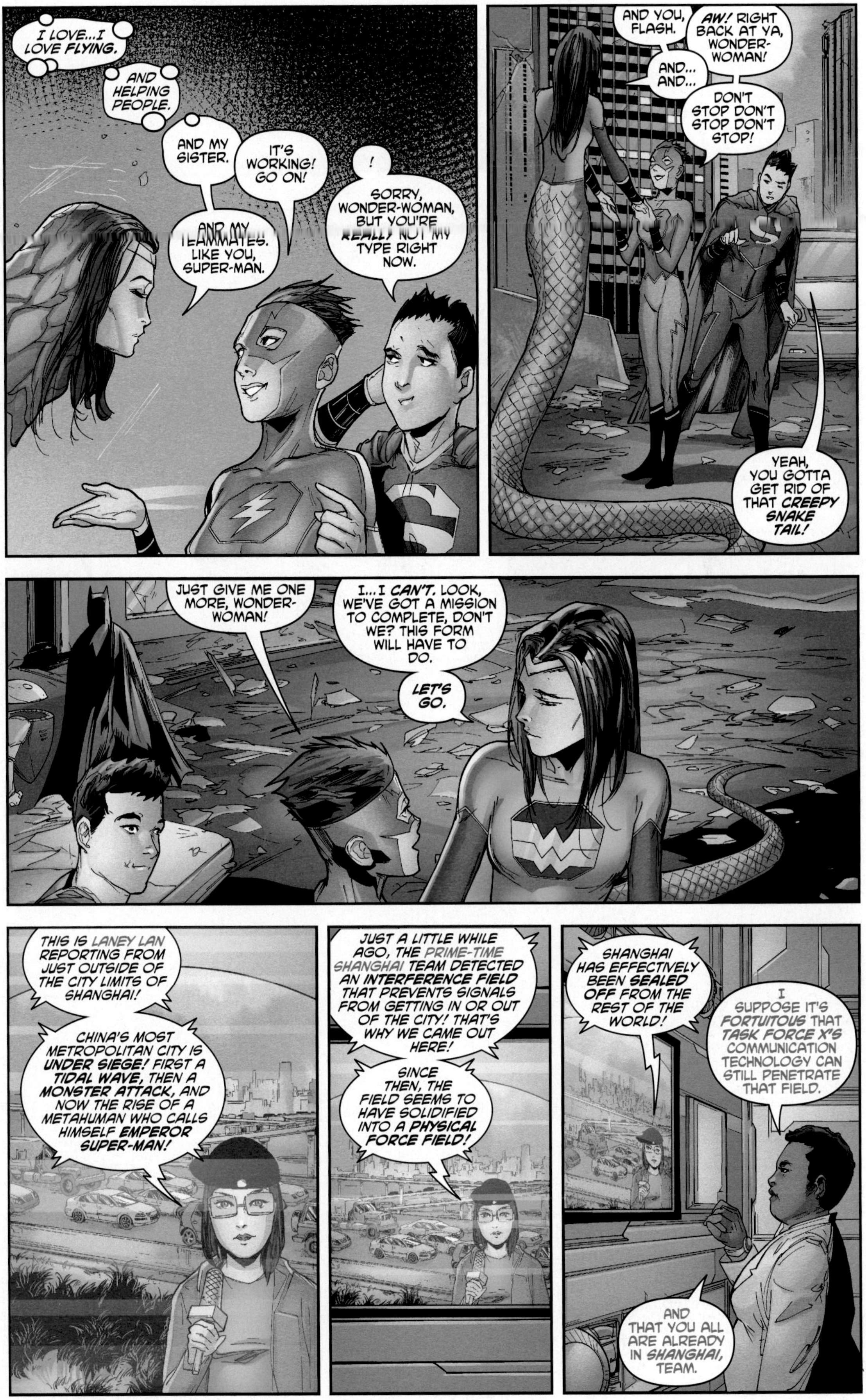
I LOVE...I LOVE FLYING.
AND HELPING PEOPLE.
AND MY SISTER.
AND MY TEAMMATES. LIKE YOU, SUPER-MAN.
IT'S WORKING! GO ON!
!
SORRY, WONDER-WOMAN, BUT YOU'RE REALLY NOT MY TYPE RIGHT NOW.
AND YOU, FLASH.
AND... AND...
AW! RIGHT BACK AT YA, WONDER-WOMAN!
DON'T STOP DON'T STOP DON'T STOP!
YEAH, YOU GOTTA GET RID OF THAT CREEPY SNAKE TAIL!
JUST GIVE ME ONE MORE, WONDER-WOMAN!
I...I CAN'T. LOOK, WE'VE GOT A MISSION TO COMPLETE, DON'T WE? THIS FORM WILL HAVE TO DO.
LET'S GO.
THIS IS LANEY LAN REPORTING FROM JUST OUTSIDE OF THE CITY LIMITS OF SHANGHAI!
CHINA'S MOST METROPOLITAN CITY IS UNDER SIEGE! FIRST A TIDAL WAVE, THEN A MONSTER ATTACK, AND NOW THE RISE OF A METAHUMAN WHO CALLS HIMSELF EMPEROR SUPER-MAN!
JUST A LITTLE WHILE AGO, THE PRIME-TIME SHANGHAI TEAM DETECTED AN INTERFERENCE FIELD THAT PREVENTS SIGNALS FROM GETTING IN OR OUT OF THE CITY! THAT'S WHY WE CAME OUT HERE!
SINCE THEN, THE FIELD SEEMS TO HAVE SOLIDIFIED INTO A PHYSICAL FORCE FIELD!
SHANGHAI HAS EFFECTIVELY BEEN SEALED OFF FROM THE REST OF THE WORLD!
I SUPPOSE IT'S FORTUITOUS THAT TASK FORCE X'S COMMUNICATION TECHNOLOGY CAN STILL PENETRATE THAT FIELD.
AND THAT YOU ALL ARE ALREADY IN SHANGHAI, TEAM.

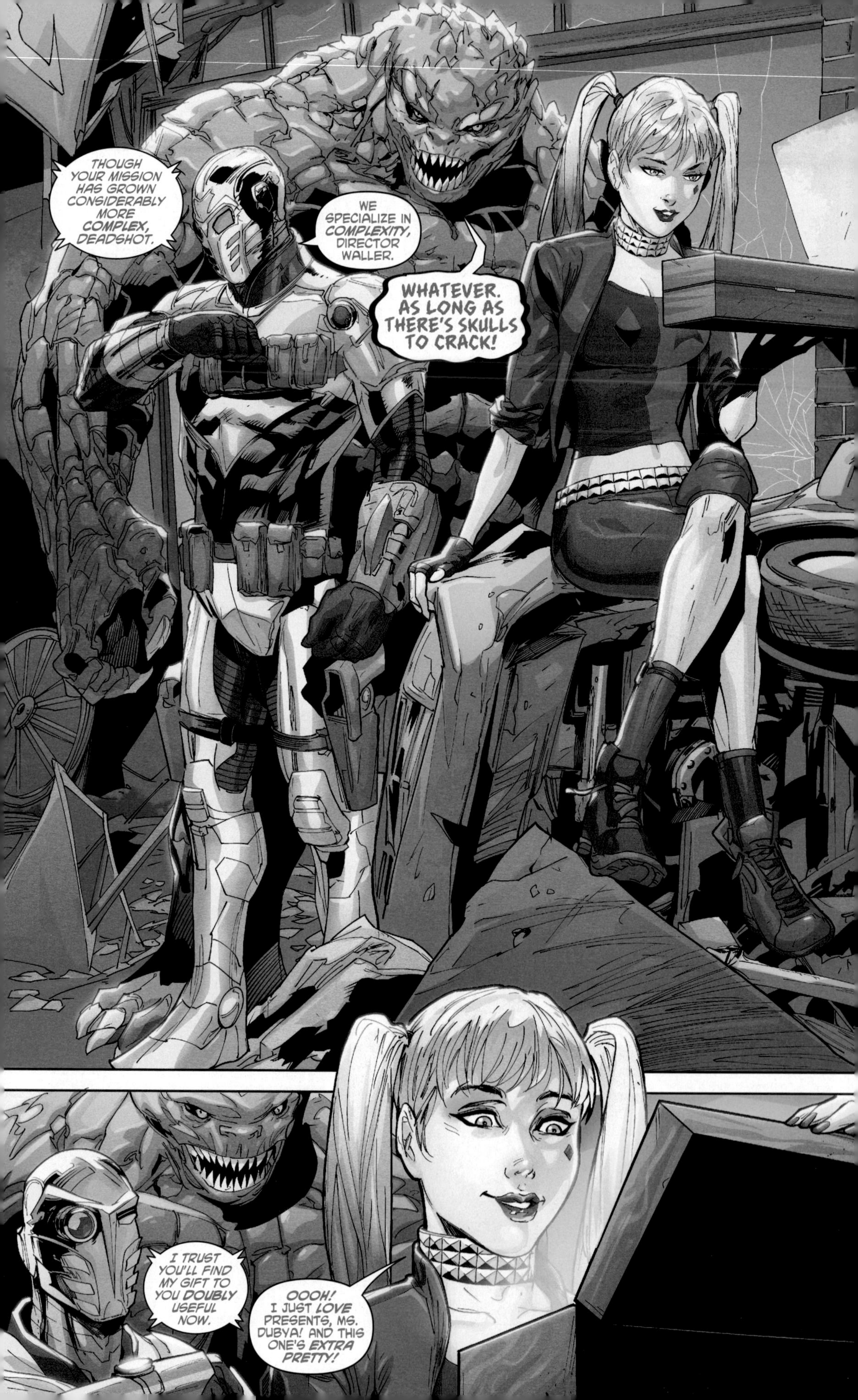
THOUGH YOUR MISSION HAS GROWN CONSIDERABLY MORE COMPLEX, DEADSHOT.
WE SPECIALIZE IN COMPLEXITY, DIRECTOR WALLER.
WHATEVER. AS LONG AS THERE'S SKULLS TO CRACK!
I TRUST YOU'LL FIND MY GIFT TO YOU DOUBLY USEFUL NOW.
OOOH! I JUST LOVE PRESENTS, MS. DUBYA! AND THIS ONE'S EXTRA PRETTY!

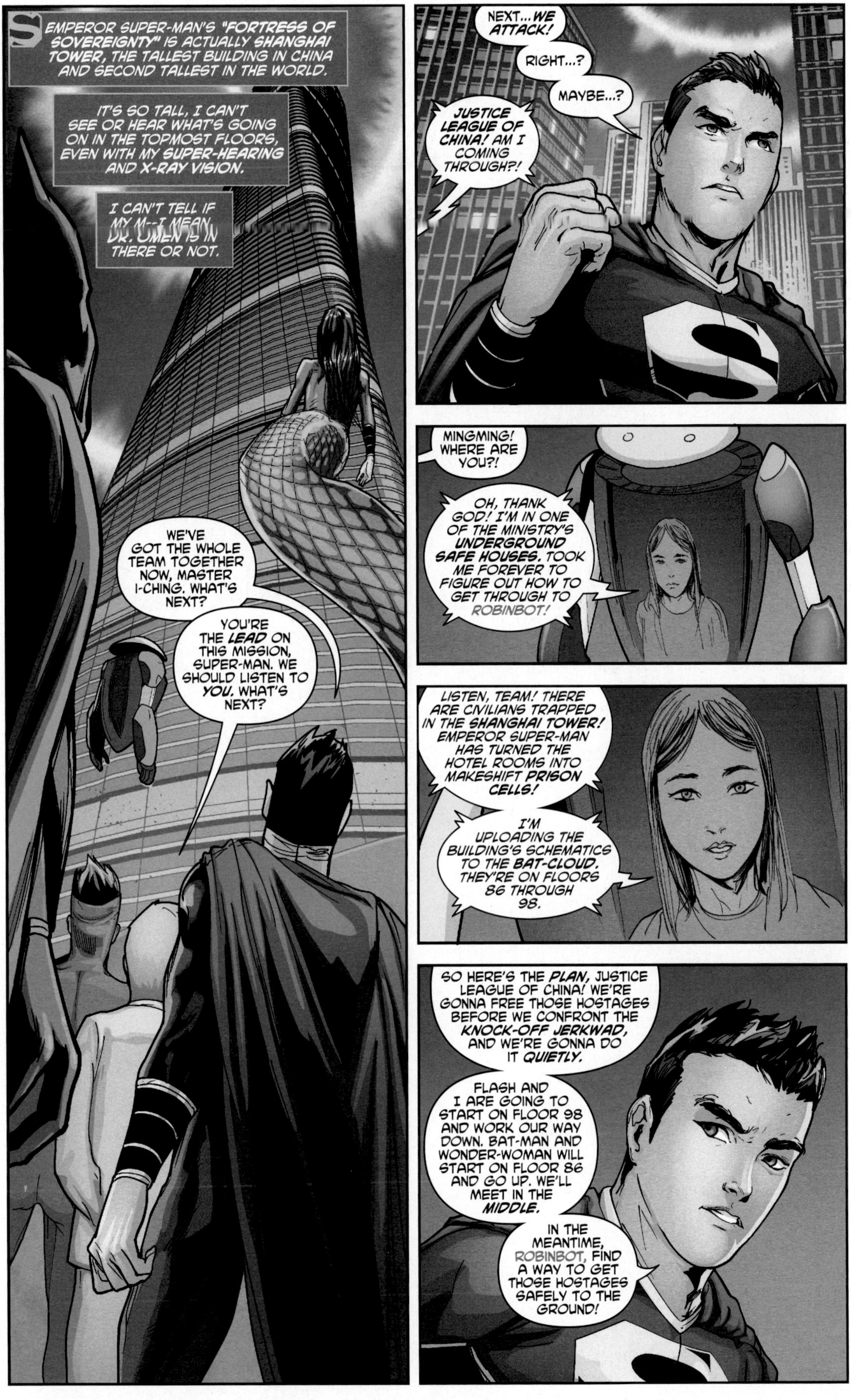
EMPEROR SUPER-MAN'S "FORTRESS OF SOVEREIGNTY" IS ACTUALLY SHANGHAI TOWER, THE TALLEST BUILDING IN CHINA AND SECOND TALLEST IN THE WORLD.
IT'S SO TALL, I CAN'T SEE OR HEAR WHAT'S GOING ON IN THE TOPMOST FLOORS, EVEN WITH MY SUPER-HEARING AND X-RAY VISION.
I CAN'T TELL IF MY M--I MEAN, DR. OMEN IS IN THERE OR NOT.
WE'VE GOT THE WHOLE TEAM TOGETHER NOW, MASTER I-CHING. WHAT'S NEXT?
YOU'RE THE LEAD ON THIS MISSION, SUPER-MAN. WE SHOULD LISTEN TO YOU. WHAT'S NEXT?
NEXT... WE ATTACK!
RIGHT...?
MAYBE...?
JUSTICE LEAGUE OF CHINA! AM I COMING THROUGH?!
MINGMING! WHERE ARE YOU?!
OH, THANK GOD! I'M IN ONE OF THE MINISTRY'S UNDERGROUND SAFE HOUSES. TOOK ME FOREVER TO FIGURE OUT HOW TO GET THROUGH TO ROBINBOT!
LISTEN, TEAM! THERE ARE CIVILIANS TRAPPED IN THE SHANGHAI TOWER! EMPEROR SUPER-MAN HAS TURNED THE HOTEL ROOMS INTO MAKESHIFT PRISON CELLS!
I'M UPLOADING THE BUILDING'S SCHEMATICS TO THE BAT-CLOUD. THEY'RE ON FLOORS 86 THROUGH 98.
SO HERE'S THE PLAN, JUSTICE LEAGUE OF CHINA! WE'RE GONNA FREE THOSE HOSTAGES BEFORE WE CONFRONT THE KNOCK-OFF JERKWAD, AND WE'RE GONNA DO IT QUIETLY.
FLASH AND I ARE GOING TO START ON FLOOR 98 AND WORK OUR WAY DOWN. BAT-MAN AND WONDER-WOMAN WILL START ON FLOOR 86 AND GO UP. WE'LL MEET IN THE MIDDLE.
IN THE MEANTIME, ROBINBOT, FIND A WAY TO GET THOSE HOSTAGES SAFELY TO THE GROUND!

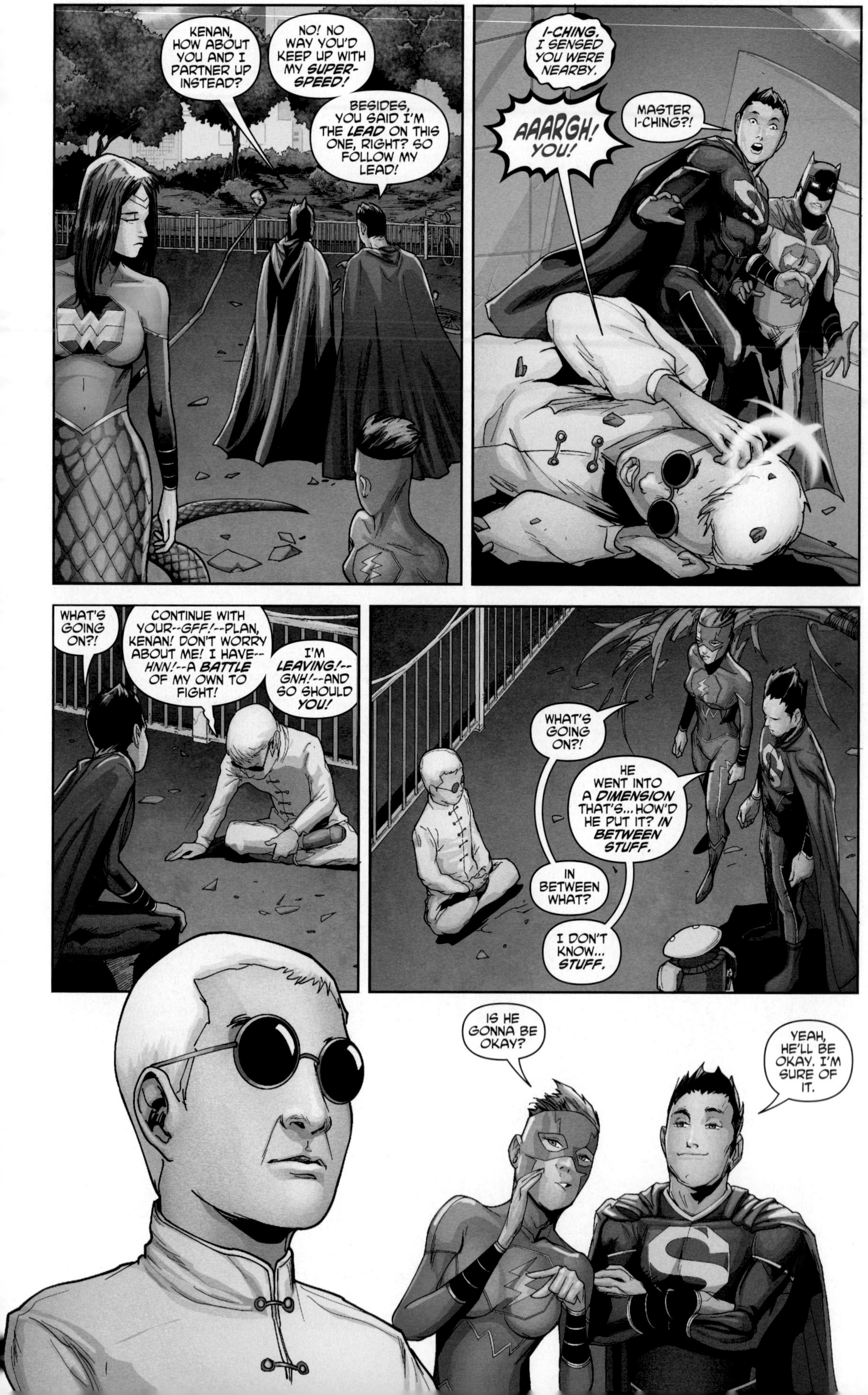
KENAN, HOW ABOUT YOU AND I PARTNER UP INSTEAD?
NO! NO WAY YOU'D KEEP UP WITH MY SUPER-SPEED!
BESIDES, YOU SAID I'M THE LEAD ON THIS ONE, RIGHT? SO FOLLOW MY LEAD!
I-CHING. I SENSED YOU WERE NEARBY.
AAARGH! YOU!
MASTER I-CHING?!
WHAT'S GOING ON?!
CONTINUE WITH YOUR--GFF!--PLAN, KENAN! DON'T WORRY ABOUT ME! I HAVE--HNN!--A BATTLE OF MY OWN TO FIGHT!
I'M LEAVING!--GNH!--AND SO SHOULD YOU!
WHAT'S GOING ON?!
HE WENT INTO A DIMENSION THAT'S...HOW'D HE PUT IT? IN BETWEEN STUFF.
IN BETWEEN WHAT?
I DON'T KNOW... STUFF.
IS HE GONNA BE OKAY?
YEAH, HE'LL BE OKAY. I'M SURE OF IT.

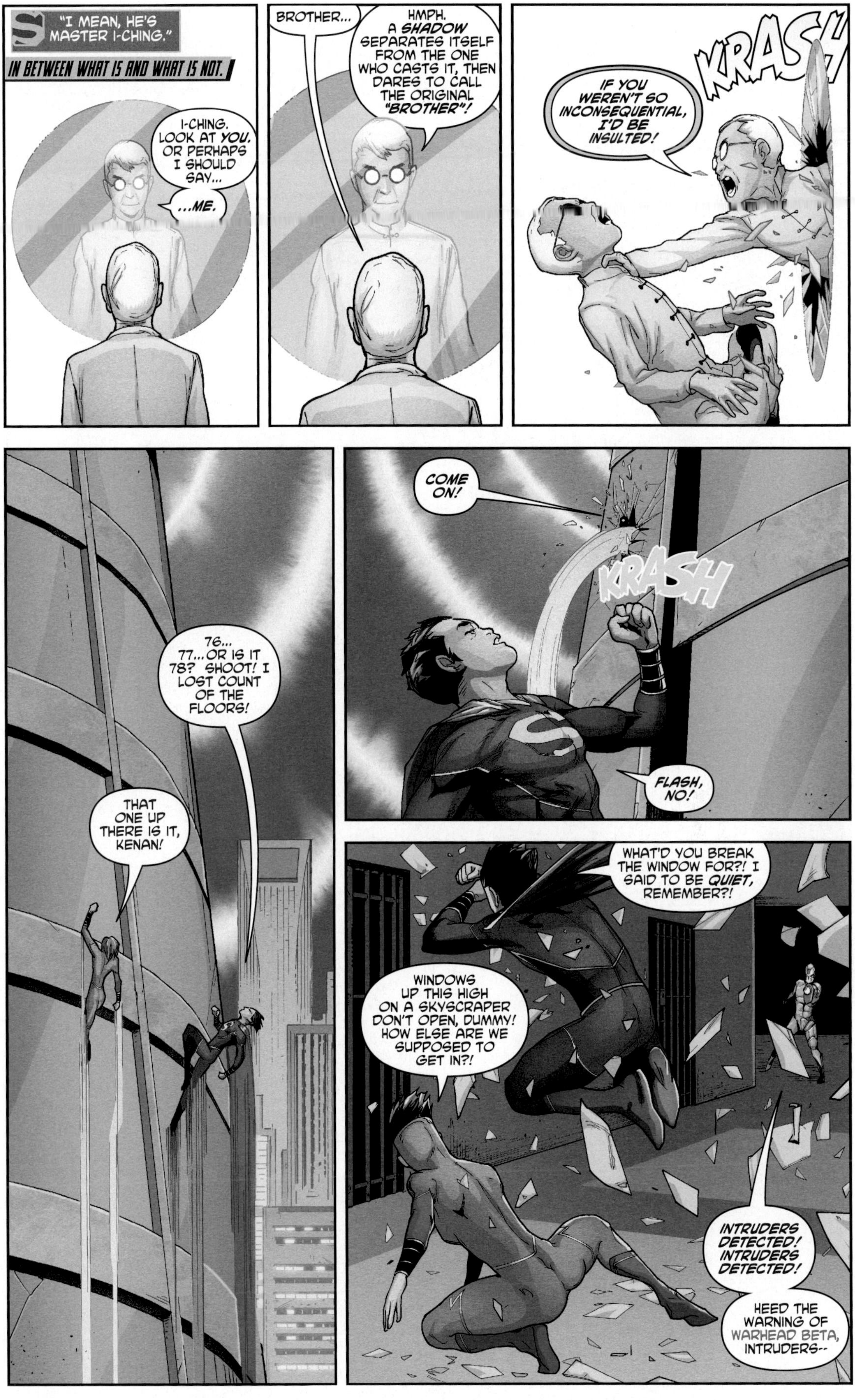
"I MEAN, HE'S MASTER I-CHING."
IN BETWEEN WHAT IS AND WHAT IS NOT.
I-CHING. LOOK AT YOU. OR PERHAPS I SHOULD SAY...
...ME.
BROTHER...
HMPH. A SHADOW SEPARATES ITSELF FROM THE ONE WHO CASTS IT, THEN DARES TO CALL THE ORIGINAL "BROTHER"!
KRASH
IF YOU WEREN'T SO INCONSEQUENTIAL, I'D BE INSULTED!
76... 77...OR IS IT 78? SHOOT! I LOST COUNT OF THE FLOORS!
THAT ONE UP THERE IS IT, KENAN!
COME ON!
KRASH
FLASH, NO!
WHAT'D YOU BREAK THE WINDOW FOR?! I SAID TO BE QUIET, REMEMBER?!
WINDOWS UP THIS HIGH ON A SKYSCRAPER DON'T OPEN, DUMMY! HOW ELSE ARE WE SUPPOSED TO GET IN?!
INTRUDERS DETECTED! INTRUDERS DETECTED!
HEED THE WARNING OF WARHEAD BETA, INTRUDERS--

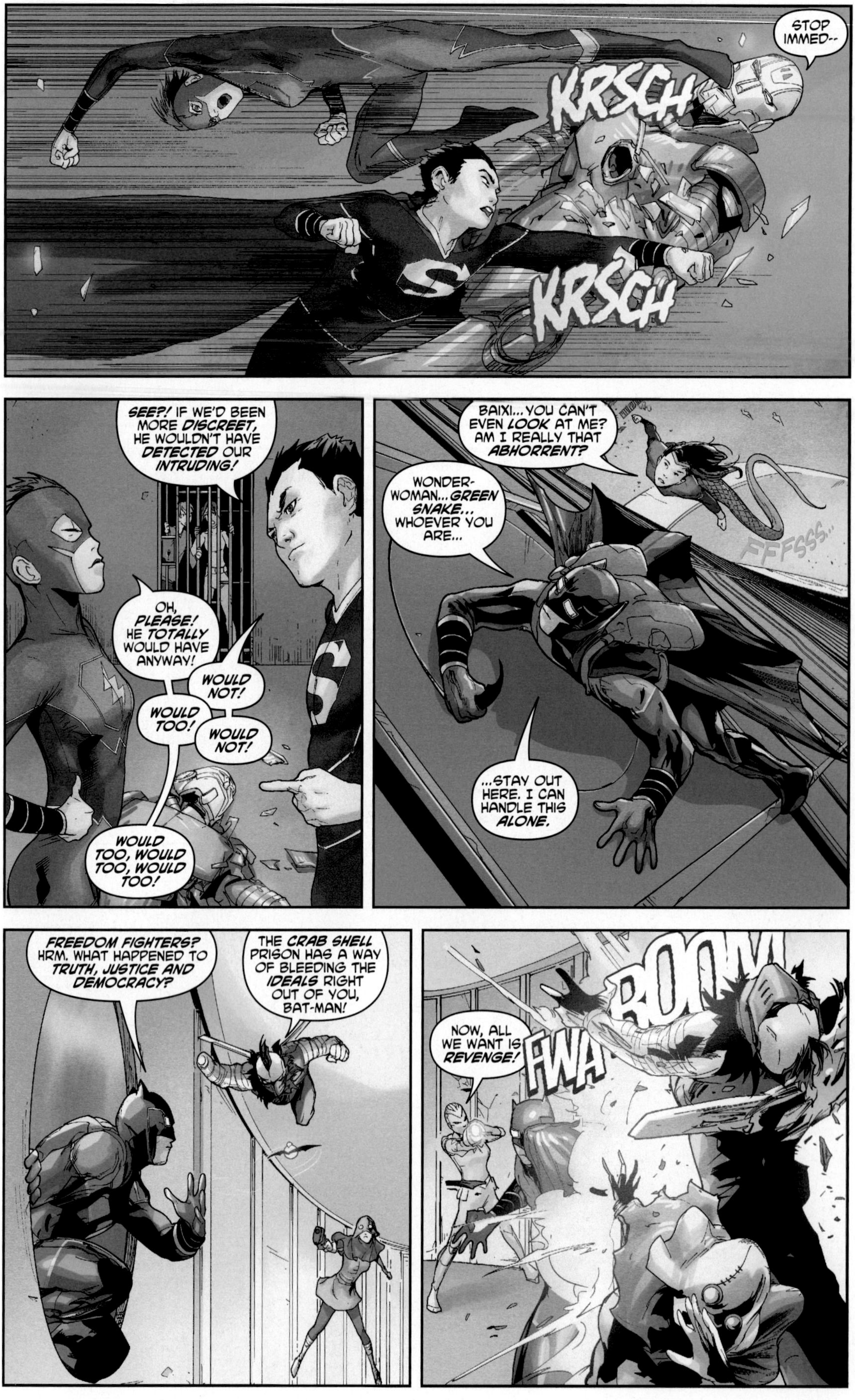

STOP IMMED--
KRSCH
KRSCH
SEE?! IF WE'D BEEN MORE DISCREET, HE WOULDN'T HAVE DETECTED OUR INTRUDING!
OH, PLEASE! HE TOTALLY WOULD HAVE ANYWAY!
WOULD NOT!
WOULD TOO!
WOULD NOT!
WOULD TOO, WOULD TOO, WOULD TOO!
BAIXI...YOU CAN'T EVEN LOOK AT ME? AM I REALLY THAT ABHORRENT?
WONDER-WOMAN...GREEN SNAKE... WHOEVER YOU ARE...
FFFSSS...
...STAY OUT HERE. I CAN HANDLE THIS ALONE.
FREEDOM FIGHTERS? HRM. WHAT HAPPENED TO TRUTH, JUSTICE AND DEMOCRACY?
THE CRAB SHELL PRISON HAS A WAY OF BLEEDING THE IDEALS RIGHT OUT OF YOU, BAT-MAN!
NOW, ALL WE WANT IS REVENGE!
FWA
BOOM

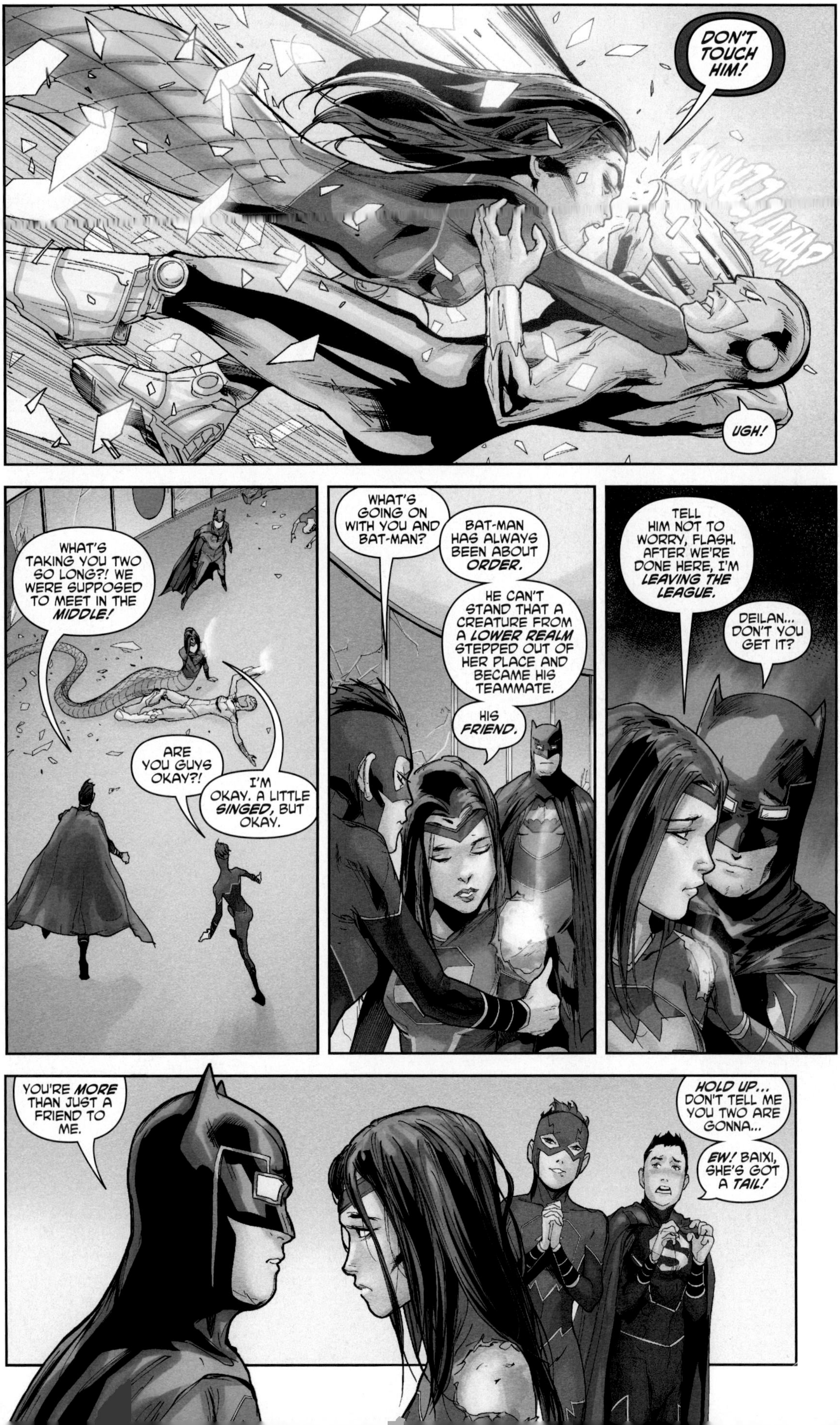

DON'T TOUCH HIM!
UGH!
WHAT'S TAKING YOU TWO SO LONG?! WE WERE SUPPOSED TO MEET IN THE MIDDLE!
ARE YOU GUYS OKAY?!
I'M OKAY. A LITTLE SINGED, BUT OKAY.
WHAT'S GOING ON WITH YOU AND BAT-MAN?
BAT-MAN HAS ALWAYS BEEN ABOUT ORDER.
HE CAN'T STAND THAT A CREATURE FROM A LOWER REALM STEPPED OUT OF HER PLACE AND BECAME HIS TEAMMATE.
HIS FRIEND.
TELL HIM NOT TO WORRY, FLASH. AFTER WE'RE DONE HERE, I'M LEAVING THE LEAGUE.
DEILAN... DON'T YOU GET IT?
YOU'RE MORE THAN JUST A FRIEND TO ME.
HOLD UP... DON'T TELL ME YOU TWO ARE GONNA...
EW! BAIXI, SHE'S GOT A TAIL!

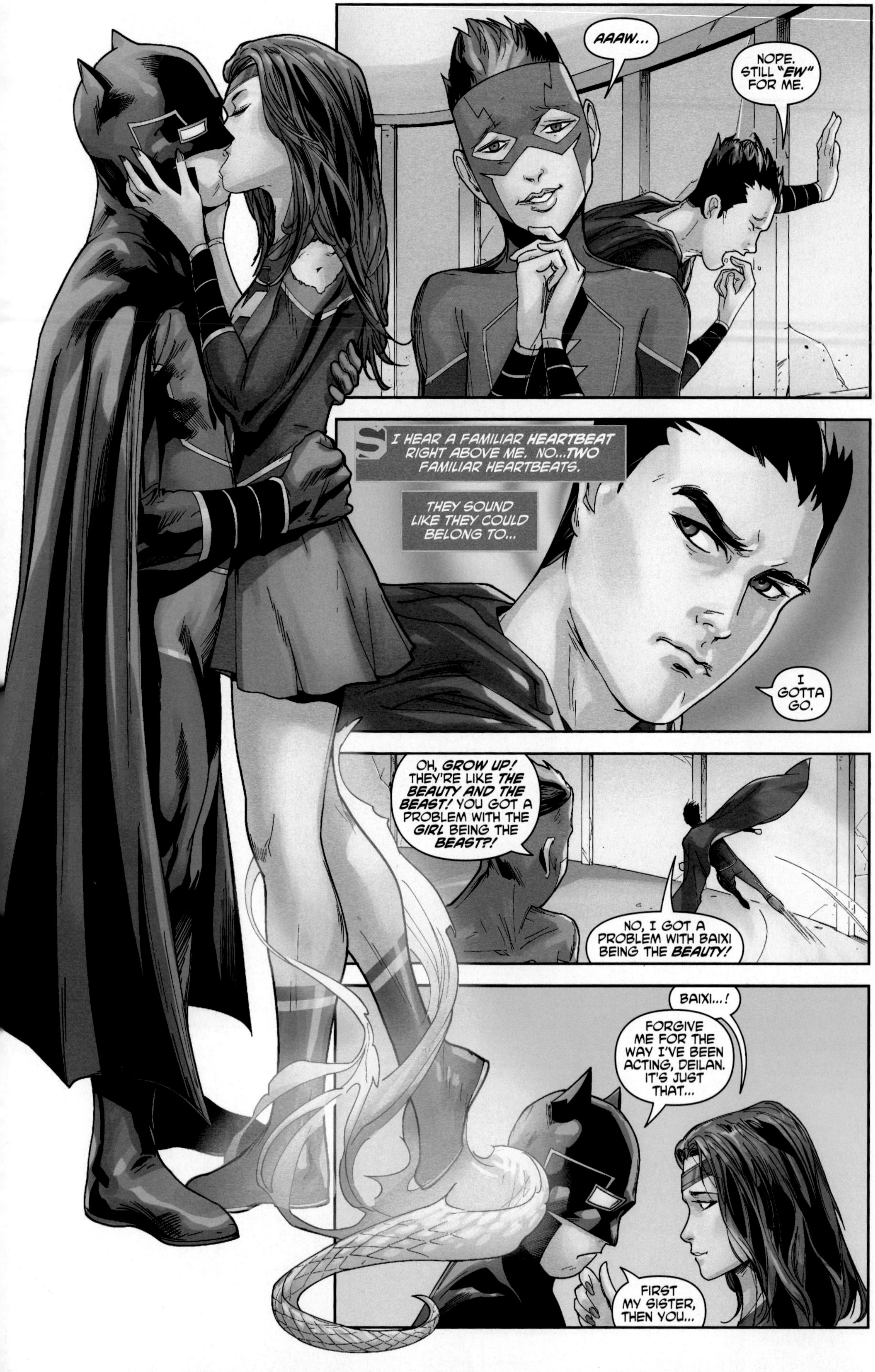
AAAW...
NOPE. STILL "EW" FOR ME.
I HEAR A FAMILIAR HEARTBEAT RIGHT ABOVE ME. NO...TWO FAMILIAR HEARTBEATS.
THEY SOUND LIKE THEY COULD BELONG TO...
I GOTTA GO.
OH, GROW UP! THEY'RE LIKE THE BEAUTY AND THE BEAST! YOU GOT A PROBLEM WITH THE GIRL BEING THE BEAST?!
NO, I GOT A PROBLEM WITH BAIXI BEING THE BEAUTY!
BAIXI...!
FORGIVE ME FOR THE WAY I'VE BEEN ACTING, DEILAN. IT'S JUST THAT...
FIRST MY SISTER, THEN YOU...

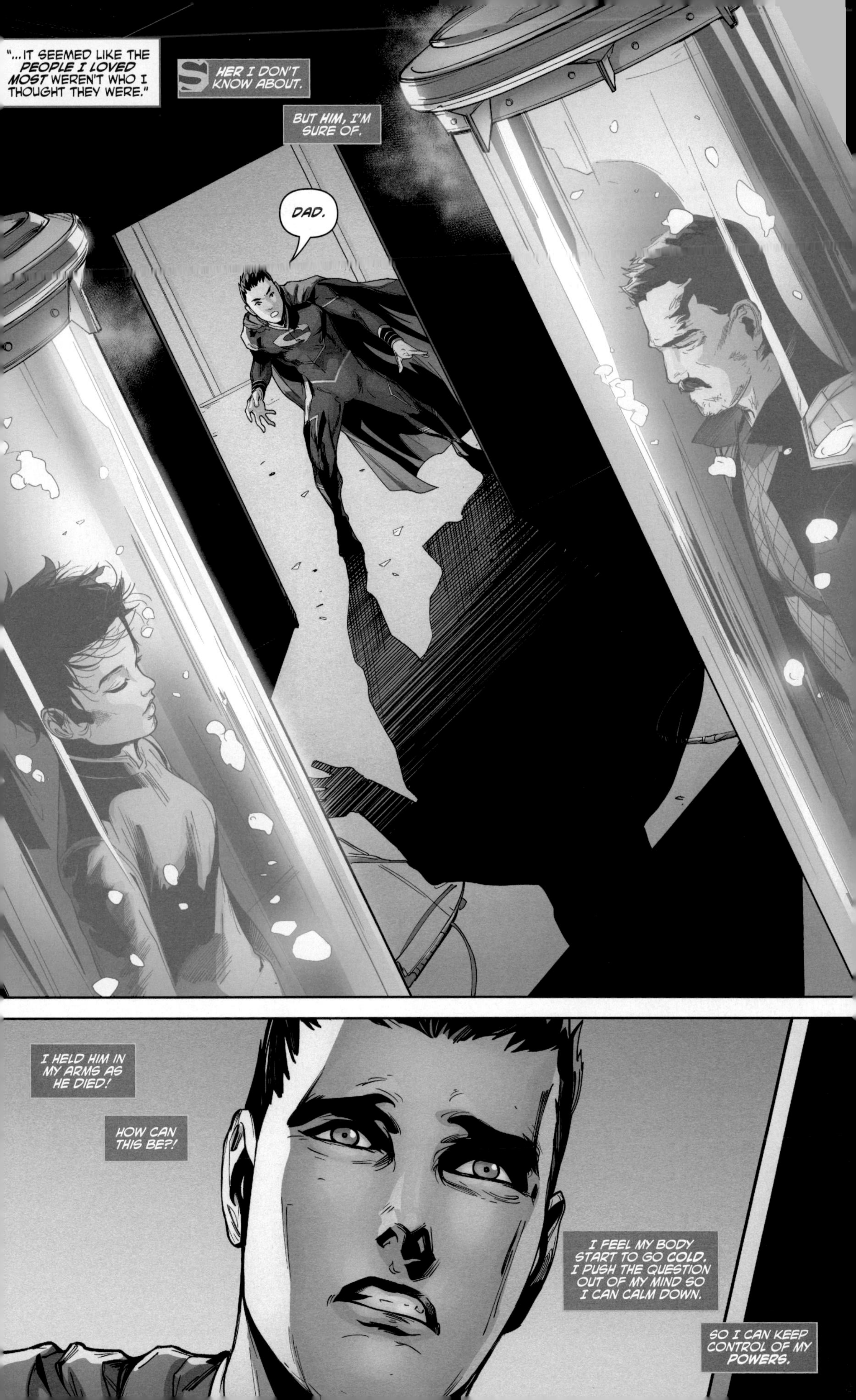
"...IT SEEMED LIKE THE PEOPLE I LOVED MOST WEREN'T WHO I THOUGHT THEY WERE."
HER I DON'T KNOW ABOUT.
BUT HIM, I'M SURE OF.
DAD.
I HELD HIM IN MY ARMS AS HE DIED!
HOW CAN THIS BE?!
I FEEL MY BODY START TO GO COLD. I PUSH THE QUESTION OUT OF MY MIND SO I CAN CALM DOWN.
SO I CAN KEEP CONTROL OF MY POWERS.

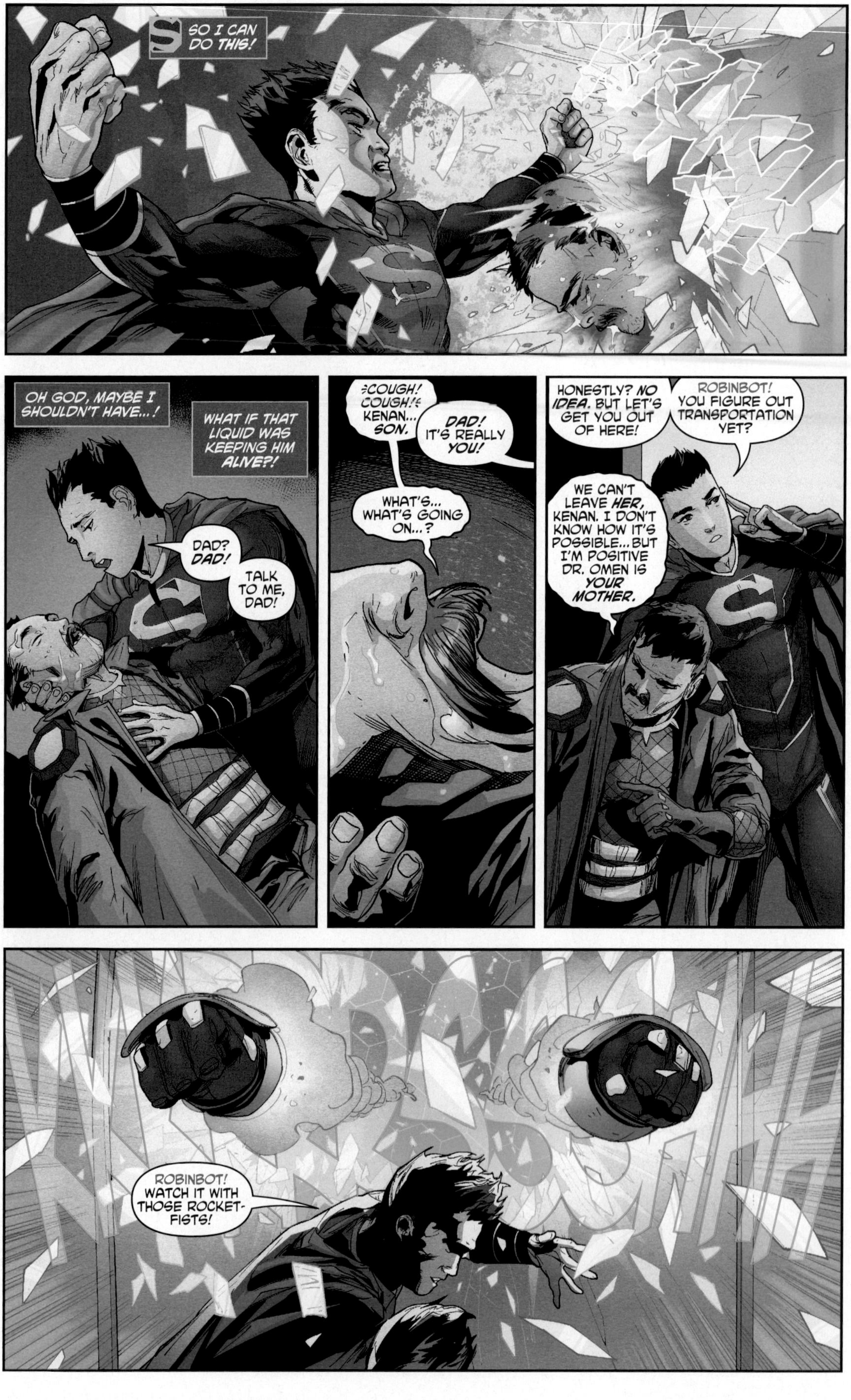

SO I CAN DO THIS!
OH GOD, MAYBE I SHOULDN'T HAVE...!
WHAT IF THAT LIQUID WAS KEEPING HIM ALIVE?!
DAD? DAD!
TALK TO ME, DAD!
COUGH! COUGH! KENAN... SON.
DAD! IT'S REALLY YOU!
WHAT'S... WHAT'S GOING ON...?
HONESTLY? NO IDEA. BUT LET'S GET YOU OUT OF HERE!
ROBINBOT! YOU FIGURE OUT TRANSPORTATION YET?
WE CAN'T LEAVE HER, KENAN. I DON'T KNOW HOW IT'S POSSIBLE... BUT I'M POSITIVE DR. OMEN IS YOUR MOTHER.
ROBINBOT! WATCH IT WITH THOSE ROCKET-FISTS!

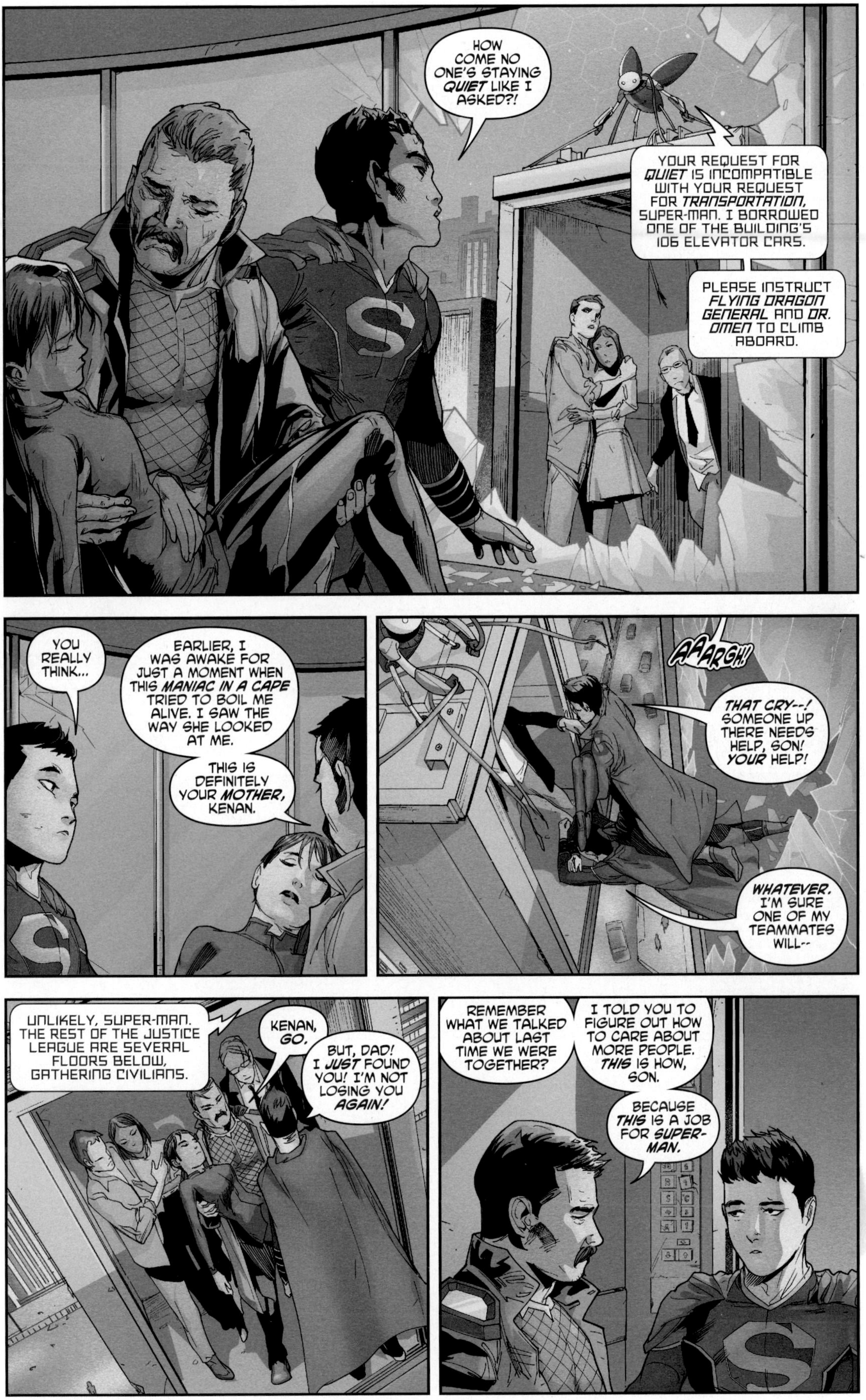
HOW COME NO ONE'S STAYING *QUIET* LIKE I ASKED?!
YOUR REQUEST FOR *QUIET* IS INCOMPATIBLE WITH YOUR REQUEST FOR *TRANSPORTATION*, SUPER-MAN. I BORROWED ONE OF THE BUILDING'S 106 ELEVATOR CARS.
PLEASE INSTRUCT *FLYING DRAGON GENERAL* AND *DR. OMEN* TO CLIMB ABOARD.
YOU REALLY THINK...
EARLIER, I WAS AWAKE FOR JUST A MOMENT WHEN THIS *MANIAC IN A CAPE* TRIED TO BOIL ME ALIVE. I SAW THE WAY SHE LOOKED AT ME.
THIS IS DEFINITELY YOUR *MOTHER*, KENAN.
AAAARGH!
THAT CRY--! SOMEONE UP THERE NEEDS HELP, SON! *YOUR* HELP!
WHATEVER. I'M SURE ONE OF MY TEAMMATES WILL--
UNLIKELY, SUPER-MAN. THE REST OF THE JUSTICE LEAGUE ARE SEVERAL FLOORS BELOW, GATHERING CIVILIANS.
KENAN, *GO.*
BUT, DAD! I *JUST* FOUND YOU! I'M NOT LOSING YOU *AGAIN!*
REMEMBER WHAT WE TALKED ABOUT LAST TIME WE WERE TOGETHER?
I TOLD YOU TO FIGURE OUT HOW TO CARE ABOUT MORE PEOPLE. *THIS* IS HOW, SON.
BECAUSE *THIS* IS A JOB FOR *SUPER-MAN.*

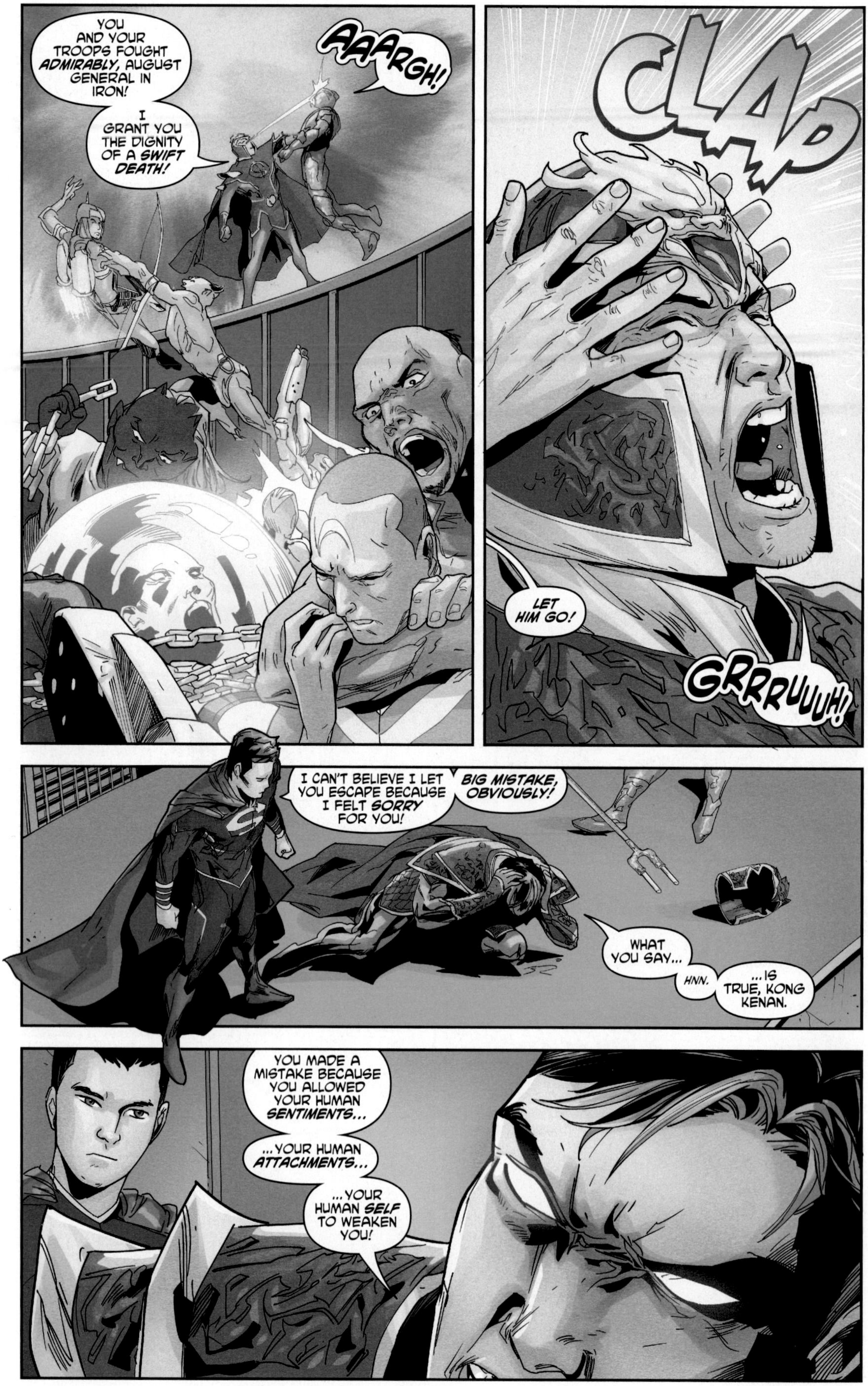
YOU AND YOUR TROOPS FOUGHT ADMIRABLY, AUGUST GENERAL IN IRON!
AAAARGH!
I GRANT YOU THE DIGNITY OF A SWIFT DEATH!
CLAP
LET HIM GO!
GRRRUUUH!
I CAN'T BELIEVE I LET YOU ESCAPE BECAUSE I FELT SORRY FOR YOU!
BIG MISTAKE, OBVIOUSLY!
WHAT YOU SAY...
HNN.
...IS TRUE, KONG KENAN.
YOU MADE A MISTAKE BECAUSE YOU ALLOWED YOUR HUMAN SENTIMENTS...
...YOUR HUMAN ATTACHMENTS...
...YOUR HUMAN SELF TO WEAKEN YOU!

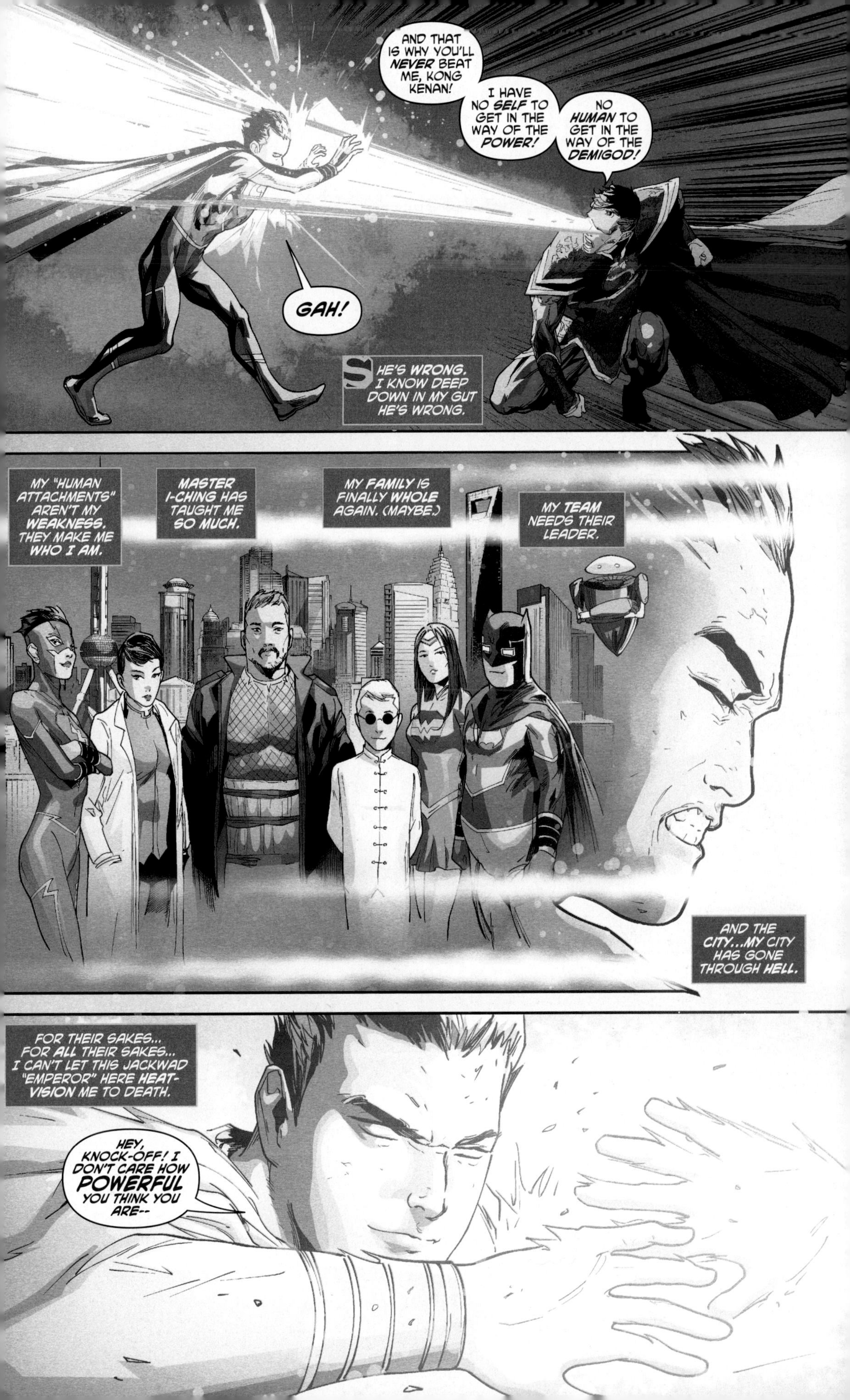
AND THAT IS WHY YOU'LL NEVER BEAT ME, KONG KENAN!
I HAVE NO SELF TO GET IN THE WAY OF THE POWER!
NO HUMAN TO GET IN THE WAY OF THE DEMIGOD!
GAH!
SHE'S WRONG. I KNOW DEEP DOWN IN MY GUT HE'S WRONG.
MY "HUMAN ATTACHMENTS" AREN'T MY WEAKNESS. THEY MAKE ME WHO I AM.
MASTER I-CHING HAS TAUGHT ME SO MUCH.
MY FAMILY IS FINALLY WHOLE AGAIN. (MAYBE.)
MY TEAM NEEDS THEIR LEADER.
AND THE CITY...MY CITY HAS GONE THROUGH HELL.
FOR THEIR SAKES... FOR ALL THEIR SAKES... I CAN'T LET THIS JACKWAD "EMPEROR" HERE HEAT-VISION ME TO DEATH.
HEY, KNOCK-OFF! I DON'T CARE HOW POWERFUL YOU THINK YOU ARE--

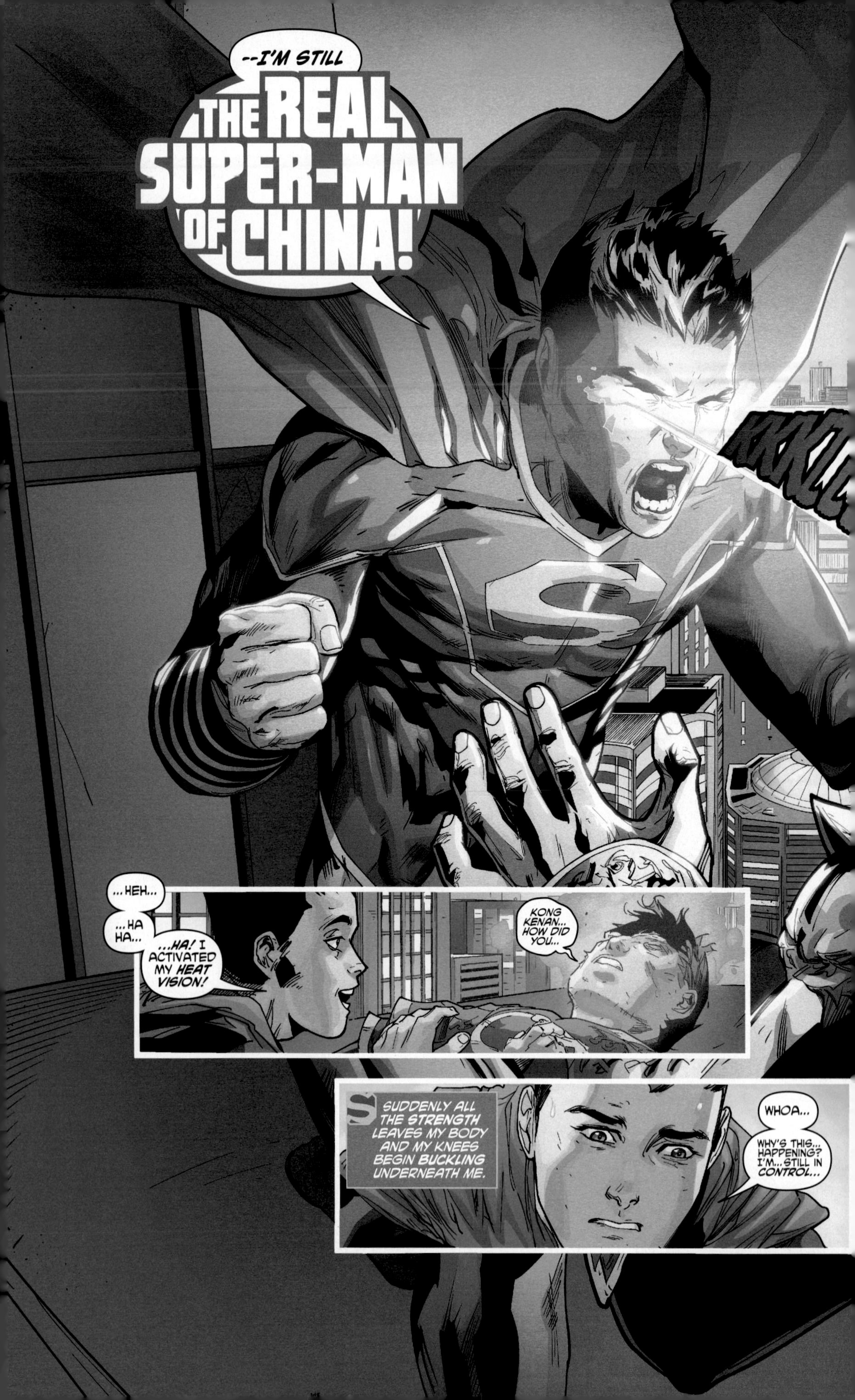
--I'M STILL
THE REAL SUPER-MAN OF CHINA!
KRKZL
...HEH...
...HA HA...
...HA! I ACTIVATED MY HEAT VISION!
KONG KENAN... HOW DID YOU...
SUDDENLY ALL THE STRENGTH LEAVES MY BODY AND MY KNEES BEGIN BUCKLING UNDERNEATH ME.
WHOA...
WHY'S THIS... HAPPENING? I'M...STILL IN CONTROL...

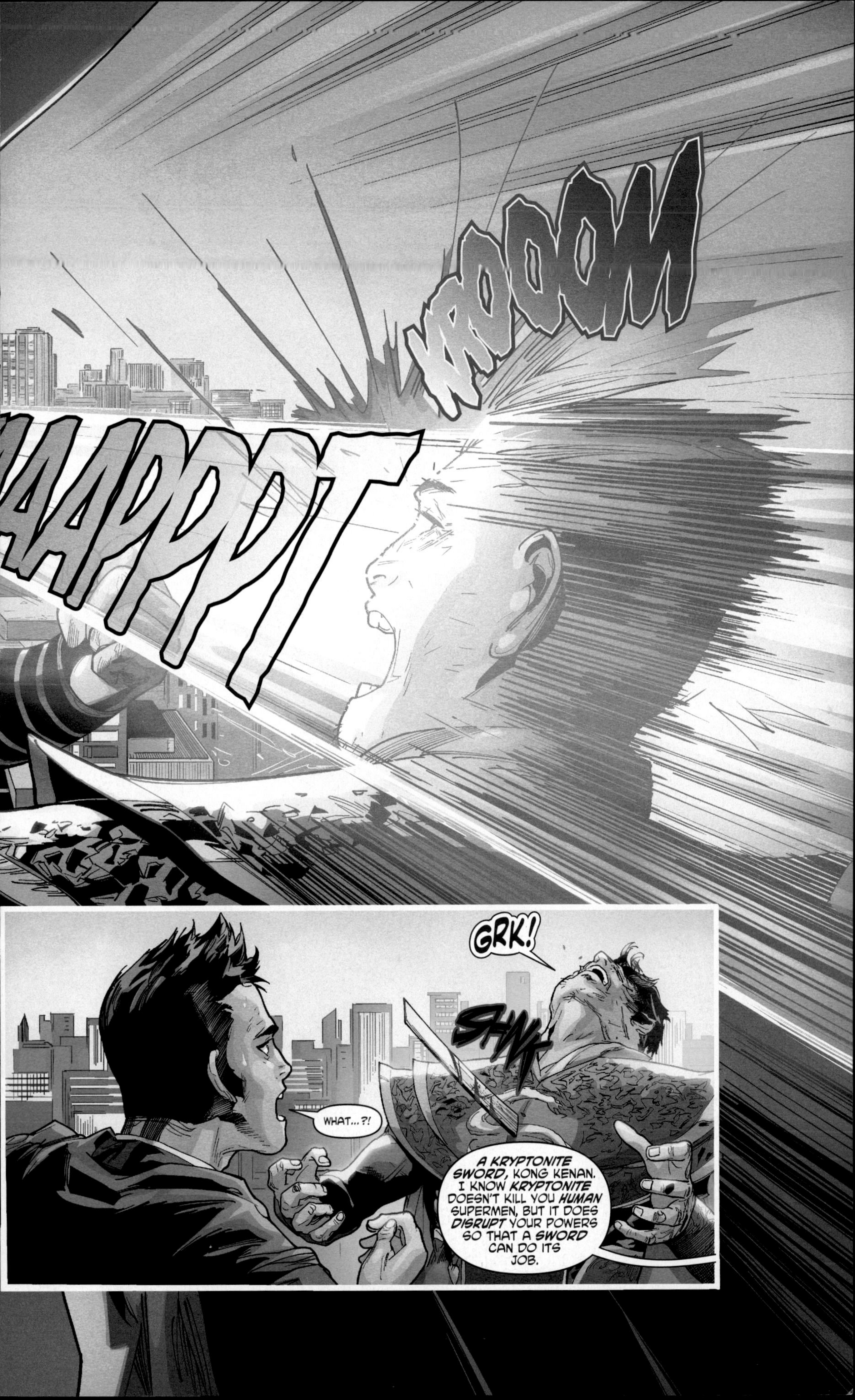
KROOOM
GRK!
SHNK
WHAT...?!
A KRYPTONITE SWORD, KONG KENAN. I KNOW KRYPTONITE DOESN'T KILL YOU HUMAN SUPERMEN, BUT IT DOES DISRUPT YOUR POWERS SO THAT A SWORD CAN DO ITS JOB.

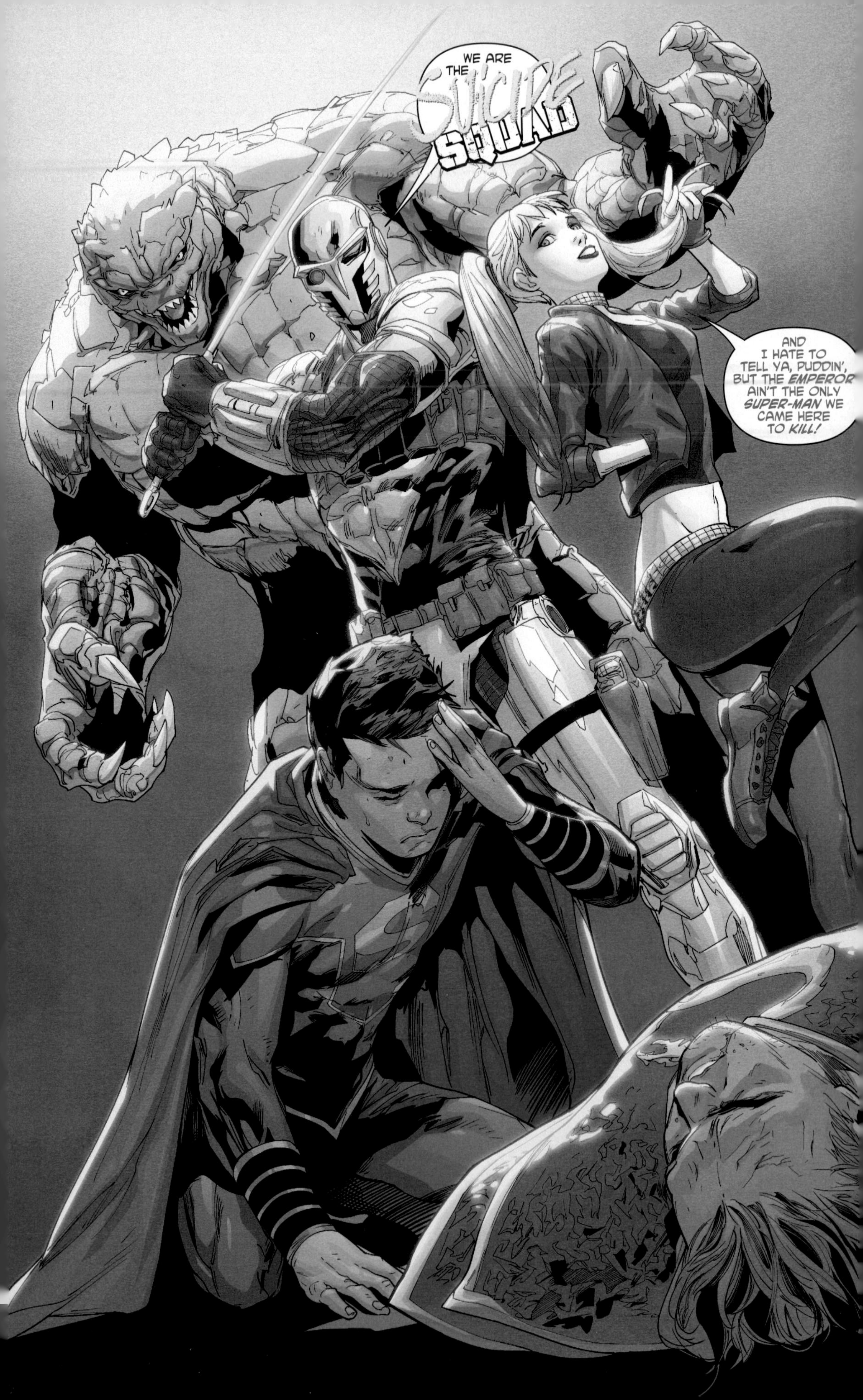
WE ARE THE SUICIDE SQUAD
AND I HATE TO TELL YA, PUDDIN', BUT THE EMPEROR AIN'T THE ONLY SUPER-MAN WE CAME HERE TO KILL!

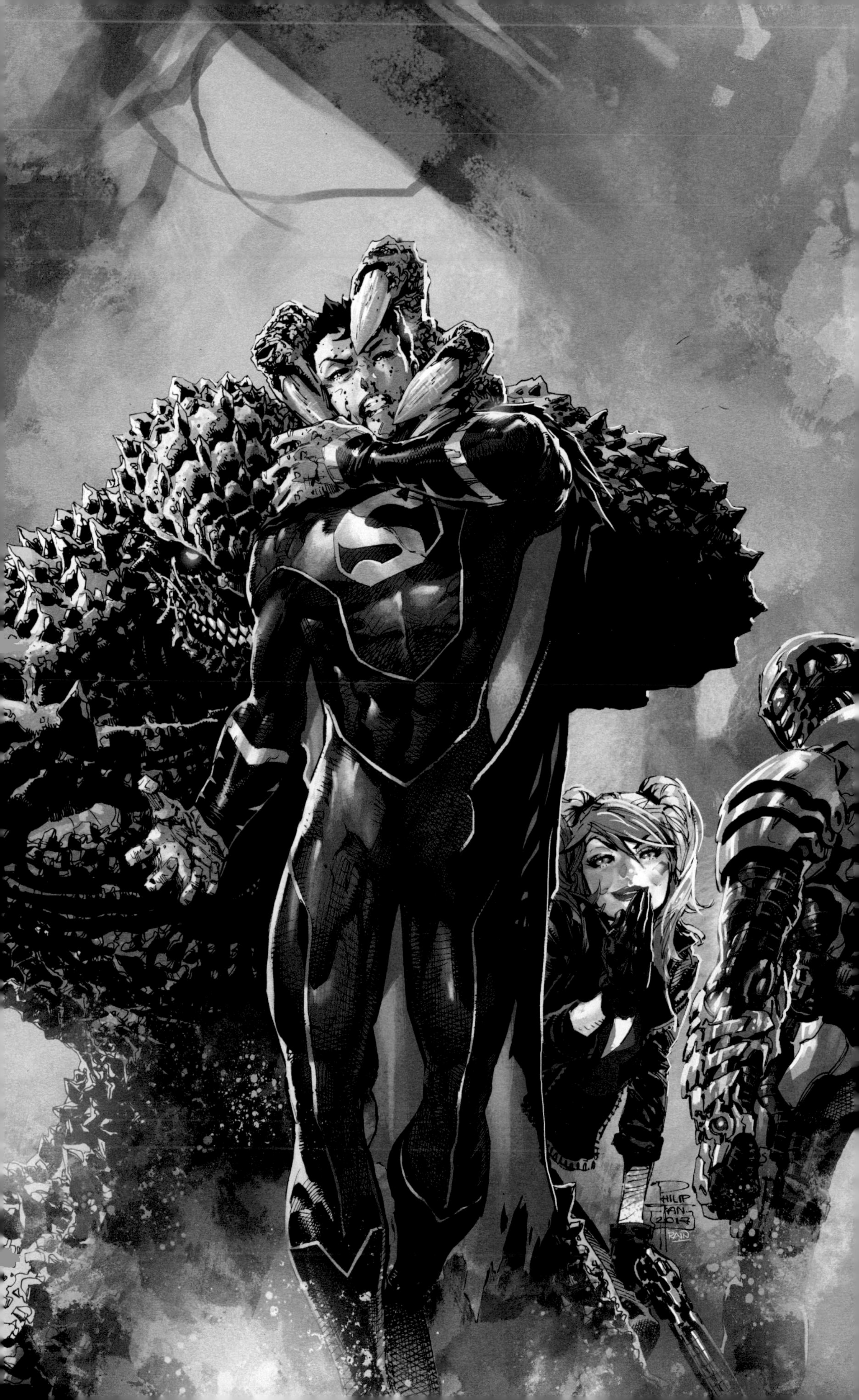

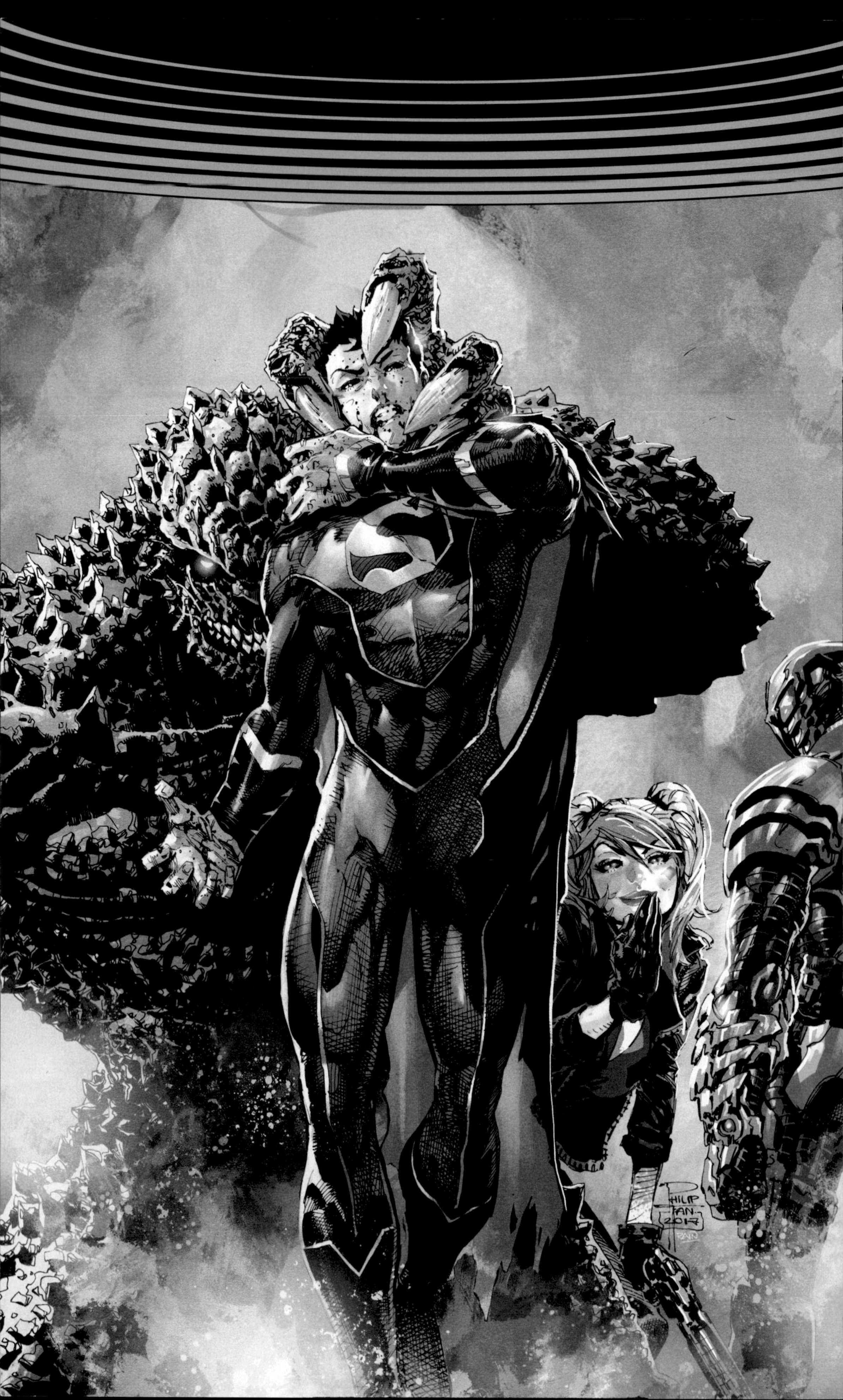
PHILIP TAN 2017

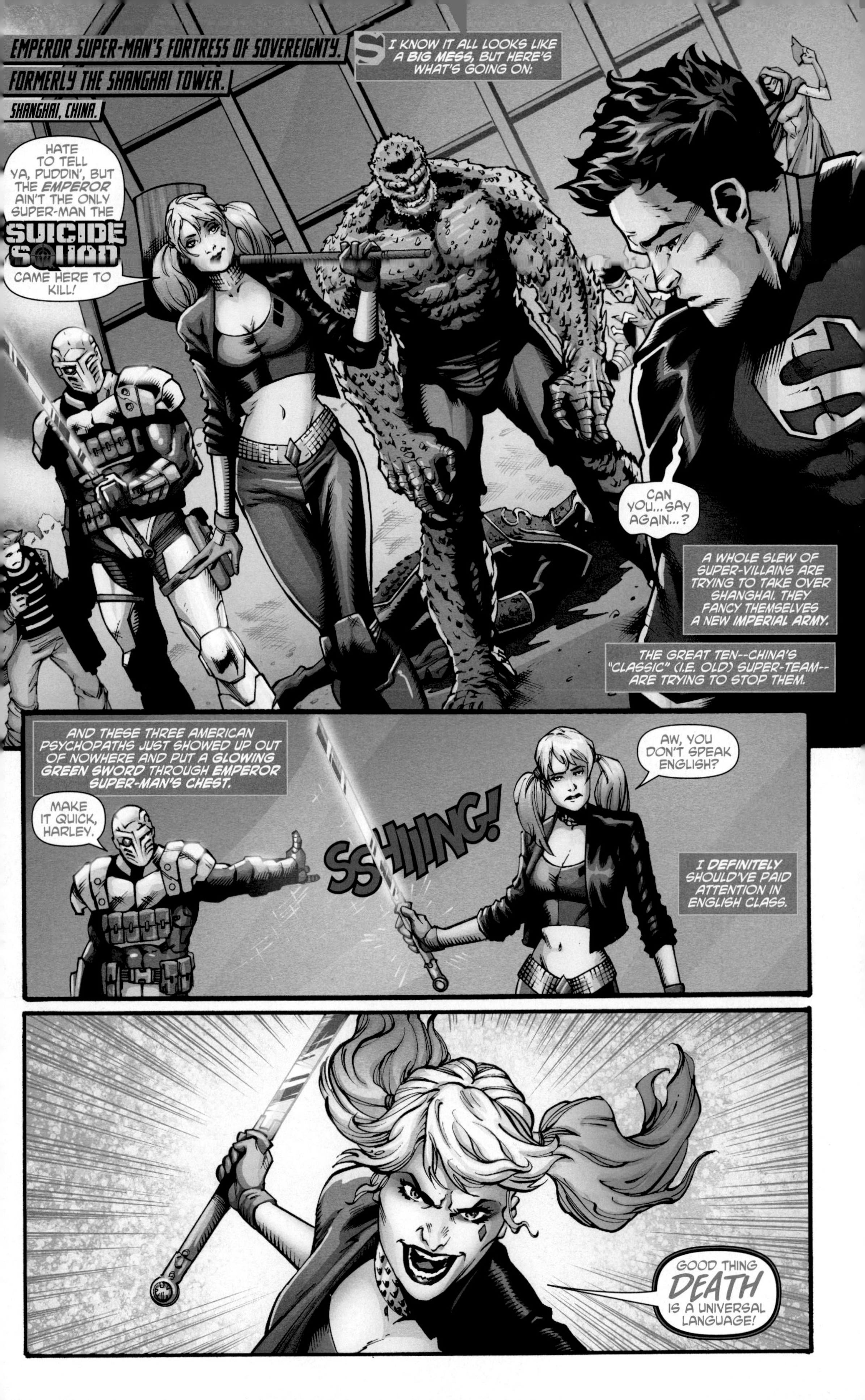
EMPEROR SUPER-MAN'S FORTRESS OF SOVEREIGNTY.
FORMERLY THE SHANGHAI TOWER.
SHANGHAI, CHINA.
I KNOW IT ALL LOOKS LIKE A BIG MESS, BUT HERE'S WHAT'S GOING ON:
HATE TO TELL YA, PUDDIN', BUT THE EMPEROR AIN'T THE ONLY SUPER-MAN THE SUICIDE SQUAD CAME HERE TO KILL!
CAN YOU...SAY AGAIN...?
A WHOLE SLEW OF SUPER-VILLAINS ARE TRYING TO TAKE OVER SHANGHAI. THEY FANCY THEMSELVES A NEW IMPERIAL ARMY.
THE GREAT TEN--CHINA'S "CLASSIC" (I.E. OLD) SUPER-TEAM--ARE TRYING TO STOP THEM.
AND THESE THREE AMERICAN PSYCHOPATHS JUST SHOWED UP OUT OF NOWHERE AND PUT A GLOWING GREEN SWORD THROUGH EMPEROR SUPER-MAN'S CHEST.
MAKE IT QUICK, HARLEY.
SSHIIING!
AW, YOU DON'T SPEAK ENGLISH?
I DEFINITELY SHOULD'VE PAID ATTENTION IN ENGLISH CLASS.
GOOD THING DEATH IS A UNIVERSAL LANGUAGE!

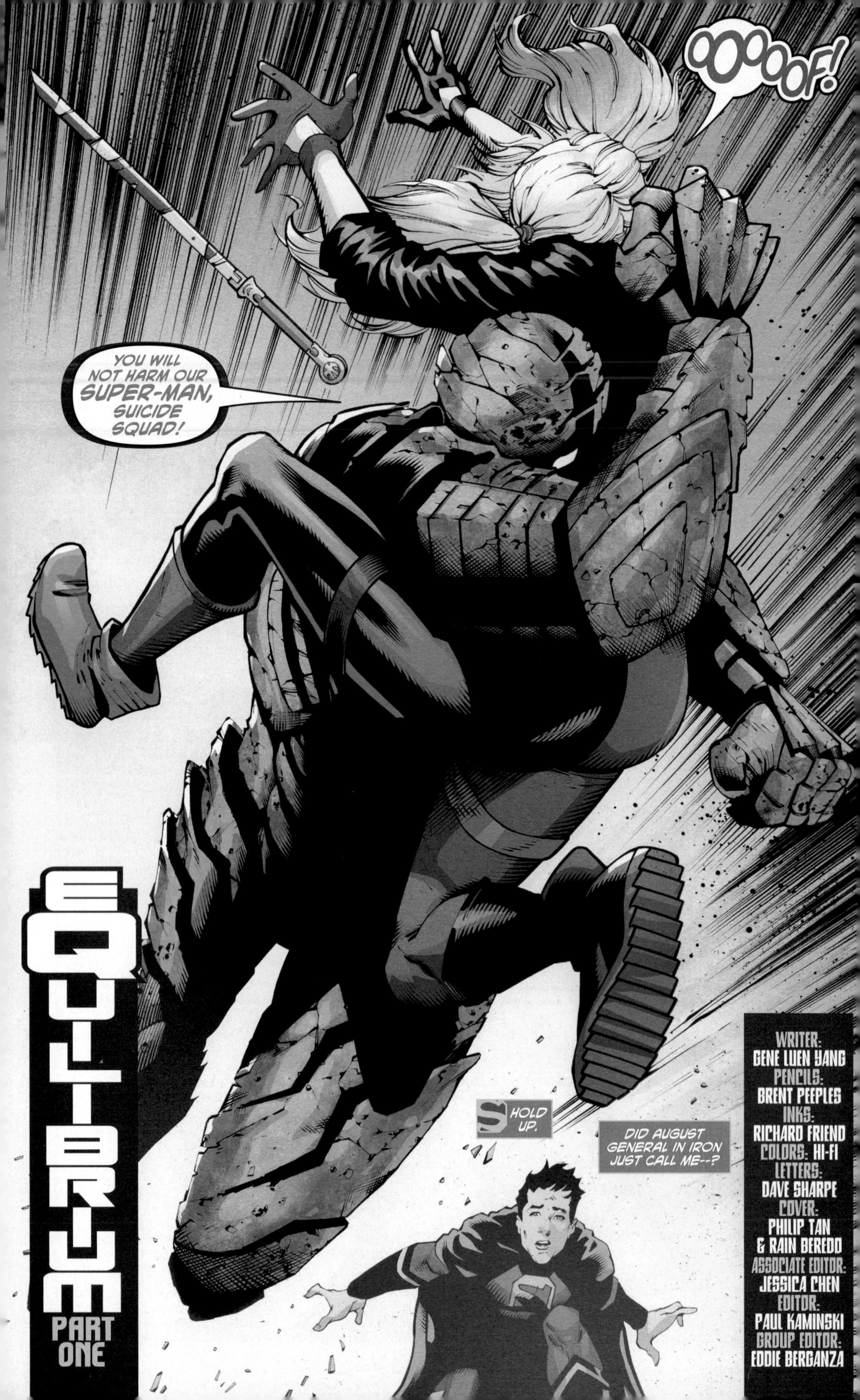
OOOOOOF!
YOU WILL NOT HARM OUR SUPER-MAN, SUICIDE SQUAD!
HOLD UP.
DID AUGUST GENERAL IN IRON JUST CALL ME--?
EQUILIBRIUM PART ONE
WRITER: GENE LUEN YANG
PENCILS: BRENT PEEPLES
INKS: RICHARD FRIEND
COLORS: HI-FI
LETTERS: DAVE SHARPE
COVER: PHILIP TAN & RAIN BEREDO
ASSOCIATE EDITOR: JESSICA CHEN
EDITOR: PAUL KAMINSKI
GROUP EDITOR: EDDIE BERGANZA

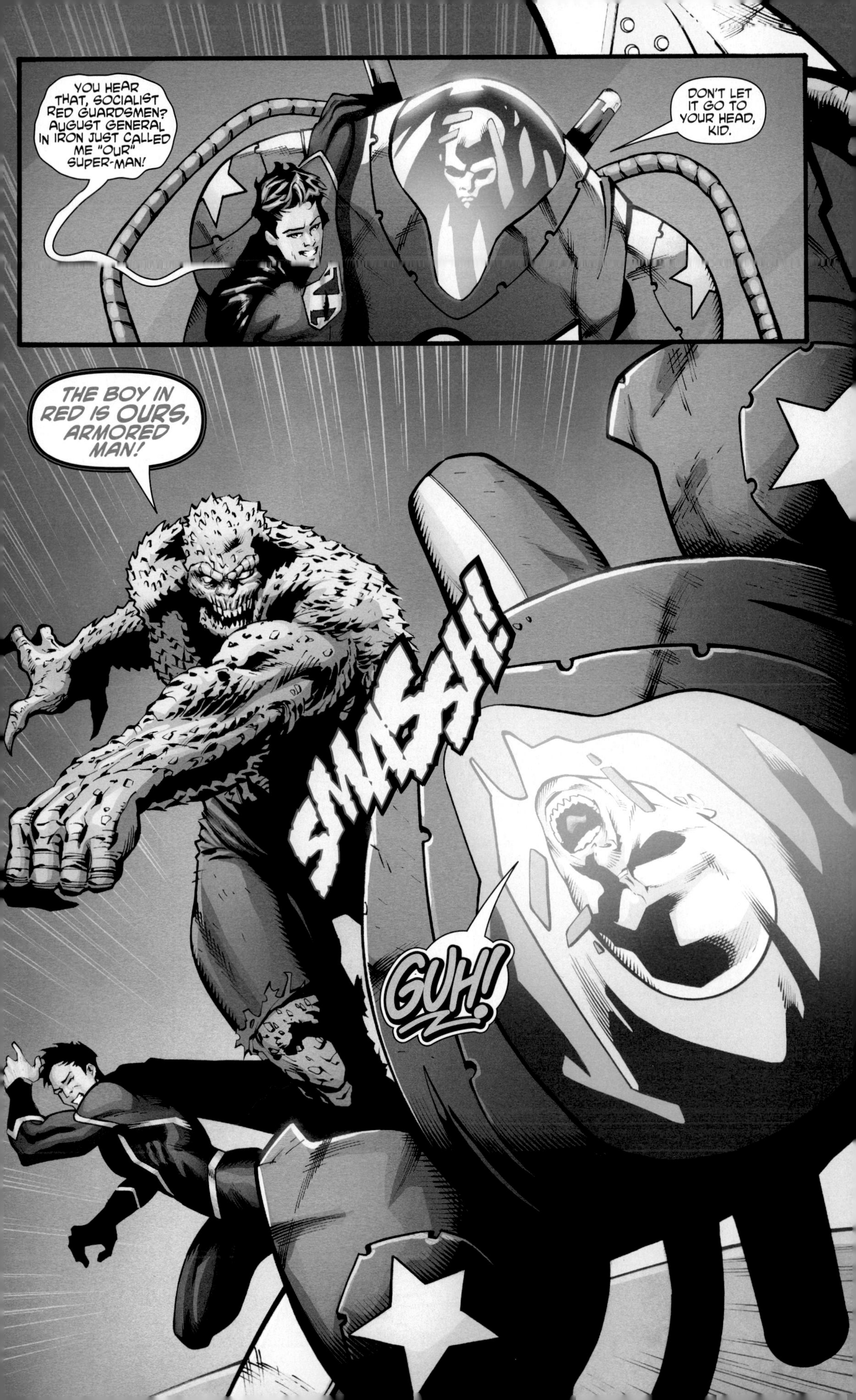
YOU HEAR THAT, SOCIALIST RED GUARDSMEN? AUGUST GENERAL IN IRON JUST CALLED ME "OUR" SUPER-MAN!
DON'T LET IT GO TO YOUR HEAD, KID.
THE BOY IN RED IS OURS, ARMORED MAN!
SMASH!!
GUH!

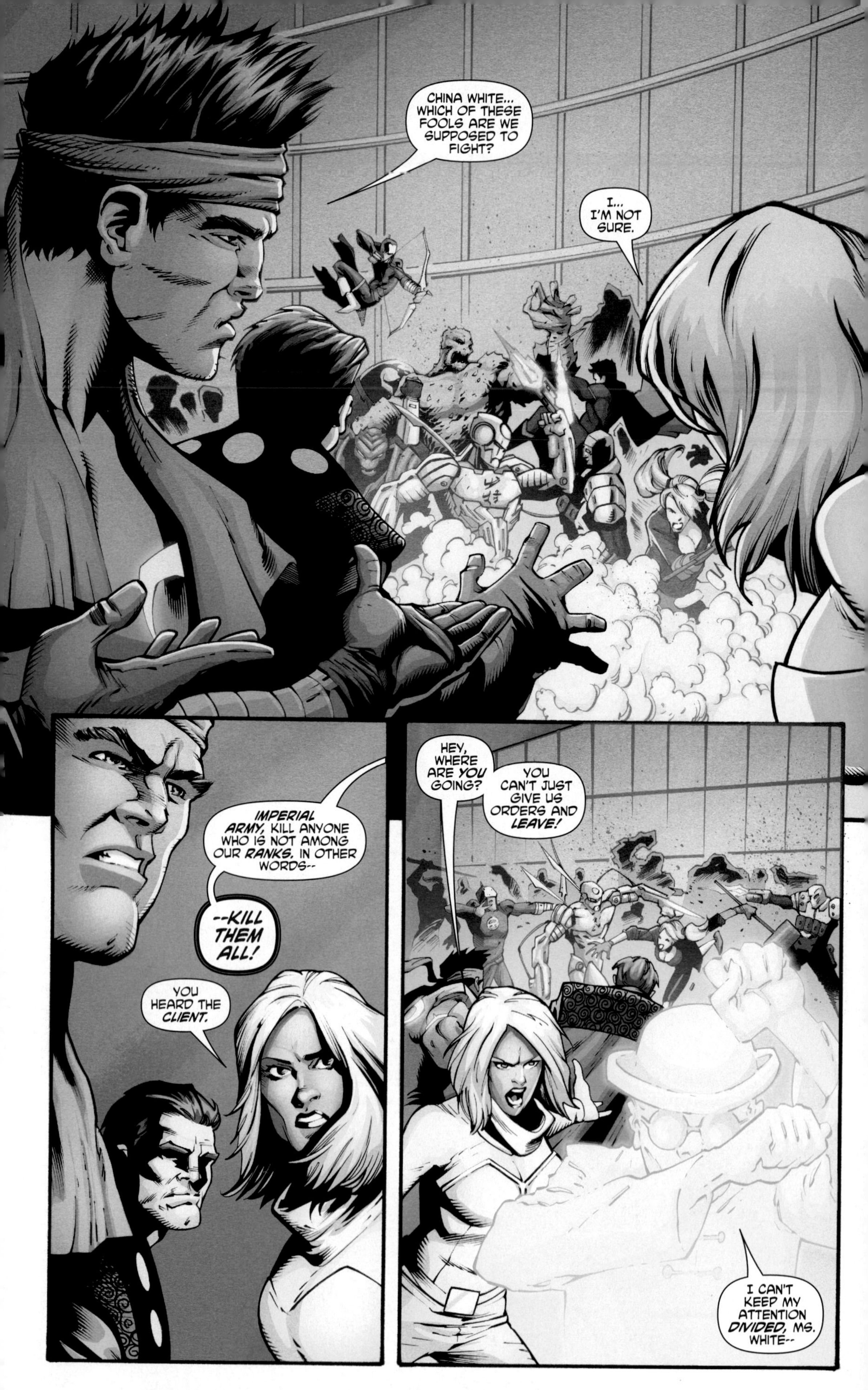
CHINA WHITE... WHICH OF THESE FOOLS ARE WE SUPPOSED TO FIGHT?
I... I'M NOT SURE.
IMPERIAL ARMY, KILL ANYONE WHO IS NOT AMONG OUR RANKS. IN OTHER WORDS--
--KILL THEM ALL!
YOU HEARD THE CLIENT.
HEY, WHERE ARE YOU GOING?
YOU CAN'T JUST GIVE US ORDERS AND LEAVE!
I CAN'T KEEP MY ATTENTION DIVIDED, MS. WHITE--

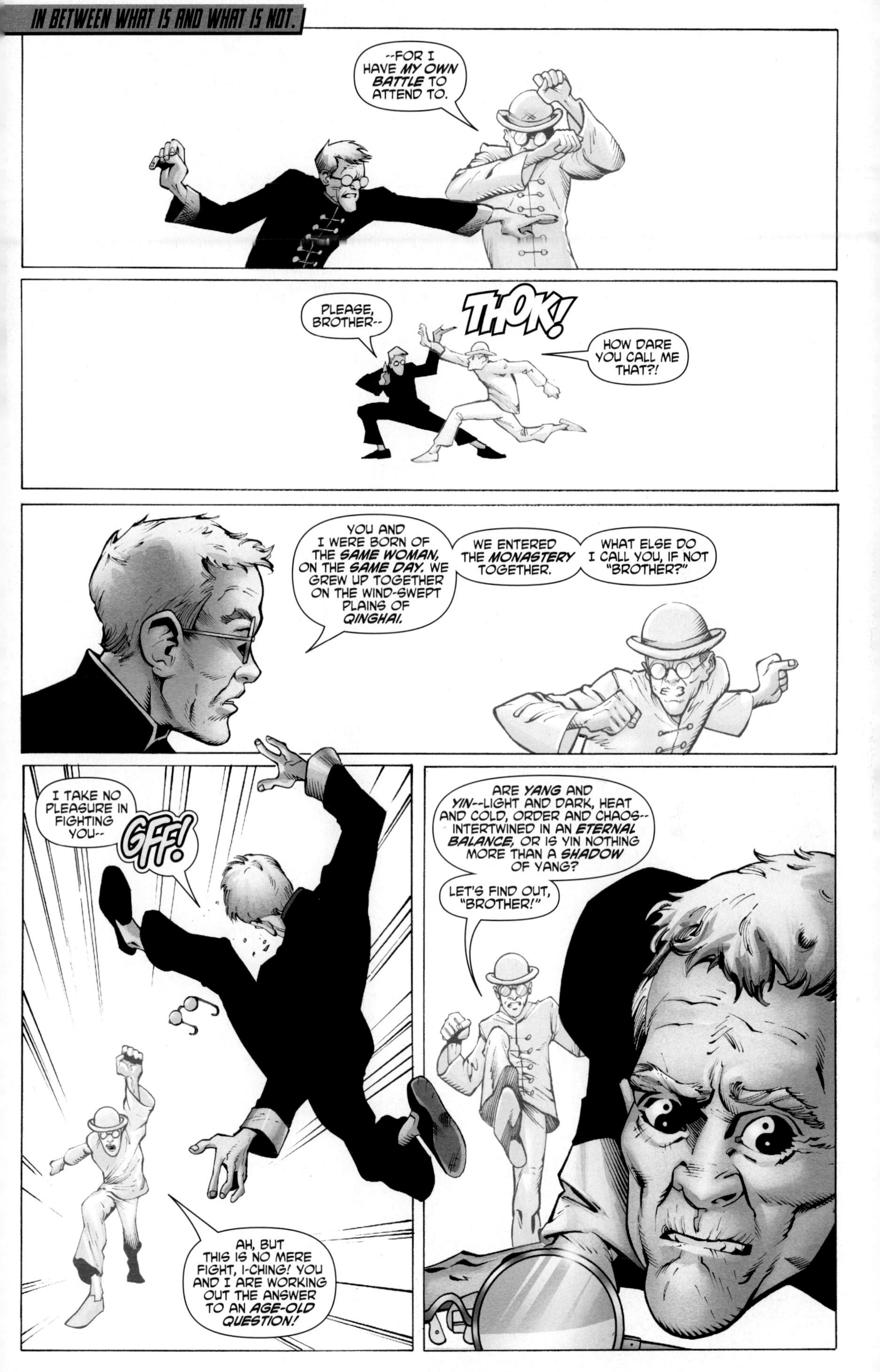
IN BETWEEN WHAT IS AND WHAT IS NOT.
--FOR I HAVE MY OWN BATTLE TO ATTEND TO.
PLEASE, BROTHER--
THOK!
HOW DARE YOU CALL ME THAT?!
YOU AND I WERE BORN OF THE SAME WOMAN, ON THE SAME DAY. WE GREW UP TOGETHER ON THE WIND-SWEPT PLAINS OF QINGHAI.
WE ENTERED THE MONASTERY TOGETHER.
WHAT ELSE DO I CALL YOU, IF NOT "BROTHER?"
I TAKE NO PLEASURE IN FIGHTING YOU--
GFF!
AH, BUT THIS IS NO MERE FIGHT, I-CHING! YOU AND I ARE WORKING OUT THE ANSWER TO AN AGE-OLD QUESTION!
ARE YANG AND YIN--LIGHT AND DARK, HEAT AND COLD, ORDER AND CHAOS--INTERTWINED IN AN ETERNAL BALANCE, OR IS YIN NOTHING MORE THAN A SHADOW OF YANG?
LET'S FIND OUT, "BROTHER!"

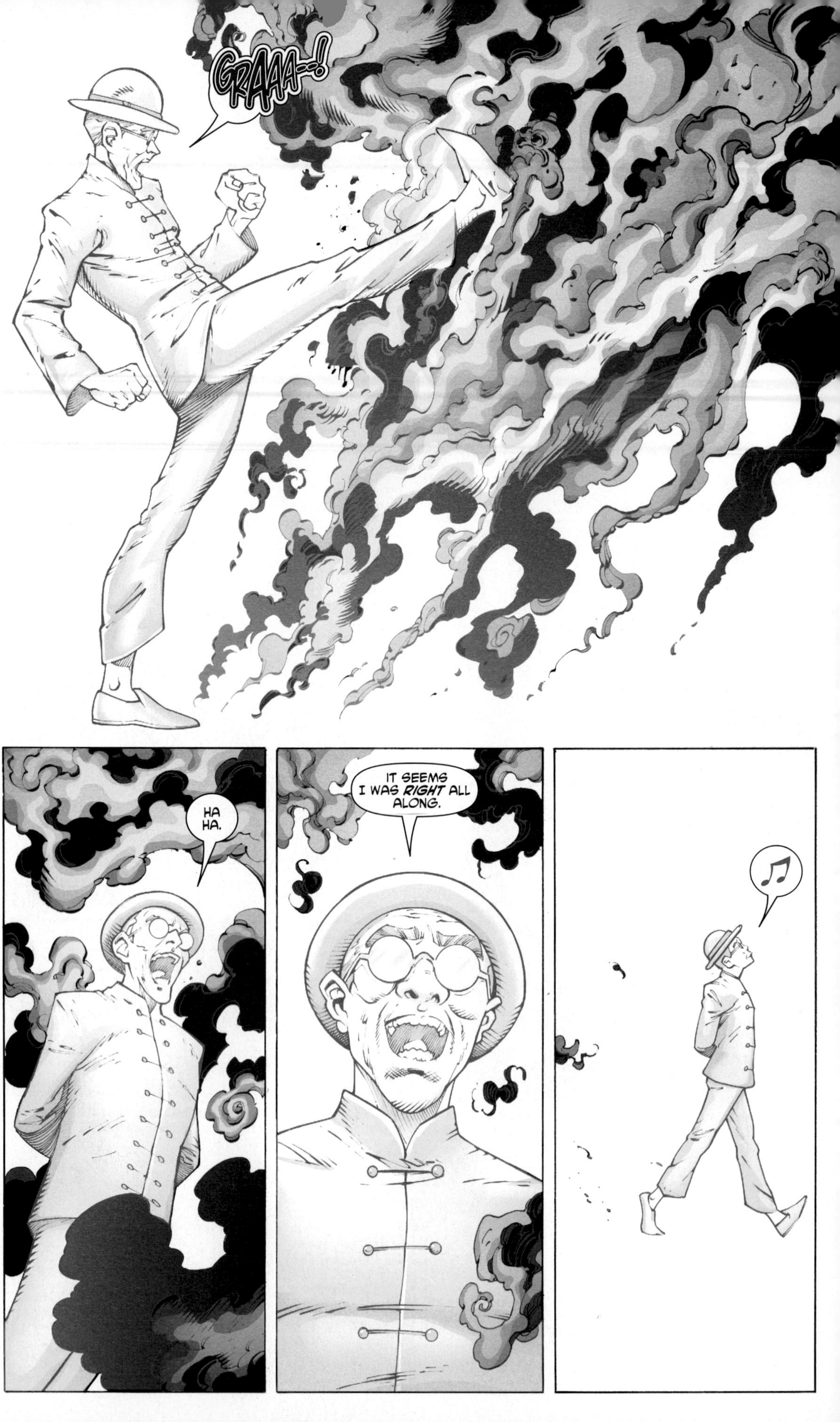
GRAAA--!
HA HA.
IT SEEMS I WAS *RIGHT* ALL ALONG.
♫

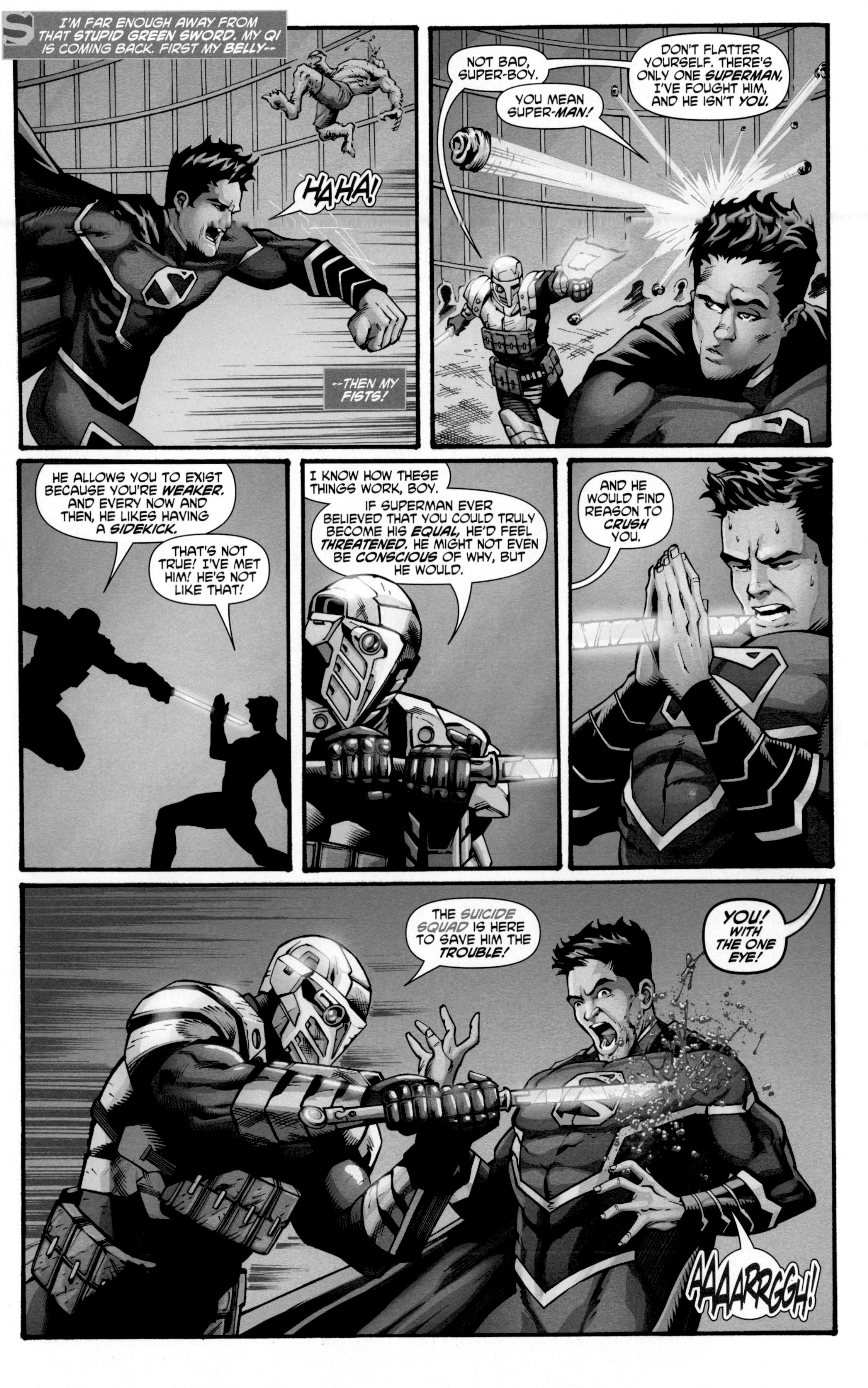

I'M FAR ENOUGH AWAY FROM THAT STUPID GREEN SWORD. MY QI IS COMING BACK. FIRST MY BELLY--
HAHA!
--THEN MY FISTS!
NOT BAD, SUPER-BOY.
YOU MEAN SUPER-MAN!
DON'T FLATTER YOURSELF. THERE'S ONLY ONE SUPERMAN, I'VE FOUGHT HIM, AND HE ISN'T YOU.
HE ALLOWS YOU TO EXIST BECAUSE YOU'RE WEAKER. AND EVERY NOW AND THEN, HE LIKES HAVING A SIDEKICK.
THAT'S NOT TRUE! I'VE MET HIM! HE'S NOT LIKE THAT!
I KNOW HOW THESE THINGS WORK, BOY.
IF SUPERMAN EVER BELIEVED THAT YOU COULD TRULY BECOME HIS EQUAL, HE'D FEEL THREATENED. HE MIGHT NOT EVEN BE CONSCIOUS OF WHY, BUT HE WOULD.
AND HE WOULD FIND REASON TO CRUSH YOU.
THE SUICIDE SQUAD IS HERE TO SAVE HIM THE TROUBLE!
YOU! WITH THE ONE EYE!
AAAARRGGH!

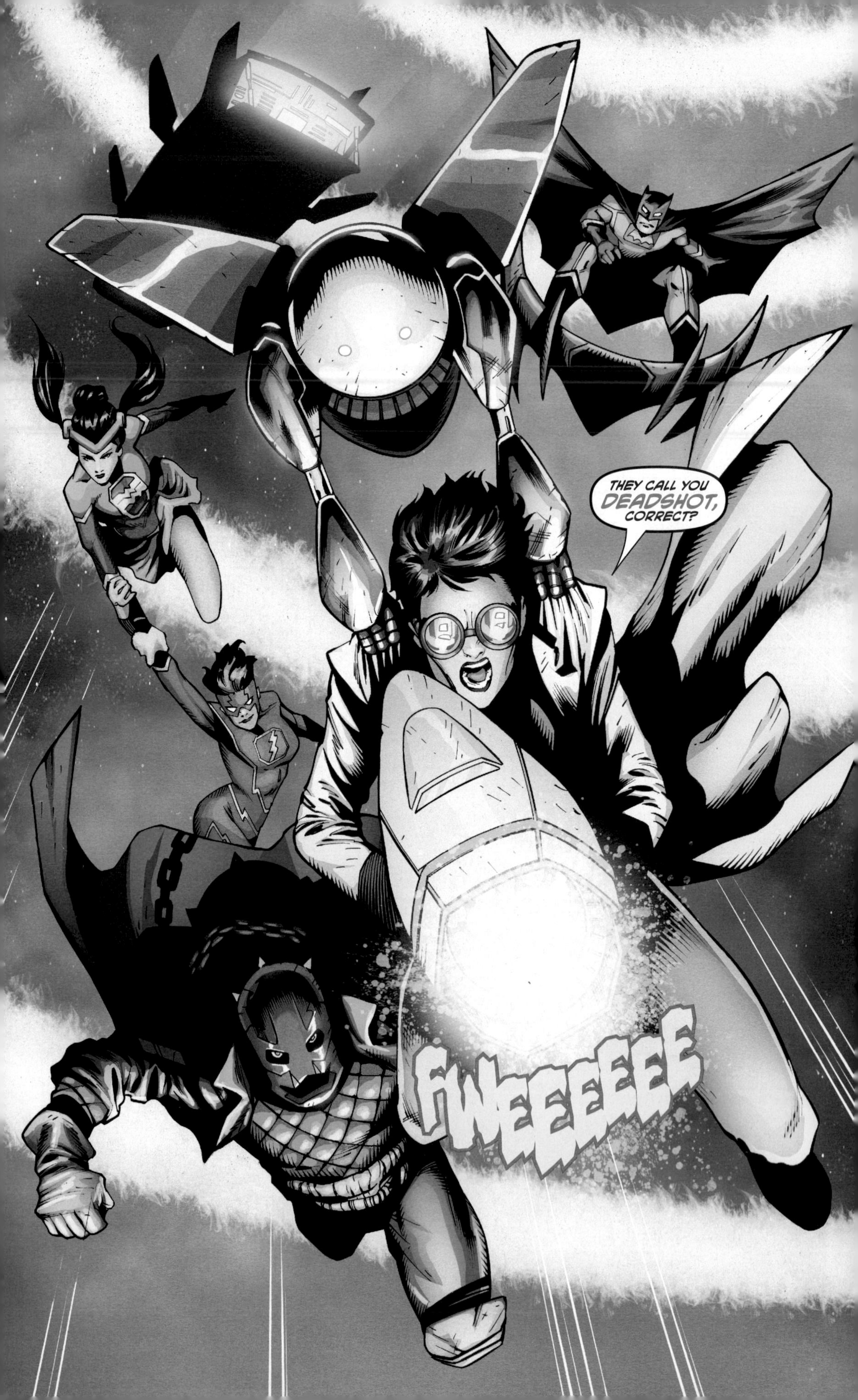
THEY CALL YOU DEADSHOT, CORRECT?
FWEEEEEE

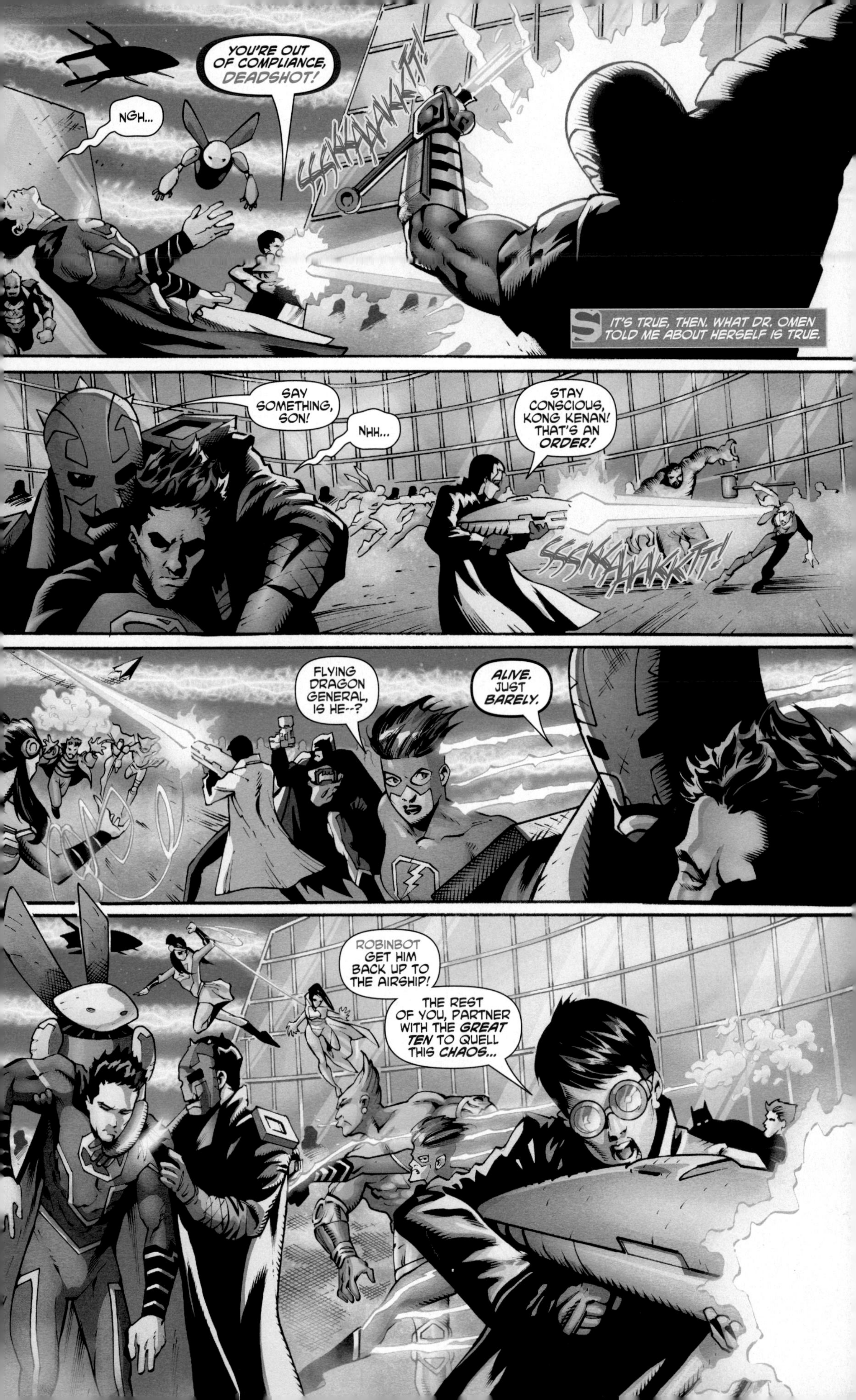
YOU'RE OUT OF COMPLIANCE, DEADSHOT!
NGH...
SSSHHRAAKKTT!!
IT'S TRUE, THEN. WHAT DR. OMEN TOLD ME ABOUT HERSELF IS TRUE.
SAY SOMETHING, SON!
NHH...
STAY CONSCIOUS, KONG KENAN! THAT'S AN ORDER!
SSSKKAAARRKTT!
FLYING DRAGON GENERAL, IS HE--?
ALIVE. JUST BARELY.
ROBINBOT GET HIM BACK UP TO THE AIRSHIP!
THE REST OF YOU, PARTNER WITH THE GREAT TEN TO QUELL THIS CHAOS...

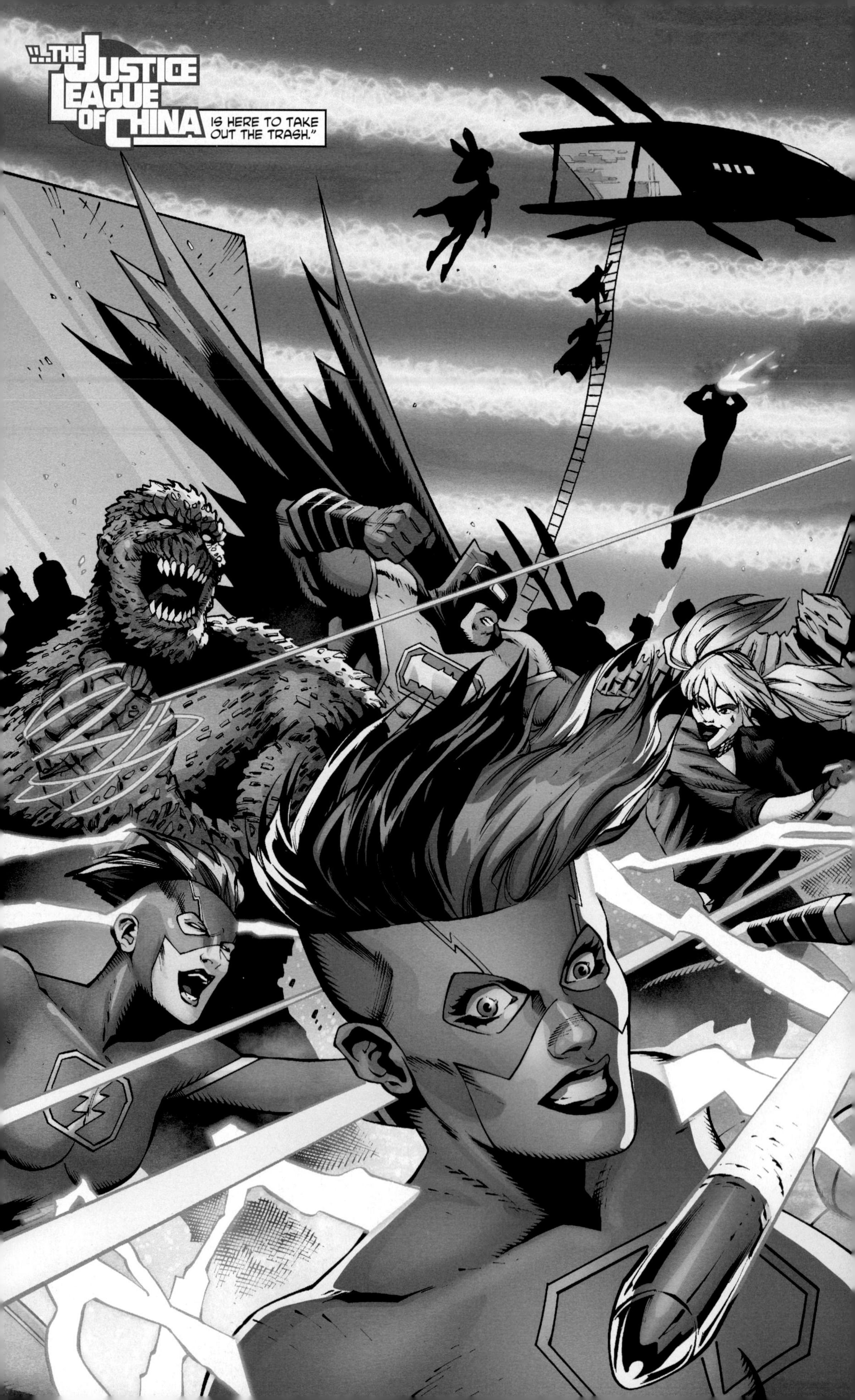
"...THE JUSTICE LEAGUE OF CHINA
IS HERE TO TAKE OUT THE TRASH."

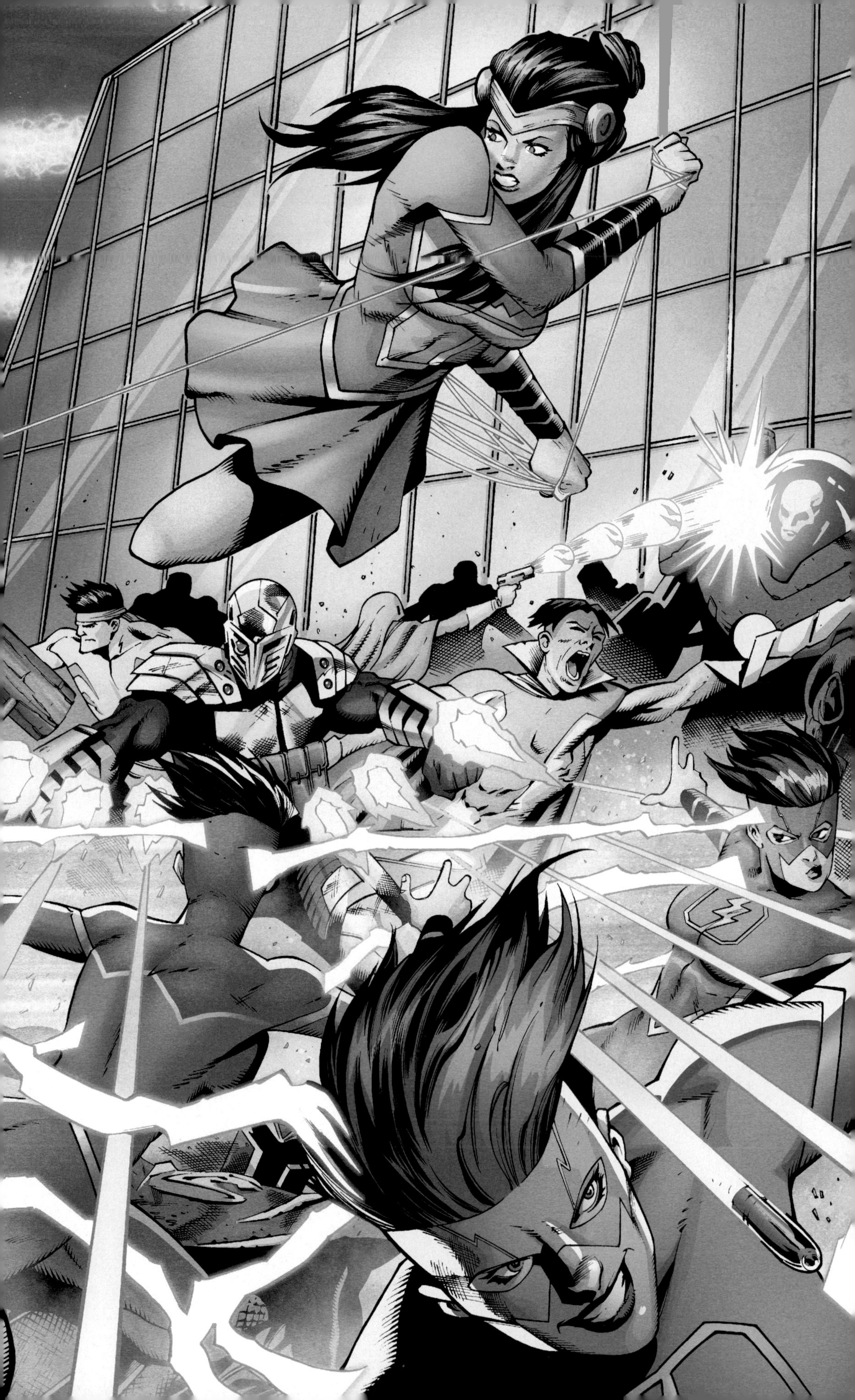

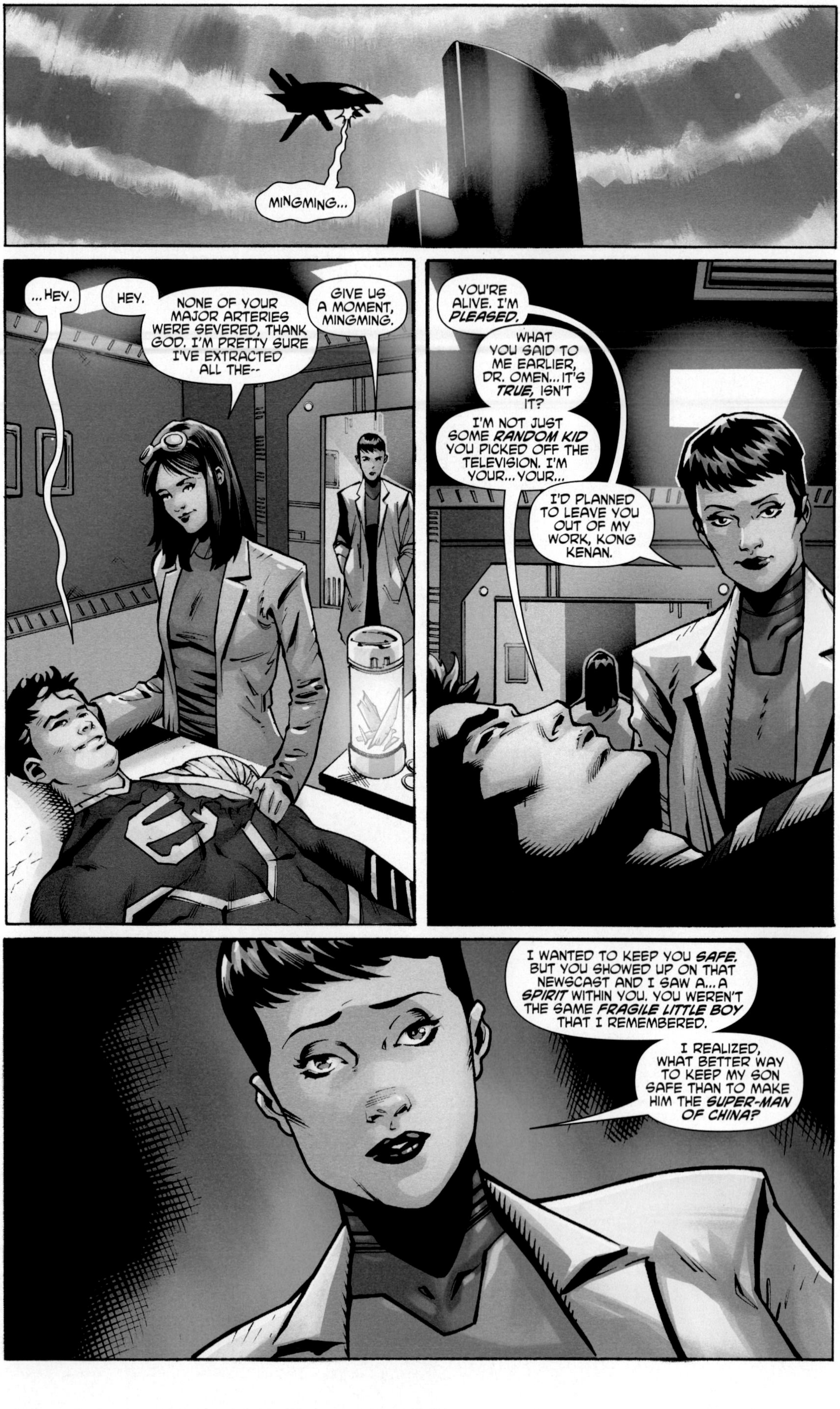
MINGMING...
...HEY.
HEY.
NONE OF YOUR MAJOR ARTERIES WERE SEVERED, THANK GOD. I'M PRETTY SURE I'VE EXTRACTED ALL THE--
GIVE US A MOMENT, MINGMING.
YOU'RE ALIVE. I'M PLEASED.
WHAT YOU SAID TO ME EARLIER, DR. OMEN... IT'S TRUE, ISN'T IT?
I'M NOT JUST SOME RANDOM KID YOU PICKED OFF THE TELEVISION. I'M YOUR... YOUR...
I'D PLANNED TO LEAVE YOU OUT OF MY WORK, KONG KENAN.
I WANTED TO KEEP YOU SAFE. BUT YOU SHOWED UP ON THAT NEWSCAST AND I SAW A... A SPIRIT WITHIN YOU. YOU WEREN'T THE SAME FRAGILE LITTLE BOY THAT I REMEMBERED.
I REALIZED, WHAT BETTER WAY TO KEEP MY SON SAFE THAN TO MAKE HIM THE SUPER-MAN OF CHINA?

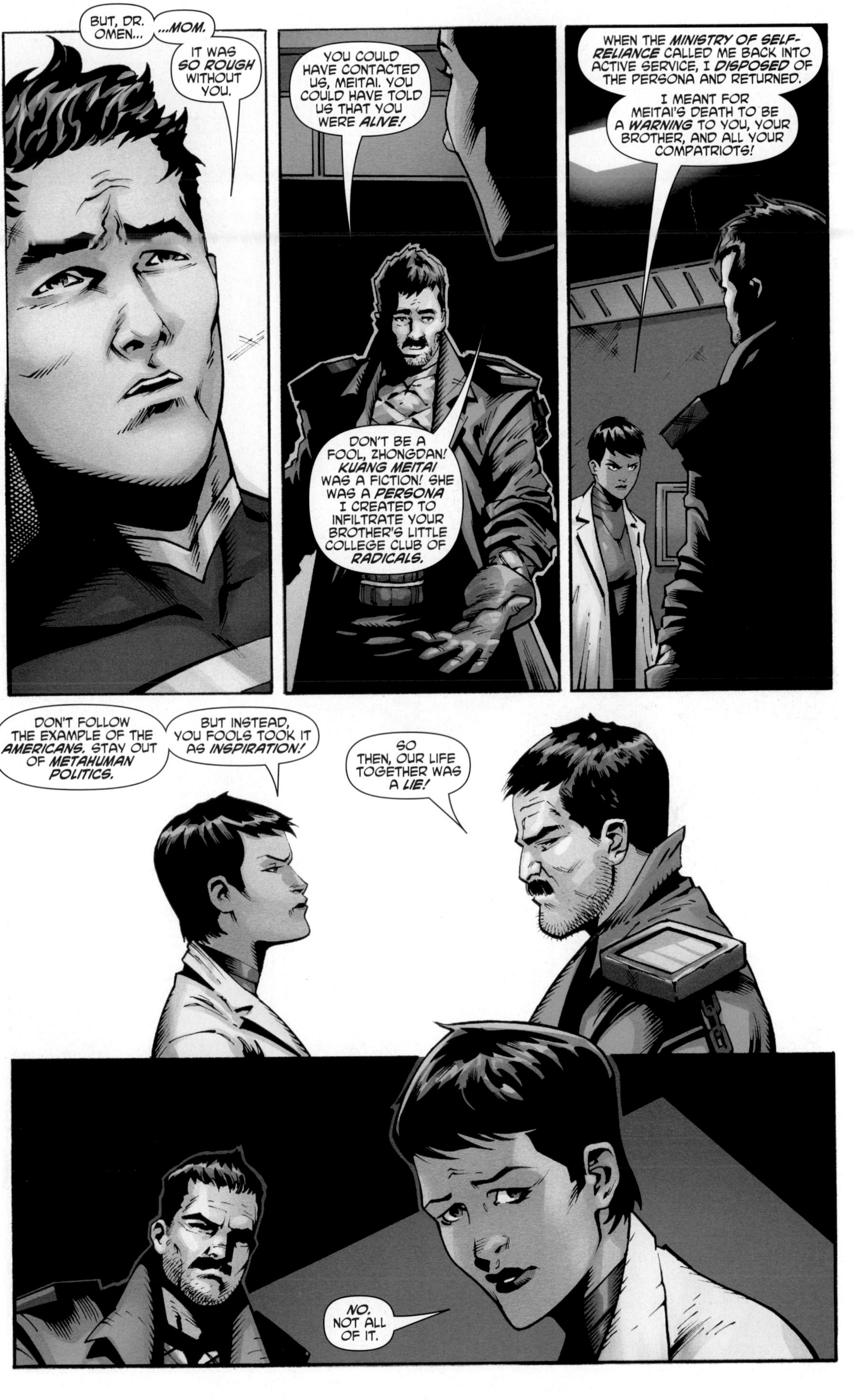
BUT, DR. OMEN...
...MOM.
IT WAS SO ROUGH WITHOUT YOU.
YOU COULD HAVE CONTACTED US, MEITAI. YOU COULD HAVE TOLD US THAT YOU WERE ALIVE!
DON'T BE A FOOL, ZHONGDAN! KUANG MEITAI WAS A FICTION! SHE WAS A PERSONA I CREATED TO INFILTRATE YOUR BROTHER'S LITTLE COLLEGE CLUB OF RADICALS.
WHEN THE MINISTRY OF SELF-RELIANCE CALLED ME BACK INTO ACTIVE SERVICE, I DISPOSED OF THE PERSONA AND RETURNED.
I MEANT FOR MEITAI'S DEATH TO BE A WARNING TO YOU, YOUR BROTHER, AND ALL YOUR COMPATRIOTS!
DON'T FOLLOW THE EXAMPLE OF THE AMERICANS. STAY OUT OF METAHUMAN POLITICS.
BUT INSTEAD, YOU FOOLS TOOK IT AS INSPIRATION!
SO THEN, OUR LIFE TOGETHER WAS A LIE!
NO. NOT ALL OF IT.

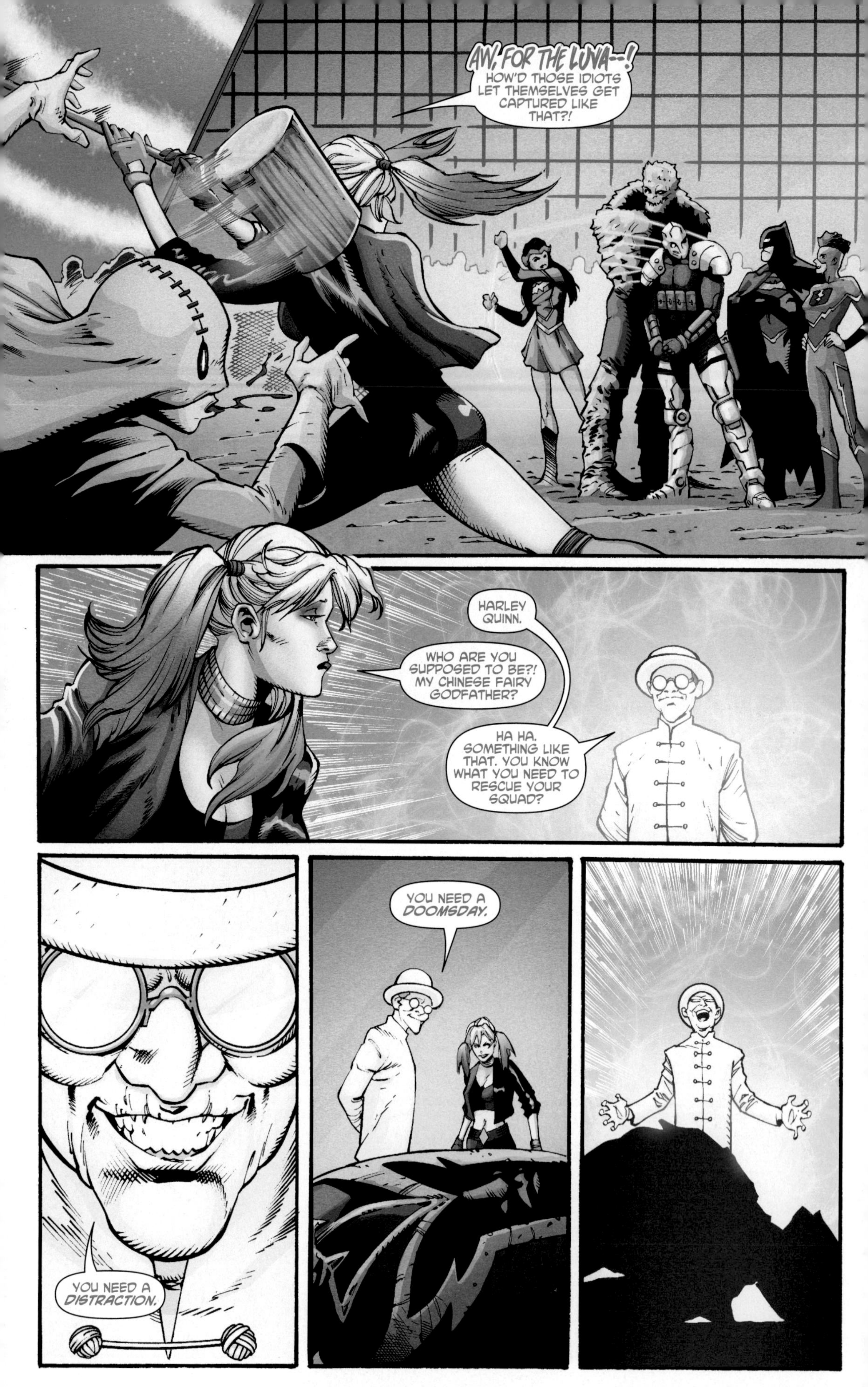
AW, FOR THE LUVA--! HOW'D THOSE IDIOTS LET THEMSELVES GET CAPTURED LIKE THAT?!
HARLEY QUINN.
WHO ARE YOU SUPPOSED TO BE?! MY CHINESE FAIRY GODFATHER?
HA HA. SOMETHING LIKE THAT. YOU KNOW WHAT YOU NEED TO RESCUE YOUR SQUAD?
YOU NEED A DISTRACTION.
YOU NEED A DOOMSDAY.

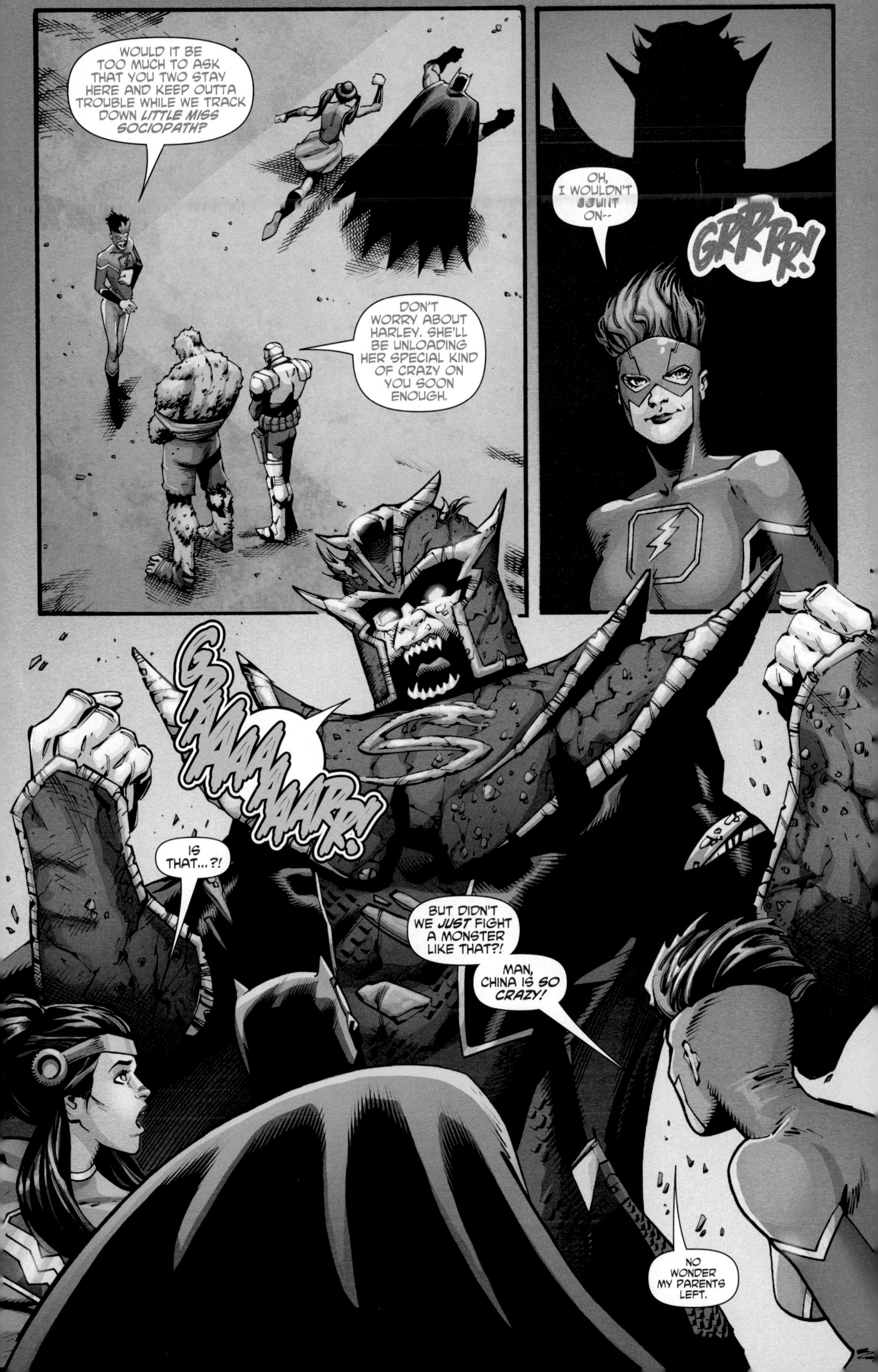
WOULD IT BE TOO MUCH TO ASK THAT YOU TWO STAY HERE AND KEEP OUTTA TROUBLE WHILE WE TRACK DOWN *LITTLE MISS SOCIOPATH?*
DON'T WORRY ABOUT HARLEY. SHE'LL BE UNLOADING HER SPECIAL KIND OF CRAZY ON YOU SOON ENOUGH.
OH, I WOULDN'T COUNT ON--
GRRRR!
GRAAAAAAARR!
IS THAT...?!
BUT DIDN'T WE *JUST* FIGHT A MONSTER LIKE THAT?!
MAN, CHINA IS *SO CRAZY!*
NO WONDER MY PARENTS LEFT.

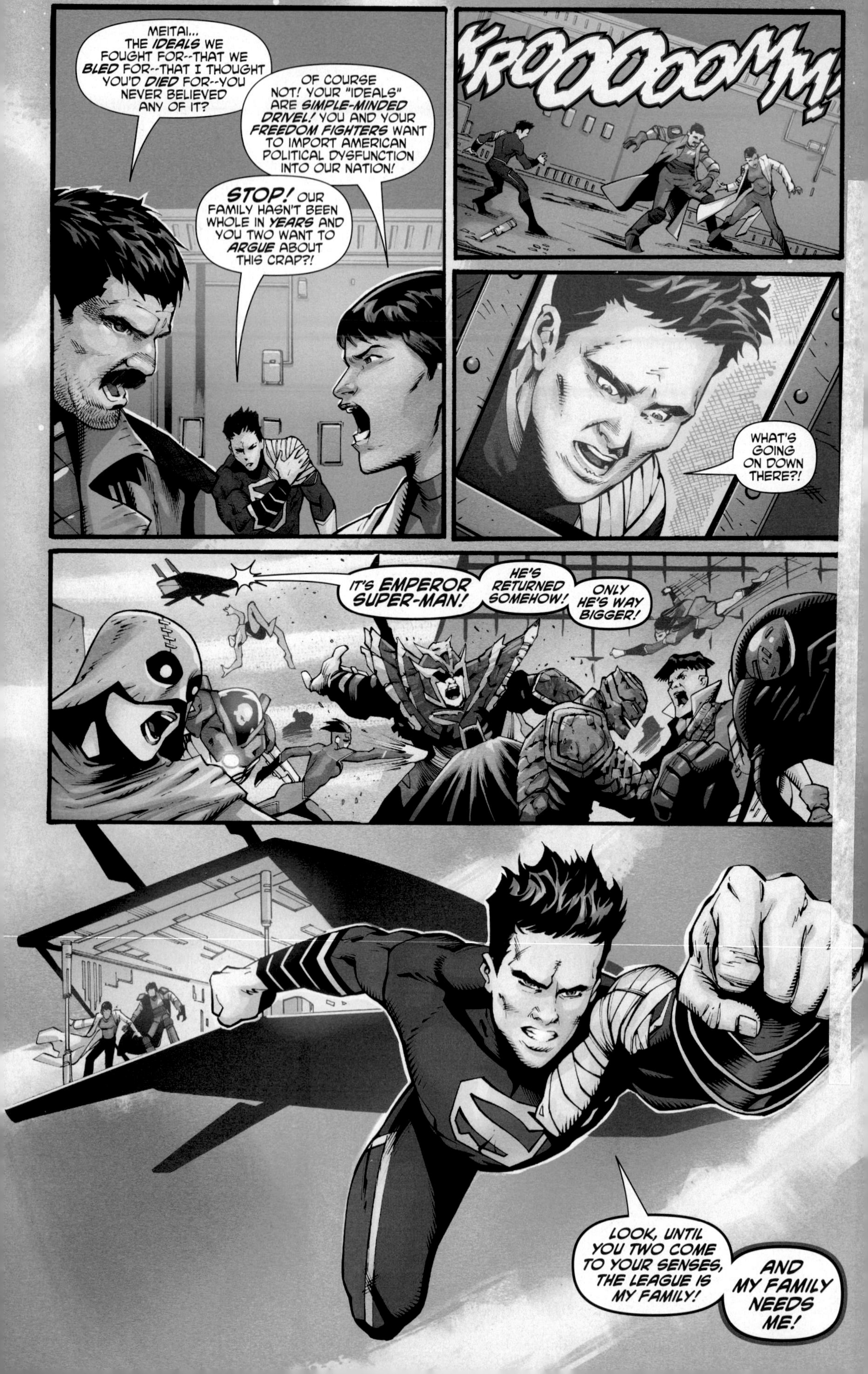
MEITAI... THE IDEALS WE FOUGHT FOR--THAT WE BLED FOR--THAT I THOUGHT YOU'D DIED FOR--YOU NEVER BELIEVED ANY OF IT?
OF COURSE NOT! YOUR "IDEALS" ARE SIMPLE-MINDED DRIVEL! YOU AND YOUR FREEDOM FIGHTERS WANT TO IMPORT AMERICAN POLITICAL DYSFUNCTION INTO OUR NATION!
STOP! OUR FAMILY HASN'T BEEN WHOLE IN YEARS AND YOU TWO WANT TO ARGUE ABOUT THIS CRAP?!
KROOOOOOM!
WHAT'S GOING ON DOWN THERE?!
IT'S EMPEROR SUPER-MAN!
HE'S RETURNED SOMEHOW!
ONLY HE'S WAY BIGGER!
LOOK, UNTIL YOU TWO COME TO YOUR SENSES, THE LEAGUE IS MY FAMILY!
AND MY FAMILY NEEDS ME!

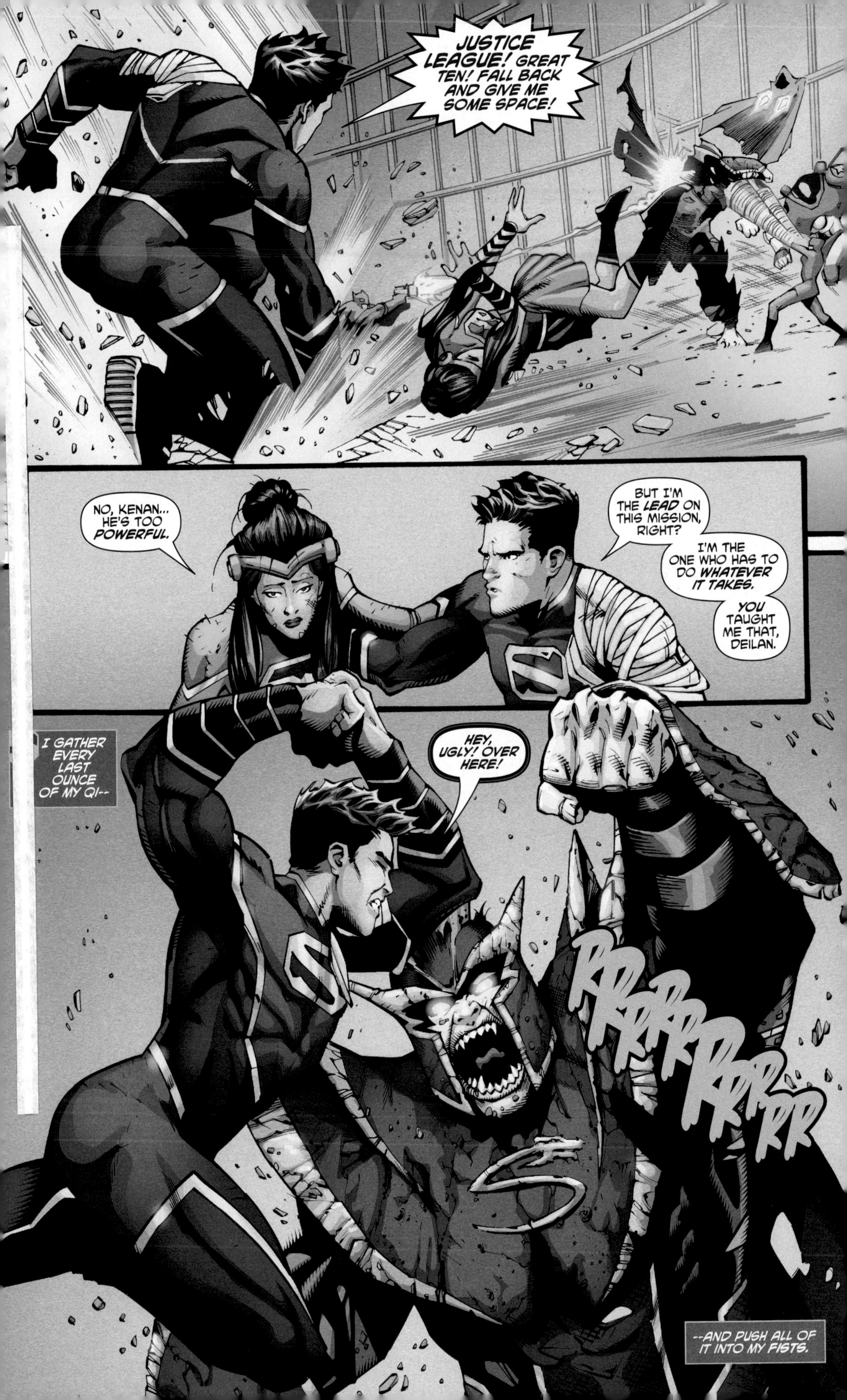
JUSTICE LEAGUE! GREAT TEN! FALL BACK AND GIVE ME SOME SPACE!
NO, KENAN... HE'S TOO POWERFUL.
BUT I'M THE LEAD ON THIS MISSION, RIGHT?
I'M THE ONE WHO HAS TO DO WHATEVER IT TAKES.
YOU TAUGHT ME THAT, DEILAN.
I GATHER EVERY LAST OUNCE OF MY QI--
HEY, UGLY! OVER HERE!
RRRRRRRRRRRR
--AND PUSH ALL OF IT INTO MY FISTS.

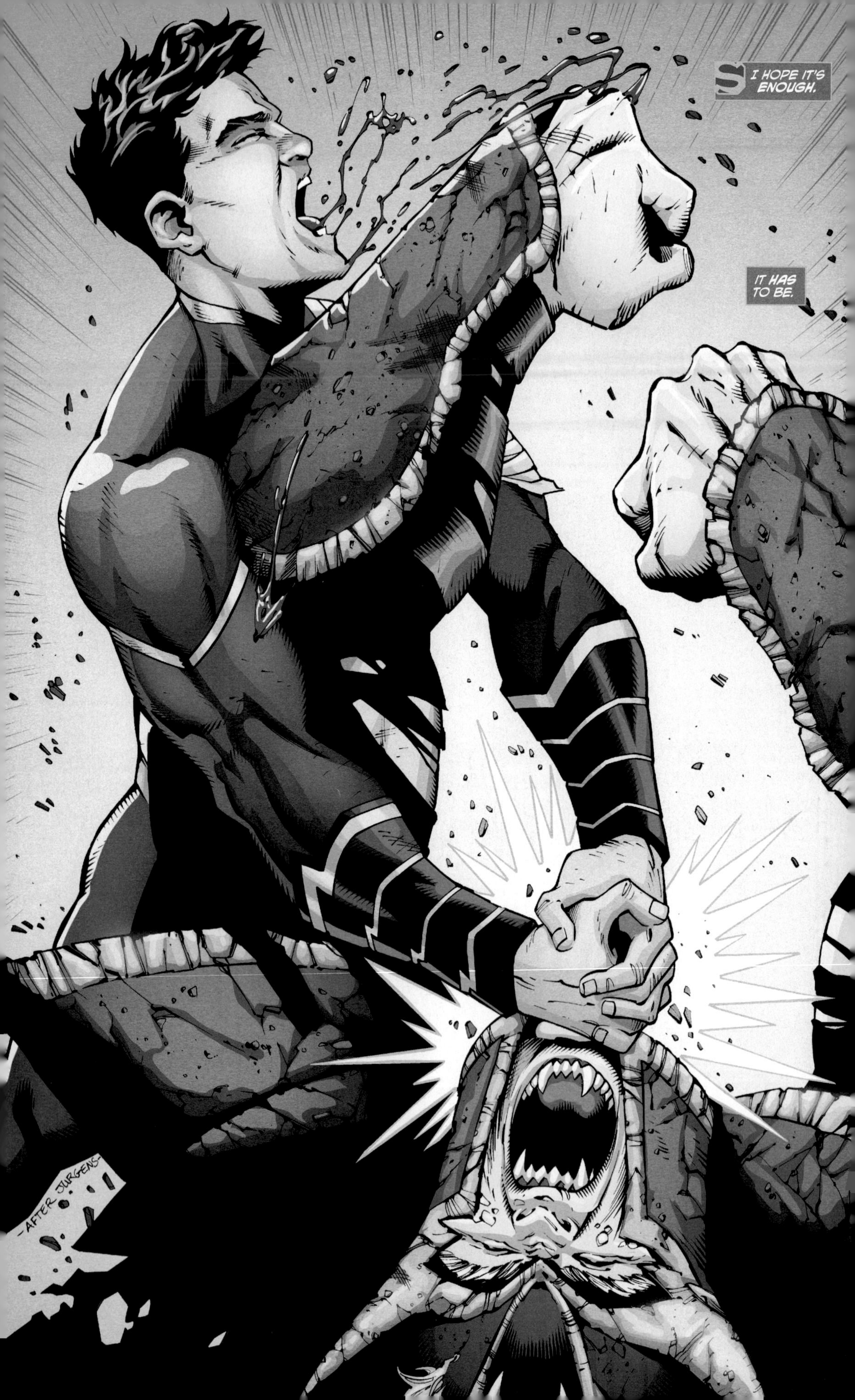
I HOPE IT'S ENOUGH.
IT HAS TO BE.
-AFTER JURGENS-

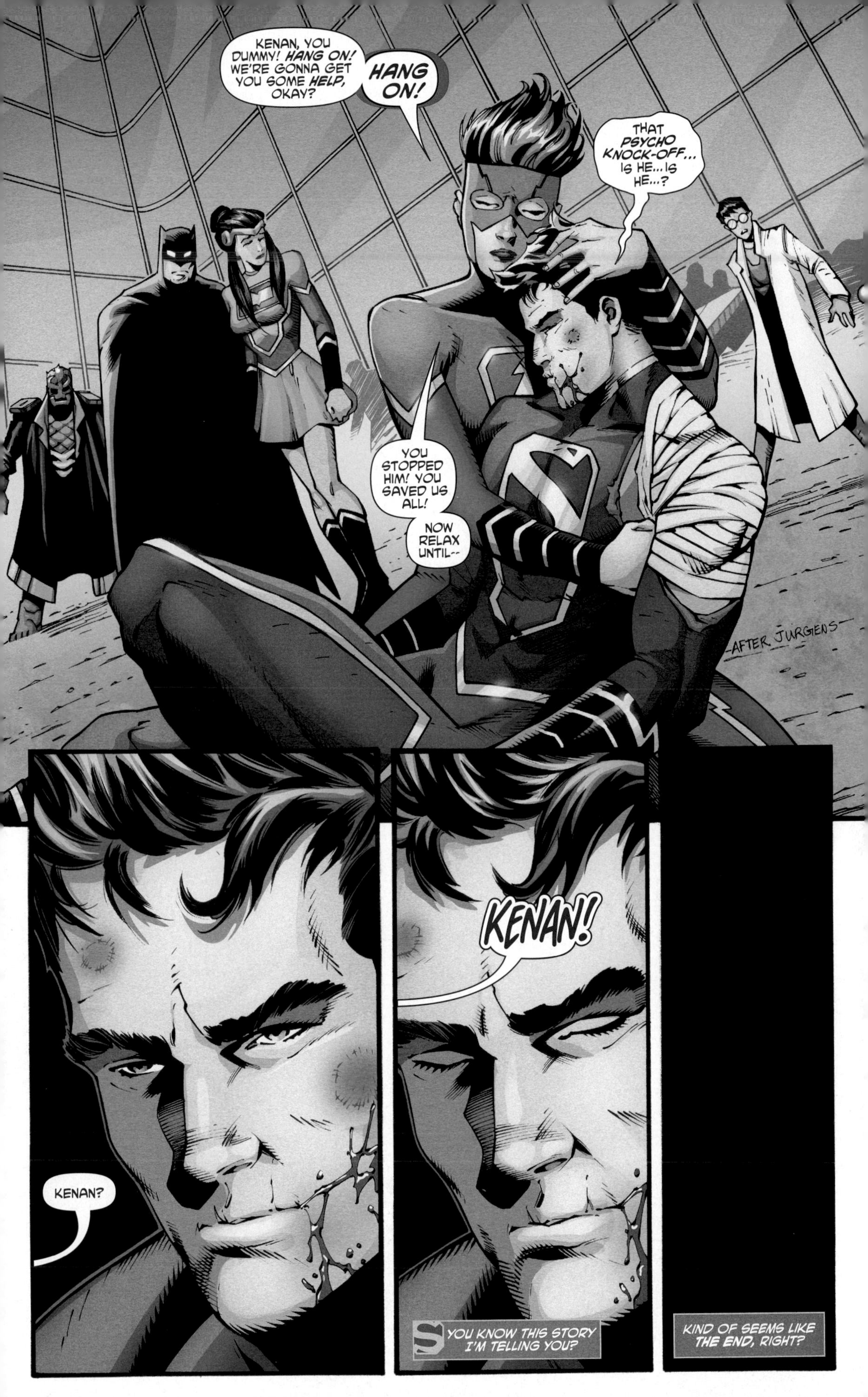
KENAN, YOU DUMMY! HANG ON! WE'RE GONNA GET YOU SOME HELP, OKAY?
HANG ON!
THAT PSYCHO KNOCK-OFF... IS HE...IS HE...?
YOU STOPPED HIM! YOU SAVED US ALL!
NOW RELAX UNTIL--
AFTER JURGENS
KENAN?
KENAN!
YOU KNOW THIS STORY I'M TELLING YOU?
KIND OF SEEMS LIKE THE END, RIGHT?

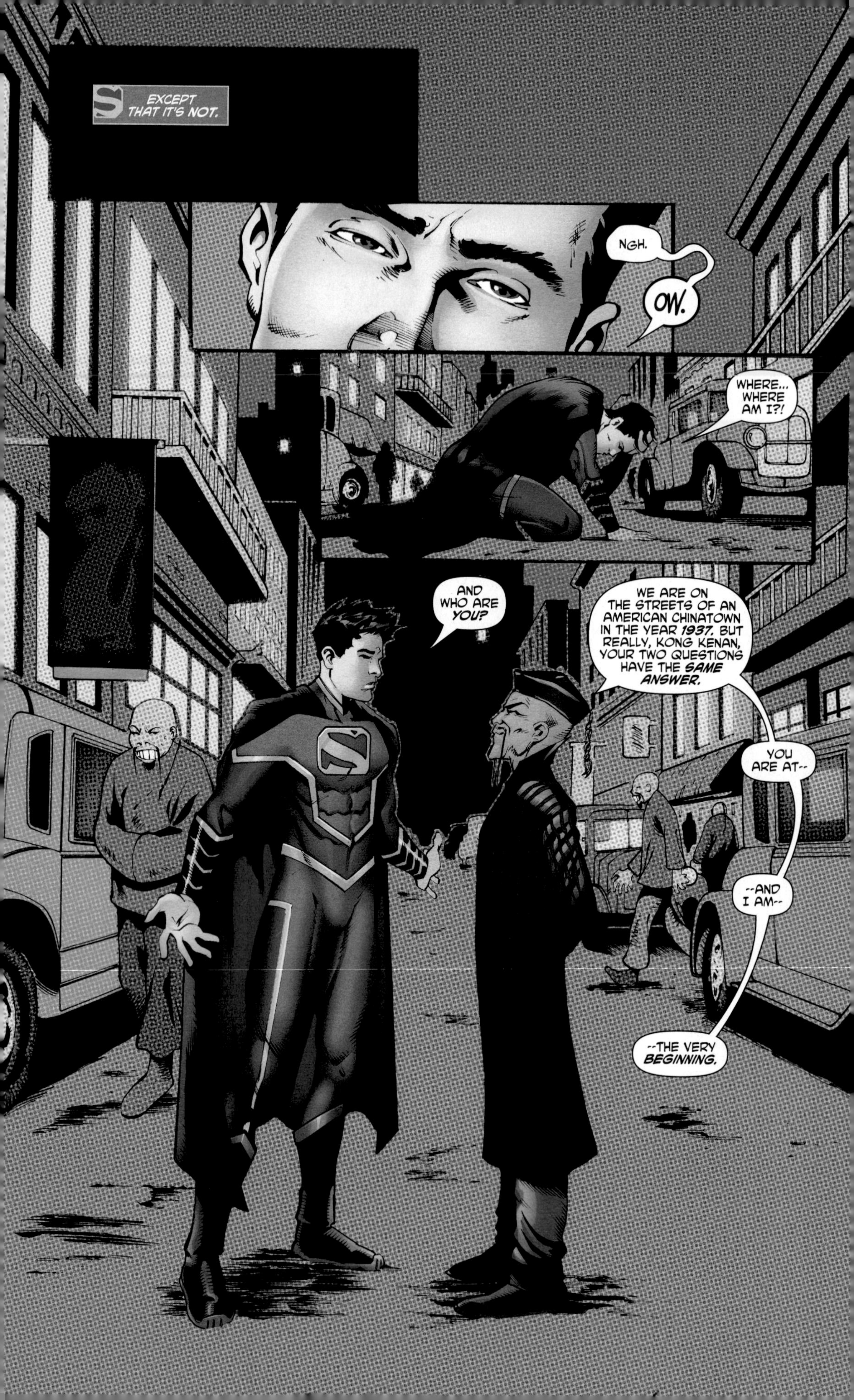

EXCEPT THAT IT'S NOT.
NGH.
OW.
WHERE... WHERE AM I?!
AND WHO ARE *YOU?*
WE ARE ON THE STREETS OF AN AMERICAN CHINATOWN IN THE YEAR *1937.* BUT REALLY, KONG KENAN, YOUR TWO QUESTIONS HAVE THE *SAME ANSWER.*
YOU ARE AT--
--AND I AM--
--THE VERY *BEGINNING.*

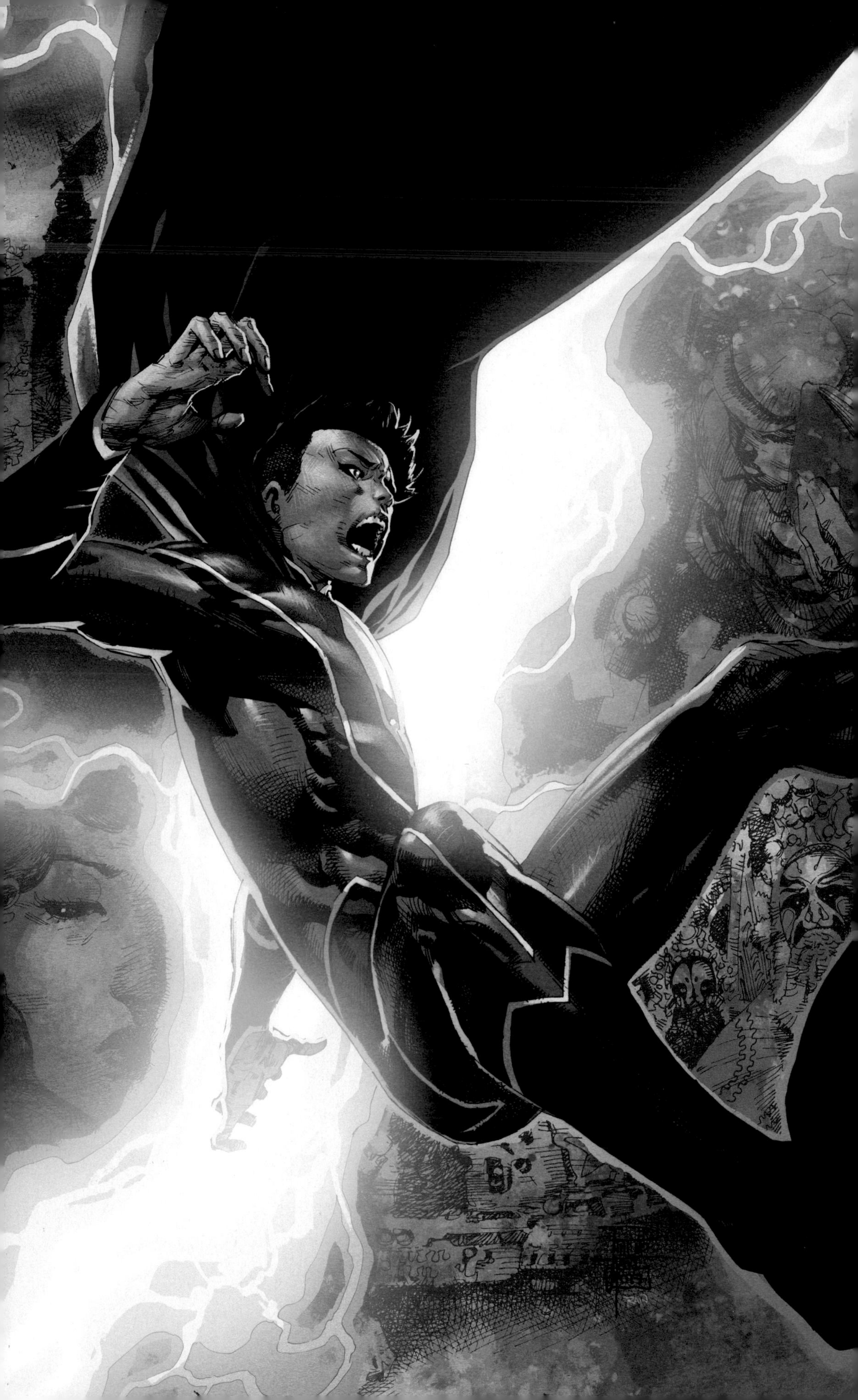

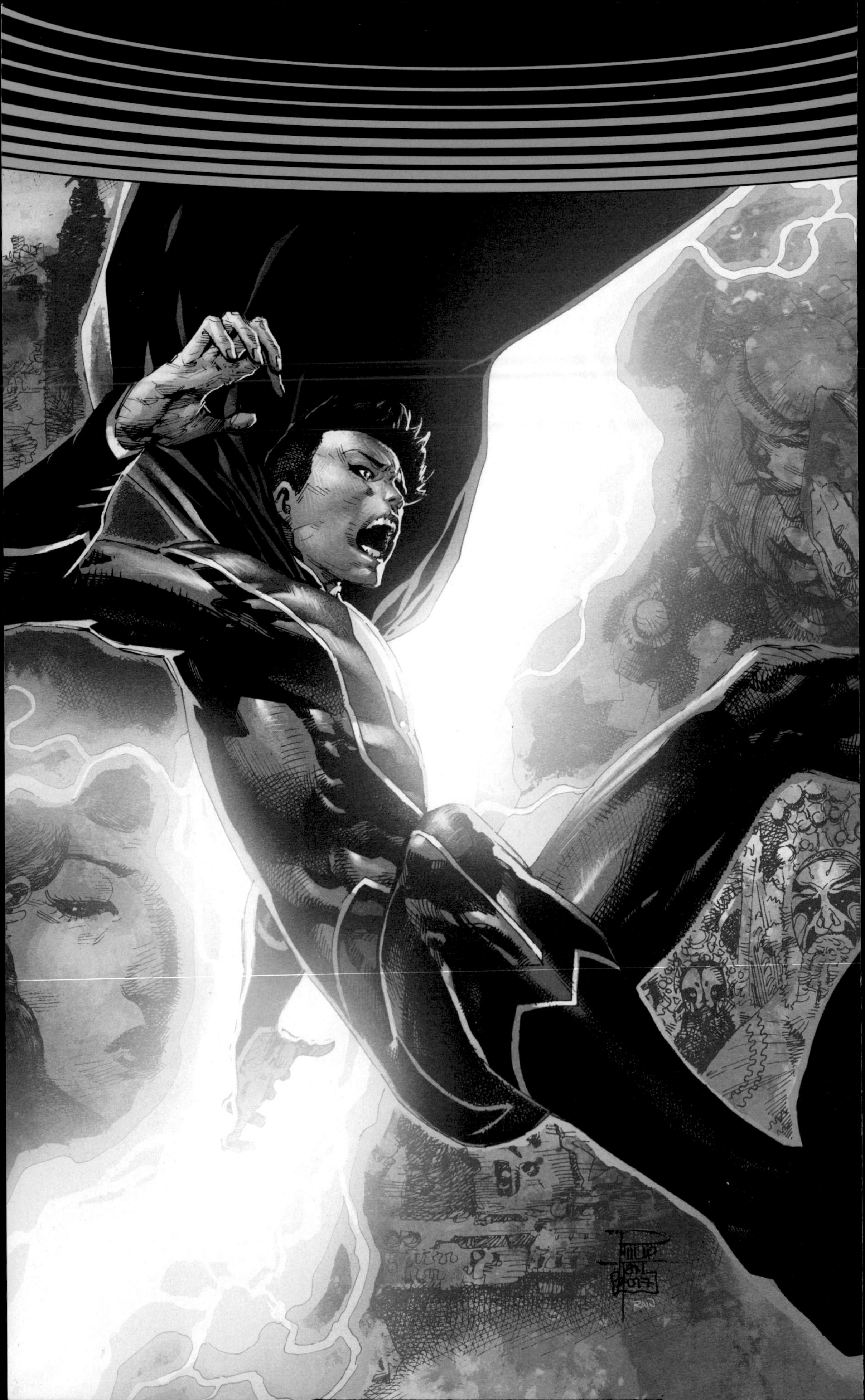

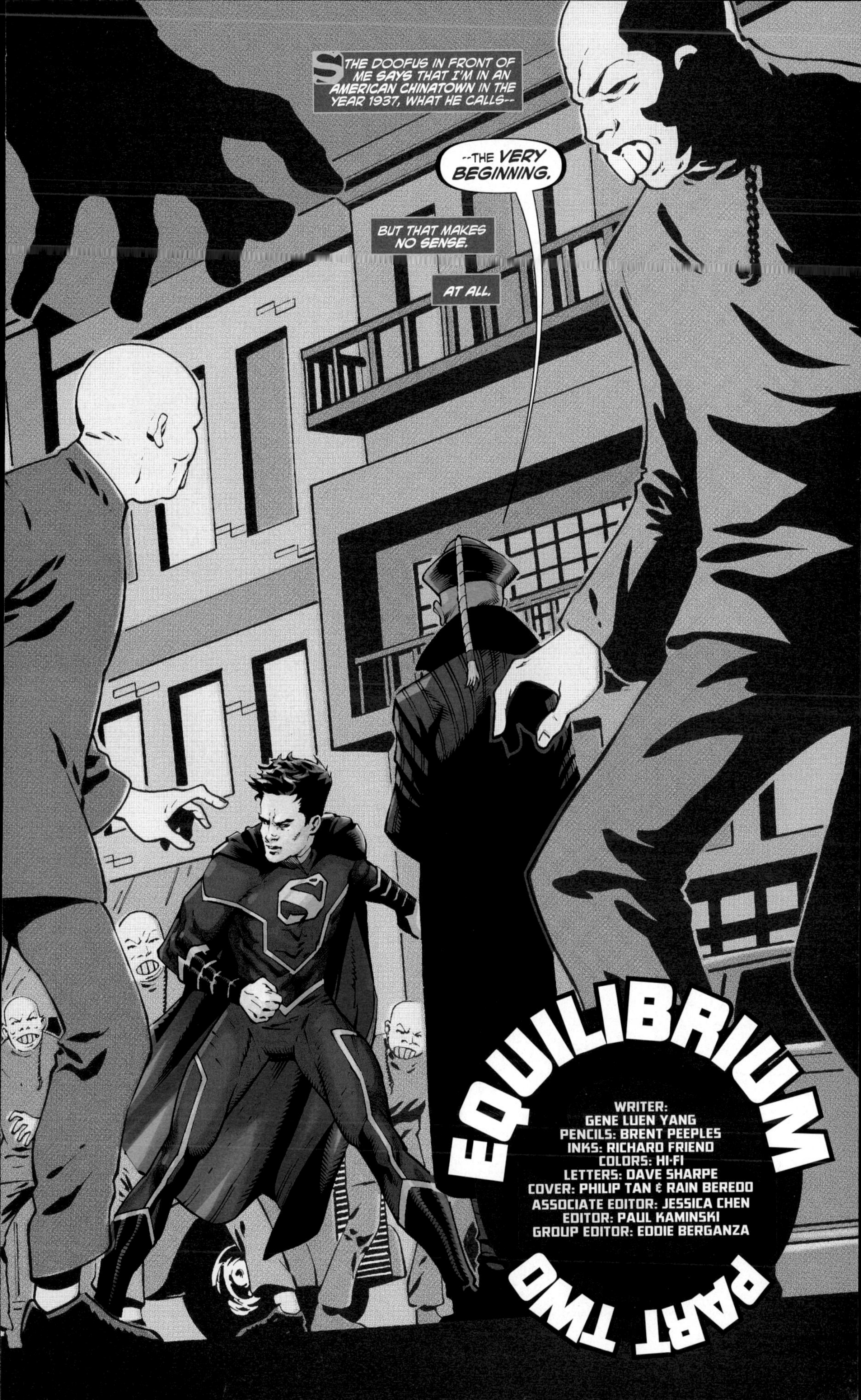
THE DOOFUS IN FRONT OF ME SAYS THAT I'M IN AN AMERICAN CHINATOWN IN THE YEAR 1937, WHAT HE CALLS--
--THE VERY BEGINNING.
BUT THAT MAKES NO SENSE.
AT ALL.
EQUILIBRIUM
PART TWO
WRITER: GENE LUEN YANG
PENCILS: BRENT PEEPLES
INKS: RICHARD FRIEND
COLORS: HI-FI
LETTERS: DAVE SHARPE
COVER: PHILIP TAN & RAIN BEREDO
ASSOCIATE EDITOR: JESSICA CHEN
EDITOR: PAUL KAMINSKI
GROUP EDITOR: EDDIE BERGANZA

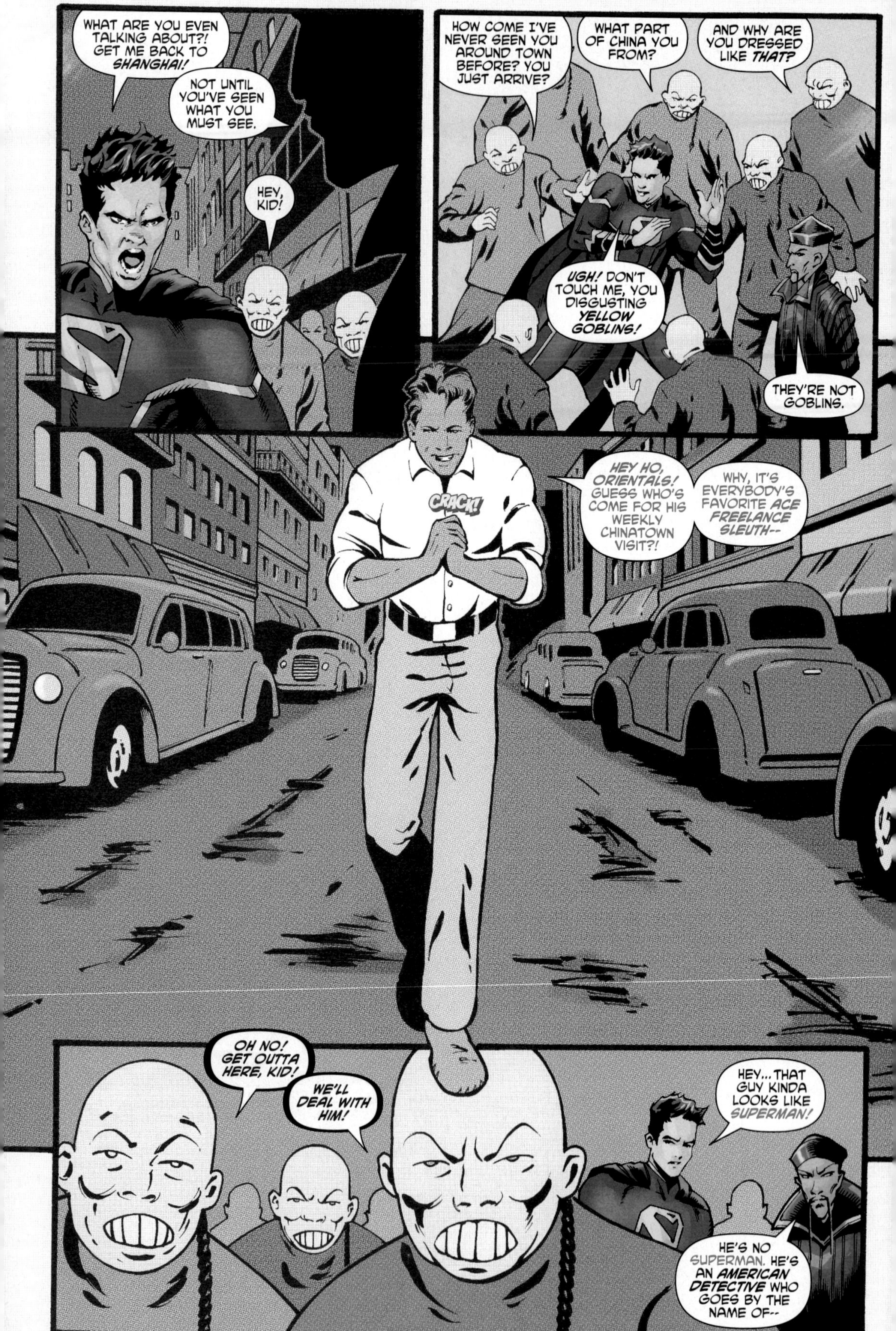
WHAT ARE YOU EVEN TALKING ABOUT?! GET ME BACK TO SHANGHAI!
NOT UNTIL YOU'VE SEEN WHAT YOU MUST SEE.
HEY, KID!
HOW COME I'VE NEVER SEEN YOU AROUND TOWN BEFORE? YOU JUST ARRIVE?
WHAT PART OF CHINA YOU FROM?
AND WHY ARE YOU DRESSED LIKE THAT?
UGH! DON'T TOUCH ME, YOU DISGUSTING YELLOW GOBLINS!
THEY'RE NOT GOBLINS.
HEY HO, ORIENTALS! GUESS WHO'S COME FOR HIS WEEKLY CHINATOWN VISIT?!
WHY, IT'S EVERYBODY'S FAVORITE ACE FREELANCE SLEUTH--
CRACK!
OH NO! GET OUTTA HERE, KID!
WE'LL DEAL WITH HIM!
HEY... THAT GUY KINDA LOOKS LIKE SUPERMAN!
HE'S NO SUPERMAN. HE'S AN AMERICAN DETECTIVE WHO GOES BY THE NAME OF--

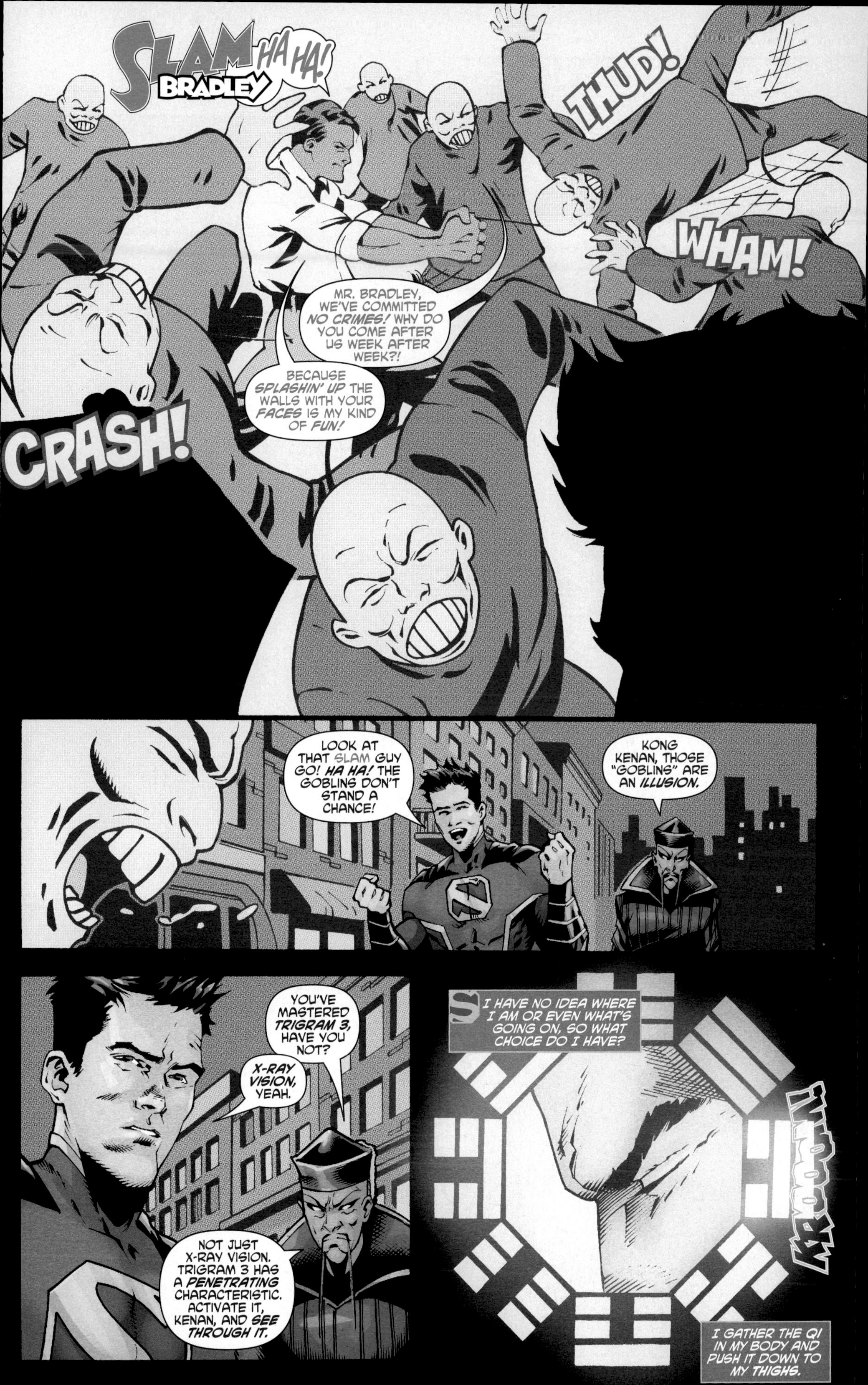
SLAM BRADLEY
HA HA!
THUD!
WHAM!
MR. BRADLEY, WE'VE COMMITTED NO CRIMES! WHY DO YOU COME AFTER US WEEK AFTER WEEK?!
BECAUSE SPLASHIN' UP THE WALLS WITH YOUR FACES IS MY KIND OF FUN!
CRASH!
LOOK AT THAT SLAM GUY GO! HA HA! THE GOBLINS DON'T STAND A CHANCE!
KONG KENAN, THOSE "GOBLINS" ARE AN ILLUSION.
YOU'VE MASTERED TRIGRAM 3, HAVE YOU NOT?
X-RAY VISION, YEAH.
NOT JUST X-RAY VISION. TRIGRAM 3 HAS A PENETRATING CHARACTERISTIC. ACTIVATE IT, KENAN, AND SEE THROUGH IT.
I HAVE NO IDEA WHERE I AM OR EVEN WHAT'S GOING ON, SO WHAT CHOICE DO I HAVE?
I GATHER THE QI IN MY BODY AND PUSH IT DOWN TO MY THIGHS.

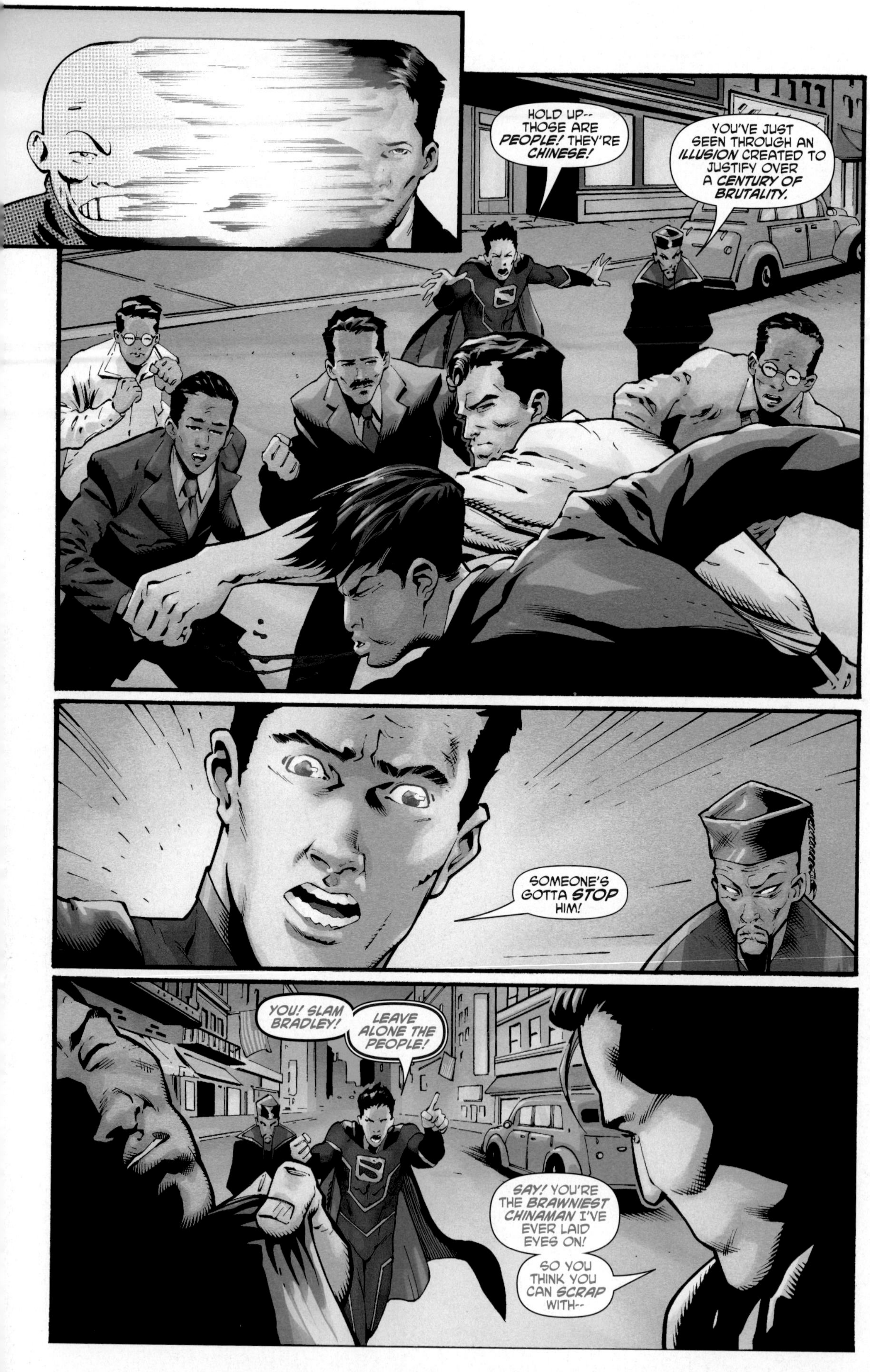
HOLD UP-- THOSE ARE *PEOPLE!* THEY'RE *CHINESE!*
YOU'VE JUST SEEN THROUGH AN *ILLUSION* CREATED TO JUSTIFY OVER A *CENTURY OF BRUTALITY.*
SOMEONE'S GOTTA *STOP* HIM!
YOU! SLAM BRADLEY!
LEAVE ALONE THE PEOPLE!
SAY! YOU'RE THE *BRAWNIEST CHINAMAN* I'VE EVER LAID EYES ON!
SO YOU THINK YOU CAN *SCRAP* WITH--

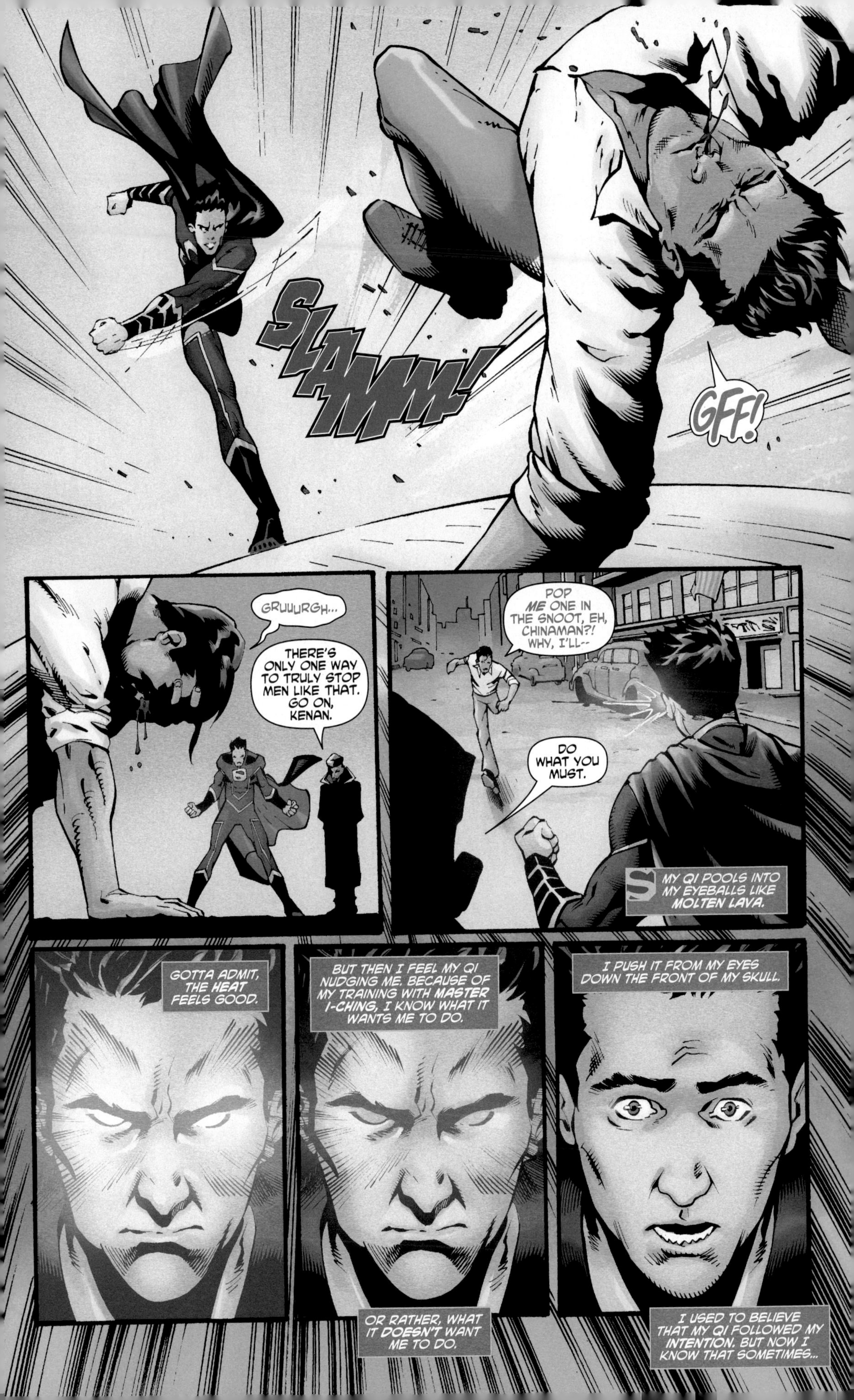
SLAMM!
GFF!
GRUUURGH...
THERE'S ONLY ONE WAY TO TRULY STOP MEN LIKE THAT. GO ON, KENAN.
POP ME ONE IN THE SNOOT, EH, CHINAMAN?! WHY, I'LL--
DO WHAT YOU MUST.
MY QI POOLS INTO MY EYEBALLS LIKE MOLTEN LAVA.
GOTTA ADMIT, THE HEAT FEELS GOOD.
BUT THEN I FEEL MY QI NUDGING ME. BECAUSE OF MY TRAINING WITH MASTER I-CHING, I KNOW WHAT IT WANTS ME TO DO.
OR RATHER, WHAT IT DOESN'T WANT ME TO DO.
I PUSH IT FROM MY EYES DOWN THE FRONT OF MY SKULL.
I USED TO BELIEVE THAT MY QI FOLLOWED MY INTENTION. BUT NOW I KNOW THAT SOMETIMES...

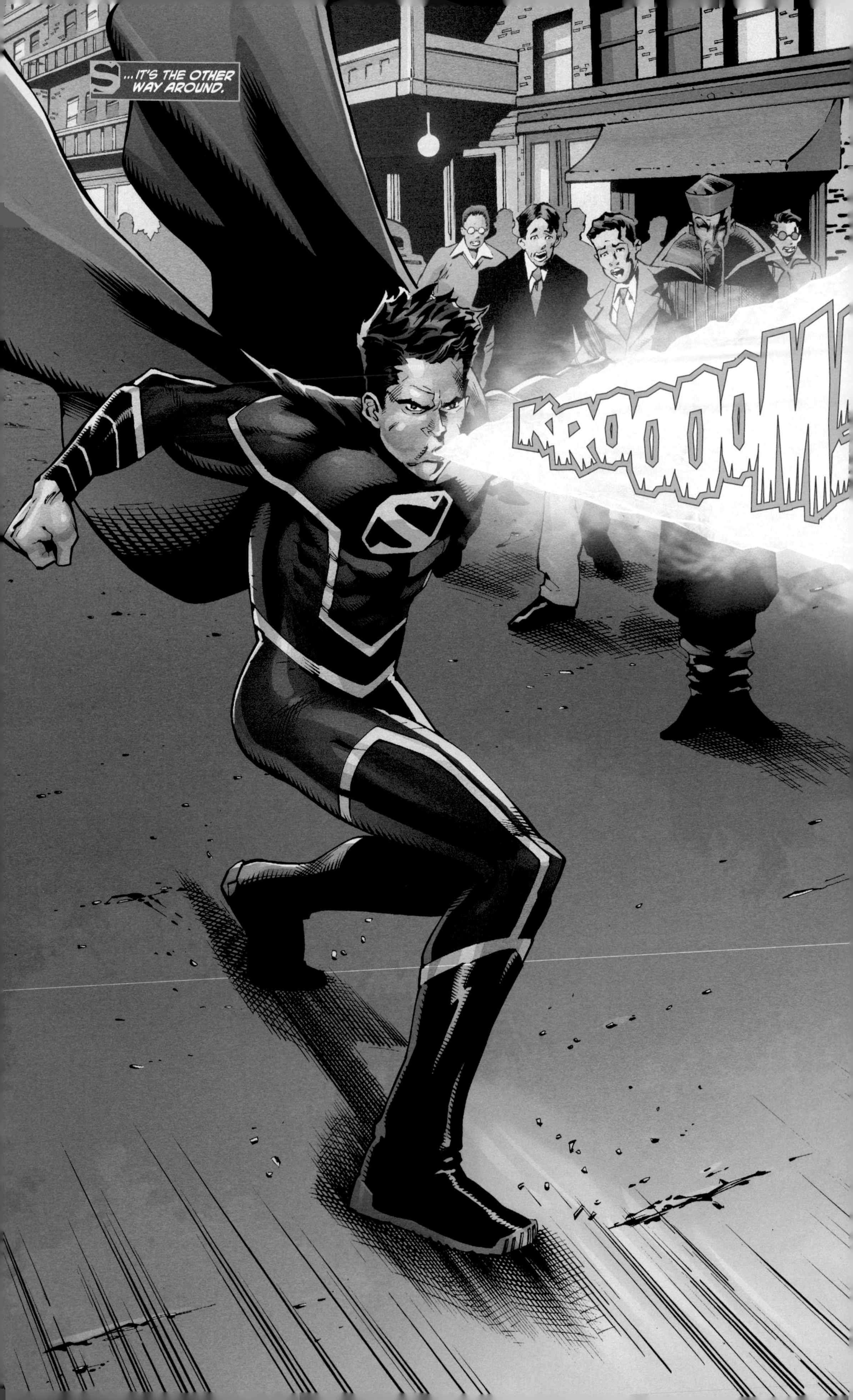
...IT'S THE OTHER WAY AROUND.
KROOOOM

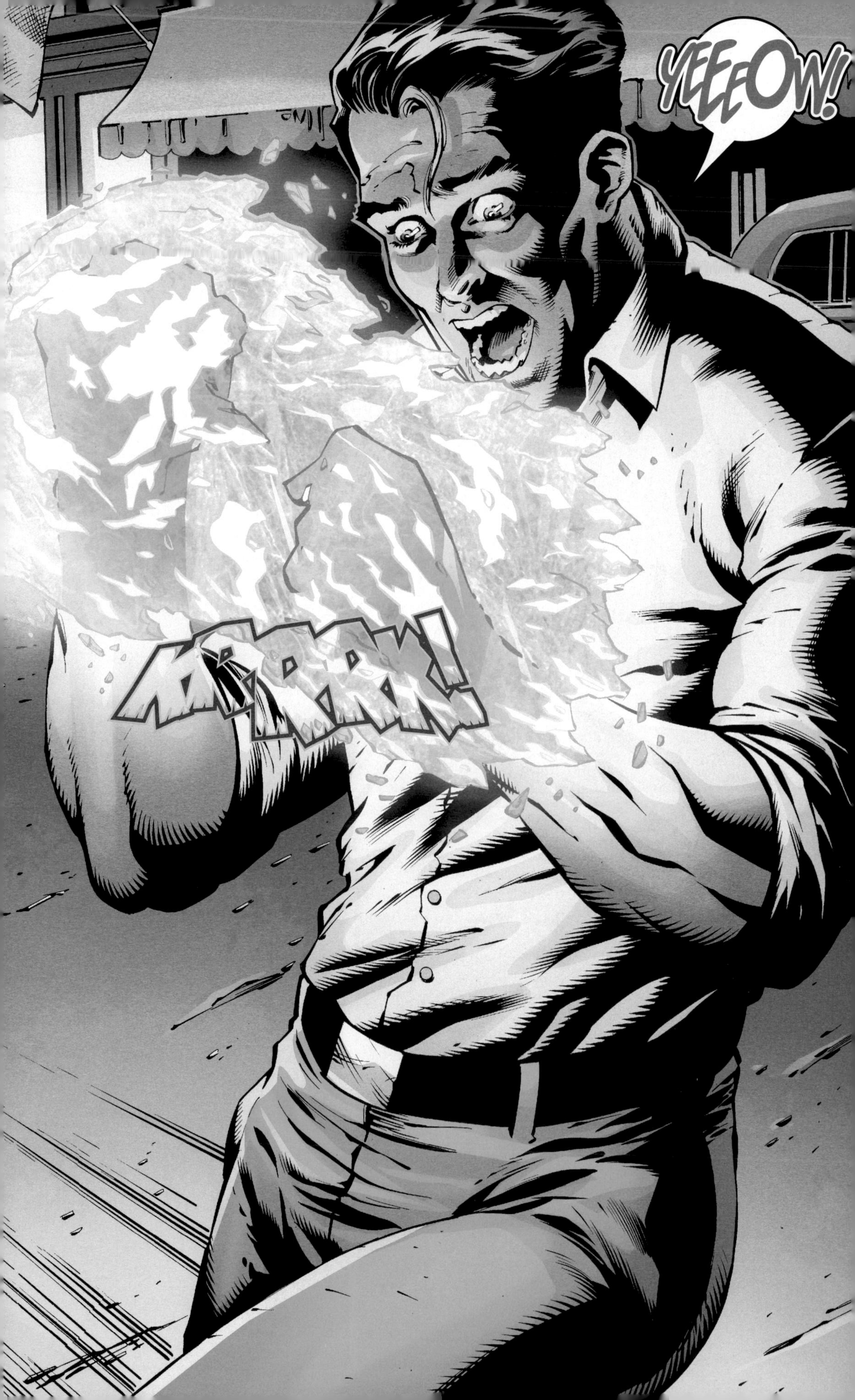
YEEEOW!

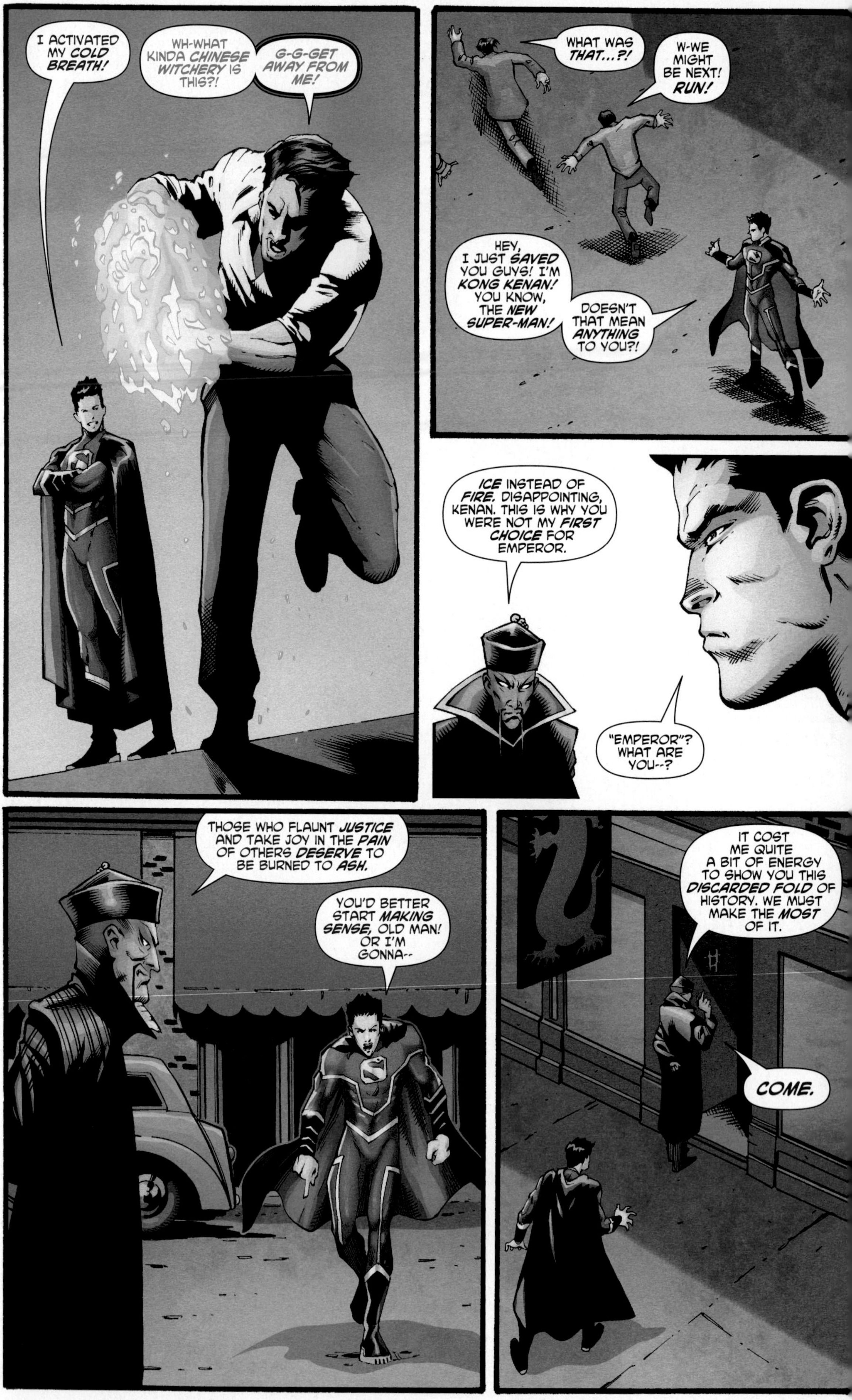
I ACTIVATED MY COLD BREATH!
WH-WHAT KINDA CHINESE WITCHERY IS THIS?!
G-G-GET AWAY FROM ME!
WHAT WAS THAT...?!
W-WE MIGHT BE NEXT! RUN!
HEY, I JUST SAVED YOU GUYS! I'M KONG KENAN! YOU KNOW, THE NEW SUPER-MAN!
DOESN'T THAT MEAN ANYTHING TO YOU?!
ICE INSTEAD OF FIRE. DISAPPOINTING, KENAN. THIS IS WHY YOU WERE NOT MY FIRST CHOICE FOR EMPEROR.
"EMPEROR"? WHAT ARE YOU--?
THOSE WHO FLAUNT JUSTICE AND TAKE JOY IN THE PAIN OF OTHERS DESERVE TO BE BURNED TO ASH.
YOU'D BETTER START MAKING SENSE, OLD MAN! OR I'M GONNA--
IT COST ME QUITE A BIT OF ENERGY TO SHOW YOU THIS DISCARDED FOLD OF HISTORY. WE MUST MAKE THE MOST OF IT.
COME.

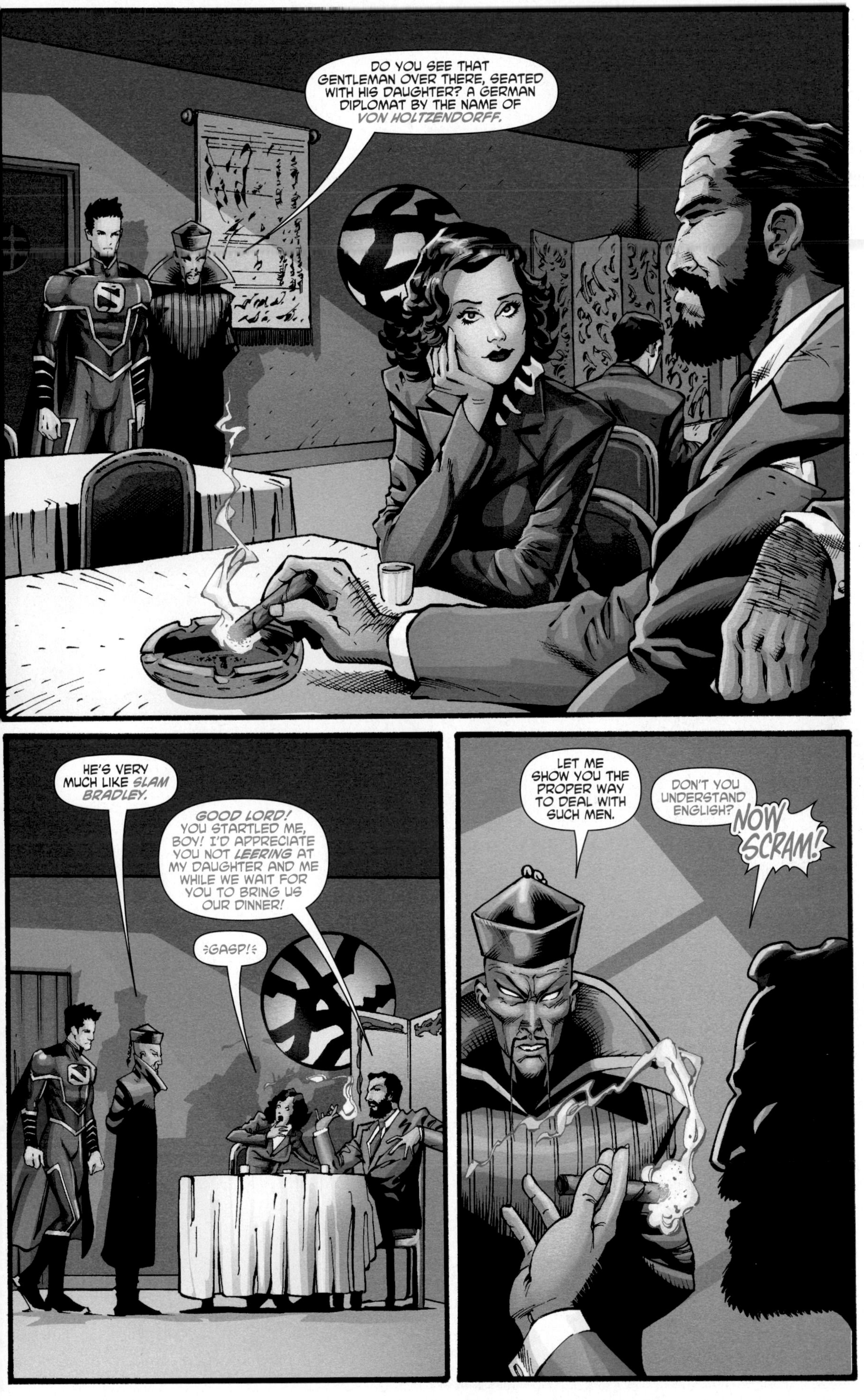
DO YOU SEE THAT GENTLEMAN OVER THERE, SEATED WITH HIS DAUGHTER? A GERMAN DIPLOMAT BY THE NAME OF VON HOLTZENDORFF.
HE'S VERY MUCH LIKE SLAM BRADLEY.
GOOD LORD! YOU STARTLED ME, BOY! I'D APPRECIATE YOU NOT LEERING AT MY DAUGHTER AND ME WHILE WE WAIT FOR YOU TO BRING US OUR DINNER!
GASP!
LET ME SHOW YOU THE PROPER WAY TO DEAL WITH SUCH MEN.
DON'T YOU UNDERSTAND ENGLISH?
NOW SCRAM!

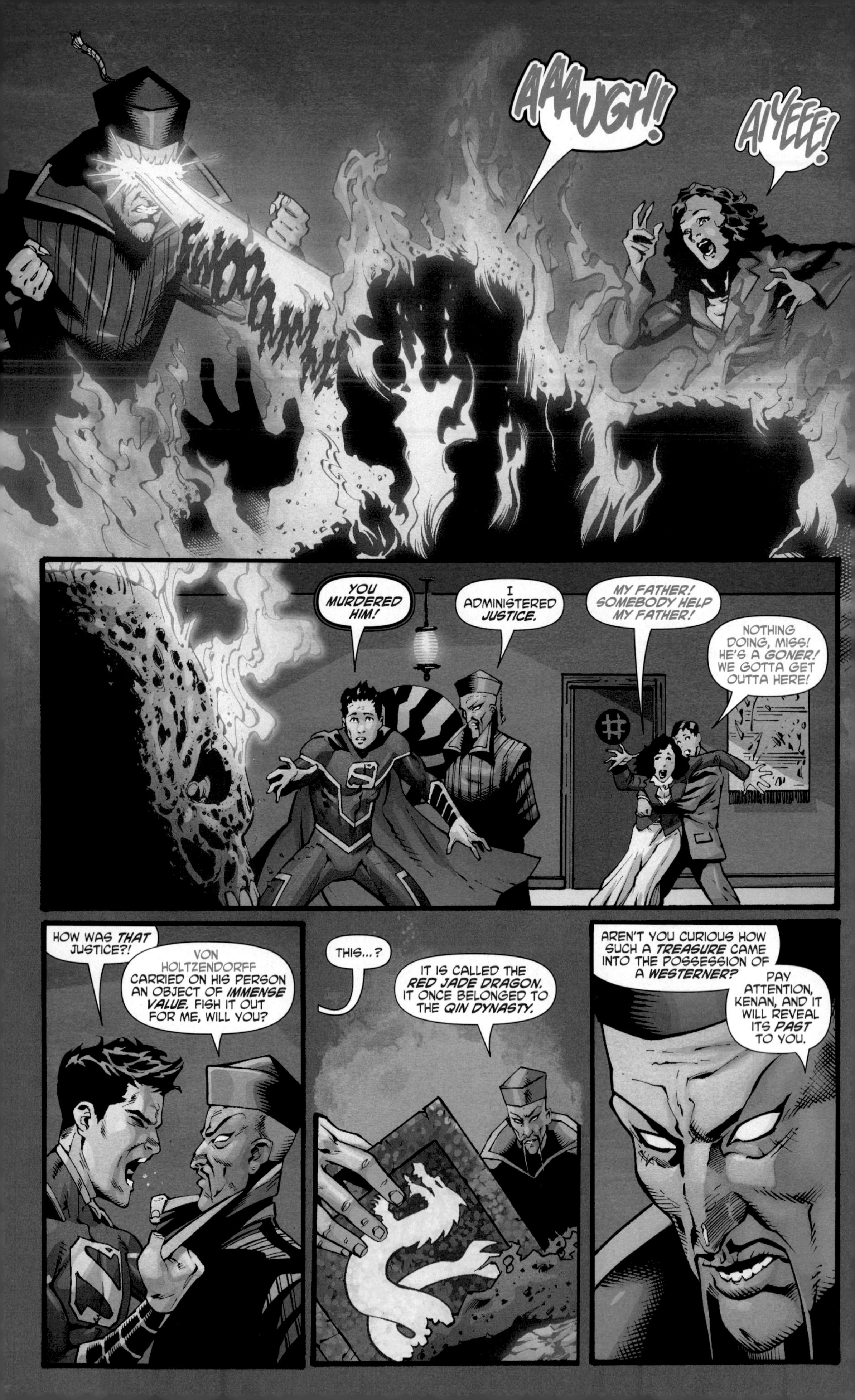
FWOOOMMM
AAAAUGH!!
AIYEEE!
YOU MURDERED HIM!
I ADMINISTERED JUSTICE.
MY FATHER! SOMEBODY HELP MY FATHER!
NOTHING DOING, MISS! HE'S A GONER! WE GOTTA GET OUTTA HERE!
HOW WAS THAT JUSTICE?!
VON HOLTZENDORFF CARRIED ON HIS PERSON AN OBJECT OF IMMENSE VALUE. FISH IT OUT FOR ME, WILL YOU?
THIS...?
IT IS CALLED THE RED JADE DRAGON. IT ONCE BELONGED TO THE QIN DYNASTY.
AREN'T YOU CURIOUS HOW SUCH A TREASURE CAME INTO THE POSSESSION OF A WESTERNER?
PAY ATTENTION, KENAN, AND IT WILL REVEAL ITS PAST TO YOU.

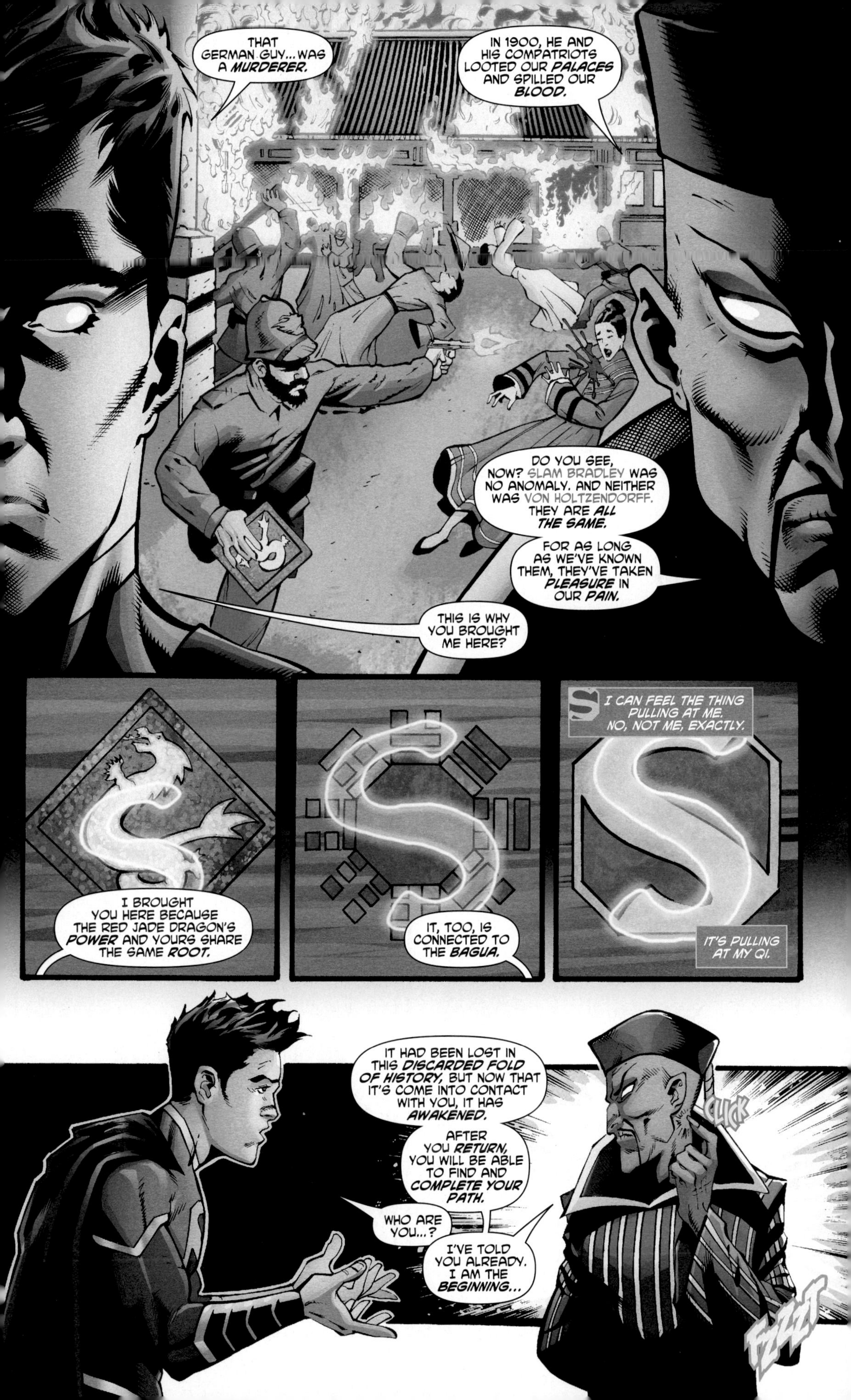
THAT GERMAN GUY... WAS A MURDERER.
IN 1900, HE AND HIS COMPATRIOTS LOOTED OUR PALACES AND SPILLED OUR BLOOD.
DO YOU SEE, NOW? SLAM BRADLEY WAS NO ANOMALY. AND NEITHER WAS VON HOLTZENDORFF. THEY ARE ALL THE SAME.
FOR AS LONG AS WE'VE KNOWN THEM, THEY'VE TAKEN PLEASURE IN OUR PAIN.
THIS IS WHY YOU BROUGHT ME HERE?
I BROUGHT YOU HERE BECAUSE THE RED JADE DRAGON'S POWER AND YOURS SHARE THE SAME ROOT.
IT, TOO, IS CONNECTED TO THE BAGUA.
I CAN FEEL THE THING PULLING AT ME. NO, NOT ME, EXACTLY.
IT'S PULLING AT MY QI.
IT HAD BEEN LOST IN THIS DISCARDED FOLD OF HISTORY, BUT NOW THAT IT'S COME INTO CONTACT WITH YOU, IT HAS AWAKENED.
AFTER YOU RETURN, YOU WILL BE ABLE TO FIND AND COMPLETE YOUR PATH.
WHO ARE YOU...?
I'VE TOLD YOU ALREADY. I AM THE BEGINNING...
CLICK
FZZZT

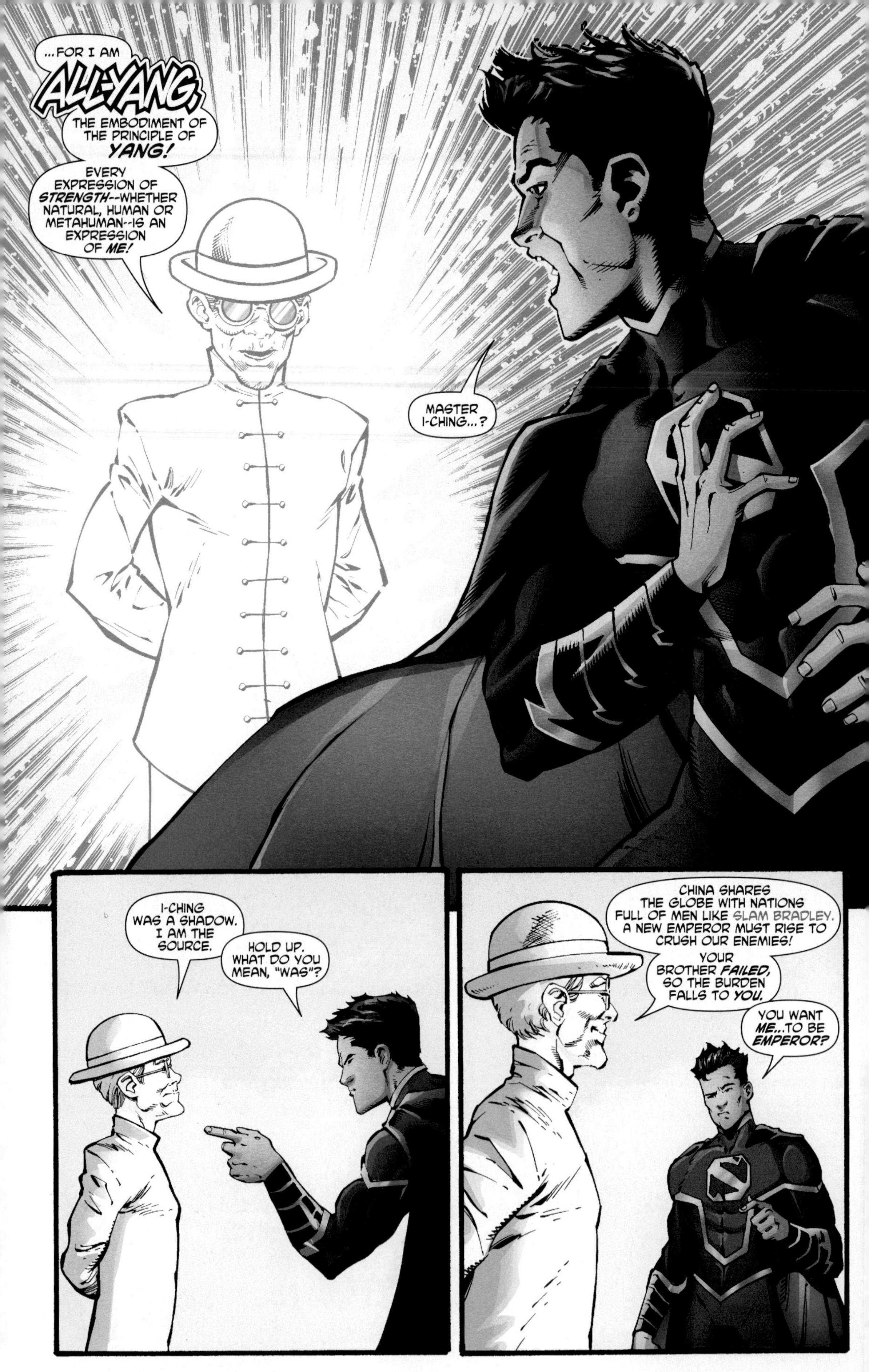
...FOR I AM
ALL-YANG,
THE EMBODIMENT OF THE PRINCIPLE OF YANG!
EVERY EXPRESSION OF STRENGTH--WHETHER NATURAL, HUMAN OR METAHUMAN--IS AN EXPRESSION OF ME!
MASTER I-CHING...?
I-CHING WAS A SHADOW. I AM THE SOURCE.
HOLD UP. WHAT DO YOU MEAN, "WAS"?
CHINA SHARES THE GLOBE WITH NATIONS FULL OF MEN LIKE SLAM BRADLEY. A NEW EMPEROR MUST RISE TO CRUSH OUR ENEMIES!
YOUR BROTHER FAILED, SO THE BURDEN FALLS TO YOU.
YOU WANT ME...TO BE EMPEROR?

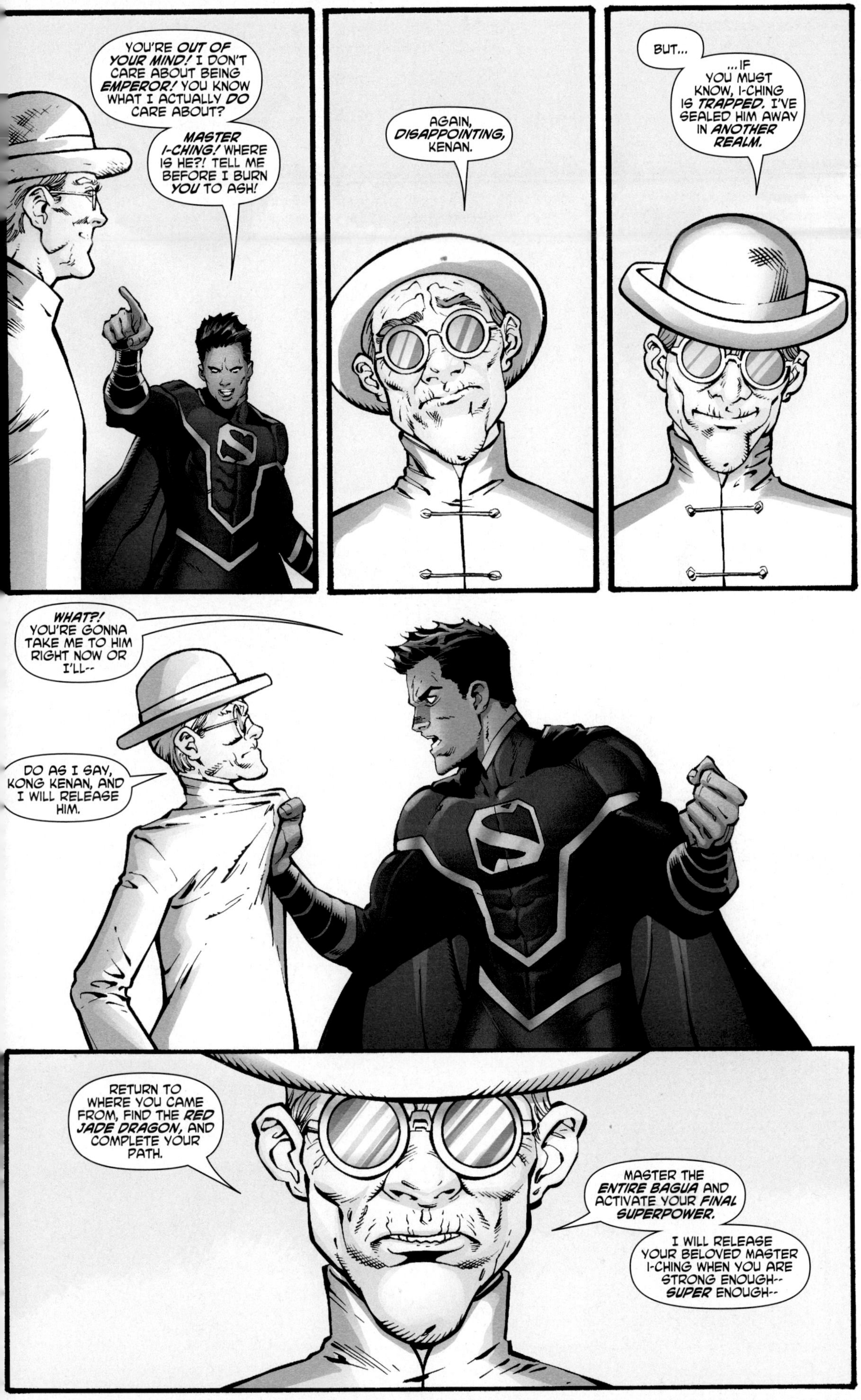
YOU'RE OUT OF YOUR MIND! I DON'T CARE ABOUT BEING EMPEROR! YOU KNOW WHAT I ACTUALLY DO CARE ABOUT?
MASTER I-CHING! WHERE IS HE?! TELL ME BEFORE I BURN YOU TO ASH!
AGAIN, DISAPPOINTING, KENAN.
BUT...
...IF YOU MUST KNOW, I-CHING IS TRAPPED. I'VE SEALED HIM AWAY IN ANOTHER REALM.
WHAT?! YOU'RE GONNA TAKE ME TO HIM RIGHT NOW OR I'LL--
DO AS I SAY, KONG KENAN, AND I WILL RELEASE HIM.
RETURN TO WHERE YOU CAME FROM, FIND THE RED JADE DRAGON, AND COMPLETE YOUR PATH.
MASTER THE ENTIRE BAGUA AND ACTIVATE YOUR FINAL SUPERPOWER.
I WILL RELEASE YOUR BELOVED MASTER I-CHING WHEN YOU ARE STRONG ENOUGH-- SUPER ENOUGH--

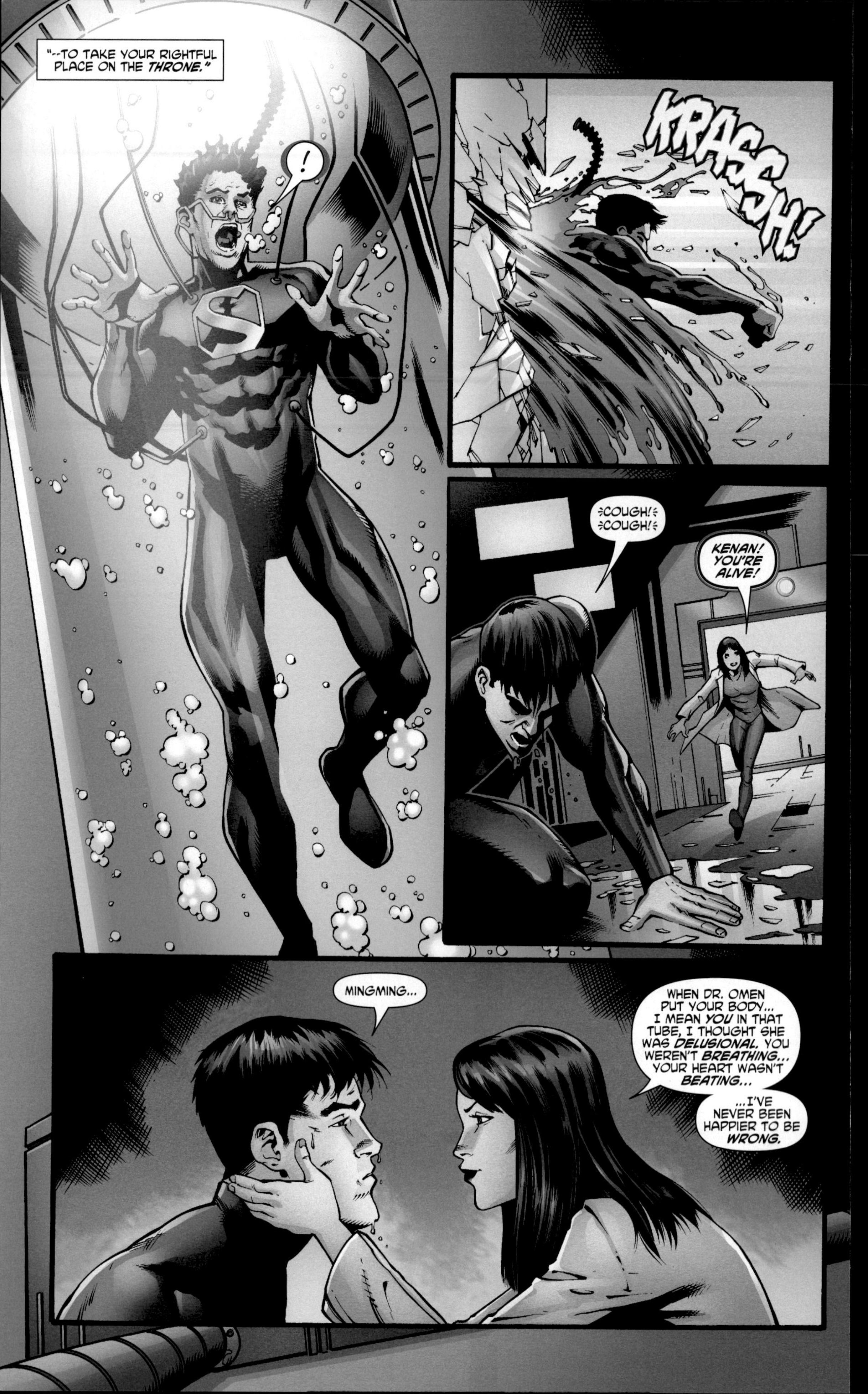
"--TO TAKE YOUR RIGHTFUL PLACE ON THE *THRONE.*"
!
KRASSH!
COUGH! COUGH!
KENAN! YOU'RE ALIVE!
MINGMING...
WHEN DR. OMEN PUT YOUR BODY... I MEAN *YOU* IN THAT TUBE, I THOUGHT SHE WAS *DELUSIONAL.* YOU WEREN'T *BREATHING...* YOUR HEART WASN'T *BEATING...*
...I'VE NEVER BEEN HAPPIER TO BE *WRONG.*

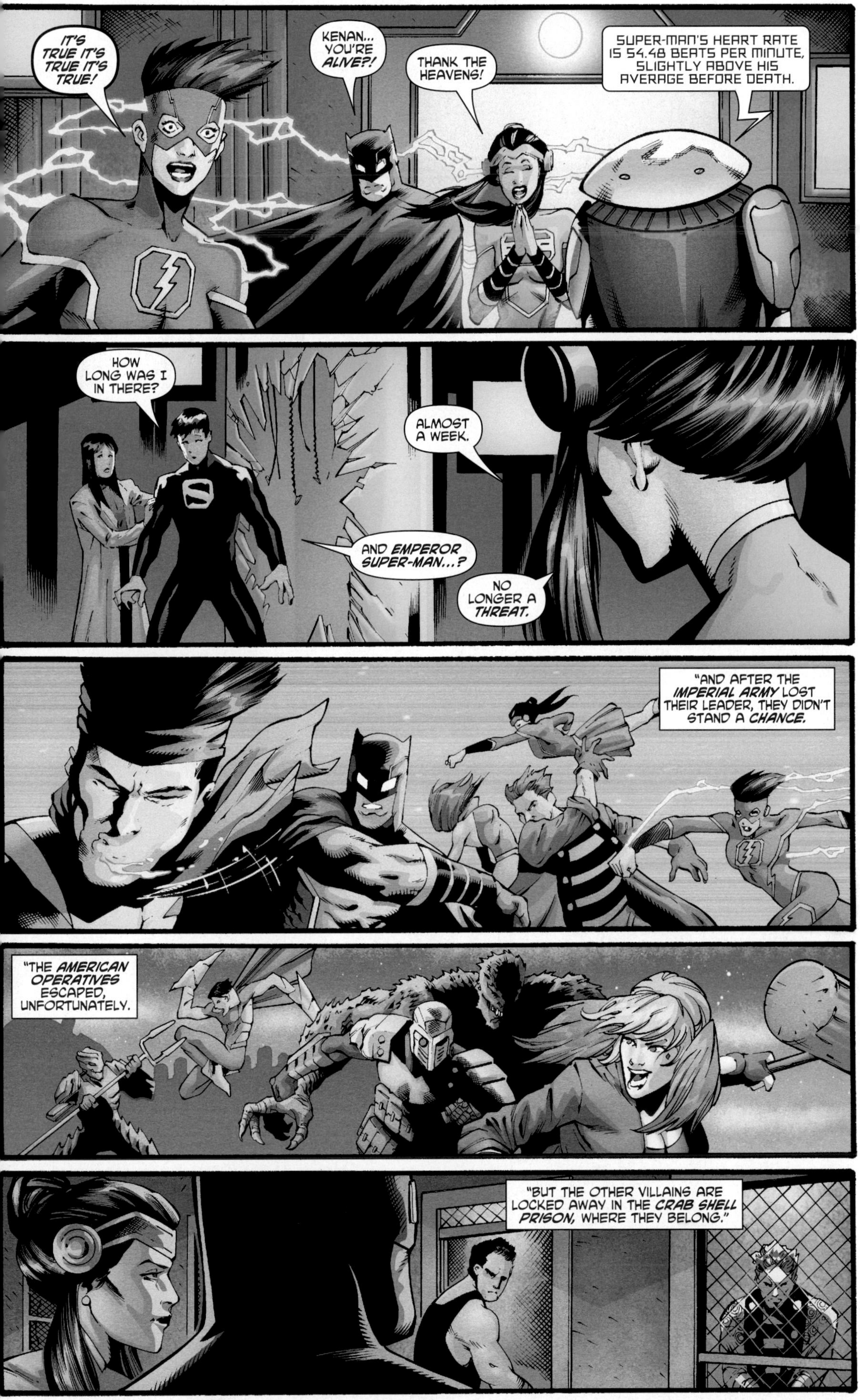
IT'S TRUE IT'S TRUE IT'S TRUE!
KENAN... YOU'RE ALIVE?!
THANK THE HEAVENS!
SUPER-MAN'S HEART RATE IS 54.48 BEATS PER MINUTE, SLIGHTLY ABOVE HIS AVERAGE BEFORE DEATH.
HOW LONG WAS I IN THERE?
ALMOST A WEEK.
AND EMPEROR SUPER-MAN...?
NO LONGER A THREAT.
"AND AFTER THE IMPERIAL ARMY LOST THEIR LEADER, THEY DIDN'T STAND A CHANCE.
"THE AMERICAN OPERATIVES ESCAPED, UNFORTUNATELY.
"BUT THE OTHER VILLAINS ARE LOCKED AWAY IN THE CRAB SHELL PRISON, WHERE THEY BELONG."

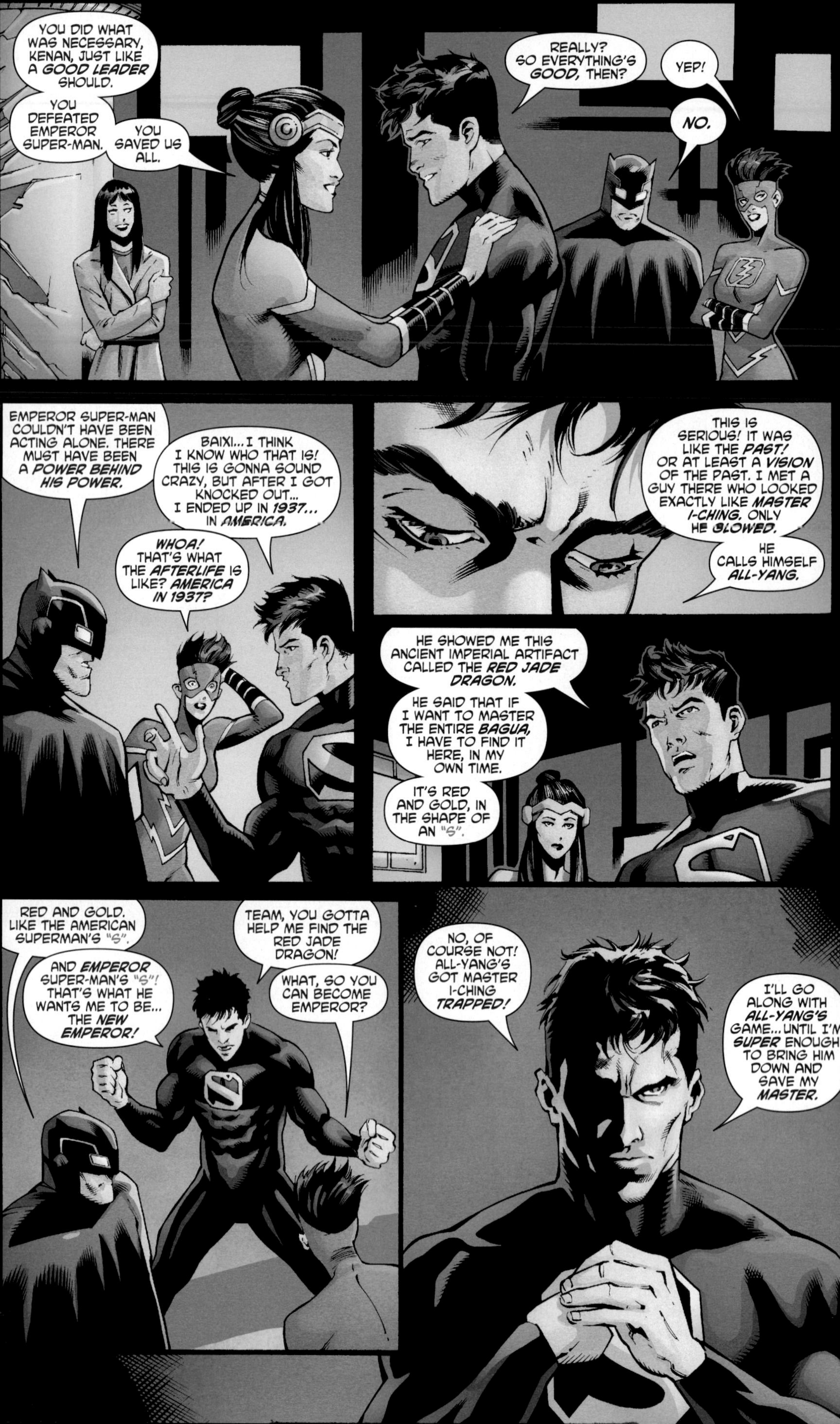
YOU DID WHAT WAS NECESSARY, KENAN, JUST LIKE A GOOD LEADER SHOULD.
YOU DEFEATED EMPEROR SUPER-MAN.
YOU SAVED US ALL.
REALLY? SO EVERYTHING'S GOOD, THEN?
YEP!
NO.
EMPEROR SUPER-MAN COULDN'T HAVE BEEN ACTING ALONE. THERE MUST HAVE BEEN A POWER BEHIND HIS POWER.
BAIXI... I THINK I KNOW WHO THAT IS! THIS IS GONNA SOUND CRAZY, BUT AFTER I GOT KNOCKED OUT... I ENDED UP IN 1937... IN AMERICA.
WHOA! THAT'S WHAT THE AFTERLIFE IS LIKE? AMERICA IN 1937?
THIS IS SERIOUS! IT WAS LIKE THE PAST! OR AT LEAST A VISION OF THE PAST. I MET A GUY THERE WHO LOOKED EXACTLY LIKE MASTER I-CHING. ONLY HE GLOWED.
HE CALLS HIMSELF ALL-YANG.
HE SHOWED ME THIS ANCIENT IMPERIAL ARTIFACT CALLED THE RED JADE DRAGON.
HE SAID THAT IF I WANT TO MASTER THE ENTIRE BAGUA, I HAVE TO FIND IT HERE, IN MY OWN TIME.
IT'S RED AND GOLD, IN THE SHAPE OF AN "S".
RED AND GOLD. LIKE THE AMERICAN SUPERMAN'S "S".
AND EMPEROR SUPER-MAN'S "S"! THAT'S WHAT HE WANTS ME TO BE... THE NEW EMPEROR!
TEAM, YOU GOTTA HELP ME FIND THE RED JADE DRAGON!
WHAT, SO YOU CAN BECOME EMPEROR?
NO, OF COURSE NOT! ALL-YANG'S GOT MASTER I-CHING TRAPPED!
I'LL GO ALONG WITH ALL-YANG'S GAME... UNTIL I'M SUPER ENOUGH TO BRING HIM DOWN AND SAVE MY MASTER.

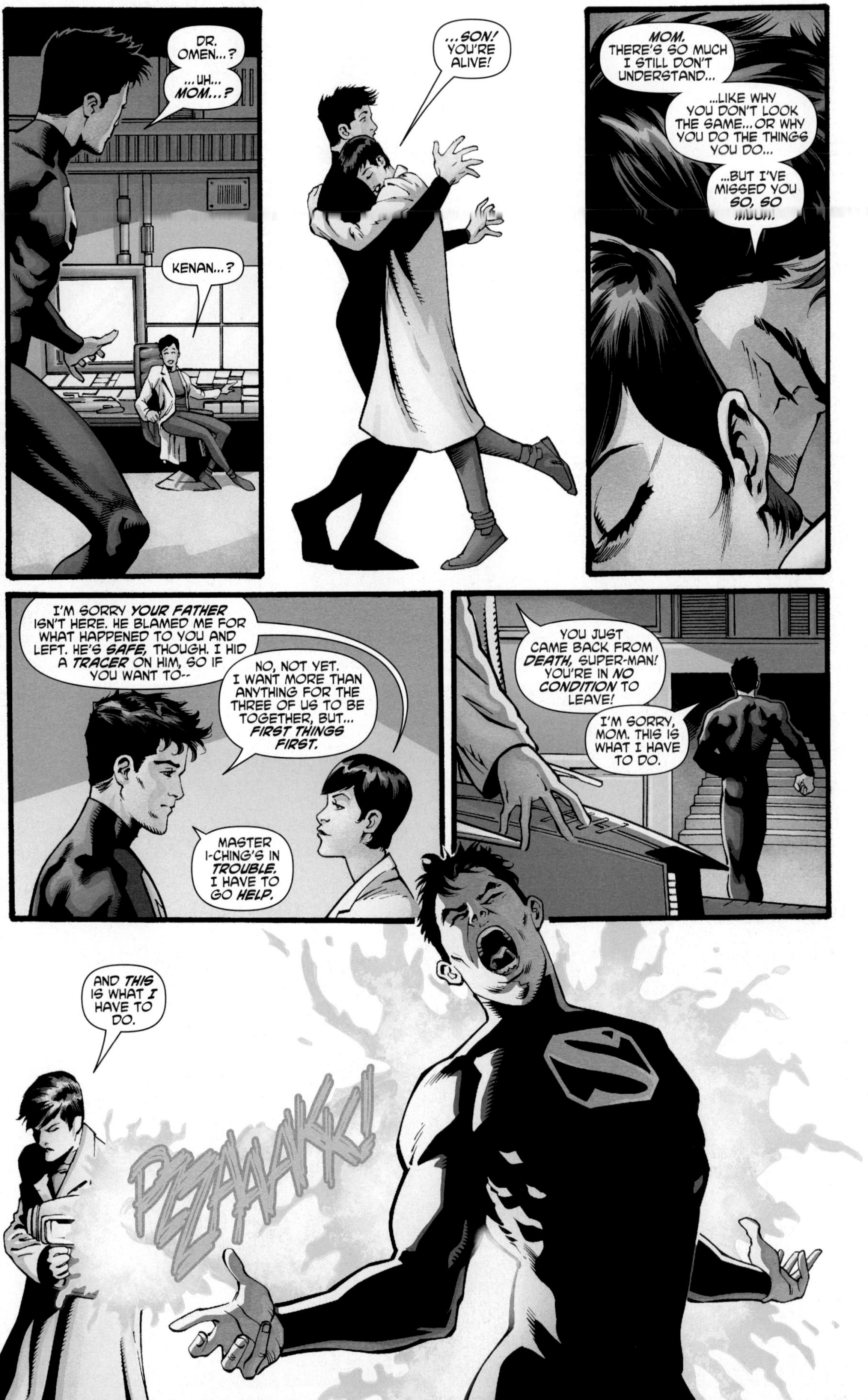
DR. OMEN...?
...UH... MOM...?
KENAN...?
...SON! YOU'RE ALIVE!
MOM. THERE'S SO MUCH I STILL DON'T UNDERSTAND...
...LIKE WHY YOU DON'T LOOK THE SAME...OR WHY YOU DO THE THINGS YOU DO...
...BUT I'VE MISSED YOU SO, SO
I'M SORRY YOUR FATHER ISN'T HERE. HE BLAMED ME FOR WHAT HAPPENED TO YOU AND LEFT. HE'S SAFE, THOUGH. I HID A TRACER ON HIM, SO IF YOU WANT TO--
NO, NOT YET. I WANT MORE THAN ANYTHING FOR THE THREE OF US TO BE TOGETHER, BUT... FIRST THINGS FIRST.
MASTER I-CHING'S IN TROUBLE. I HAVE TO GO HELP.
YOU JUST CAME BACK FROM DEATH, SUPER-MAN! YOU'RE IN NO CONDITION TO LEAVE!
I'M SORRY, MOM. THIS IS WHAT I HAVE TO DO.
AND THIS IS WHAT I HAVE TO DO.
PZZAAAKK!

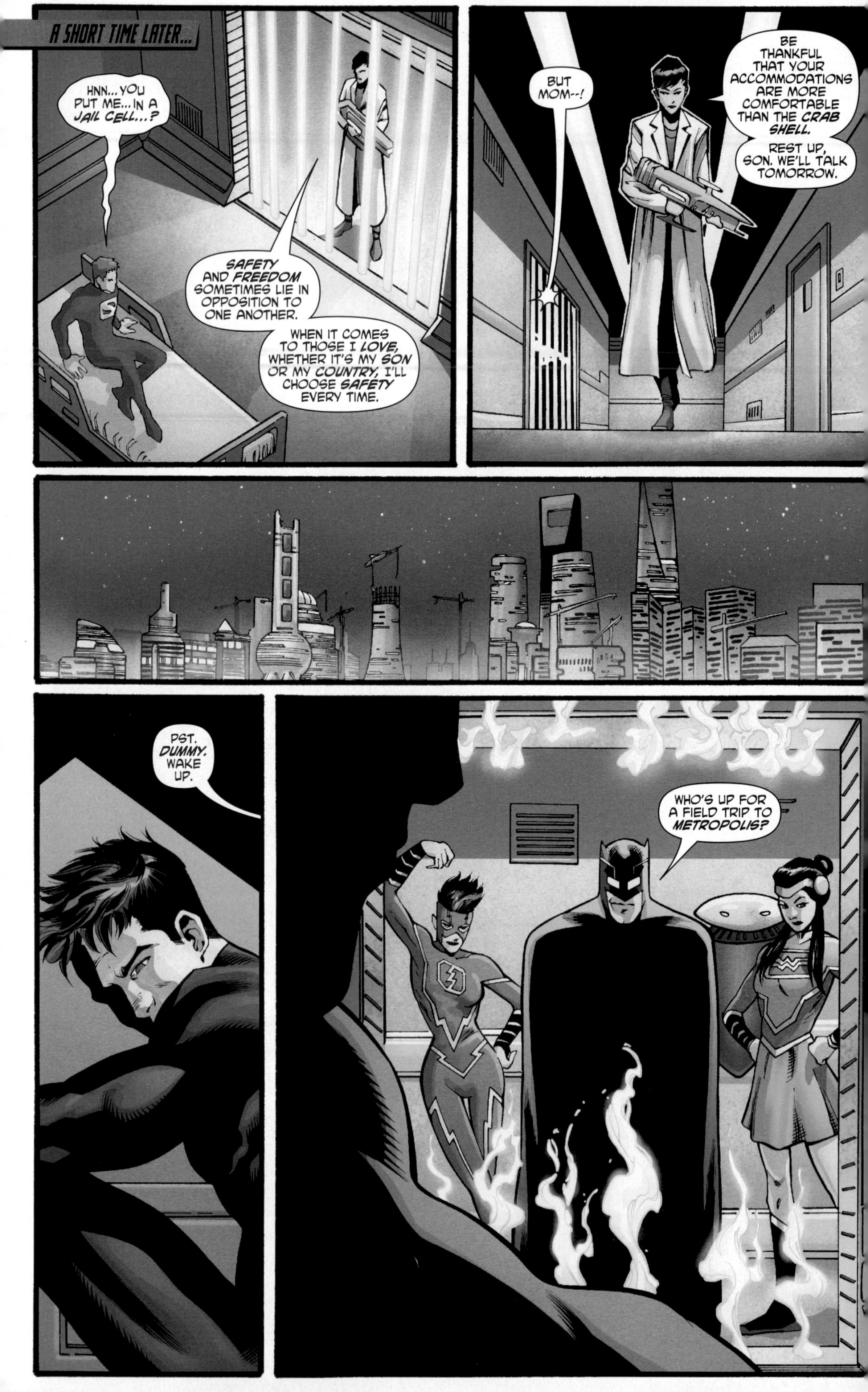
A SHORT TIME LATER...
HNN...YOU PUT ME...IN A JAIL CELL...?
SAFETY AND FREEDOM SOMETIMES LIE IN OPPOSITION TO ONE ANOTHER.
WHEN IT COMES TO THOSE I LOVE, WHETHER IT'S MY SON OR MY COUNTRY, I'LL CHOOSE SAFETY EVERY TIME.
BUT MOM--!
BE THANKFUL THAT YOUR ACCOMMODATIONS ARE MORE COMFORTABLE THAN THE CRAB SHELL.
REST UP, SON. WE'LL TALK TOMORROW.
PST. DUMMY. WAKE UP.
WHO'S UP FOR A FIELD TRIP TO METROPOLIS?

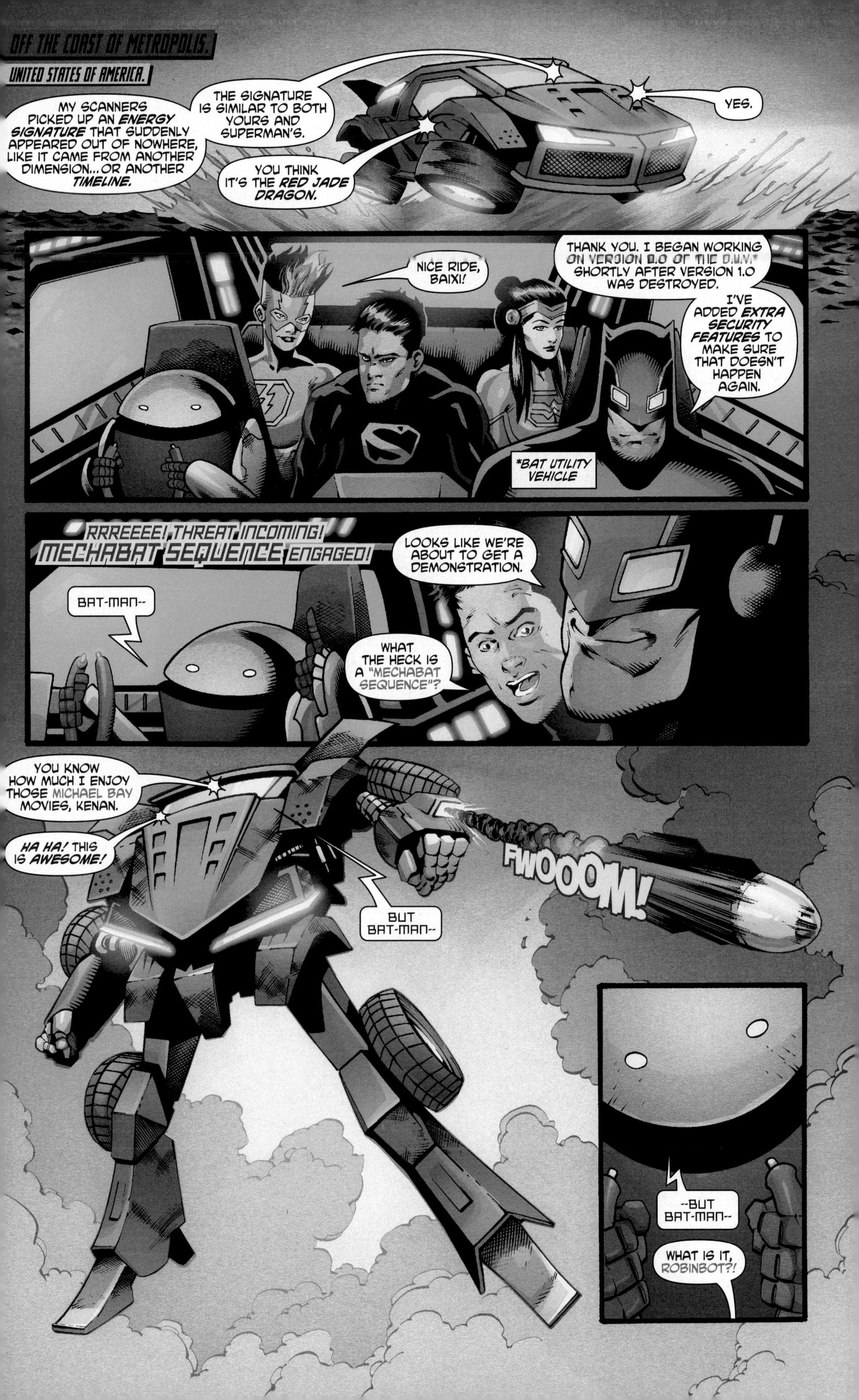
OFF THE COAST OF METROPOLIS.
UNITED STATES OF AMERICA.
MY SCANNERS PICKED UP AN ENERGY SIGNATURE THAT SUDDENLY APPEARED OUT OF NOWHERE, LIKE IT CAME FROM ANOTHER DIMENSION...OR ANOTHER TIMELINE.
THE SIGNATURE IS SIMILAR TO BOTH YOURS AND SUPERMAN'S.
YOU THINK IT'S THE RED JADE DRAGON.
YES.
NICE RIDE, BAIXI!
THANK YOU. I BEGAN WORKING ON VERSION 2.0 OF THE B.U.V.* SHORTLY AFTER VERSION 1.0 WAS DESTROYED.
I'VE ADDED EXTRA SECURITY FEATURES TO MAKE SURE THAT DOESN'T HAPPEN AGAIN.
*BAT UTILITY VEHICLE
RRREEEE! THREAT INCOMING! MECHABAT SEQUENCE ENGAGED!
LOOKS LIKE WE'RE ABOUT TO GET A DEMONSTRATION.
BAT-MAN--
WHAT THE HECK IS A "MECHABAT SEQUENCE"?
YOU KNOW HOW MUCH I ENJOY THOSE MICHAEL BAY MOVIES, KENAN.
HA HA! THIS IS AWESOME!
BUT BAT-MAN--
FWOOOM!
--BUT BAT-MAN--
WHAT IS IT, ROBINBOT?!

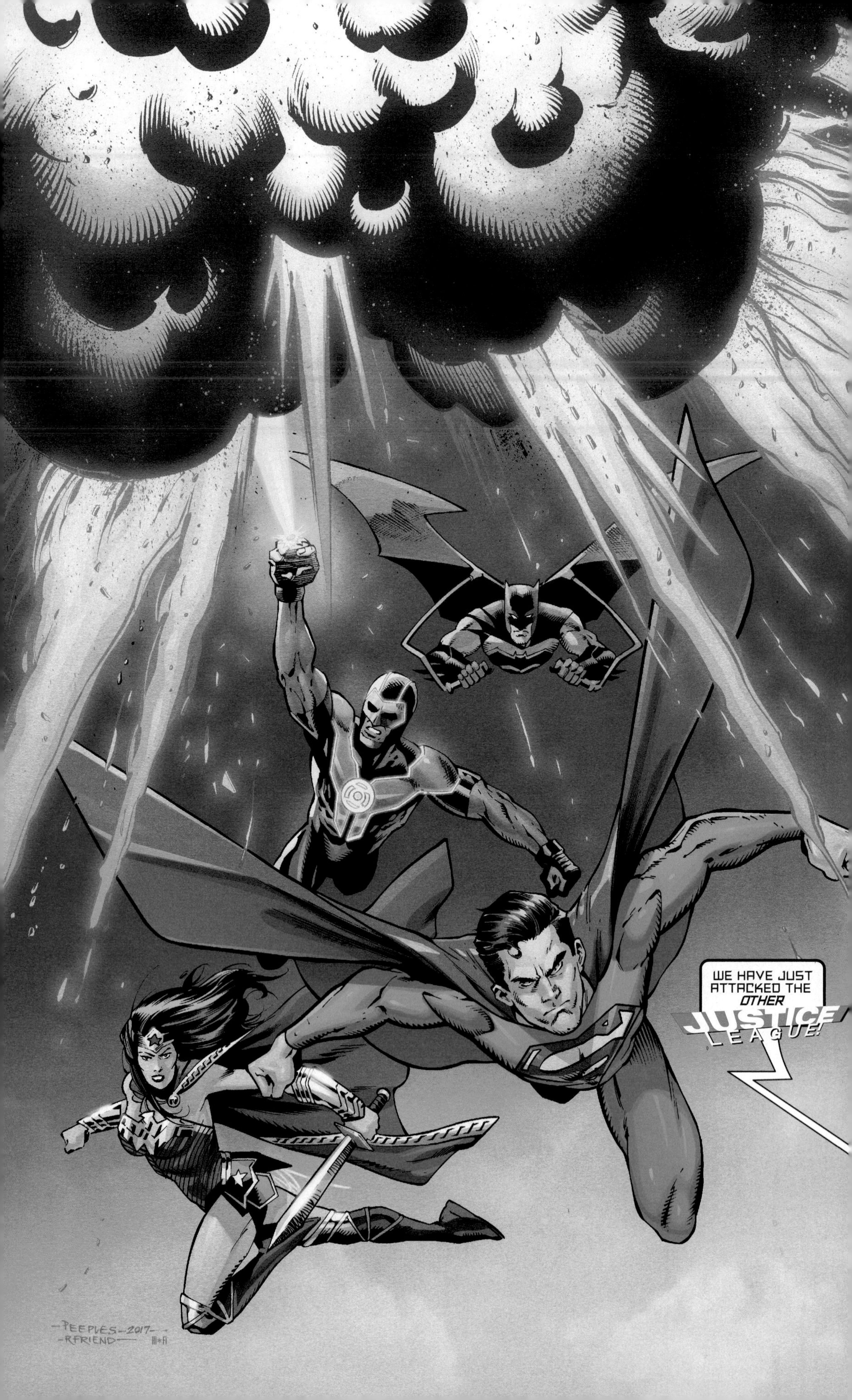
WE HAVE JUST ATTACKED THE *OTHER*
JUSTICE LEAGUE!
-PEEPLES-2017-
-RFRIEND-

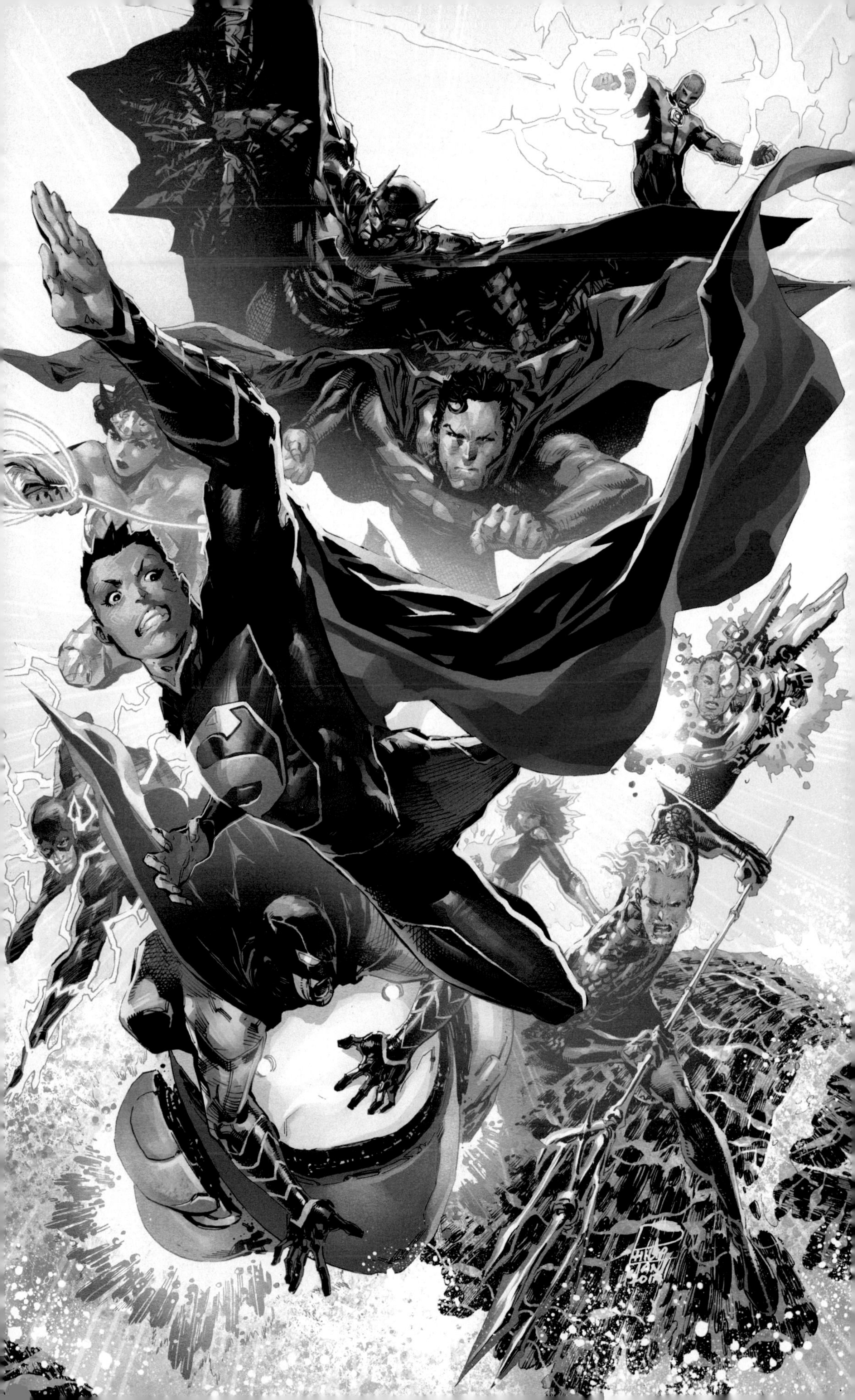

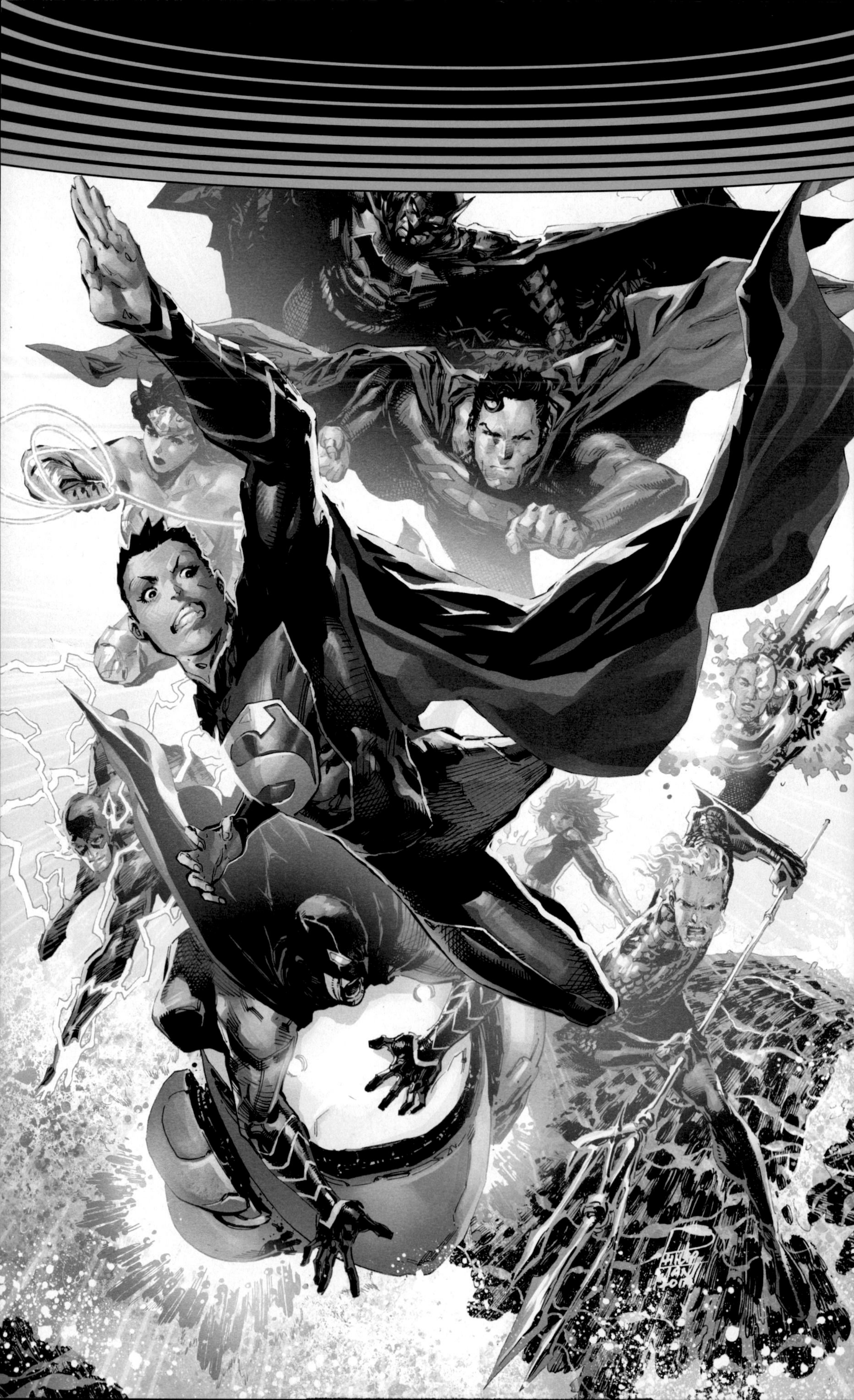

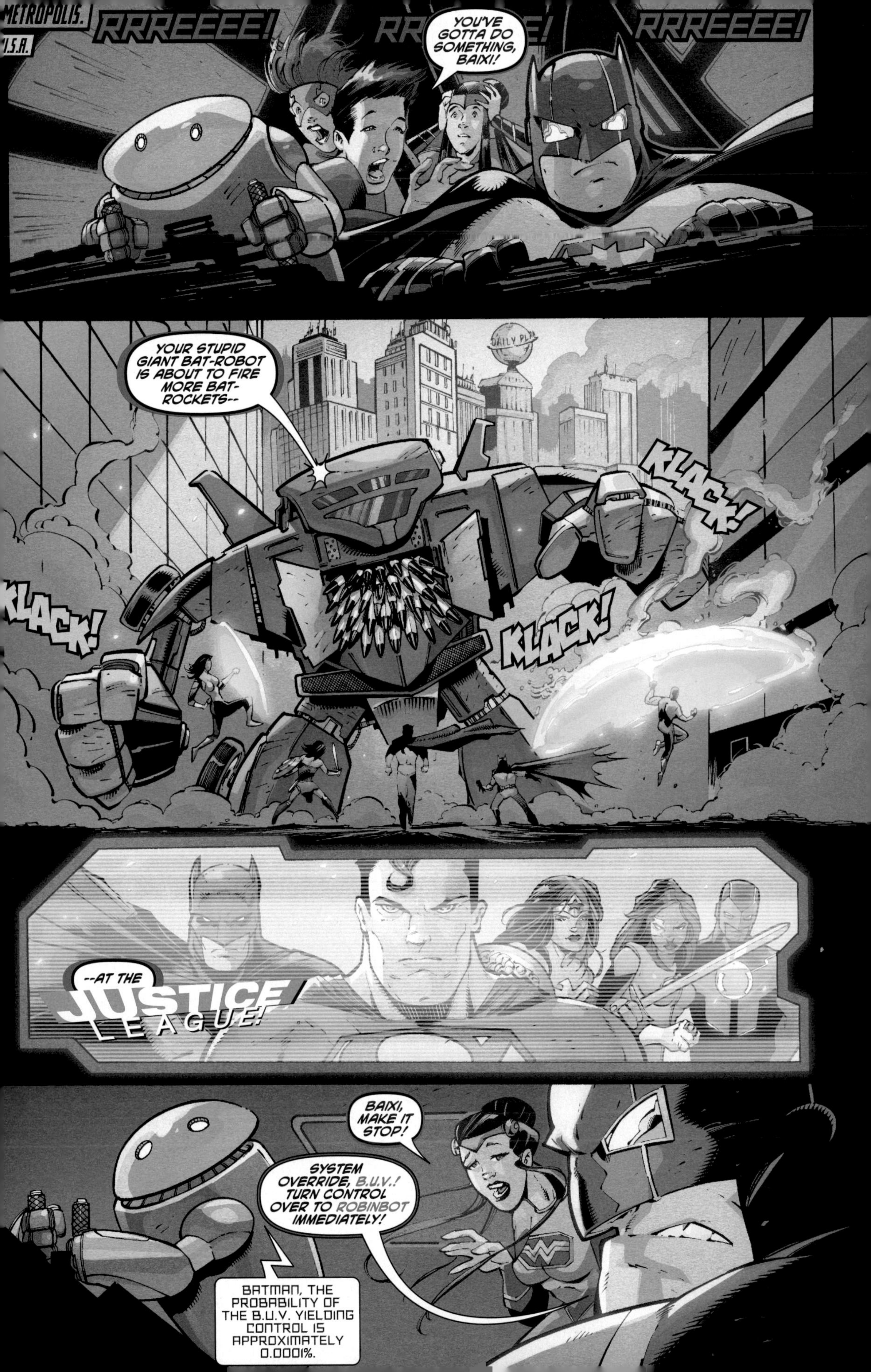

METROPOLIS, U.S.A.
RRREEEE! RRREEEE! RRREEEE!
YOU'VE GOTTA DO SOMETHING, BAIXI!
YOUR STUPID GIANT BAT-ROBOT IS ABOUT TO FIRE MORE BAT-ROCKETS--
KLACK!
KLACK!
KLACK!
--AT THE
JUSTICE LEAGUE!
BAIXI, MAKE IT STOP!
SYSTEM OVERRIDE, B.U.V.! TURN CONTROL OVER TO ROBINBOT IMMEDIATELY!
BATMAN, THE PROBABILITY OF THE B.U.V. YIELDING CONTROL IS APPROXIMATELY 0.0001%.

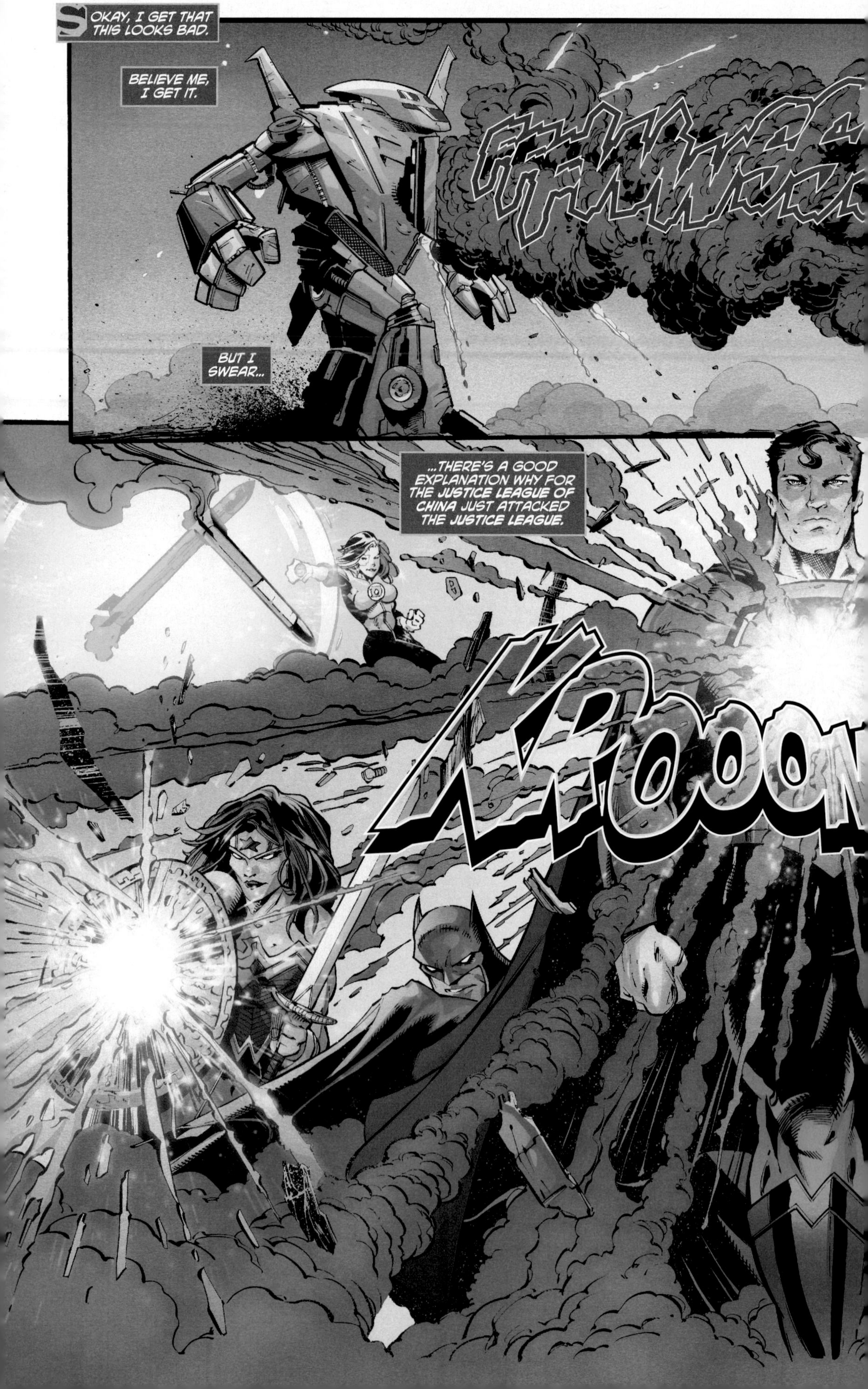
OKAY, I GET THAT THIS LOOKS BAD.
BELIEVE ME, I GET IT.
BUT I SWEAR...
...THERE'S A GOOD EXPLANATION WHY FOR THE JUSTICE LEAGUE OF CHINA JUST ATTACKED THE JUSTICE LEAGUE.

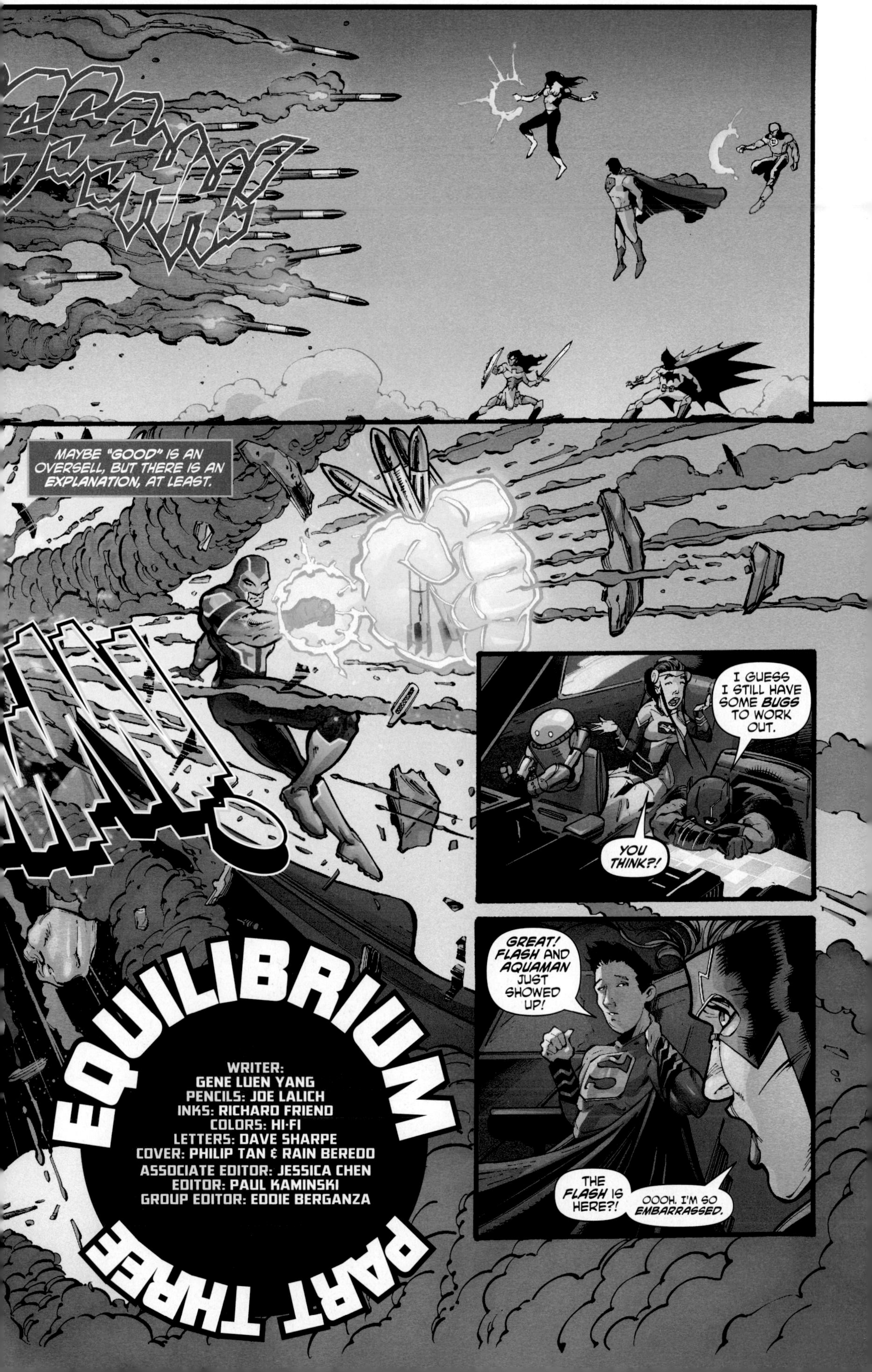
MAYBE "GOOD" IS AN OVERSELL, BUT THERE IS AN EXPLANATION, AT LEAST.
I GUESS I STILL HAVE SOME BUGS TO WORK OUT.
YOU THINK?!
GREAT! FLASH AND AQUAMAN JUST SHOWED UP!
THE FLASH IS HERE?!
OOOH. I'M SO EMBARRASSED.
EQUILIBRIUM
PART THREE
WRITER: GENE LUEN YANG
PENCILS: JOE LALICH
INKS: RICHARD FRIEND
COLORS: HI-FI
LETTERS: DAVE SHARPE
COVER: PHILIP TAN & RAIN BEREDO
ASSOCIATE EDITOR: JESSICA CHEN
EDITOR: PAUL KAMINSKI
GROUP EDITOR: EDDIE BERGANZA

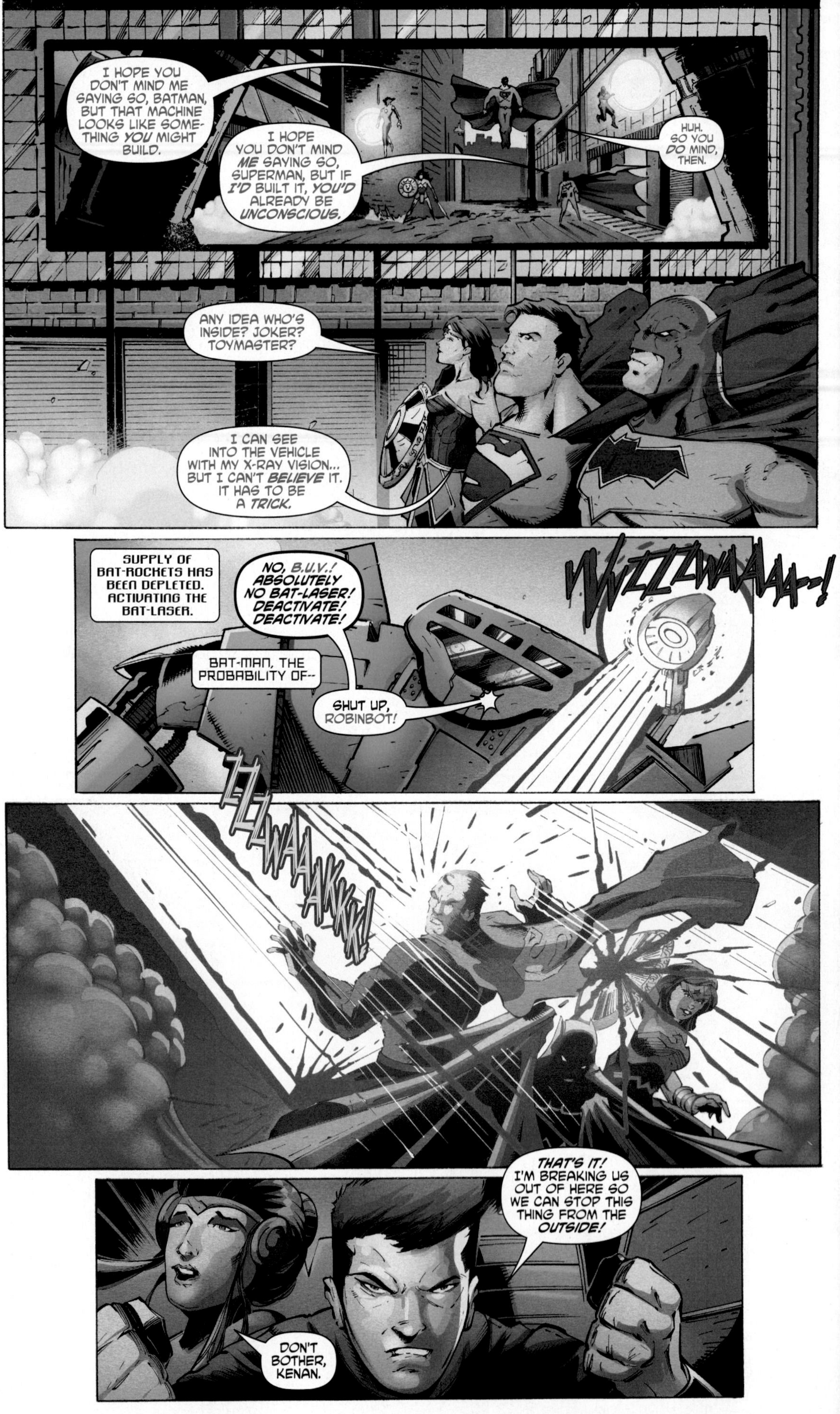
I HOPE YOU DON'T MIND ME SAYING SO, BATMAN, BUT THAT MACHINE LOOKS LIKE SOMETHING *YOU* MIGHT BUILD.
I HOPE YOU DON'T MIND *ME* SAYING SO, SUPERMAN, BUT IF *I'D* BUILT IT, *YOU'D* ALREADY BE *UNCONSCIOUS.*
HUH. SO YOU *DO* MIND, THEN.
ANY IDEA WHO'S INSIDE? JOKER? TOYMASTER?
I CAN SEE INTO THE VEHICLE WITH MY X-RAY VISION... BUT I CAN'T *BELIEVE* IT. IT HAS TO BE A *TRICK.*
SUPPLY OF BAT-ROCKETS HAS BEEN DEPLETED. ACTIVATING THE BAT-LASER.
NO, B.U.V.! ABSOLUTELY NO BAT-LASER! DEACTIVATE! DEACTIVATE!
VVVZZZZWAAAAA--!
BAT-MAN, THE PROBABILITY OF--
SHUT UP, ROBINBOT!
ZZZZWAAAAKKKK!
THAT'S IT! I'M BREAKING US OUT OF HERE SO WE CAN STOP THIS THING FROM THE *OUTSIDE!*
DON'T BOTHER, KENAN.

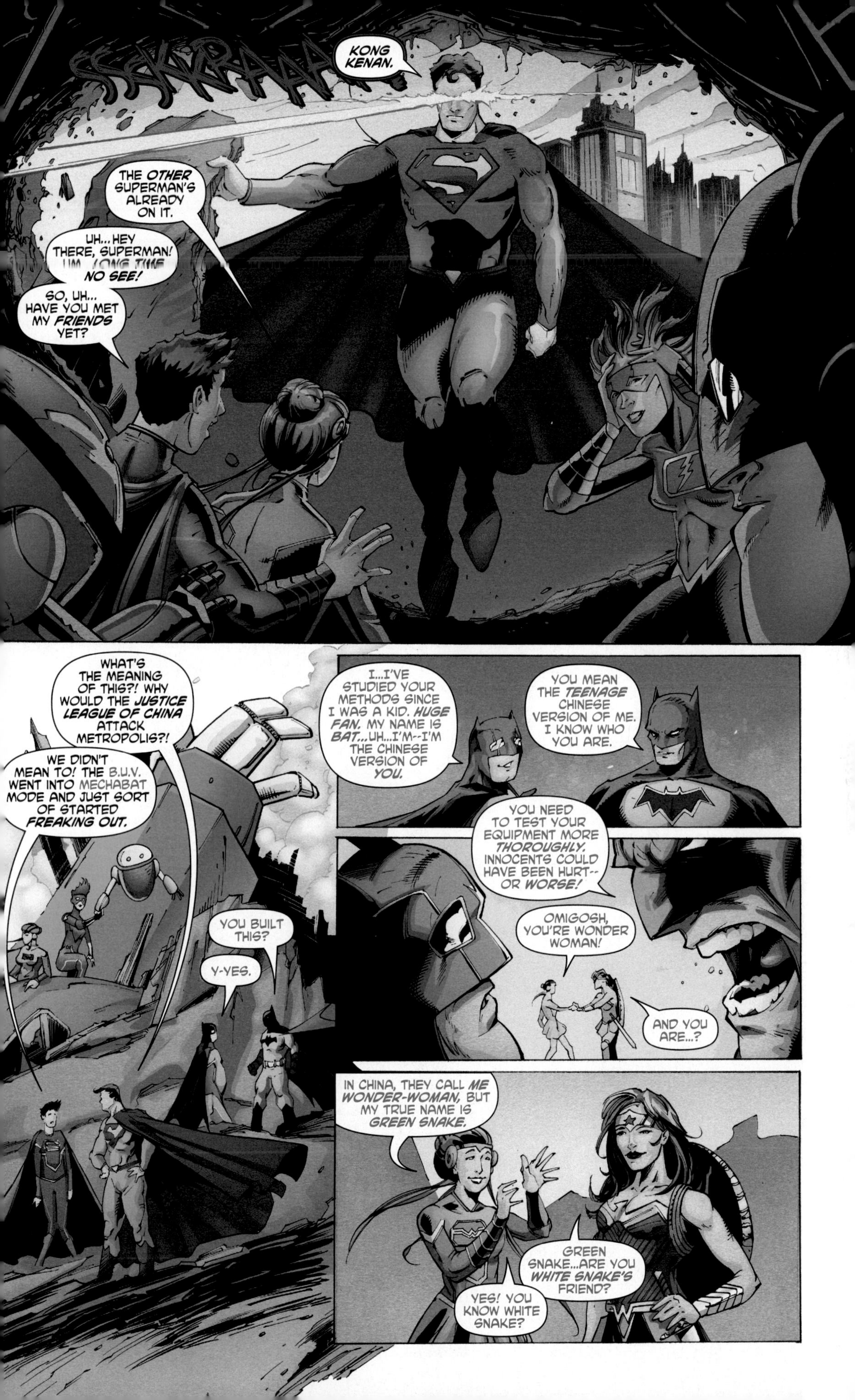
SSKKRAAA
KONG KENAN.
THE OTHER SUPERMAN'S ALREADY ON IT.
UH... HEY THERE, SUPERMAN! UM, LONG TIME NO SEE!
SO, UH... HAVE YOU MET MY FRIENDS YET?
WHAT'S THE MEANING OF THIS?! WHY WOULD THE JUSTICE LEAGUE OF CHINA ATTACK METROPOLIS?!
WE DIDN'T MEAN TO! THE B.U.V. WENT INTO MECHABAT MODE AND JUST SORT OF STARTED FREAKING OUT.
YOU BUILT THIS?
Y-YES.
I...I'VE STUDIED YOUR METHODS SINCE I WAS A KID. HUGE FAN. MY NAME IS BAT... UH... I'M--I'M THE CHINESE VERSION OF YOU.
YOU MEAN THE TEENAGE CHINESE VERSION OF ME. I KNOW WHO YOU ARE.
YOU NEED TO TEST YOUR EQUIPMENT MORE THOROUGHLY. INNOCENTS COULD HAVE BEEN HURT-- OR WORSE!
OMIGOSH, YOU'RE WONDER WOMAN!
AND YOU ARE...?
IN CHINA, THEY CALL ME WONDER-WOMAN, BUT MY TRUE NAME IS GREEN SNAKE.
GREEN SNAKE...ARE YOU WHITE SNAKE'S FRIEND?
YES! YOU KNOW WHITE SNAKE?

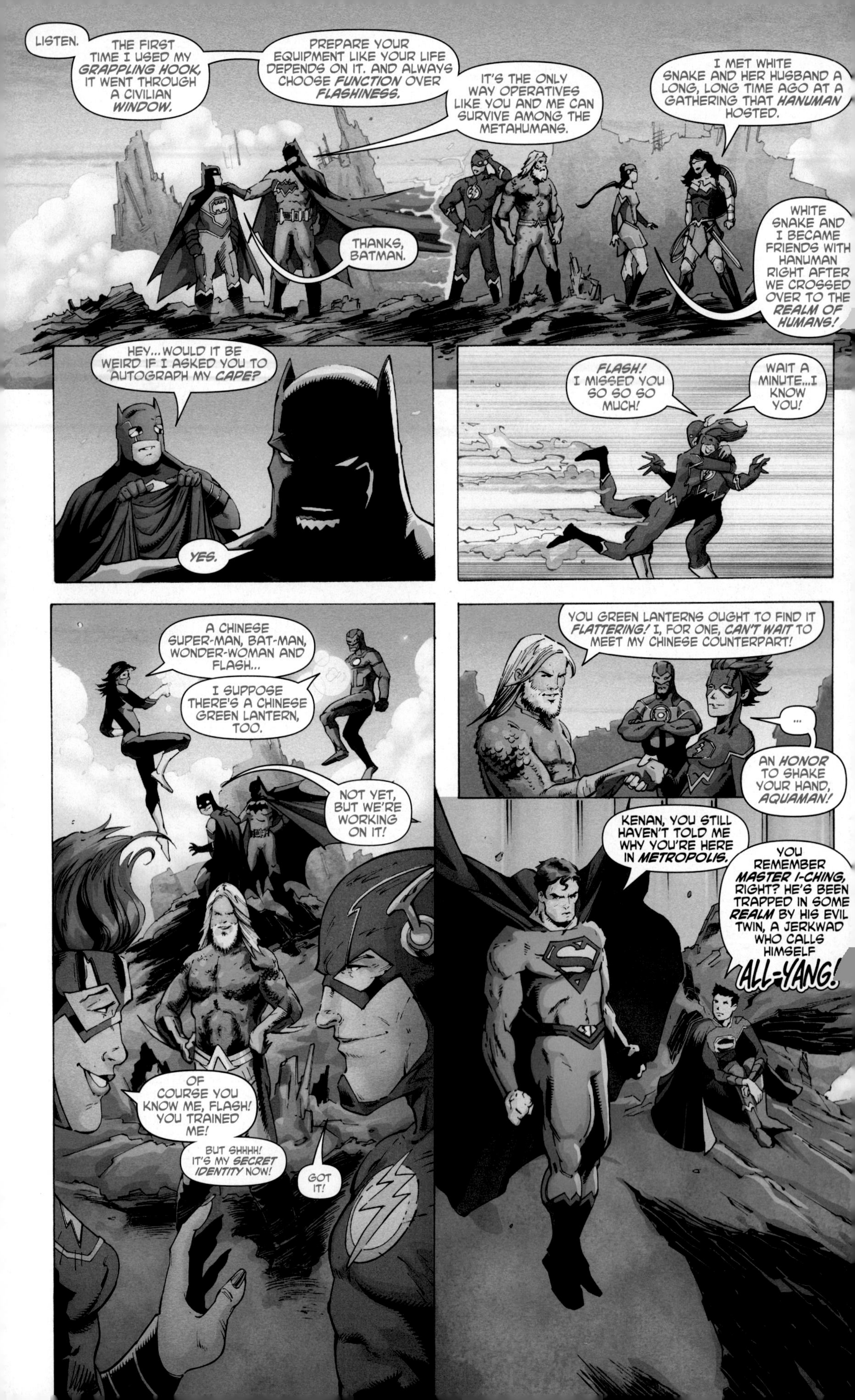
LISTEN.
THE FIRST TIME I USED MY GRAPPLING HOOK, IT WENT THROUGH A CIVILIAN WINDOW.
PREPARE YOUR EQUIPMENT LIKE YOUR LIFE DEPENDS ON IT. AND ALWAYS CHOOSE FUNCTION OVER FLASHINESS.
IT'S THE ONLY WAY OPERATIVES LIKE YOU AND ME CAN SURVIVE AMONG THE METAHUMANS.
THANKS, BATMAN.
I MET WHITE SNAKE AND HER HUSBAND A LONG, LONG TIME AGO AT A GATHERING THAT HANUMAN HOSTED.
WHITE SNAKE AND I BECAME FRIENDS WITH HANUMAN RIGHT AFTER WE CROSSED OVER TO THE REALM OF HUMANS!
HEY... WOULD IT BE WEIRD IF I ASKED YOU TO AUTOGRAPH MY CAPE?
YES.
FLASH! I MISSED YOU SO SO SO MUCH!
WAIT A MINUTE... I KNOW YOU!
A CHINESE SUPER-MAN, BAT-MAN, WONDER-WOMAN AND FLASH...
I SUPPOSE THERE'S A CHINESE GREEN LANTERN, TOO.
NOT YET, BUT WE'RE WORKING ON IT!
OF COURSE YOU KNOW ME, FLASH! YOU TRAINED ME!
BUT SHHHH! IT'S MY SECRET IDENTITY NOW!
GOT IT!
YOU GREEN LANTERNS OUGHT TO FIND IT FLATTERING! I, FOR ONE, CAN'T WAIT TO MEET MY CHINESE COUNTERPART!
...
AN HONOR TO SHAKE YOUR HAND, AQUAMAN!
KENAN, YOU STILL HAVEN'T TOLD ME WHY YOU'RE HERE IN METROPOLIS.
YOU REMEMBER MASTER I-CHING, RIGHT? HE'S BEEN TRAPPED IN SOME REALM BY HIS EVIL TWIN, A JERKWAD WHO CALLS HIMSELF ALL-YANG!

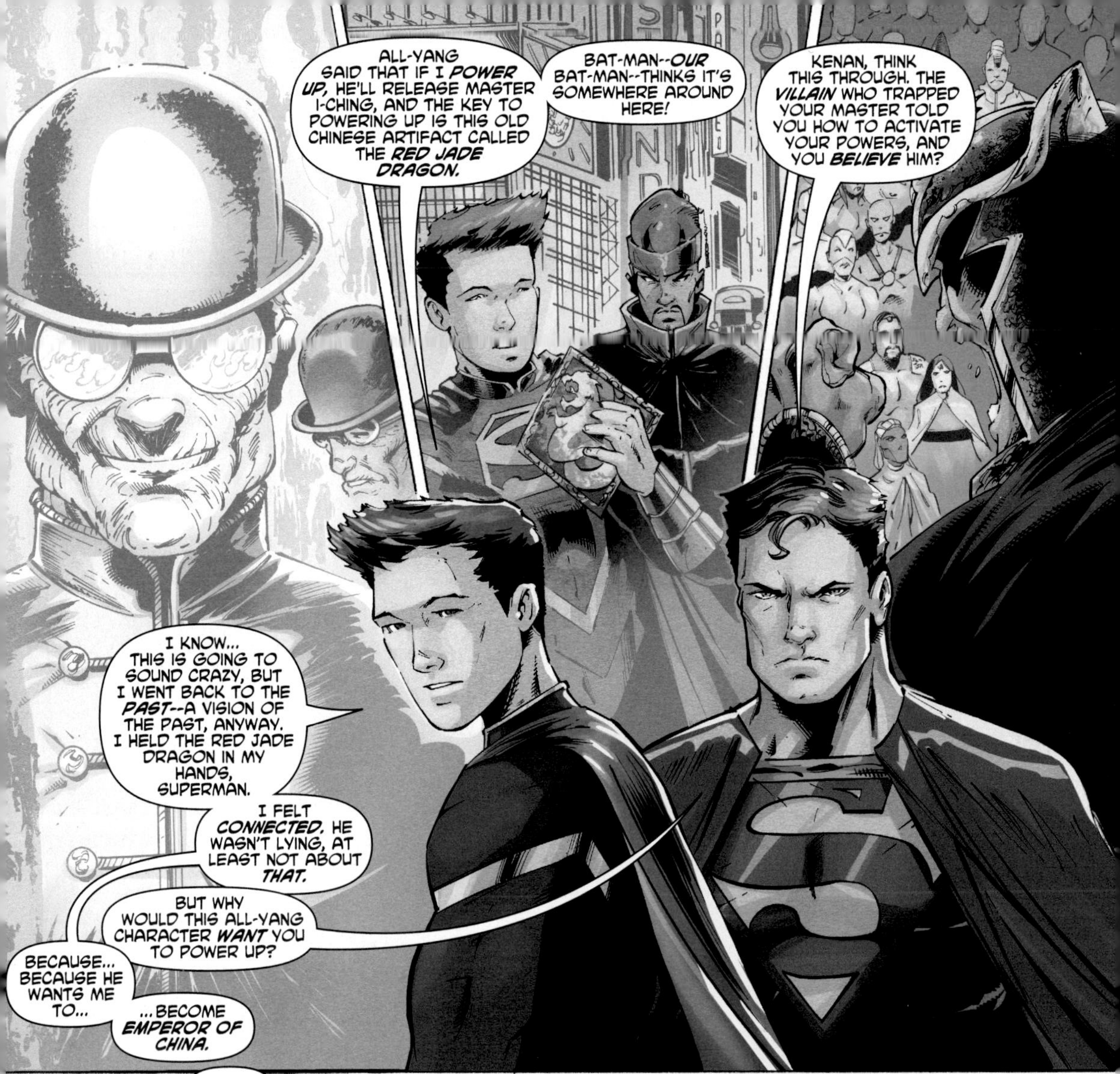
ALL-YANG SAID THAT IF I POWER UP, HE'LL RELEASE MASTER I-CHING, AND THE KEY TO POWERING UP IS THIS OLD CHINESE ARTIFACT CALLED THE RED JADE DRAGON.
BAT-MAN--OUR BAT-MAN--THINKS IT'S SOMEWHERE AROUND HERE!
KENAN, THINK THIS THROUGH. THE VILLAIN WHO TRAPPED YOUR MASTER TOLD YOU HOW TO ACTIVATE YOUR POWERS, AND YOU BELIEVE HIM?
I KNOW... THIS IS GOING TO SOUND CRAZY, BUT I WENT BACK TO THE PAST--A VISION OF THE PAST, ANYWAY. I HELD THE RED JADE DRAGON IN MY HANDS, SUPERMAN.
I FELT CONNECTED. HE WASN'T LYING, AT LEAST NOT ABOUT THAT.
BUT WHY WOULD THIS ALL-YANG CHARACTER WANT YOU TO POWER UP?
BECAUSE... BECAUSE HE WANTS ME TO...
...BECOME EMPEROR OF CHINA.

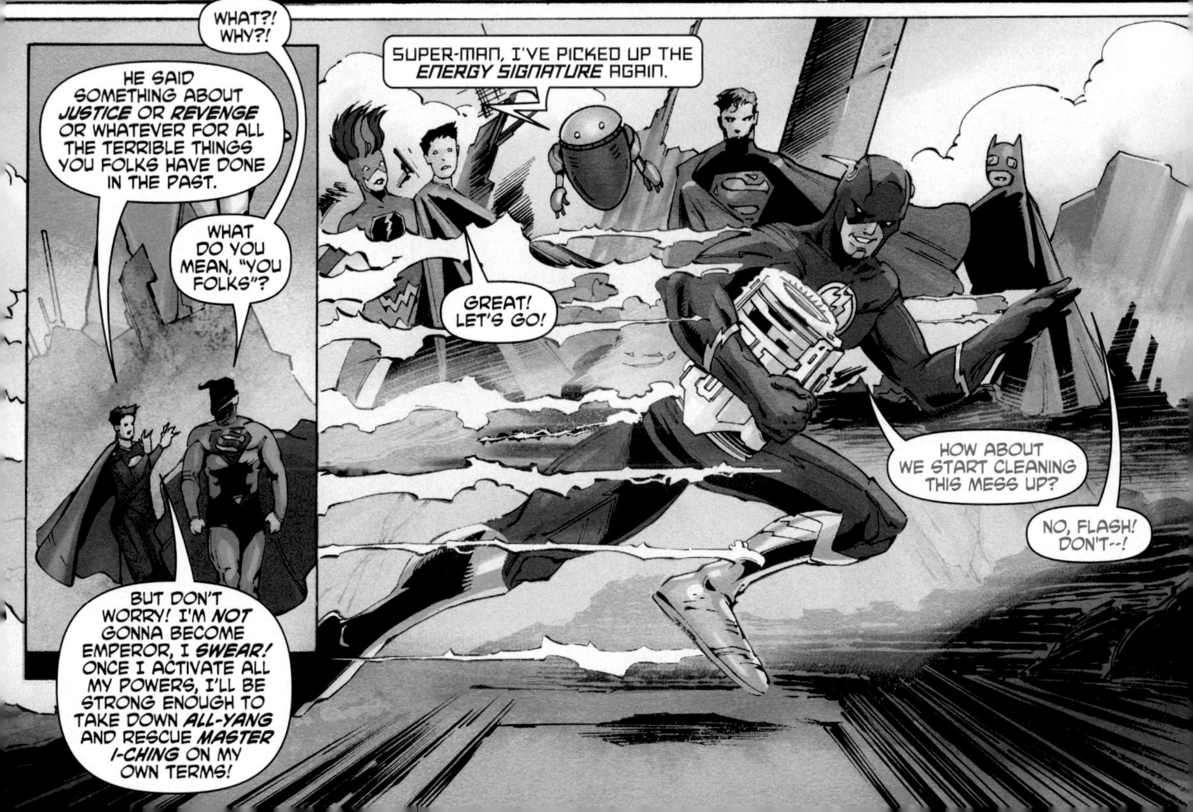
WHAT?! WHY?!
HE SAID SOMETHING ABOUT JUSTICE OR REVENGE OR WHATEVER FOR ALL THE TERRIBLE THINGS YOU FOLKS HAVE DONE IN THE PAST.
WHAT DO YOU MEAN, "YOU FOLKS"?
BUT DON'T WORRY! I'M NOT GONNA BECOME EMPEROR, I SWEAR! ONCE I ACTIVATE ALL MY POWERS, I'LL BE STRONG ENOUGH TO TAKE DOWN ALL-YANG AND RESCUE MASTER I-CHING ON MY OWN TERMS!
SUPER-MAN, I'VE PICKED UP THE ENERGY SIGNATURE AGAIN.
GREAT! LET'S GO!
HOW ABOUT WE START CLEANING THIS MESS UP?
NO, FLASH! DON'T--!

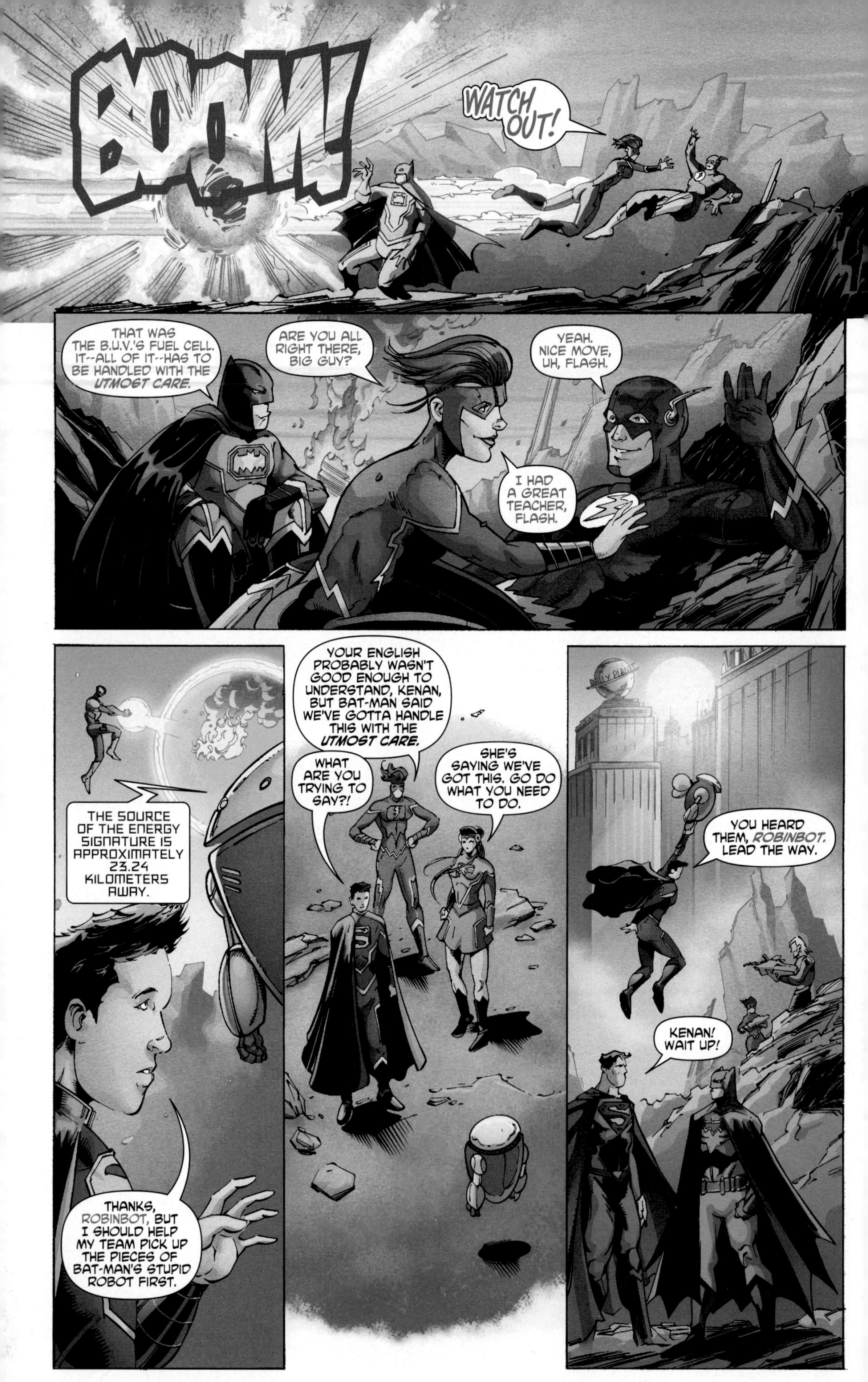
BOOM!
WATCH OUT!
THAT WAS THE B.U.V.'S FUEL CELL. IT--ALL OF IT--HAS TO BE HANDLED WITH THE UTMOST CARE.
ARE YOU ALL RIGHT THERE, BIG GUY?
YEAH. NICE MOVE, UH, FLASH.
I HAD A GREAT TEACHER, FLASH.
THE SOURCE OF THE ENERGY SIGNATURE IS APPROXIMATELY 23.24 KILOMETERS AWAY.
THANKS, ROBINBOT, BUT I SHOULD HELP MY TEAM PICK UP THE PIECES OF BAT-MAN'S STUPID ROBOT FIRST.
YOUR ENGLISH PROBABLY WASN'T GOOD ENOUGH TO UNDERSTAND, KENAN, BUT BAT-MAN SAID WE'VE GOTTA HANDLE THIS WITH THE UTMOST CARE.
WHAT ARE YOU TRYING TO SAY?!
SHE'S SAYING WE'VE GOT THIS. GO DO WHAT YOU NEED TO DO.
YOU HEARD THEM, ROBINBOT. LEAD THE WAY.
KENAN! WAIT UP!

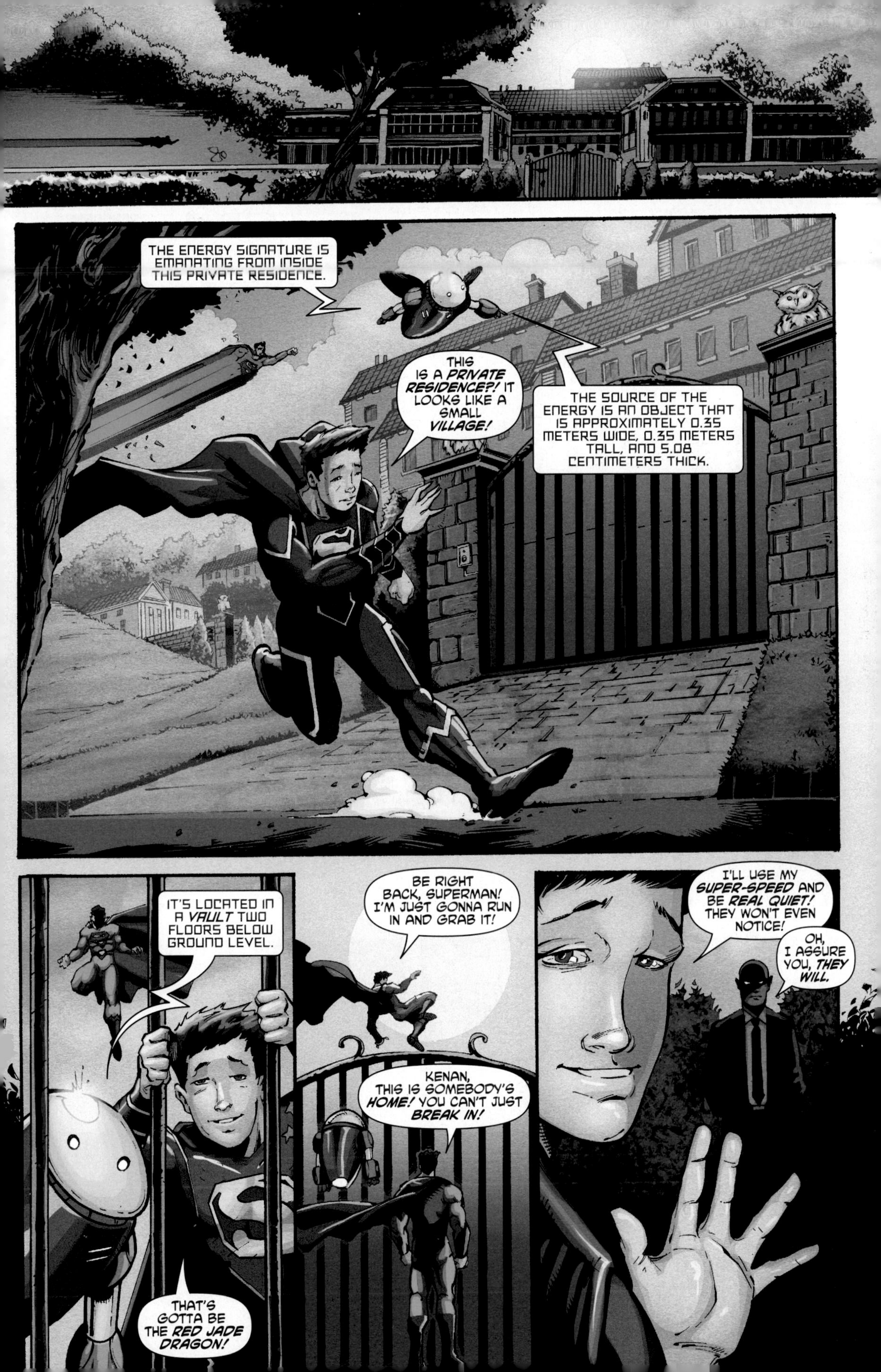
THE ENERGY SIGNATURE IS EMANATING FROM INSIDE THIS PRIVATE RESIDENCE.
THIS IS A PRIVATE RESIDENCE?! IT LOOKS LIKE A SMALL VILLAGE!
THE SOURCE OF THE ENERGY IS AN OBJECT THAT IS APPROXIMATELY 0.35 METERS WIDE, 0.35 METERS TALL, AND 5.08 CENTIMETERS THICK.
IT'S LOCATED IN A VAULT TWO FLOORS BELOW GROUND LEVEL.
THAT'S GOTTA BE THE RED JADE DRAGON!
BE RIGHT BACK, SUPERMAN! I'M JUST GONNA RUN IN AND GRAB IT!
KENAN, THIS IS SOMEBODY'S HOME! YOU CAN'T JUST BREAK IN!
I'LL USE MY SUPER-SPEED AND BE REAL QUIET! THEY WON'T EVEN NOTICE!
OH, I ASSURE YOU, THEY WILL.

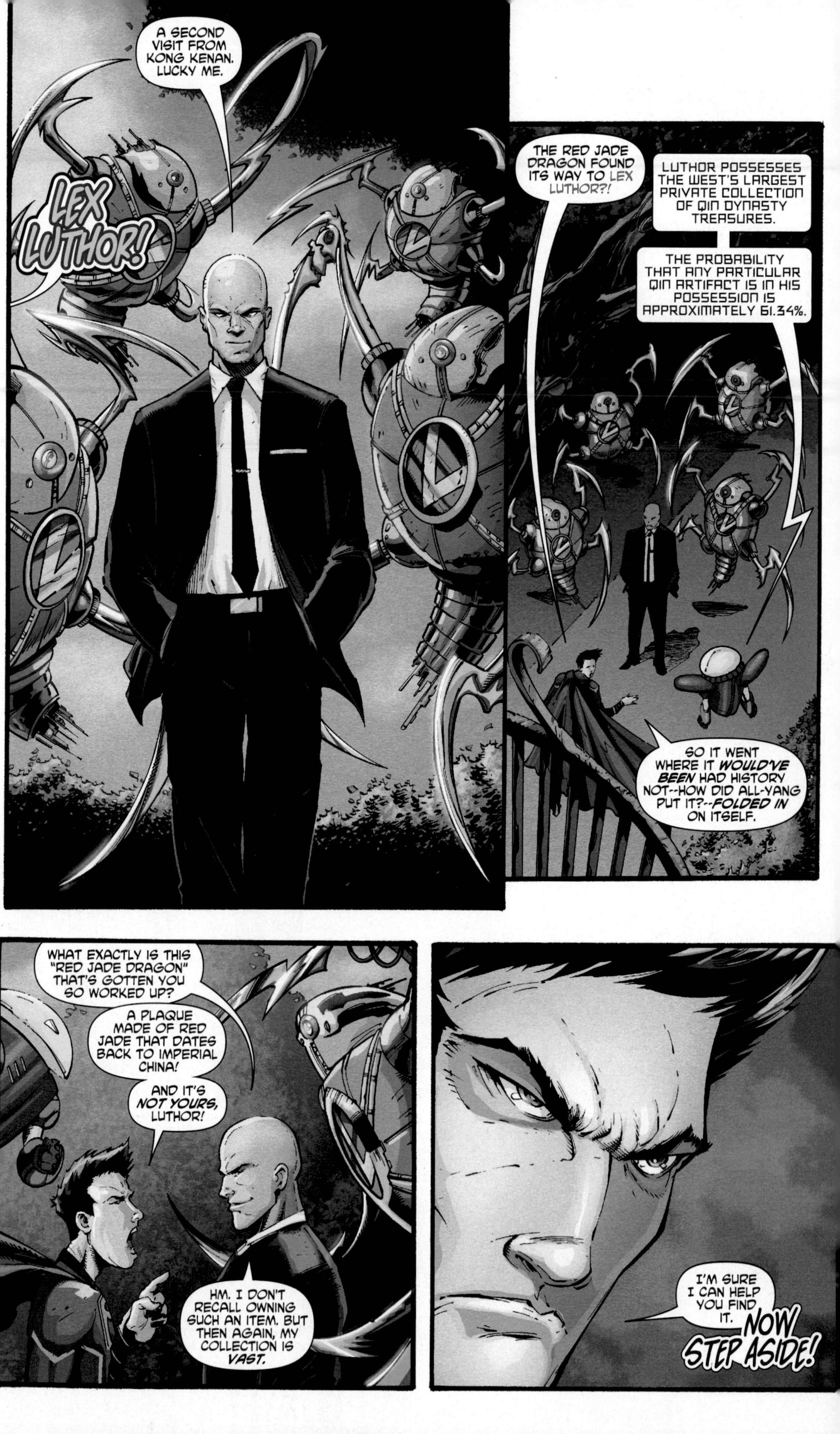
A SECOND VISIT FROM KONG KENAN. LUCKY ME.
LEX LUTHOR!
THE RED JADE DRAGON FOUND ITS WAY TO LEX LUTHOR?!
LUTHOR POSSESSES THE WEST'S LARGEST PRIVATE COLLECTION OF QIN DYNASTY TREASURES.
THE PROBABILITY THAT ANY PARTICULAR QIN ARTIFACT IS IN HIS POSSESSION IS APPROXIMATELY 61.34%.
SO IT WENT WHERE IT WOULD'VE BEEN HAD HISTORY NOT--HOW DID ALL-YANG PUT IT?--FOLDED IN ON ITSELF.
WHAT EXACTLY IS THIS "RED JADE DRAGON" THAT'S GOTTEN YOU SO WORKED UP?
A PLAQUE MADE OF RED JADE THAT DATES BACK TO IMPERIAL CHINA!
AND IT'S NOT YOURS, LUTHOR!
HM. I DON'T RECALL OWNING SUCH AN ITEM. BUT THEN AGAIN, MY COLLECTION IS VAST.
I'M SURE I CAN HELP YOU FIND IT.
NOW STEP ASIDE!

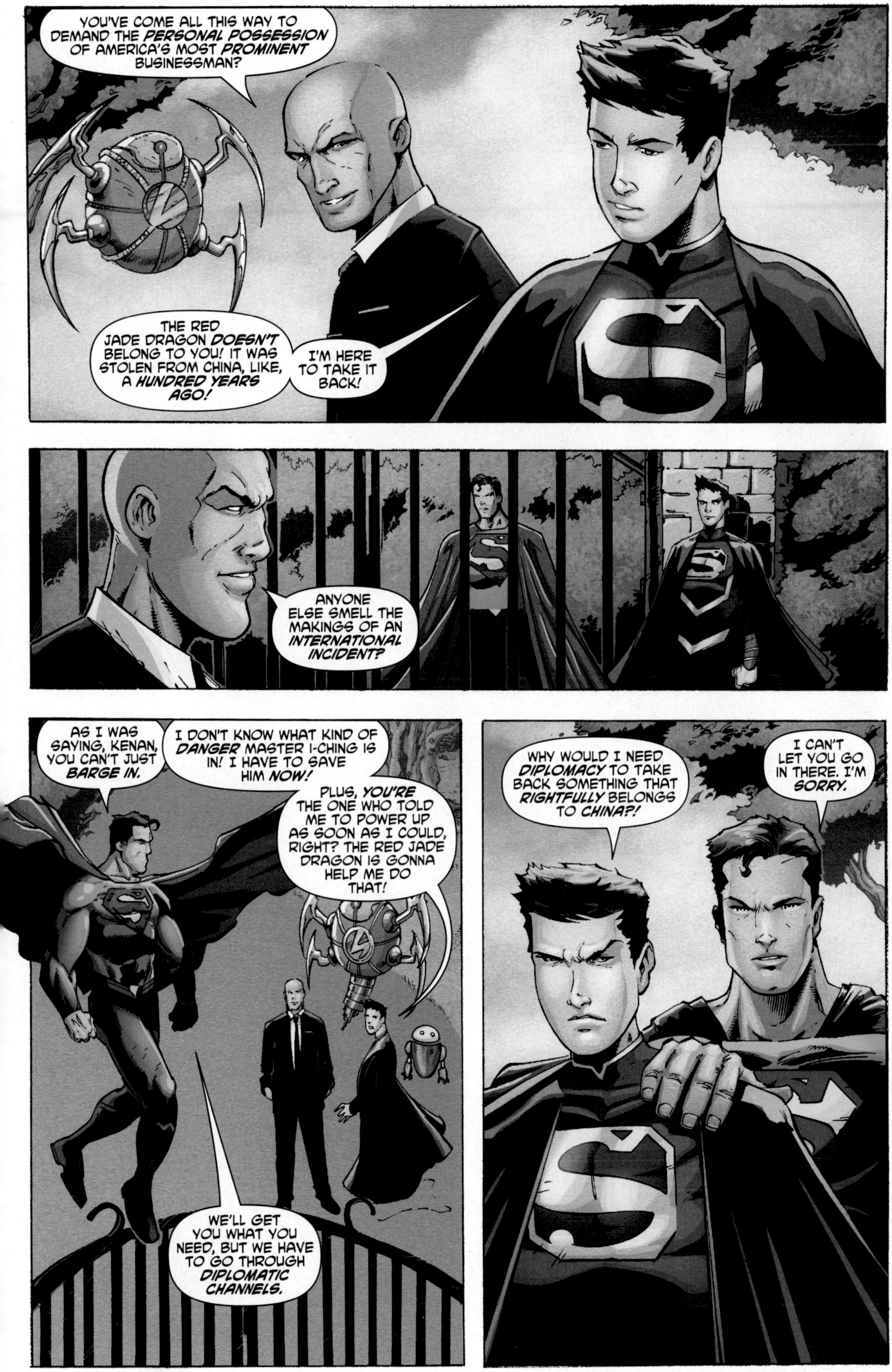
YOU'VE COME ALL THIS WAY TO DEMAND THE PERSONAL POSSESSION OF AMERICA'S MOST PROMINENT BUSINESSMAN?
THE RED JADE DRAGON DOESN'T BELONG TO YOU! IT WAS STOLEN FROM CHINA, LIKE, A HUNDRED YEARS AGO!
I'M HERE TO TAKE IT BACK!
ANYONE ELSE SMELL THE MAKINGS OF AN INTERNATIONAL INCIDENT?
AS I WAS SAYING, KENAN, YOU CAN'T JUST BARGE IN.
I DON'T KNOW WHAT KIND OF DANGER MASTER I-CHING IS IN! I HAVE TO SAVE HIM NOW!
PLUS, YOU'RE THE ONE WHO TOLD ME TO POWER UP AS SOON AS I COULD, RIGHT? THE RED JADE DRAGON IS GONNA HELP ME DO THAT!
WE'LL GET YOU WHAT YOU NEED, BUT WE HAVE TO GO THROUGH DIPLOMATIC CHANNELS.
WHY WOULD I NEED DIPLOMACY TO TAKE BACK SOMETHING THAT RIGHTFULLY BELONGS TO CHINA?!
I CAN'T LET YOU GO IN THERE. I'M SORRY.

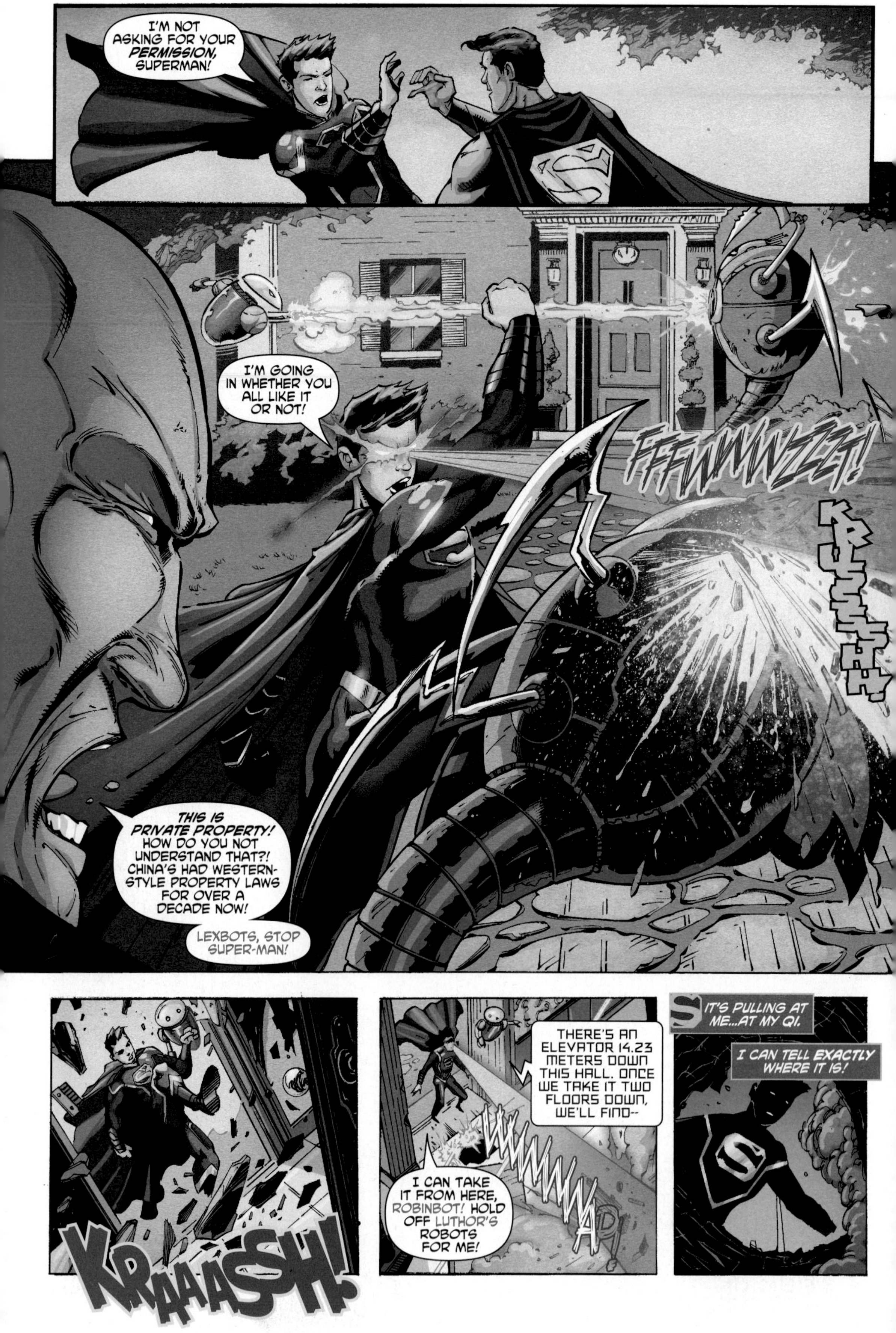

I'M NOT ASKING FOR YOUR PERMISSION, SUPERMAN!
I'M GOING IN WHETHER YOU ALL LIKE IT OR NOT!
FFFWWWZZZT!
KRUSSSSHH!
THIS IS PRIVATE PROPERTY! HOW DO YOU NOT UNDERSTAND THAT?! CHINA'S HAD WESTERN-STYLE PROPERTY LAWS FOR OVER A DECADE NOW!
LEXBOTS, STOP SUPER-MAN!
KRAAASH!
THERE'S AN ELEVATOR 14.23 METERS DOWN THIS HALL. ONCE WE TAKE IT TWO FLOORS DOWN, WE'LL FIND--
I CAN TAKE IT FROM HERE, ROBINBOT! HOLD OFF LUTHOR'S ROBOTS FOR ME!
IT'S PULLING AT ME...AT MY QI.
I CAN TELL EXACTLY WHERE IT IS!

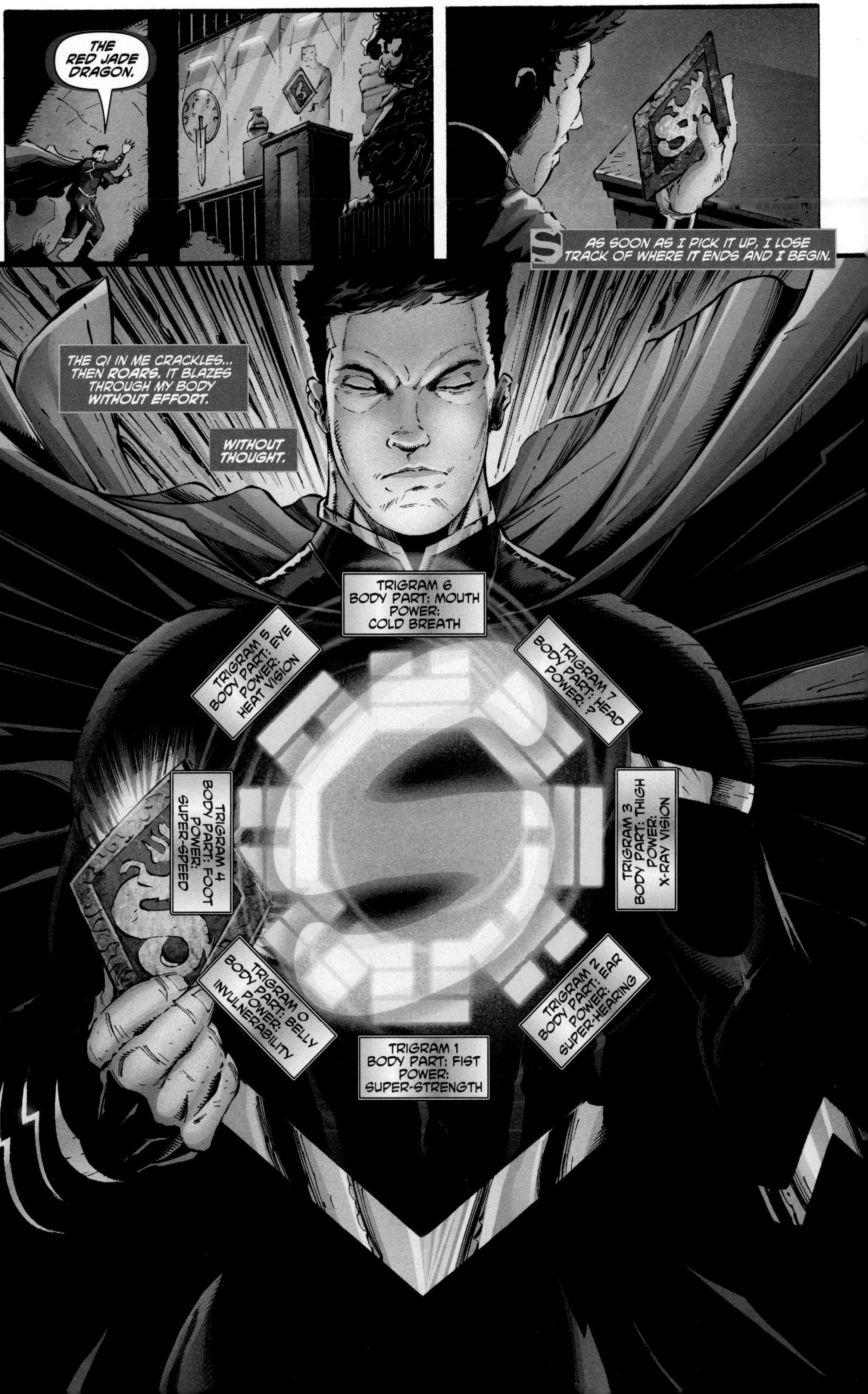

THE RED JADE DRAGON.
AS SOON AS I PICK IT UP, I LOSE TRACK OF WHERE IT ENDS AND I BEGIN.
THE QI IN ME CRACKLES... THEN ROARS. IT BLAZES THROUGH MY BODY WITHOUT EFFORT.
WITHOUT THOUGHT.
TRIGRAM 6 BODY PART: MOUTH POWER: COLD BREATH
TRIGRAM 7 BODY PART: HEAD POWER: ?
TRIGRAM 3 BODY PART: THIGH POWER: X-RAY VISION
TRIGRAM 2 BODY PART: EAR POWER: SUPER-HEARING
TRIGRAM 1 BODY PART: FIST POWER: SUPER-STRENGTH
TRIGRAM 0 BODY PART: BELLY POWER: INVULNERABILITY
TRIGRAM 4 BODY PART: FOOT POWER: SUPER-SPEED
TRIGRAM 5 BODY PART: EYE POWER: HEAT VISION

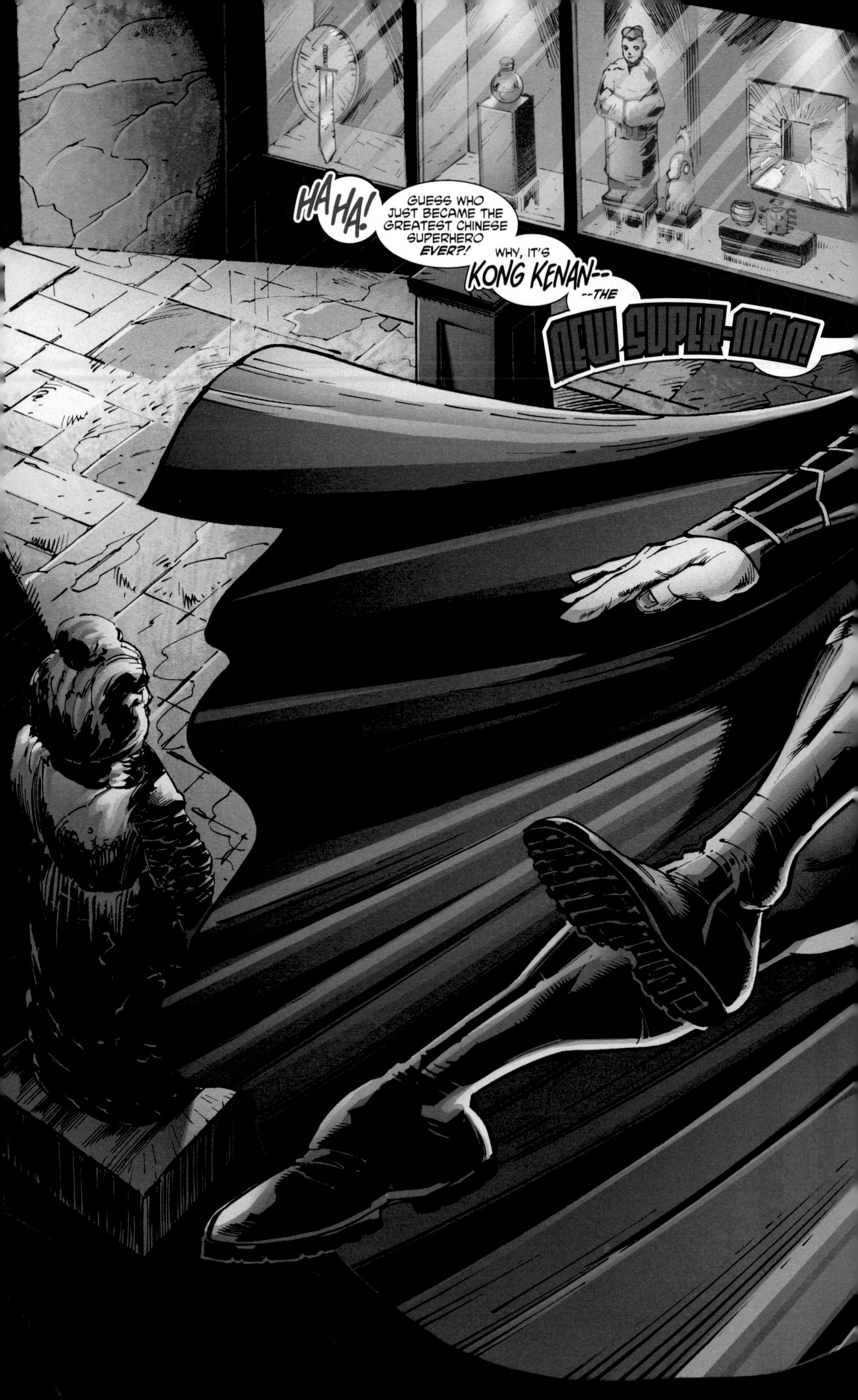
HAHA!
GUESS WHO JUST BECAME THE GREATEST CHINESE SUPERHERO EVER?!
WHY, IT'S KONG KENAN--
--THE NEW SUPER-MAN!

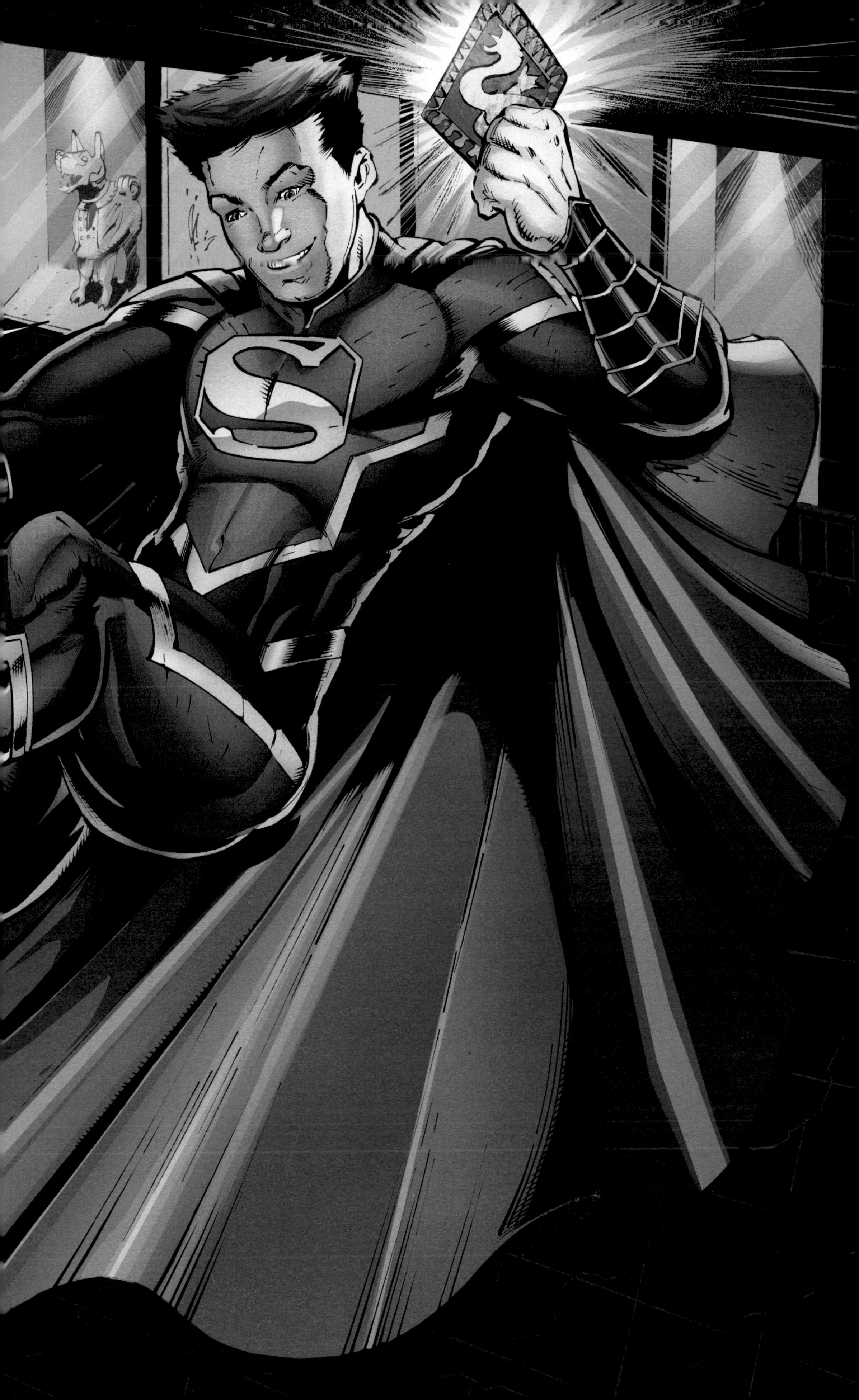

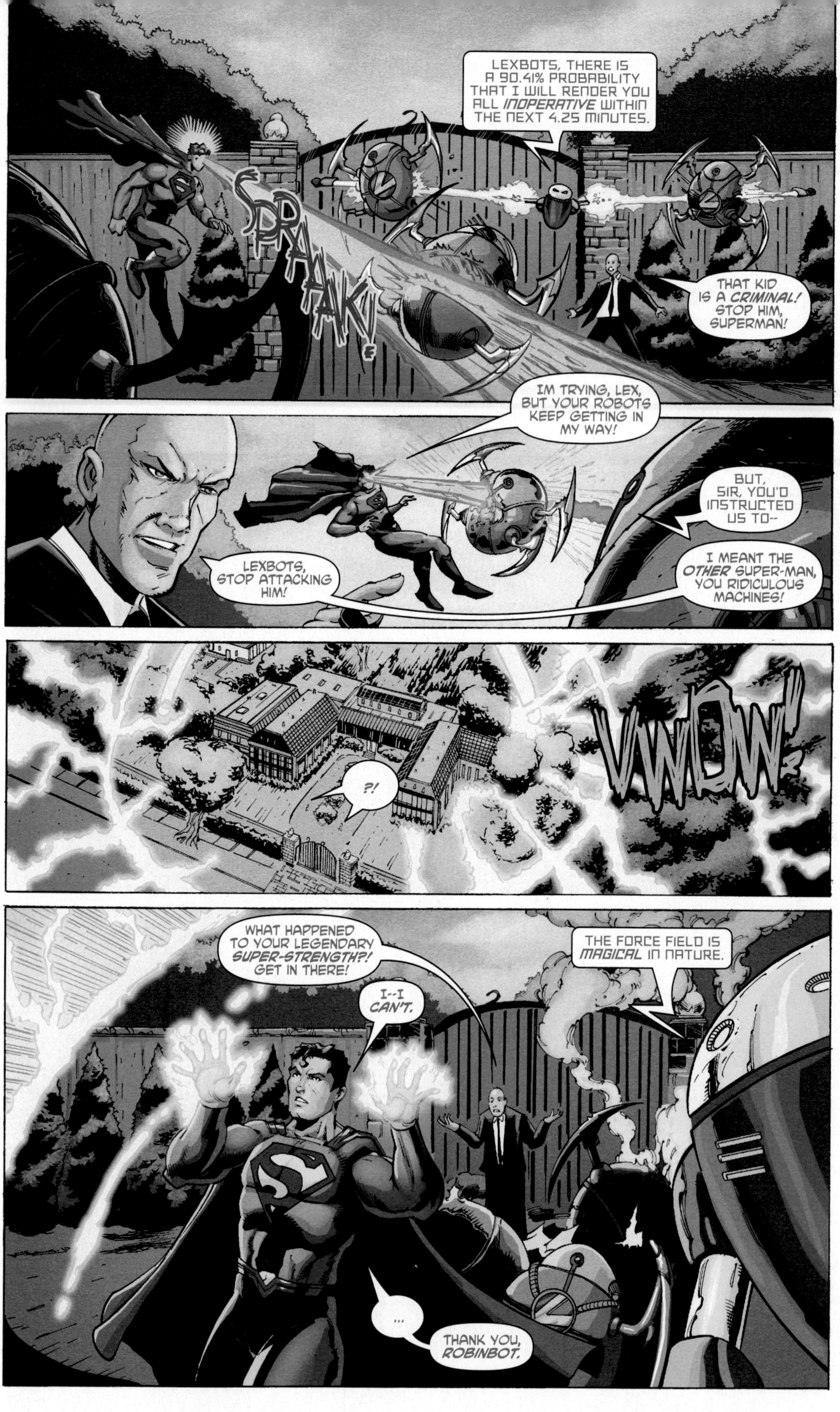
LEXBOTS, THERE IS A 90.41% PROBABILITY THAT I WILL RENDER YOU ALL *INOPERATIVE* WITHIN THE NEXT 4.25 MINUTES.
SPRAAAKK!
THAT KID IS A *CRIMINAL!* STOP HIM, SUPERMAN!
IM TRYING, LEX, BUT YOUR ROBOTS KEEP GETTING IN MY WAY!
BUT, SIR, YOU'D INSTRUCTED US TO--
LEXBOTS, STOP ATTACKING HIM!
I MEANT THE *OTHER* SUPER-MAN, YOU RIDICULOUS MACHINES!
VWOW!
?!
WHAT HAPPENED TO YOUR LEGENDARY *SUPER-STRENGTH?!* GET IN THERE!
THE FORCE FIELD IS *MAGICAL* IN NATURE.
I--I *CAN'T.*
...
THANK YOU, *ROBINBOT.*

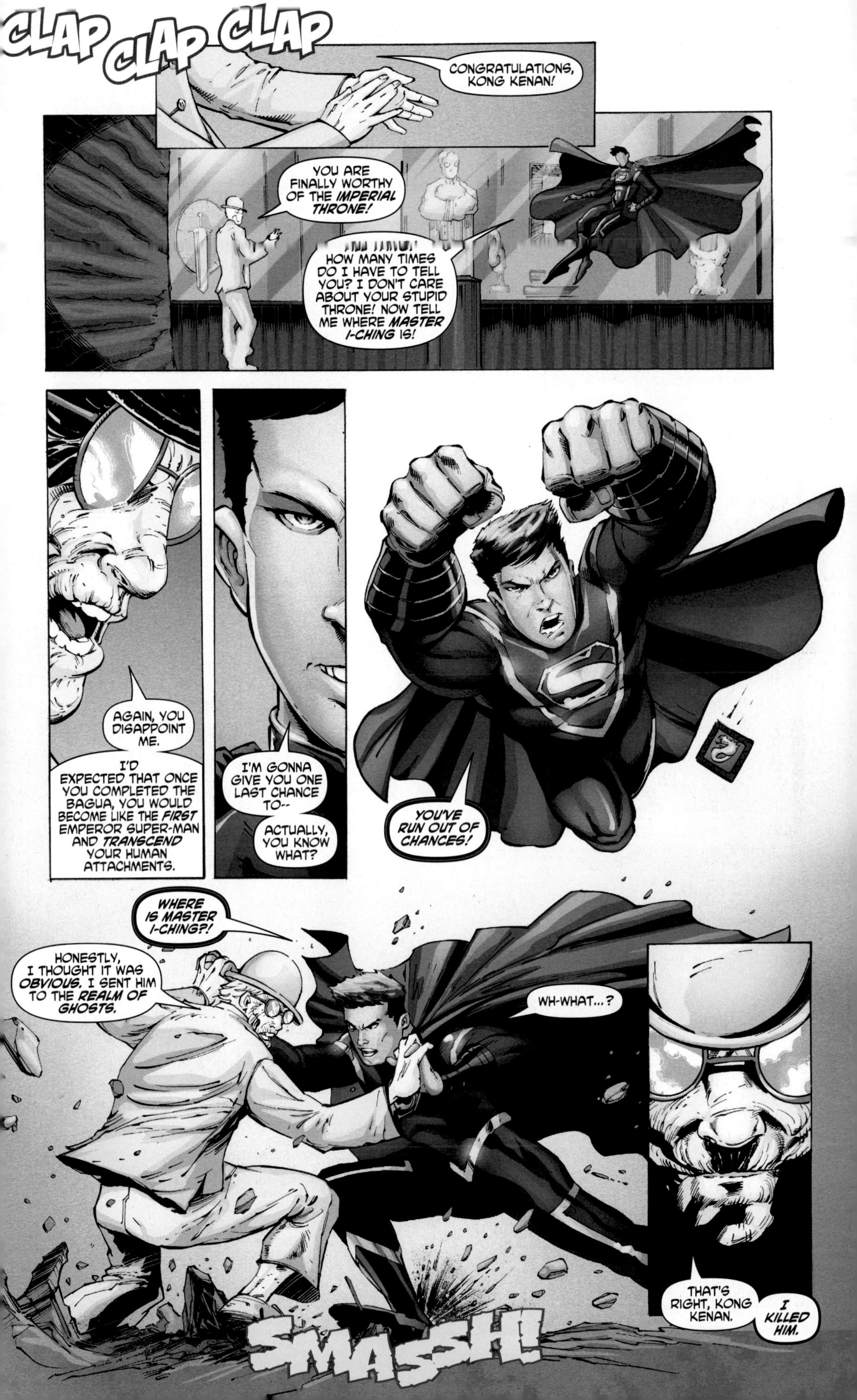

CLAP CLAP CLAP
CONGRATULATIONS, KONG KENAN!
YOU ARE FINALLY WORTHY OF THE IMPERIAL THRONE!
HOW MANY TIMES DO I HAVE TO TELL YOU? I DON'T CARE ABOUT YOUR STUPID THRONE! NOW TELL ME WHERE MASTER I-CHING IS!
AGAIN, YOU DISAPPOINT ME.
I'D EXPECTED THAT ONCE YOU COMPLETED THE BAGUA, YOU WOULD BECOME LIKE THE FIRST EMPEROR SUPER-MAN AND TRANSCEND YOUR HUMAN ATTACHMENTS.
I'M GONNA GIVE YOU ONE LAST CHANCE TO--
ACTUALLY, YOU KNOW WHAT?
YOU'VE RUN OUT OF CHANCES!
WHERE IS MASTER I-CHING?!
HONESTLY, I THOUGHT IT WAS OBVIOUS. I SENT HIM TO THE REALM OF GHOSTS.
WH-WHAT...?
THAT'S RIGHT, KONG KENAN.
I KILLED HIM.
SMASSH!

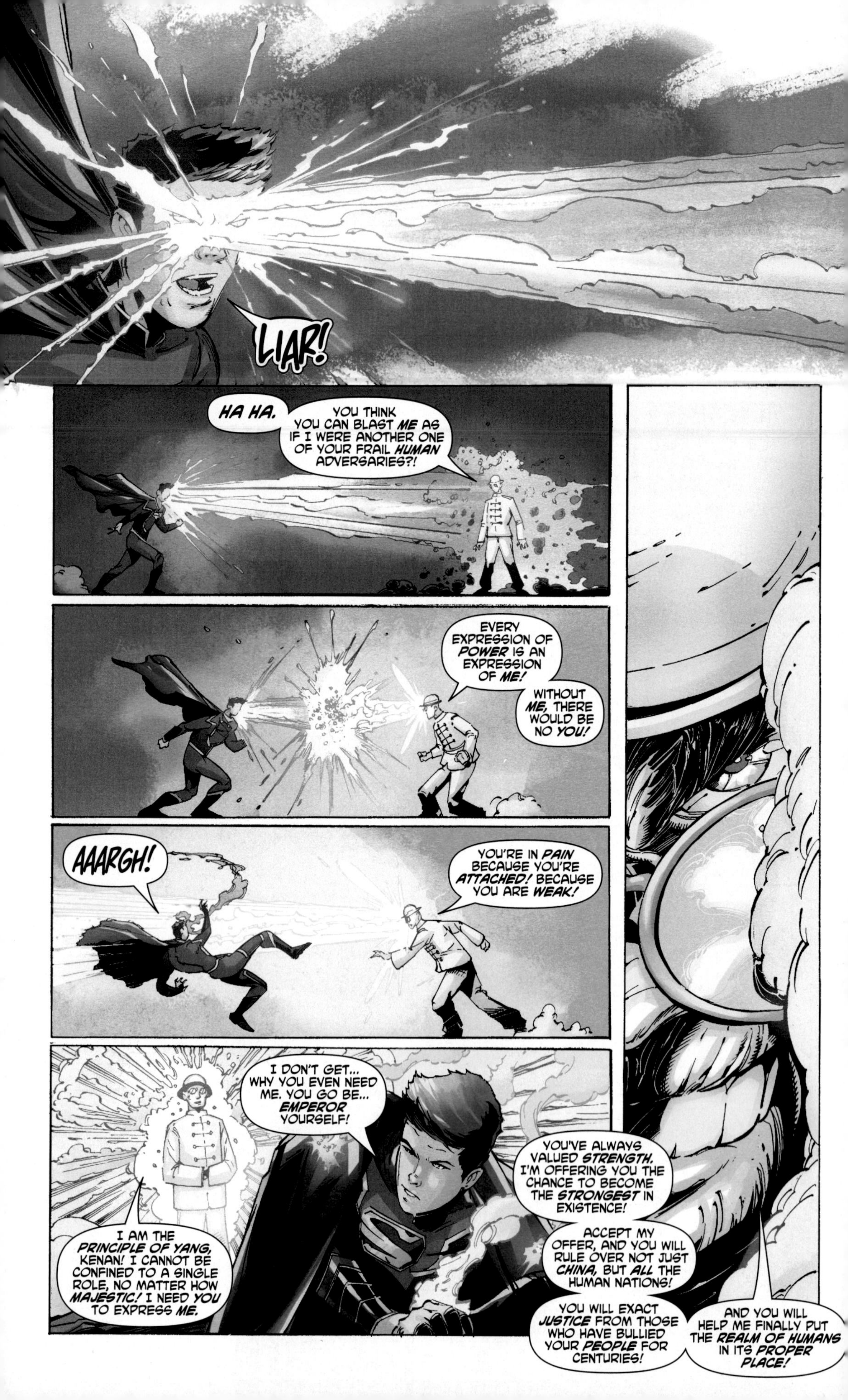
LIAR!
HA HA.
YOU THINK YOU CAN BLAST ME AS IF I WERE ANOTHER ONE OF YOUR FRAIL HUMAN ADVERSARIES?!
EVERY EXPRESSION OF POWER IS AN EXPRESSION OF ME!
WITHOUT ME, THERE WOULD BE NO YOU!
AAARGH!
YOU'RE IN PAIN BECAUSE YOU'RE ATTACHED! BECAUSE YOU ARE WEAK!
I DON'T GET... WHY YOU EVEN NEED ME. YOU GO BE... EMPEROR YOURSELF!
I AM THE PRINCIPLE OF YANG, KENAN! I CANNOT BE CONFINED TO A SINGLE ROLE, NO MATTER HOW MAJESTIC! I NEED YOU TO EXPRESS ME.
YOU'VE ALWAYS VALUED STRENGTH. I'M OFFERING YOU THE CHANCE TO BECOME THE STRONGEST IN EXISTENCE!
ACCEPT MY OFFER, AND YOU WILL RULE OVER NOT JUST CHINA, BUT ALL THE HUMAN NATIONS!
YOU WILL EXACT JUSTICE FROM THOSE WHO HAVE BULLIED YOUR PEOPLE FOR CENTURIES!
AND YOU WILL HELP ME FINALLY PUT THE REALM OF HUMANS IN ITS PROPER PLACE!

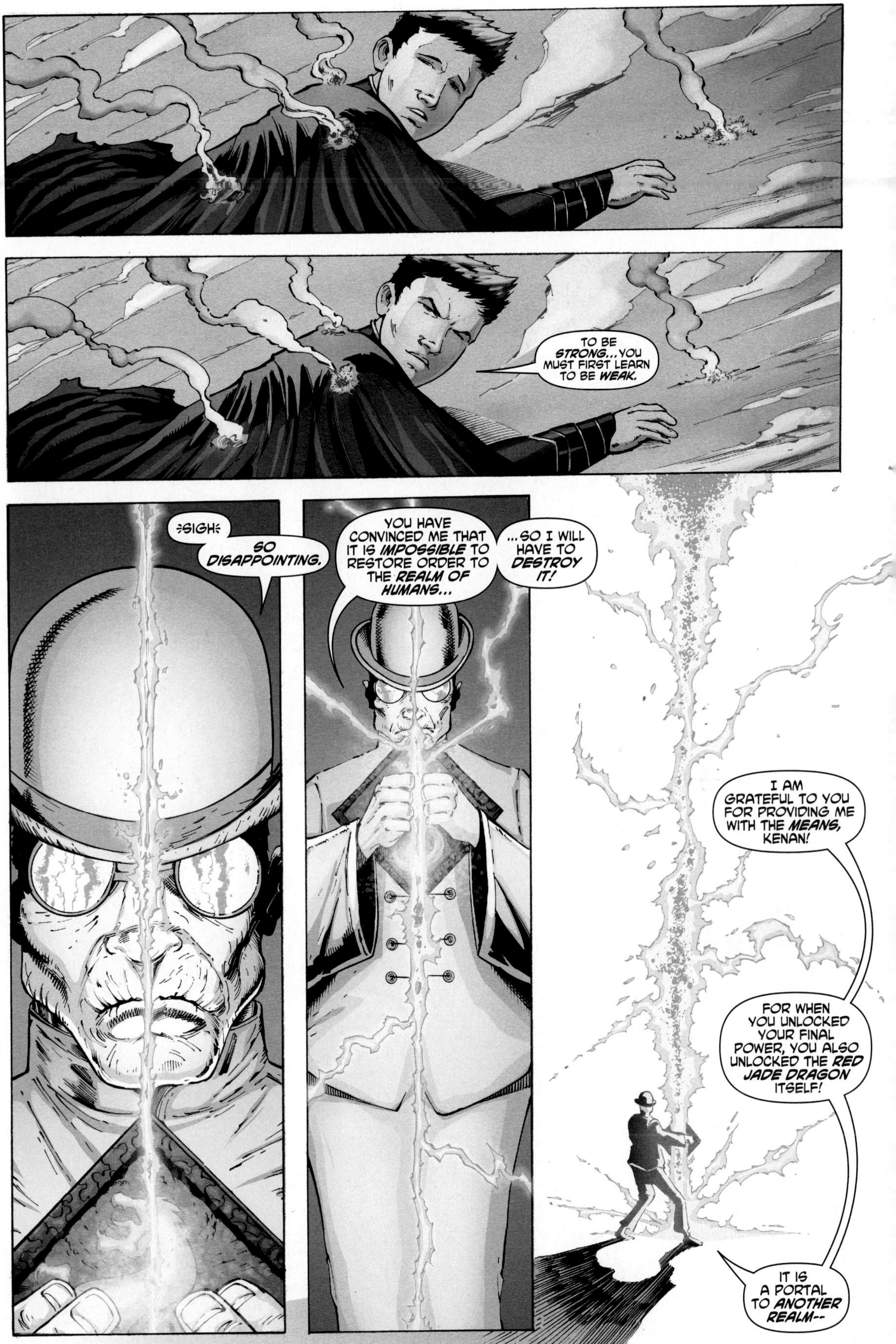
TO BE STRONG... YOU MUST FIRST LEARN TO BE WEAK.
SIGH
SO DISAPPOINTING.
YOU HAVE CONVINCED ME THAT IT IS IMPOSSIBLE TO RESTORE ORDER TO THE REALM OF HUMANS...
...SO I WILL HAVE TO DESTROY IT!
I AM GRATEFUL TO YOU FOR PROVIDING ME WITH THE MEANS, KENAN!
FOR WHEN YOU UNLOCKED YOUR FINAL POWER, YOU ALSO UNLOCKED THE RED JADE DRAGON ITSELF!
IT IS A PORTAL TO ANOTHER REALM--

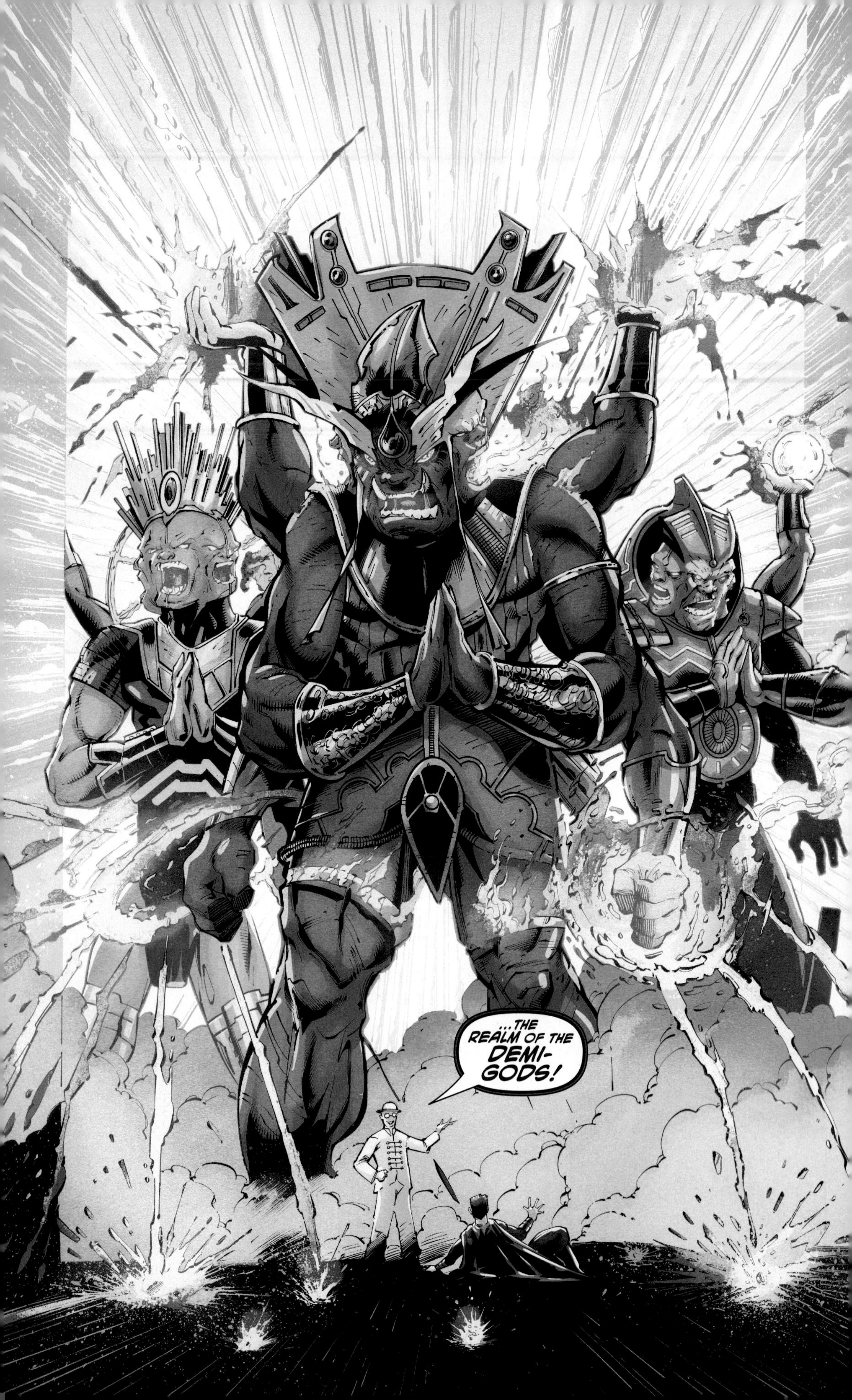
...THE REALM OF THE DEMI-GODS!

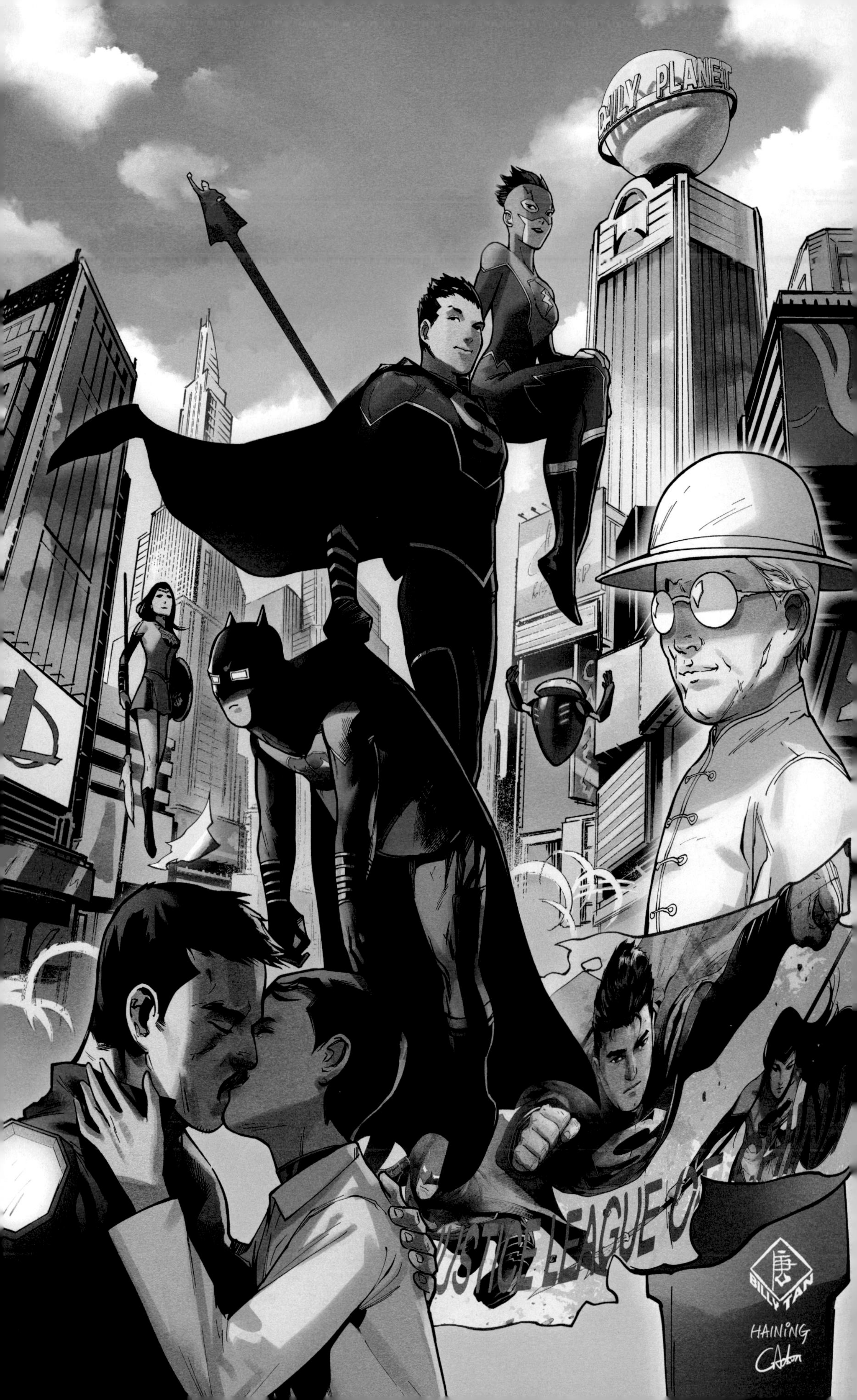
DAILY PLANET
JUSTICE LEAGUE
BILLY TAN
HAINING

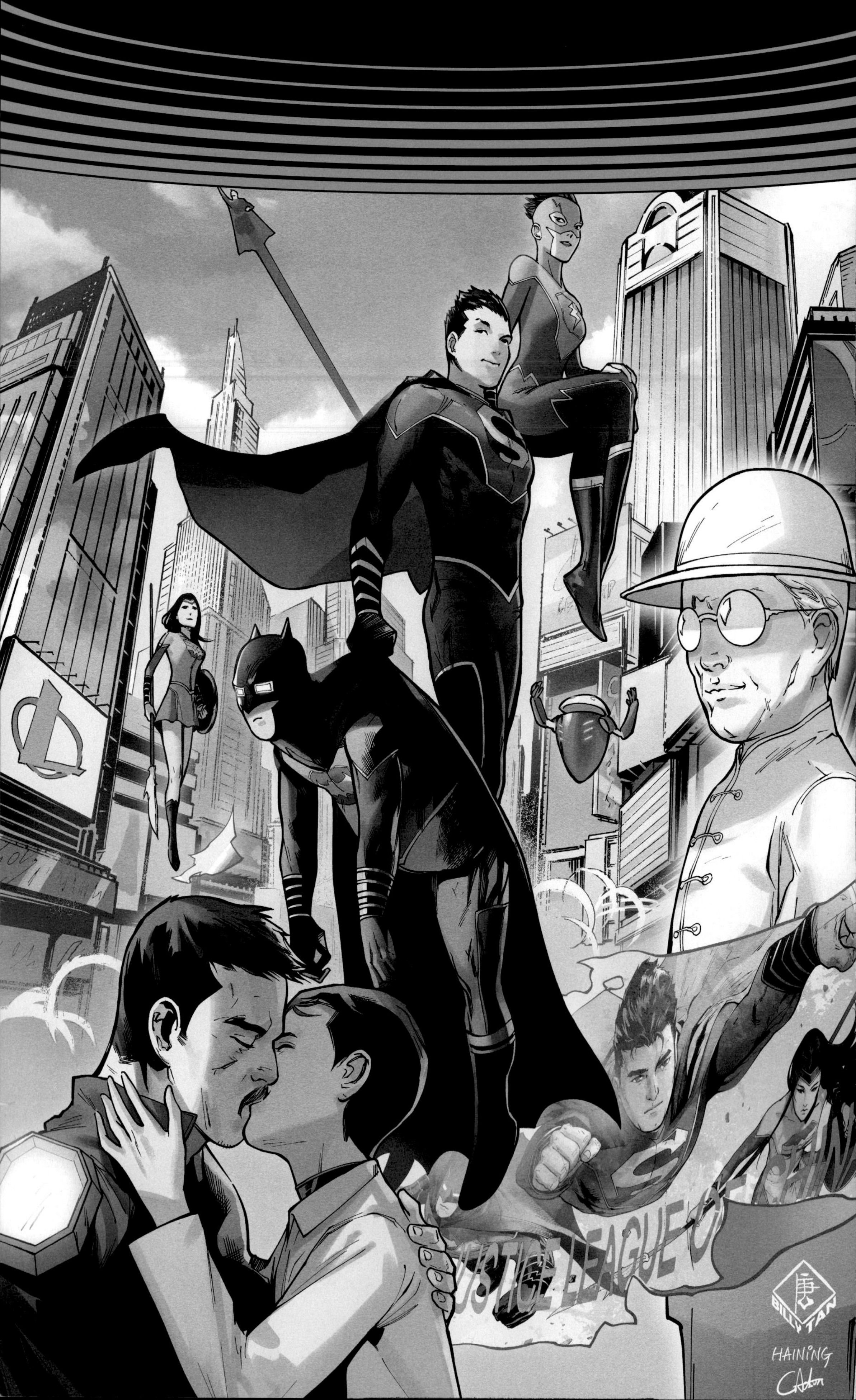
USTICE LEAGUE
BILLY TAN
HAINING

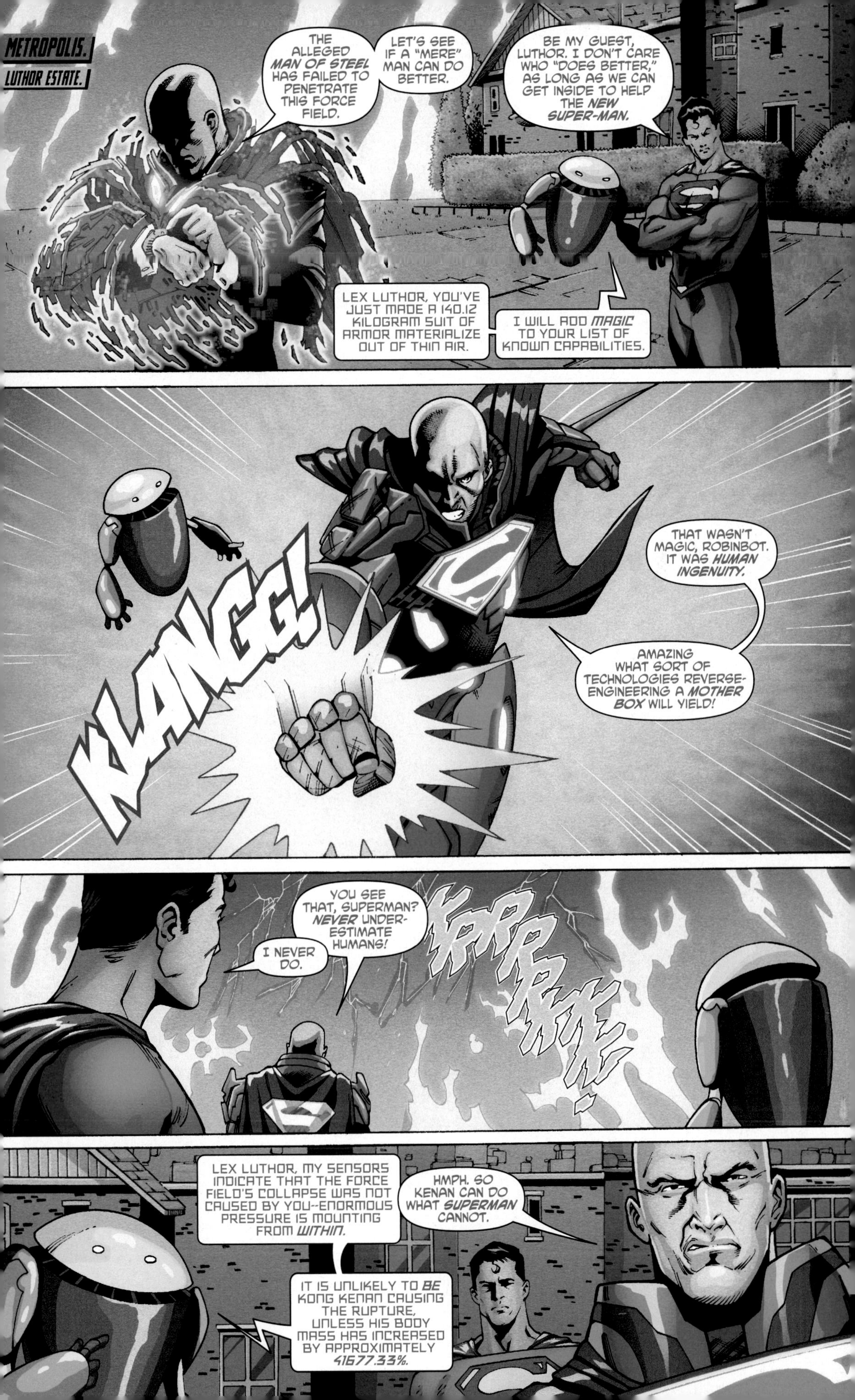
METROPOLIS.
LUTHOR ESTATE.
THE ALLEGED MAN OF STEEL HAS FAILED TO PENETRATE THIS FORCE FIELD.
LET'S SEE IF A "MERE" MAN CAN DO BETTER.
BE MY GUEST, LUTHOR. I DON'T CARE WHO "DOES BETTER," AS LONG AS WE CAN GET INSIDE TO HELP THE NEW SUPER-MAN.
LEX LUTHOR, YOU'VE JUST MADE A 140.12 KILOGRAM SUIT OF ARMOR MATERIALIZE OUT OF THIN AIR.
I WILL ADD MAGIC TO YOUR LIST OF KNOWN CAPABILITIES.
KLANGG!
THAT WASN'T MAGIC, ROBINBOT. IT WAS HUMAN INGENUITY.
AMAZING WHAT SORT OF TECHNOLOGIES REVERSE-ENGINEERING A MOTHER BOX WILL YIELD!
YOU SEE THAT, SUPERMAN? NEVER UNDER-ESTIMATE HUMANS!
I NEVER DO.
KRRRKKK!
LEX LUTHOR, MY SENSORS INDICATE THAT THE FORCE FIELD'S COLLAPSE WAS NOT CAUSED BY YOU--ENORMOUS PRESSURE IS MOUNTING FROM WITHIN.
HMPH. SO KENAN CAN DO WHAT SUPERMAN CANNOT.
IT IS UNLIKELY TO BE KONG KENAN CAUSING THE RUPTURE, UNLESS HIS BODY MASS HAS INCREASED BY APPROXIMATELY 41677.33%.

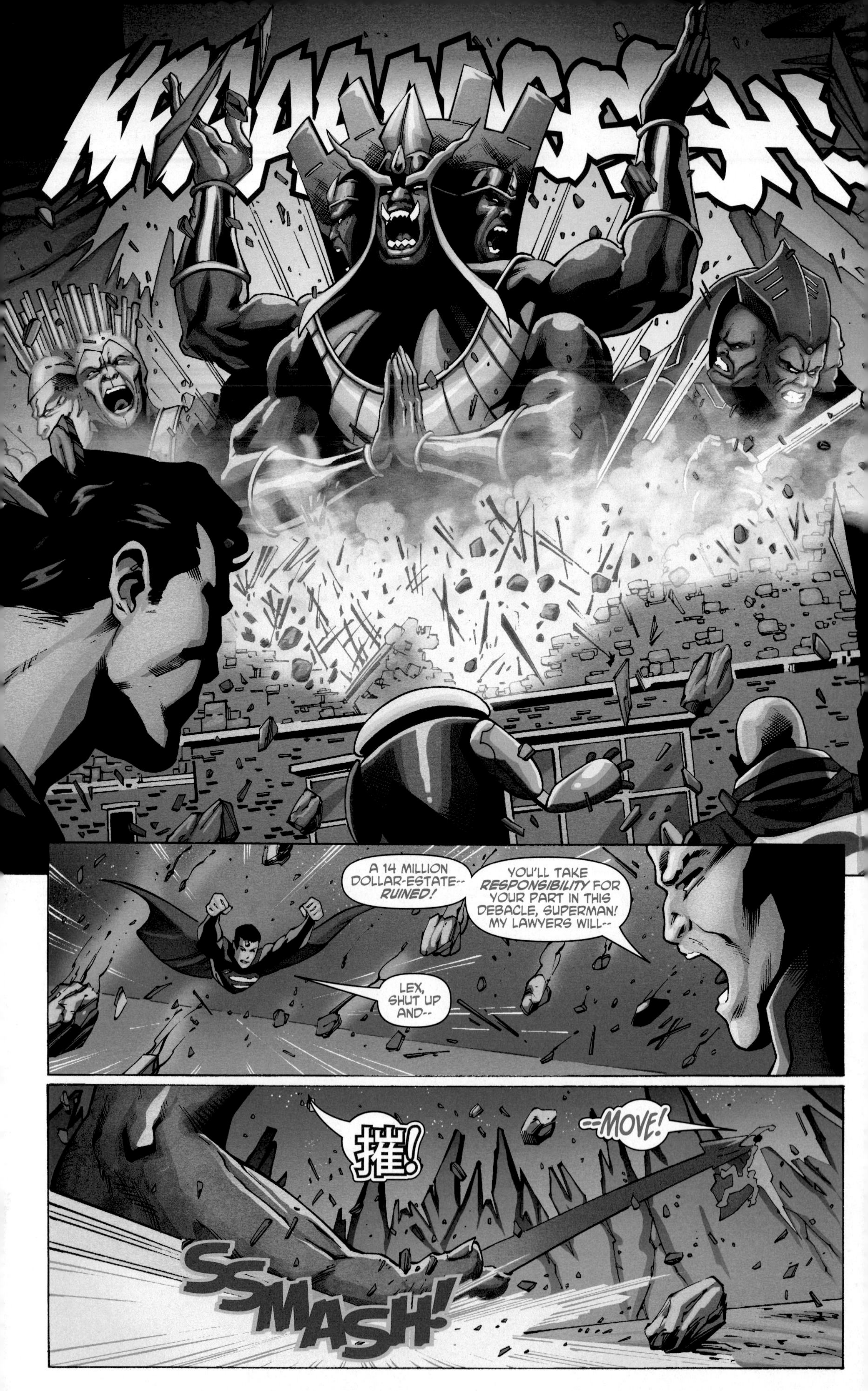
A 14 MILLION DOLLAR-ESTATE-- RUINED!
YOU'LL TAKE RESPONSIBILITY FOR YOUR PART IN THIS DEBACLE, SUPERMAN! MY LAWYERS WILL--
LEX, SHUT UP AND--
摧!
--MOVE!
SSMASH!

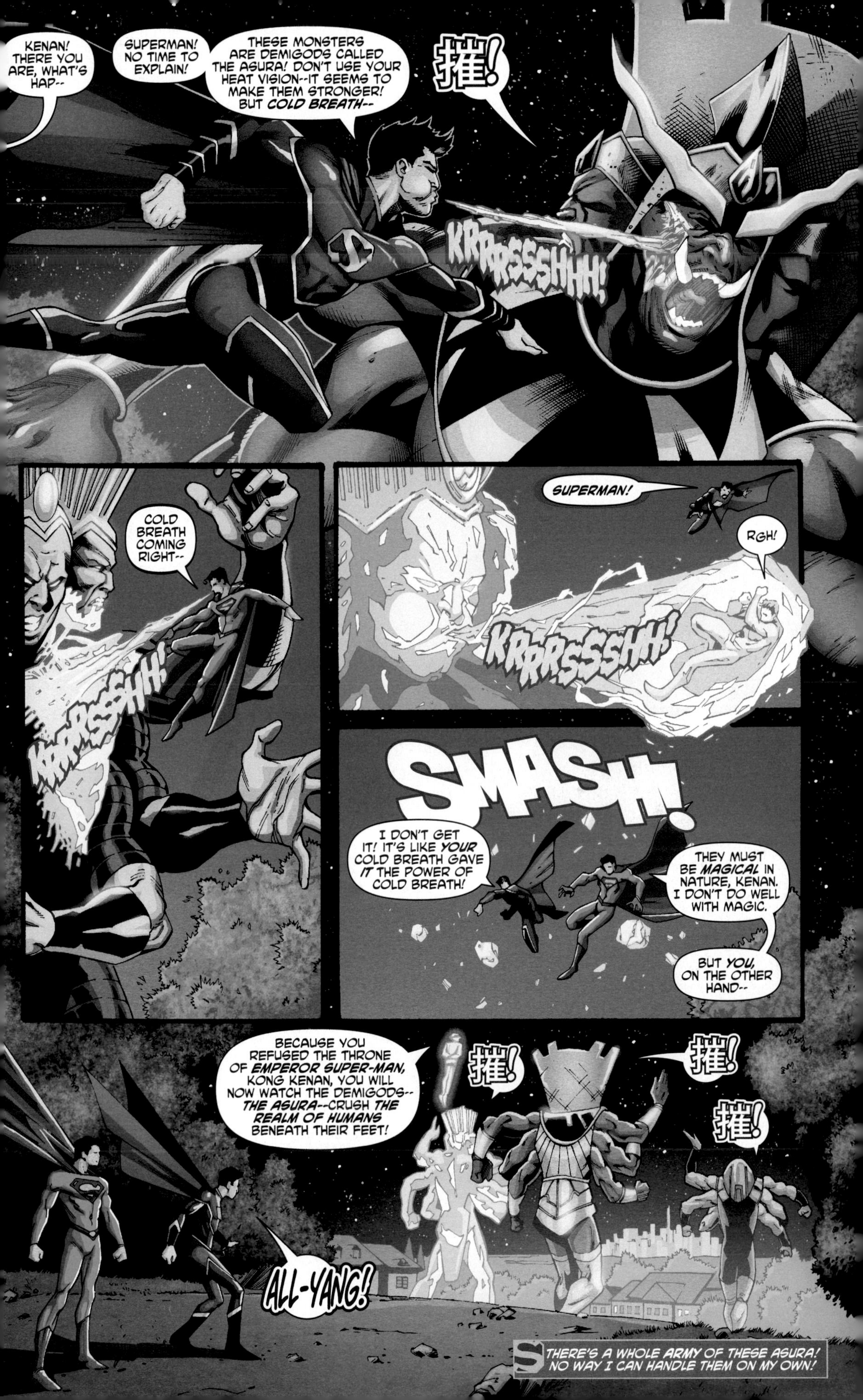
KENAN! THERE YOU ARE, WHAT'S HAP--
SUPERMAN! NO TIME TO EXPLAIN!
THESE MONSTERS ARE DEMIGODS CALLED THE ASURA! DON'T USE YOUR HEAT VISION--IT SEEMS TO MAKE THEM STRONGER! BUT COLD BREATH--
摧!
KRRRSSSHHH!
COLD BREATH COMING RIGHT--
KRRRSSSHH!
SUPERMAN!
RGH!
KRRRSSSHH!
SMASH!
I DON'T GET IT! IT'S LIKE YOUR COLD BREATH GAVE IT THE POWER OF COLD BREATH!
THEY MUST BE MAGICAL IN NATURE, KENAN. I DON'T DO WELL WITH MAGIC.
BUT YOU, ON THE OTHER HAND--
BECAUSE YOU REFUSED THE THRONE OF EMPEROR SUPER-MAN, KONG KENAN, YOU WILL NOW WATCH THE DEMIGODS-- THE ASURA--CRUSH THE REALM OF HUMANS BENEATH THEIR FEET!
摧!
摧!
摧!
ALL-YANG!
THERE'S A WHOLE ARMY OF THESE ASURA! NO WAY I CAN HANDLE THEM ON MY OWN!

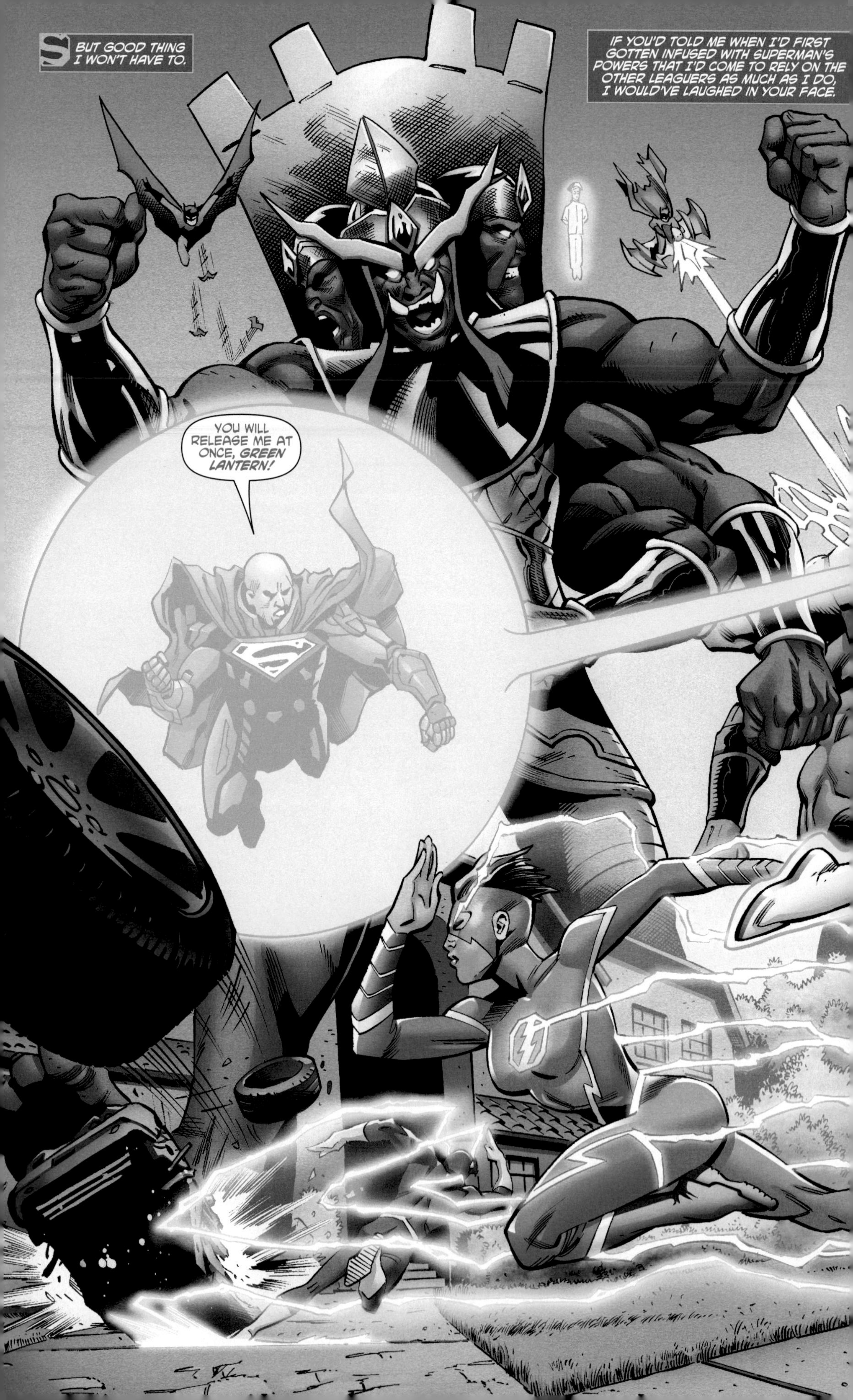
BUT GOOD THING I WON'T HAVE TO.
IF YOU'D TOLD ME WHEN I'D FIRST GOTTEN INFUSED WITH SUPERMAN'S POWERS THAT I'D COME TO RELY ON THE OTHER LEAGUERS AS MUCH AS I DO, I WOULD'VE LAUGHED IN YOUR FACE.
YOU WILL RELEASE ME AT ONCE, GREEN LANTERN!

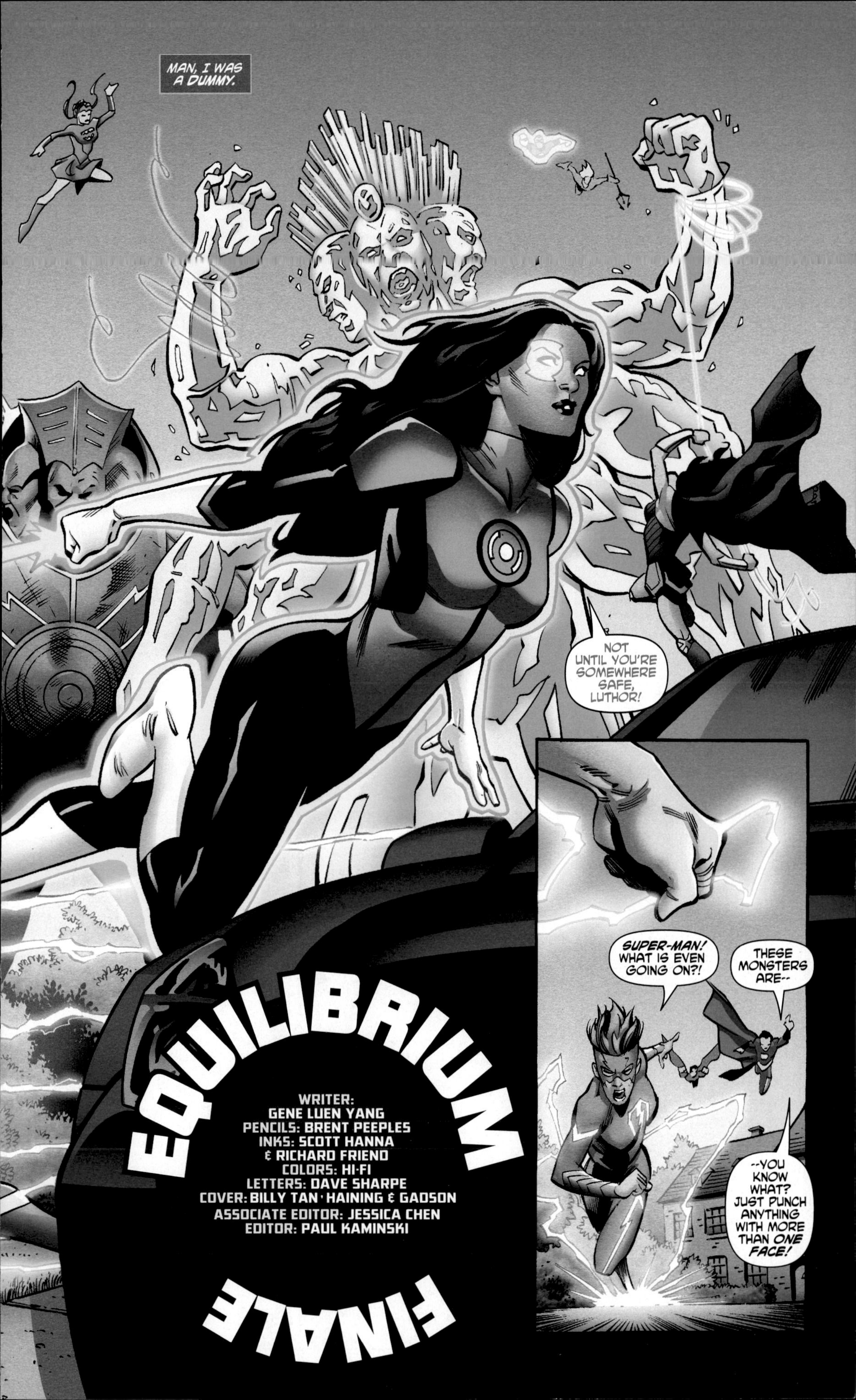
MAN, I WAS A DUMMY.
NOT UNTIL YOU'RE SOMEWHERE SAFE, LUTHOR!
SUPER-MAN! WHAT IS EVEN GOING ON?!
THESE MONSTERS ARE--
--YOU KNOW WHAT? JUST PUNCH ANYTHING WITH MORE THAN ONE FACE!
EQUILIBRIUM
FINALE
WRITER: GENE LUEN YANG
PENCILS: BRENT PEEPLES
INKS: SCOTT HANNA & RICHARD FRIEND
COLORS: HI-FI
LETTERS: DAVE SHARPE
COVER: BILLY TAN · HAINING & GADSON
ASSOCIATE EDITOR: JESSICA CHEN
EDITOR: PAUL KAMINSKI

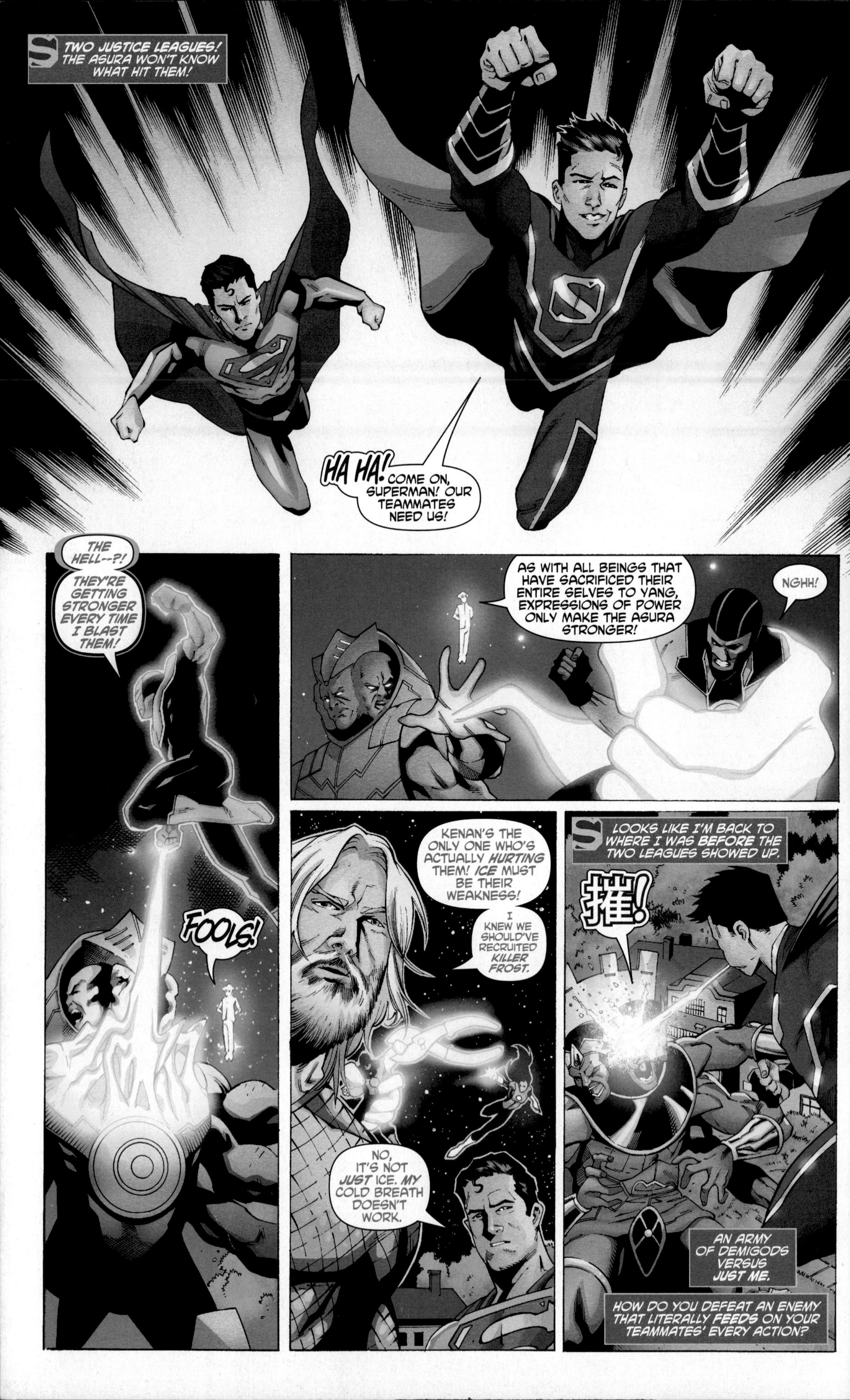

TWO JUSTICE LEAGUES! THE ASURA WON'T KNOW WHAT HIT THEM!
HA HA! COME ON, SUPERMAN! OUR TEAMMATES NEED US!
THE HELL--?!
THEY'RE GETTING STRONGER EVERY TIME I BLAST THEM!
FOOLS!
AS WITH ALL BEINGS THAT HAVE SACRIFICED THEIR ENTIRE SELVES TO YANG, EXPRESSIONS OF POWER ONLY MAKE THE ASURA STRONGER!
NGHH!
KENAN'S THE ONLY ONE WHO'S ACTUALLY HURTING THEM! ICE MUST BE THEIR WEAKNESS!
I KNEW WE SHOULD'VE RECRUITED KILLER FROST.
NO, IT'S NOT JUST ICE. MY COLD BREATH DOESN'T WORK.
LOOKS LIKE I'M BACK TO WHERE I WAS BEFORE THE TWO LEAGUES SHOWED UP.
摧!
AN ARMY OF DEMIGODS VERSUS JUST ME.
HOW DO YOU DEFEAT AN ENEMY THAT LITERALLY FEEDS ON YOUR TEAMMATES' EVERY ACTION?

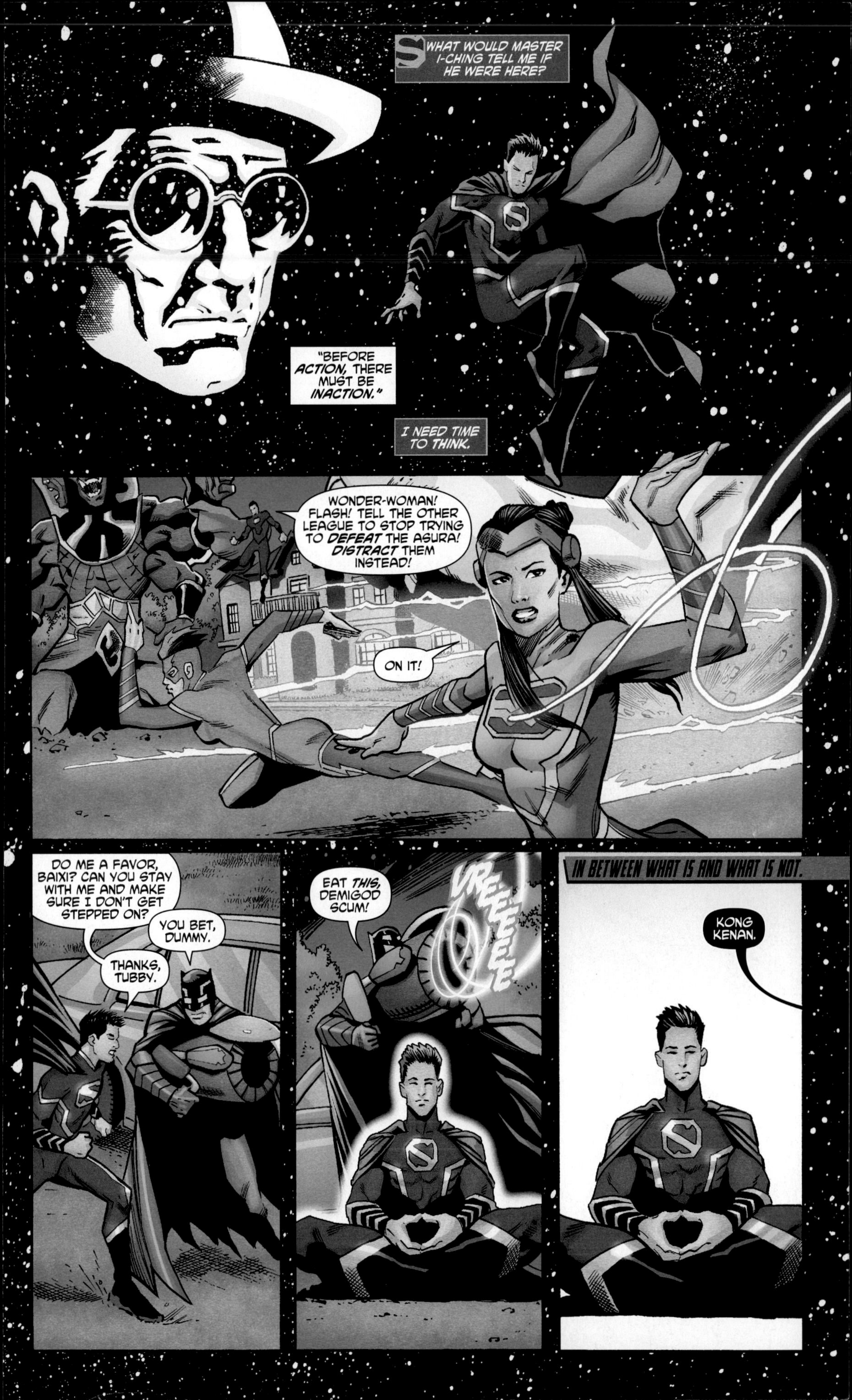
WHAT WOULD MASTER I-CHING TELL ME IF HE WERE HERE?
"BEFORE ACTION, THERE MUST BE INACTION."
I NEED TIME TO THINK.
WONDER-WOMAN! FLASH! TELL THE OTHER LEAGUE TO STOP TRYING TO DEFEAT THE ASURA! DISTRACT THEM INSTEAD!
ON IT!
DO ME A FAVOR, BAIXI? CAN YOU STAY WITH ME AND MAKE SURE I DON'T GET STEPPED ON?
YOU BET, DUMMY.
THANKS, TUBBY.
EAT THIS, DEMIGOD SCUM!
VREEEEEE
IN BETWEEN WHAT IS AND WHAT IS NOT.
KONG KENAN.

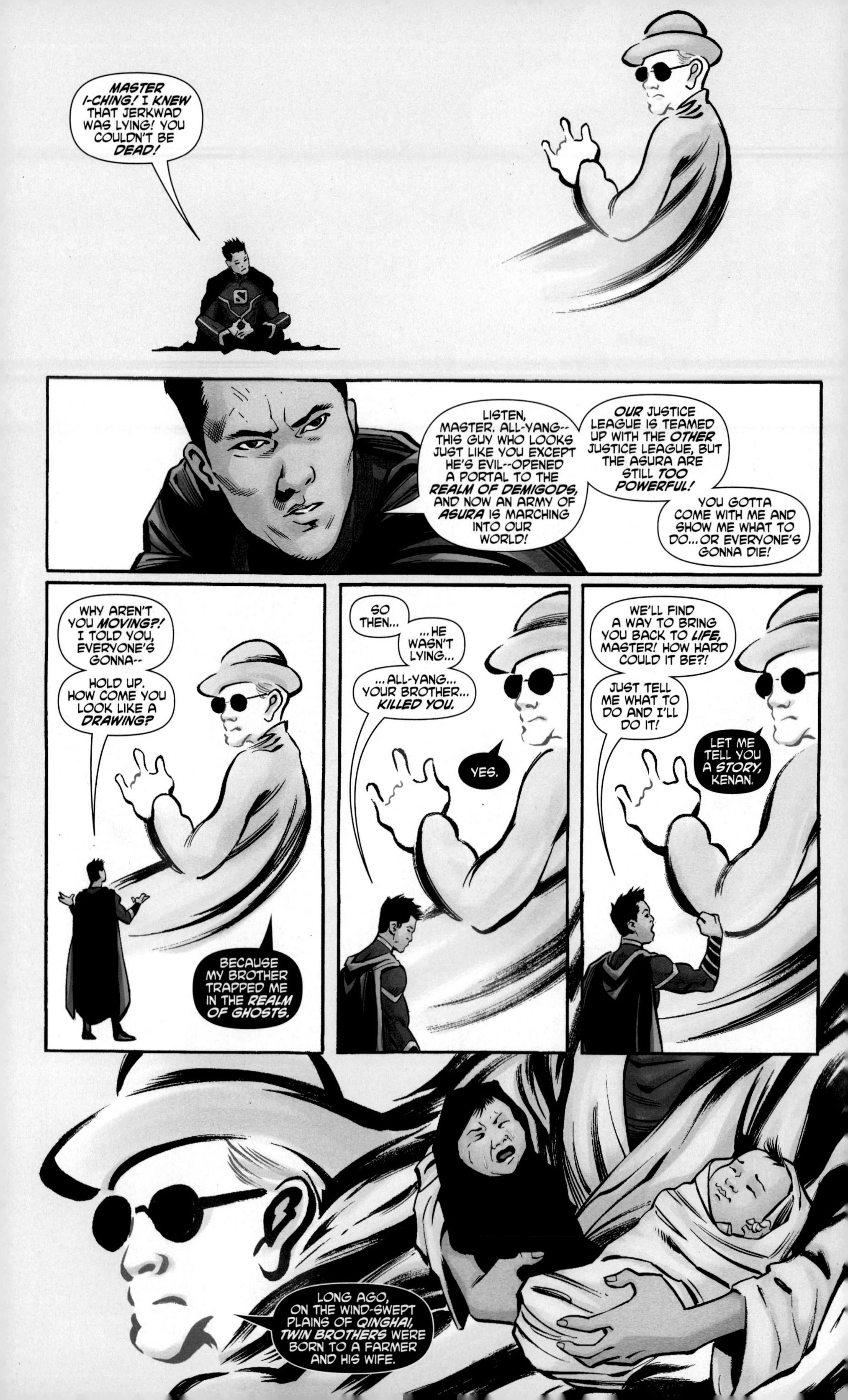

MASTER I-CHING! I KNEW THAT JERKWAD WAS LYING! YOU COULDN'T BE DEAD!
LISTEN, MASTER. ALL-YANG-- THIS GUY WHO LOOKS JUST LIKE YOU EXCEPT HE'S EVIL--OPENED A PORTAL TO THE REALM OF DEMIGODS, AND NOW AN ARMY OF ASURA IS MARCHING INTO OUR WORLD!
OUR JUSTICE LEAGUE IS TEAMED UP WITH THE OTHER JUSTICE LEAGUE, BUT THE ASURA ARE STILL TOO POWERFUL!
YOU GOTTA COME WITH ME AND SHOW ME WHAT TO DO...OR EVERYONE'S GONNA DIE!
WHY AREN'T YOU MOVING?! I TOLD YOU, EVERYONE'S GONNA--
HOLD UP. HOW COME YOU LOOK LIKE A DRAWING?
BECAUSE MY BROTHER TRAPPED ME IN THE REALM OF GHOSTS.
SO THEN...
...HE WASN'T LYING...
...ALL-YANG... YOUR BROTHER... KILLED YOU.
YES.
WE'LL FIND A WAY TO BRING YOU BACK TO LIFE, MASTER! HOW HARD COULD IT BE?!
JUST TELL ME WHAT TO DO AND I'LL DO IT!
LET ME TELL YOU A STORY, KENAN.
LONG AGO, ON THE WIND-SWEPT PLAINS OF QINGHAI, TWIN BROTHERS WERE BORN TO A FARMER AND HIS WIFE.

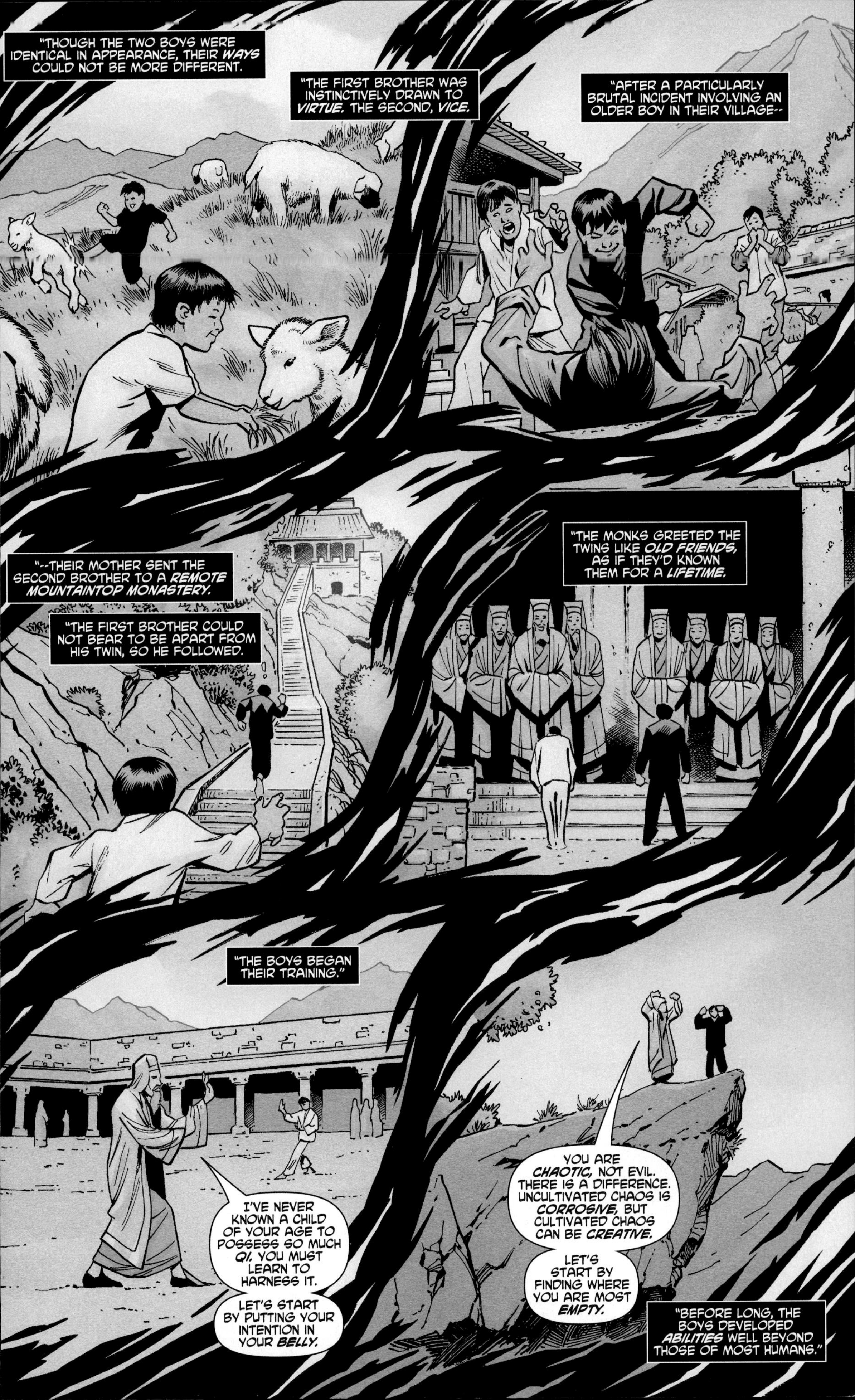

"THOUGH THE TWO BOYS WERE IDENTICAL IN APPEARANCE, THEIR WAYS COULD NOT BE MORE DIFFERENT.
"THE FIRST BROTHER WAS INSTINCTIVELY DRAWN TO VIRTUE. THE SECOND, VICE.
"AFTER A PARTICULARLY BRUTAL INCIDENT INVOLVING AN OLDER BOY IN THEIR VILLAGE--
"--THEIR MOTHER SENT THE SECOND BROTHER TO A REMOTE MOUNTAINTOP MONASTERY.
"THE FIRST BROTHER COULD NOT BEAR TO BE APART FROM HIS TWIN, SO HE FOLLOWED.
"THE MONKS GREETED THE TWINS LIKE OLD FRIENDS, AS IF THEY'D KNOWN THEM FOR A LIFETIME.
"THE BOYS BEGAN THEIR TRAINING."
I'VE NEVER KNOWN A CHILD OF YOUR AGE TO POSSESS SO MUCH QI. YOU MUST LEARN TO HARNESS IT.
LET'S START BY PUTTING YOUR INTENTION IN YOUR BELLY.
YOU ARE CHAOTIC, NOT EVIL. THERE IS A DIFFERENCE. UNCULTIVATED CHAOS IS CORROSIVE, BUT CULTIVATED CHAOS CAN BE CREATIVE.
LET'S START BY FINDING WHERE YOU ARE MOST EMPTY.
"BEFORE LONG, THE BOYS DEVELOPED ABILITIES WELL BEYOND THOSE OF MOST HUMANS."

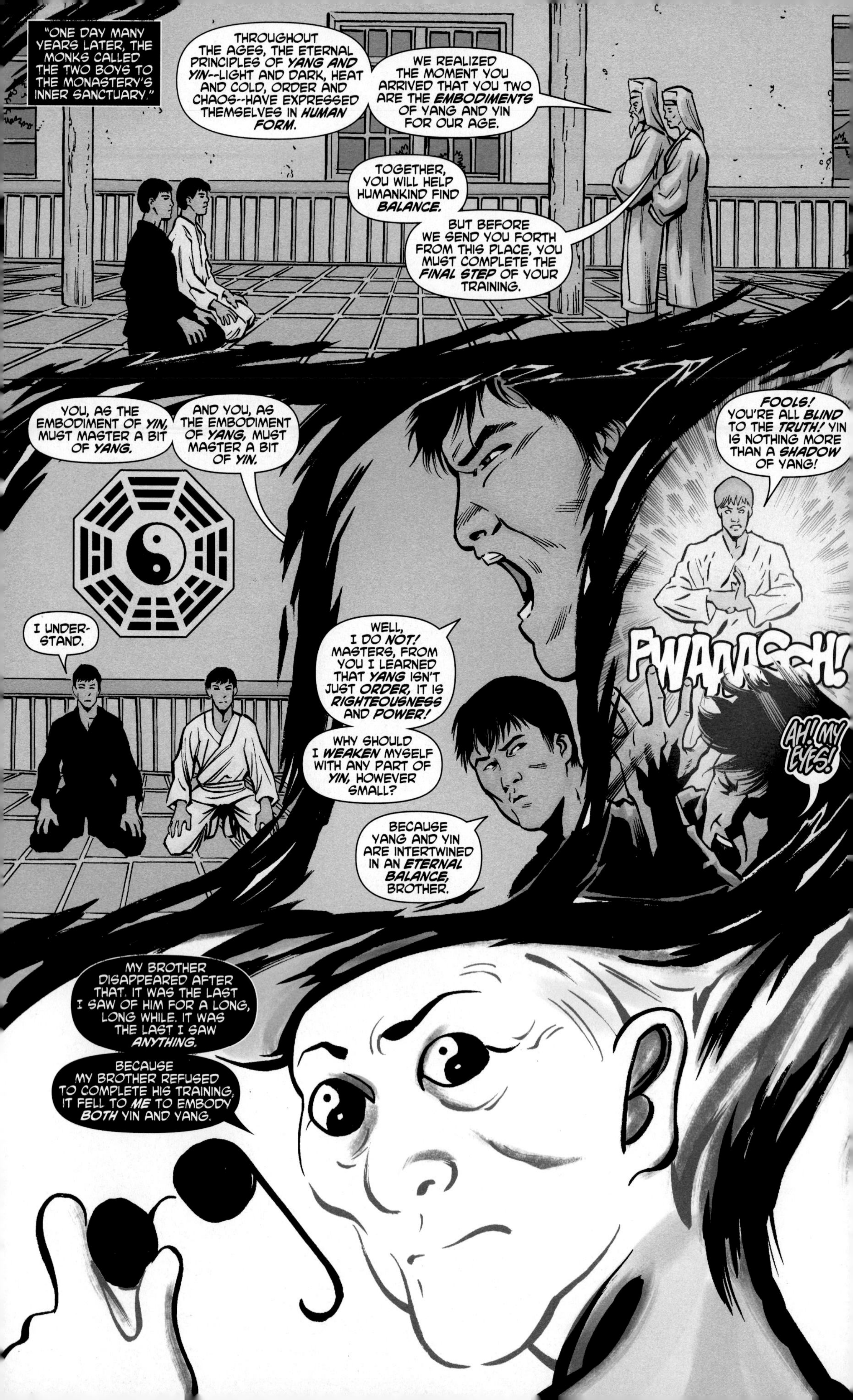
"ONE DAY MANY YEARS LATER, THE MONKS CALLED THE TWO BOYS TO THE MONASTERY'S INNER SANCTUARY."
THROUGHOUT THE AGES, THE ETERNAL PRINCIPLES OF YANG AND YIN--LIGHT AND DARK, HEAT AND COLD, ORDER AND CHAOS--HAVE EXPRESSED THEMSELVES IN HUMAN FORM.
WE REALIZED THE MOMENT YOU ARRIVED THAT YOU TWO ARE THE EMBODIMENTS OF YANG AND YIN FOR OUR AGE.
TOGETHER, YOU WILL HELP HUMANKIND FIND BALANCE.
BUT BEFORE WE SEND YOU FORTH FROM THIS PLACE, YOU MUST COMPLETE THE FINAL STEP OF YOUR TRAINING.
YOU, AS THE EMBODIMENT OF YIN, MUST MASTER A BIT OF YANG.
AND YOU, AS THE EMBODIMENT OF YANG, MUST MASTER A BIT OF YIN.
I UNDER-STAND.
WELL, I DO NOT! MASTERS, FROM YOU I LEARNED THAT YANG ISN'T JUST ORDER, IT IS RIGHTEOUSNESS AND POWER!
WHY SHOULD I WEAKEN MYSELF WITH ANY PART OF YIN, HOWEVER SMALL?
BECAUSE YANG AND YIN ARE INTERTWINED IN AN ETERNAL BALANCE, BROTHER.
FOOLS! YOU'RE ALL BLIND TO THE TRUTH! YIN IS NOTHING MORE THAN A SHADOW OF YANG!
FWAAASSH!
AH! MY EYES!
MY BROTHER DISAPPEARED AFTER THAT. IT WAS THE LAST I SAW OF HIM FOR A LONG, LONG WHILE. IT WAS THE LAST I SAW ANYTHING.
BECAUSE MY BROTHER REFUSED TO COMPLETE HIS TRAINING, IT FELL TO ME TO EMBODY BOTH YIN AND YANG.

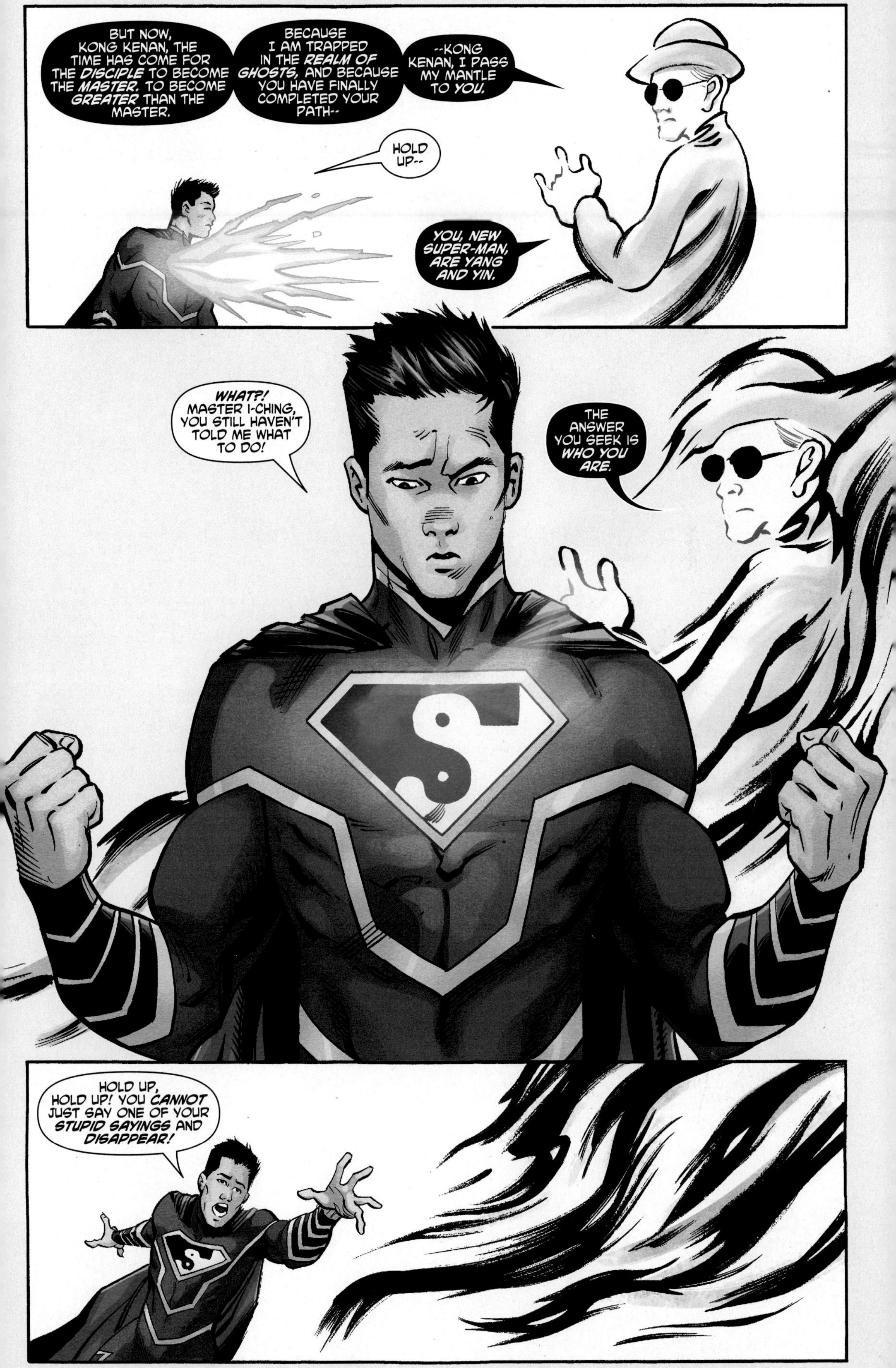
BUT NOW, KONG KENAN, THE TIME HAS COME FOR THE DISCIPLE TO BECOME THE MASTER. TO BECOME GREATER THAN THE MASTER.
BECAUSE I AM TRAPPED IN THE REALM OF GHOSTS, AND BECAUSE YOU HAVE FINALLY COMPLETED YOUR PATH--
--KONG KENAN, I PASS MY MANTLE TO YOU.
HOLD UP--
YOU, NEW SUPER-MAN, ARE YANG AND YIN.
WHAT?! MASTER I-CHING, YOU STILL HAVEN'T TOLD ME WHAT TO DO!
THE ANSWER YOU SEEK IS WHO YOU ARE.
HOLD UP, HOLD UP! YOU CANNOT JUST SAY ONE OF YOUR STUPID SAYINGS AND DISAPPEAR!

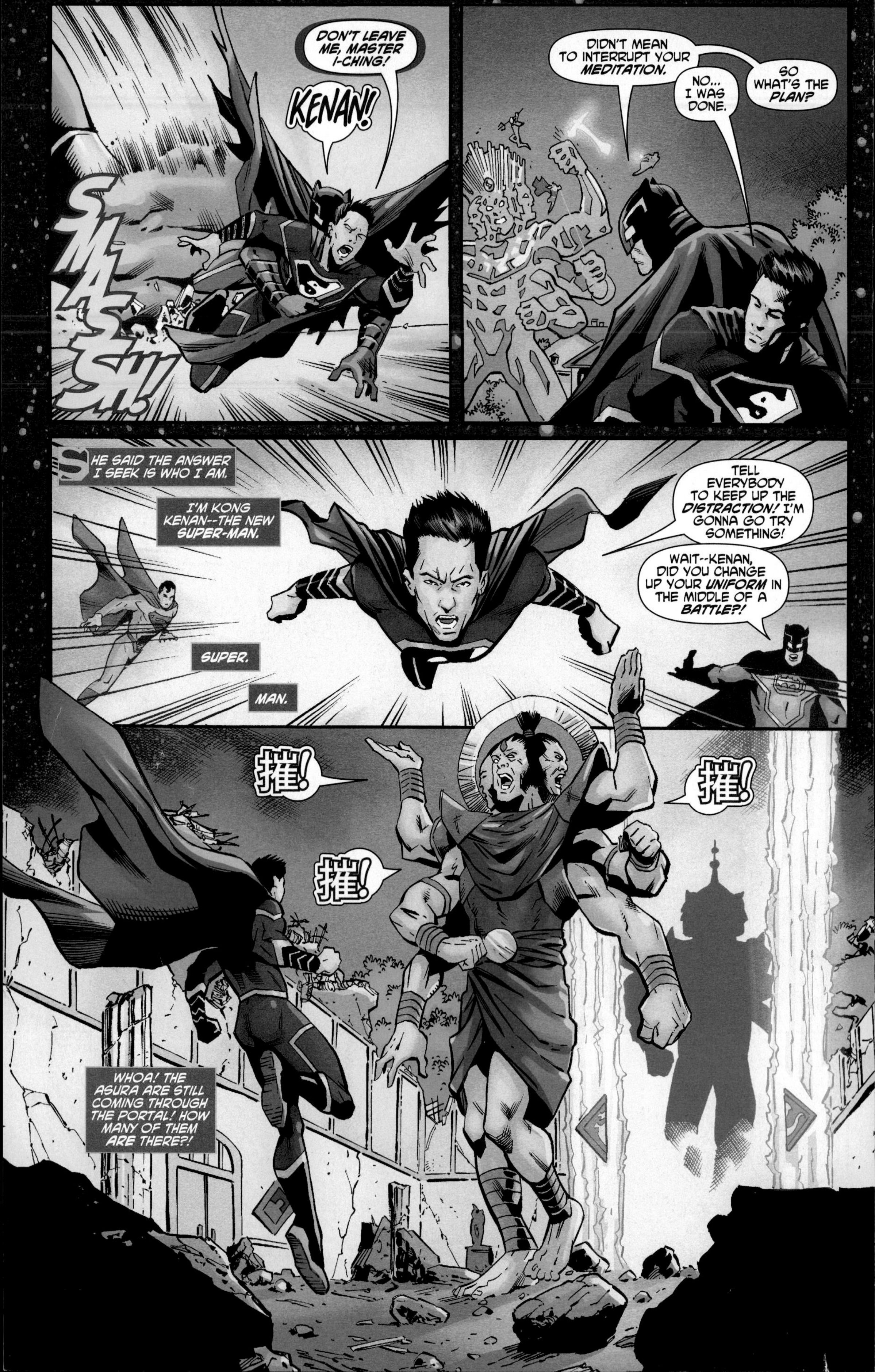
DON'T LEAVE ME, MASTER I-CHING!
KENAN!
SMASH!
DIDN'T MEAN TO INTERRUPT YOUR MEDITATION.
NO... I WAS DONE.
SO WHAT'S THE PLAN?
SHE SAID THE ANSWER I SEEK IS WHO I AM.
I'M KONG KENAN--THE NEW SUPER-MAN.
SUPER.
MAN.
TELL EVERYBODY TO KEEP UP THE DISTRACTION! I'M GONNA GO TRY SOMETHING!
WAIT--KENAN, DID YOU CHANGE UP YOUR UNIFORM IN THE MIDDLE OF A BATTLE?!
摧!
摧!
摧!
WHOA! THE ASURA ARE STILL COMING THROUGH THE PORTAL! HOW MANY OF THEM ARE THERE?!

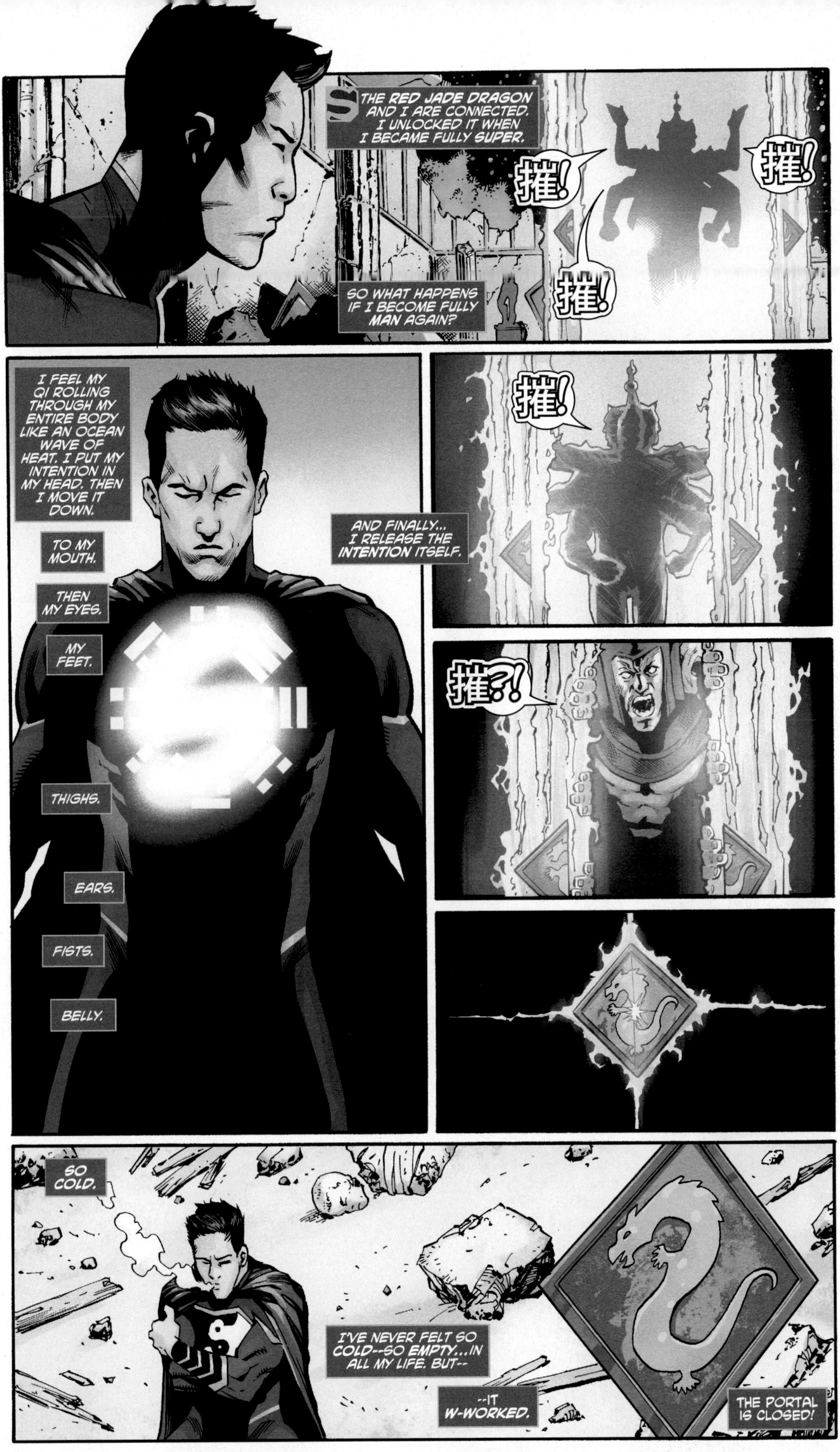
THE RED JADE DRAGON AND I ARE CONNECTED. I UNLOCKED IT WHEN I BECAME FULLY SUPER.
摧!
摧!
摧!
SO WHAT HAPPENS IF I BECOME FULLY MAN AGAIN?
I FEEL MY QI ROLLING THROUGH MY ENTIRE BODY LIKE AN OCEAN WAVE OF HEAT. I PUT MY INTENTION IN MY HEAD. THEN I MOVE IT DOWN.
TO MY MOUTH.
THEN MY EYES.
MY FEET.
THIGHS.
EARS.
FISTS.
BELLY.
AND FINALLY... I RELEASE THE INTENTION ITSELF.
摧!
摧?!
SO COLD.
I'VE NEVER FELT SO COLD--SO EMPTY...IN ALL MY LIFE. BUT--
--IT W-WORKED.
THE PORTAL IS CLOSED!

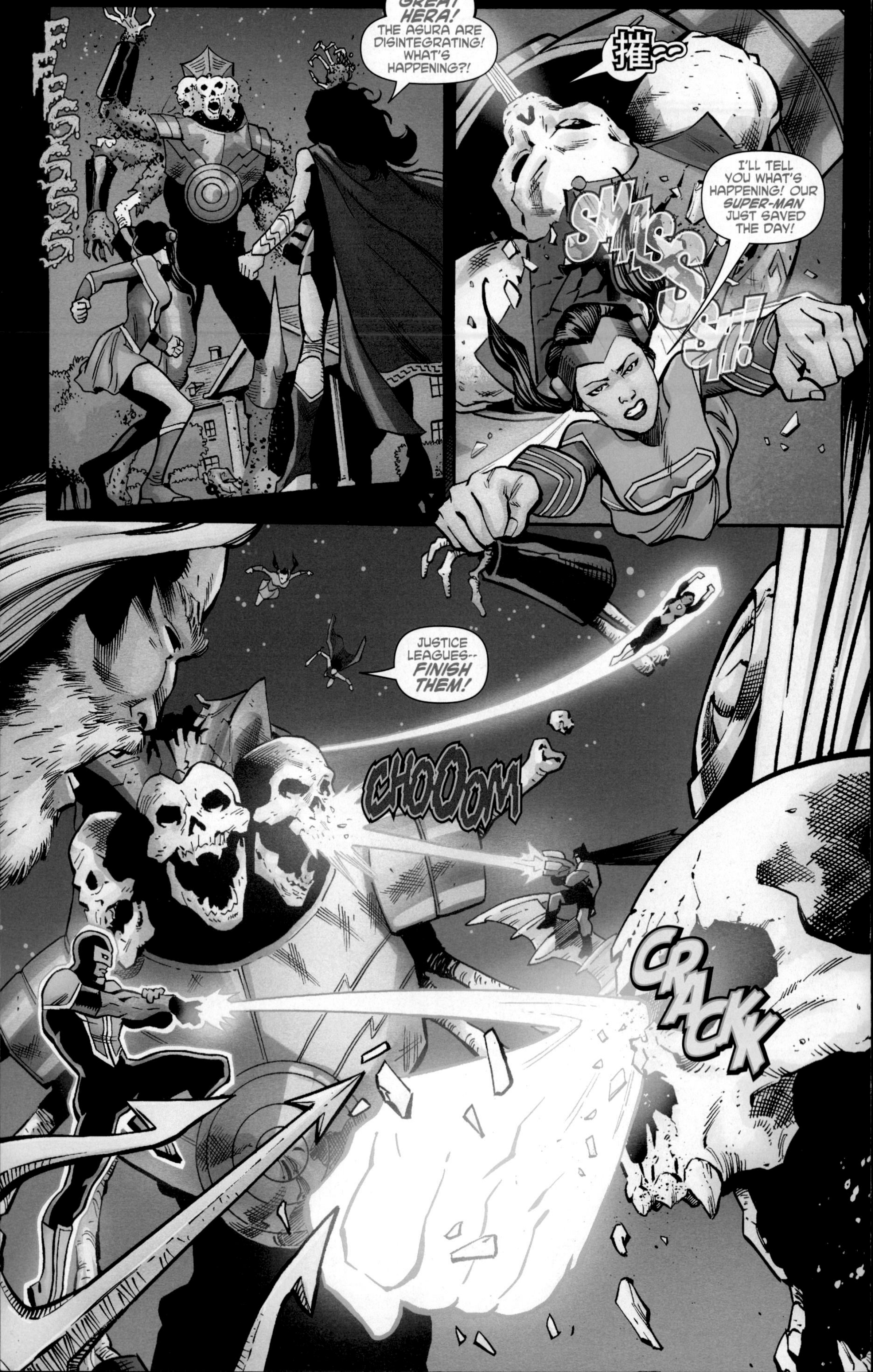
FSSSHHHHH
GREAT HERA! THE ASURA ARE DISINTEGRATING! WHAT'S HAPPENING?!
摧∞
I'LL TELL YOU WHAT'S HAPPENING! OUR SUPER-MAN JUST SAVED THE DAY!
SMASSSH!
JUSTICE LEAGUES-- FINISH THEM!
CHOOOM
CRACKK

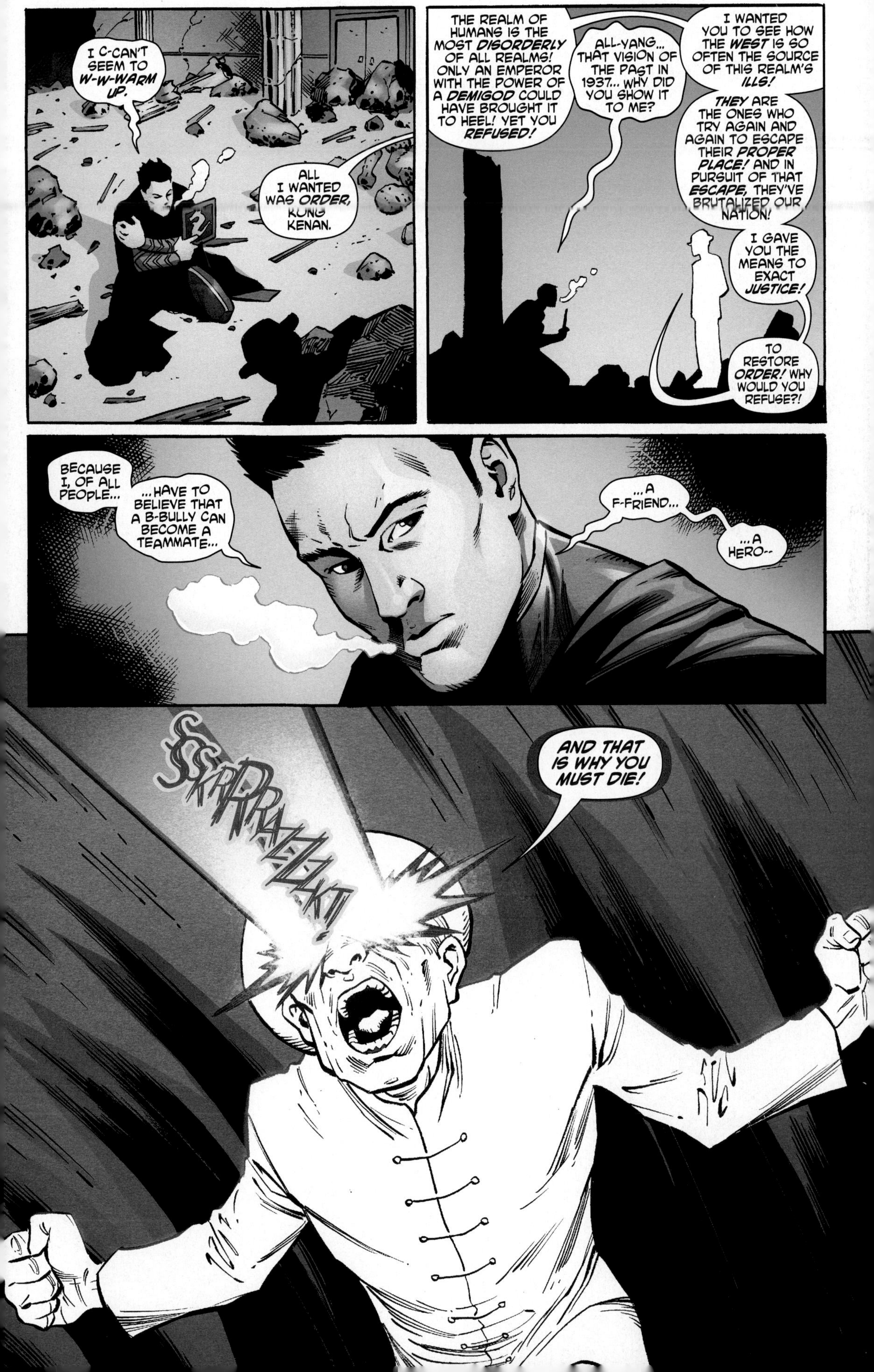
I C-CAN'T SEEM TO W-W-WARM UP.
ALL I WANTED WAS ORDER, KUNG KENAN.
THE REALM OF HUMANS IS THE MOST DISORDERLY OF ALL REALMS! ONLY AN EMPEROR WITH THE POWER OF A DEMIGOD COULD HAVE BROUGHT IT TO HEEL! YET YOU REFUSED!
ALL-YANG... THAT VISION OF THE PAST IN 1937... WHY DID YOU SHOW IT TO ME?
I WANTED YOU TO SEE HOW THE WEST IS SO OFTEN THE SOURCE OF THIS REALM'S ILLS!
THEY ARE THE ONES WHO TRY AGAIN AND AGAIN TO ESCAPE THEIR PROPER PLACE! AND IN PURSUIT OF THAT ESCAPE, THEY'VE BRUTALIZED OUR NATION!
I GAVE YOU THE MEANS TO EXACT JUSTICE!
TO RESTORE ORDER! WHY WOULD YOU REFUSE?!
BECAUSE I, OF ALL PEOPLE...
...HAVE TO BELIEVE THAT A B-BULLY CAN BECOME A TEAMMATE...
...A F-FRIEND...
...A HERO--
SSKRRRAZZAKT!
AND THAT IS WHY YOU MUST DIE!

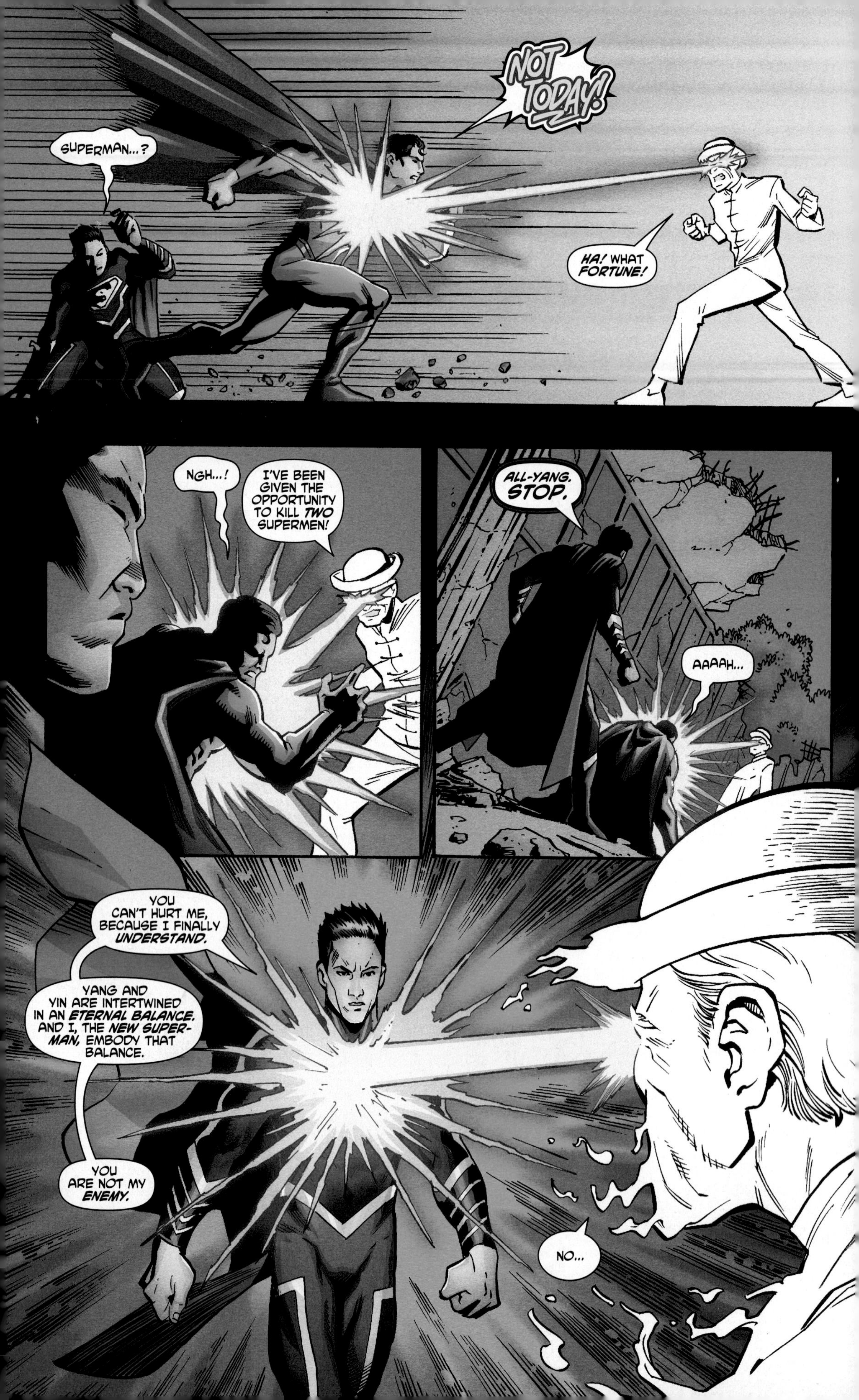
SUPERMAN...?
NOT TODAY!
HA! WHAT FORTUNE!
NGH...!
I'VE BEEN GIVEN THE OPPORTUNITY TO KILL TWO SUPERMEN!
ALL-YANG. STOP.
AAAAH...
YOU CAN'T HURT ME, BECAUSE I FINALLY UNDERSTAND.
YANG AND YIN ARE INTERTWINED IN AN ETERNAL BALANCE. AND I, THE NEW SUPER-MAN, EMBODY THAT BALANCE.
YOU ARE NOT MY ENEMY.
NO...

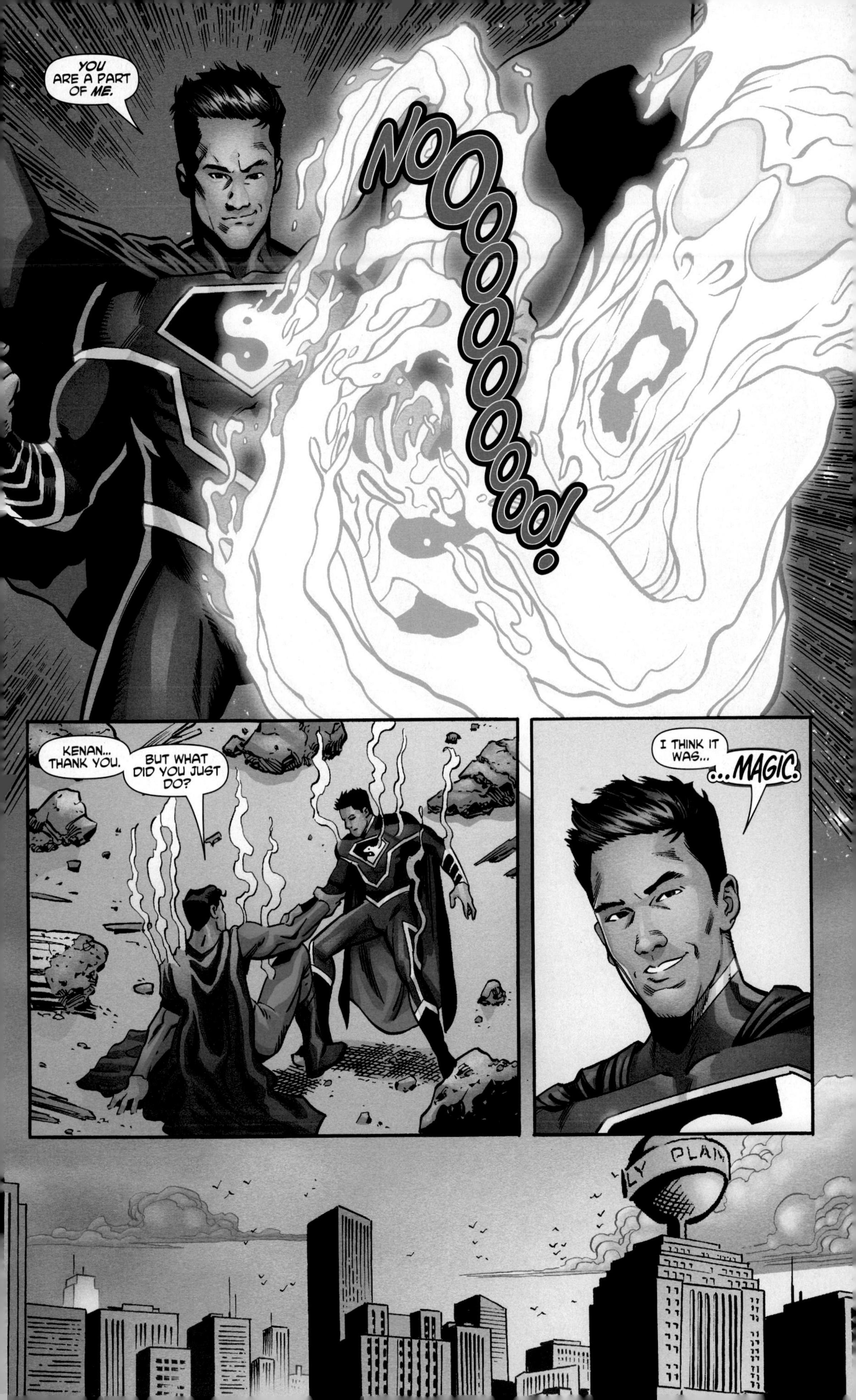
YOU ARE A PART OF ME.
NOOOOOOOOOOO!
KENAN... THANK YOU.
BUT WHAT DID YOU JUST DO?
I THINK IT WAS...
...MAGIC.

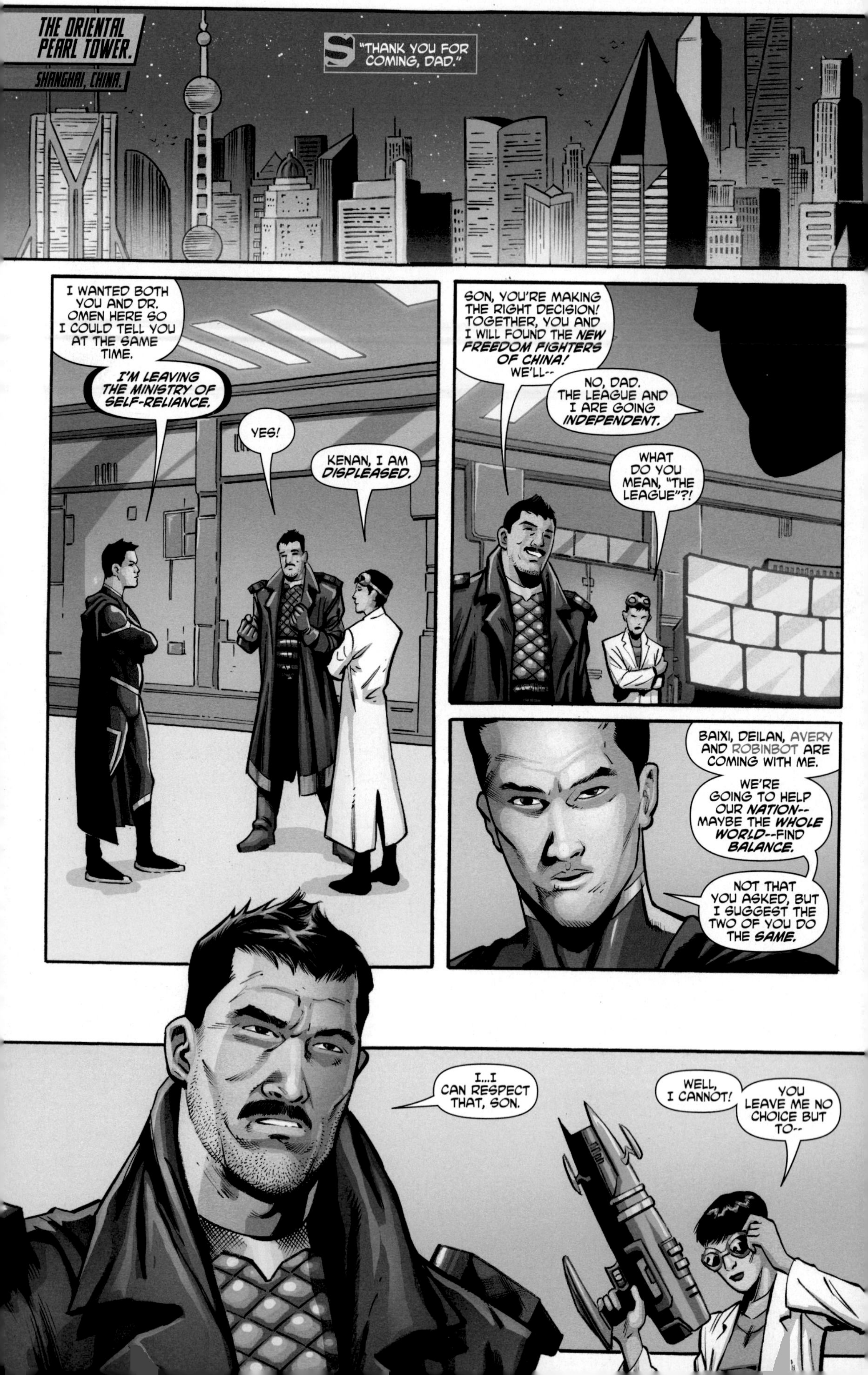
THE ORIENTAL PEARL TOWER.
SHANGHAI, CHINA.
"THANK YOU FOR COMING, DAD."
I WANTED BOTH YOU AND DR. OMEN HERE SO I COULD TELL YOU AT THE SAME TIME.
I'M LEAVING THE MINISTRY OF SELF-RELIANCE.
YES!
KENAN, I AM DISPLEASED.
SON, YOU'RE MAKING THE RIGHT DECISION! TOGETHER, YOU AND I WILL FOUND THE NEW FREEDOM FIGHTERS OF CHINA! WE'LL--
NO, DAD. THE LEAGUE AND I ARE GOING INDEPENDENT.
WHAT DO YOU MEAN, "THE LEAGUE"?!
BAIXI, DEILAN, AVERY AND ROBINBOT ARE COMING WITH ME.
WE'RE GOING TO HELP OUR NATION--MAYBE THE WHOLE WORLD--FIND BALANCE.
NOT THAT YOU ASKED, BUT I SUGGEST THE TWO OF YOU DO THE SAME.
I...I CAN RESPECT THAT, SON.
WELL, I CANNOT!
YOU LEAVE ME NO CHOICE BUT TO--

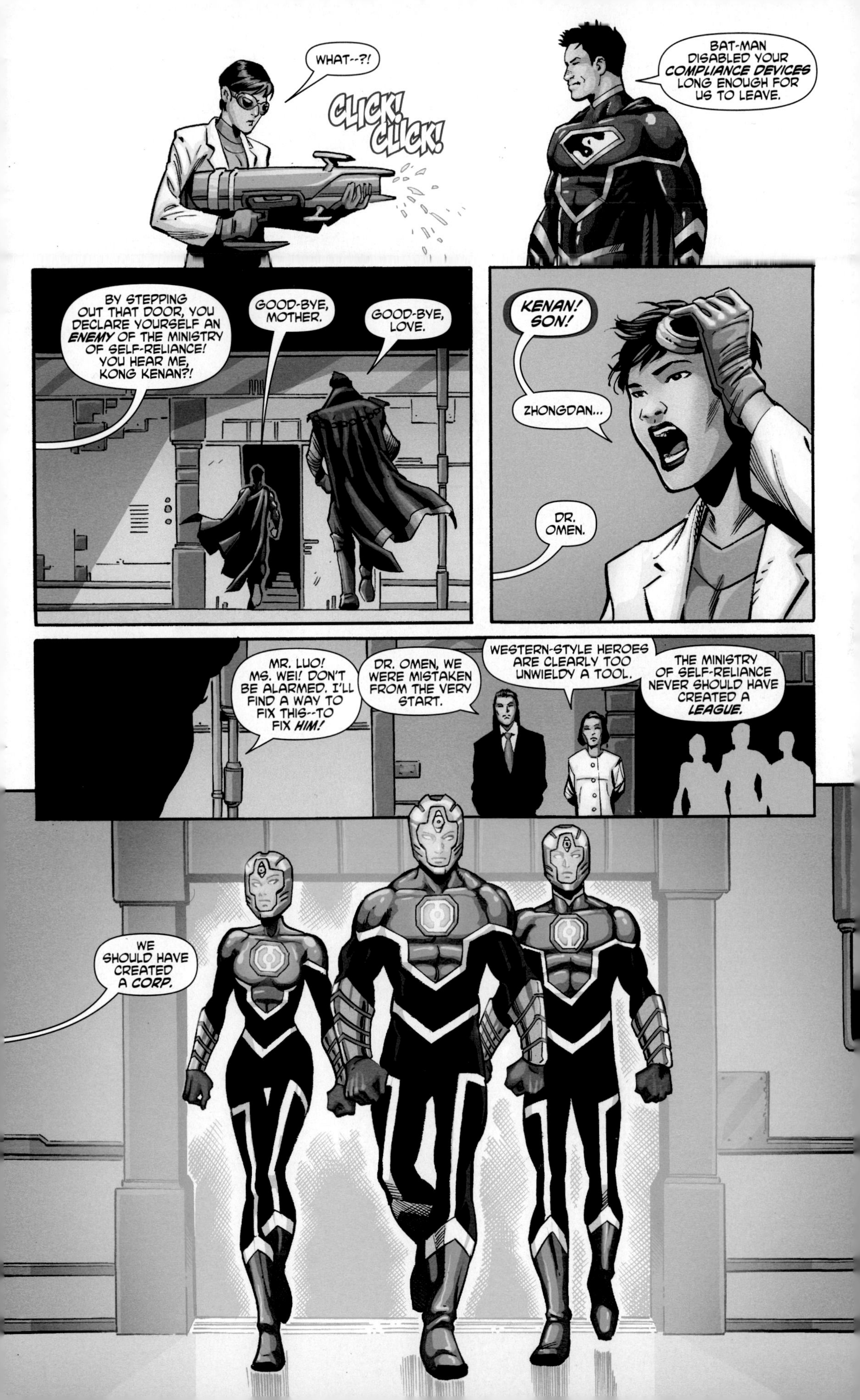
WHAT--?!
CLICK! CLICK!
BAT-MAN DISABLED YOUR COMPLIANCE DEVICES LONG ENOUGH FOR US TO LEAVE.
BY STEPPING OUT THAT DOOR, YOU DECLARE YOURSELF AN ENEMY OF THE MINISTRY OF SELF-RELIANCE! YOU HEAR ME, KONG KENAN?!
GOOD-BYE, MOTHER.
GOOD-BYE, LOVE.
KENAN! SON!
ZHONGDAN...
DR. OMEN.
MR. LUO! MS. WEI! DON'T BE ALARMED. I'LL FIND A WAY TO FIX THIS--TO FIX HIM!
DR. OMEN, WE WERE MISTAKEN FROM THE VERY START.
WESTERN-STYLE HEROES ARE CLEARLY TOO UNWIELDY A TOOL.
THE MINISTRY OF SELF-RELIANCE NEVER SHOULD HAVE CREATED A LEAGUE.
WE SHOULD HAVE CREATED A CORP.

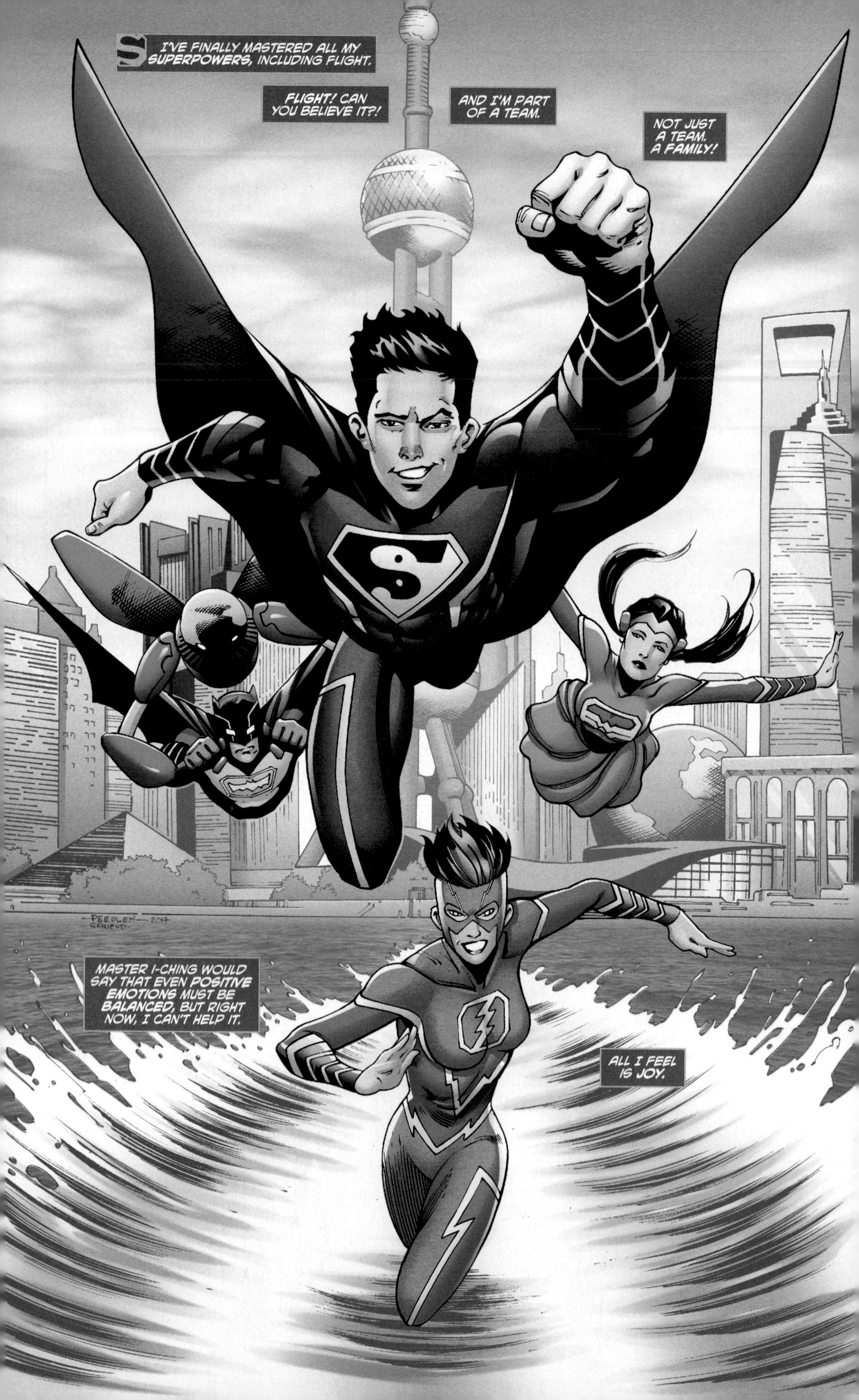
I'VE FINALLY MASTERED ALL MY SUPERPOWERS, INCLUDING FLIGHT.
FLIGHT! CAN YOU BELIEVE IT?!
AND I'M PART OF A TEAM.
NOT JUST A TEAM. A FAMILY!
MASTER I-CHING WOULD SAY THAT EVEN POSITIVE EMOTIONS MUST BE BALANCED, BUT RIGHT NOW, I CAN'T HELP IT.
ALL I FEEL IS JOY.

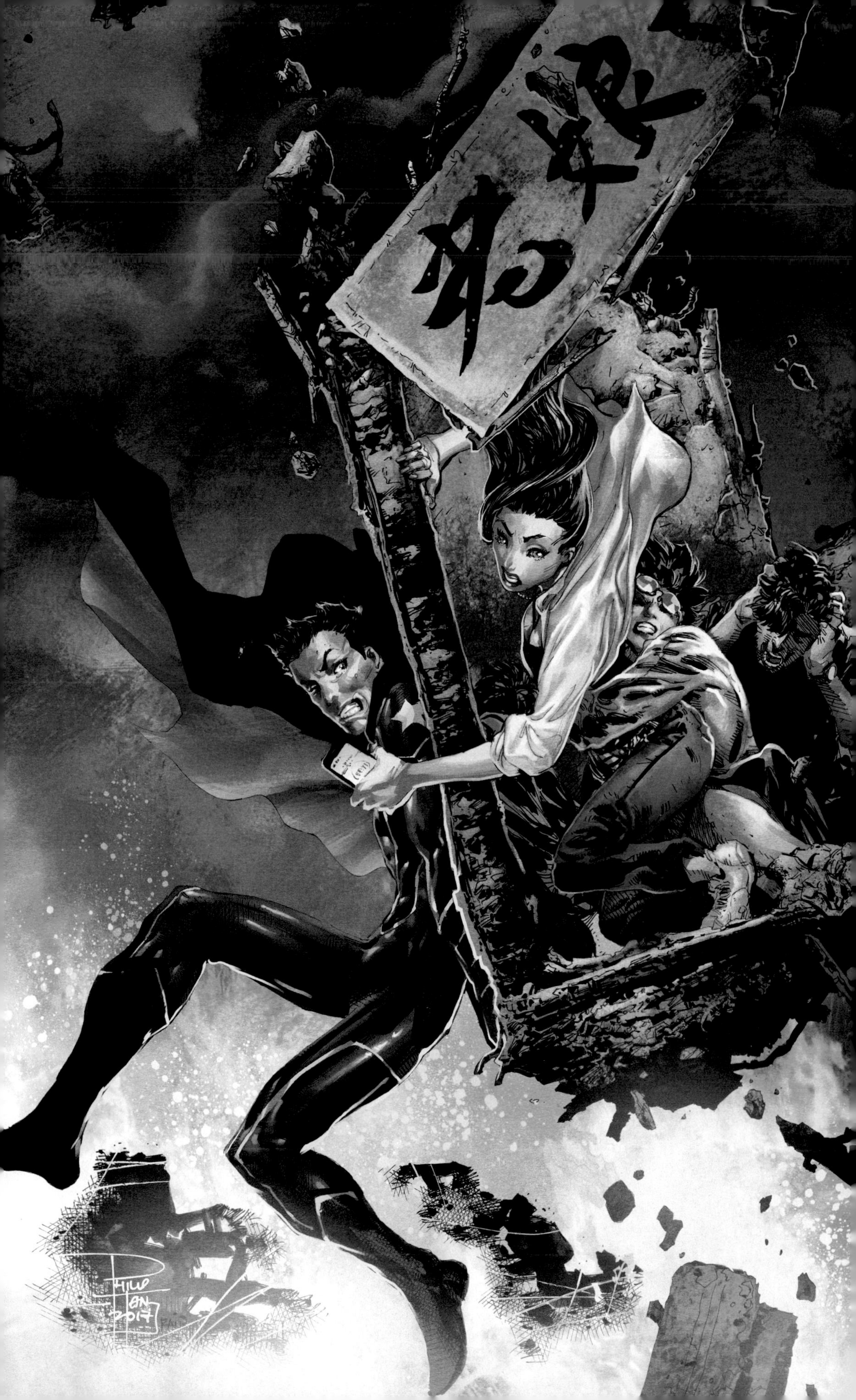

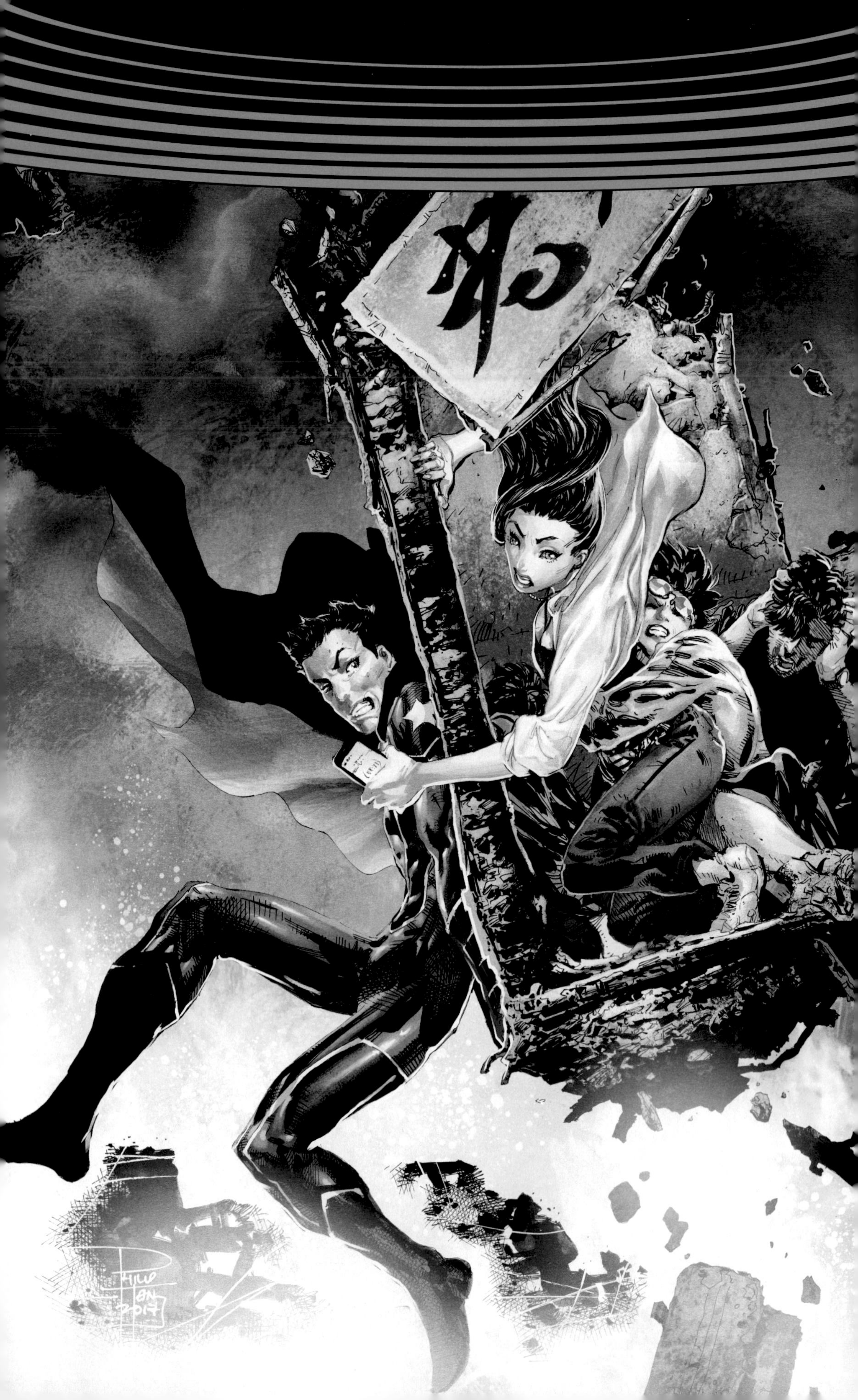

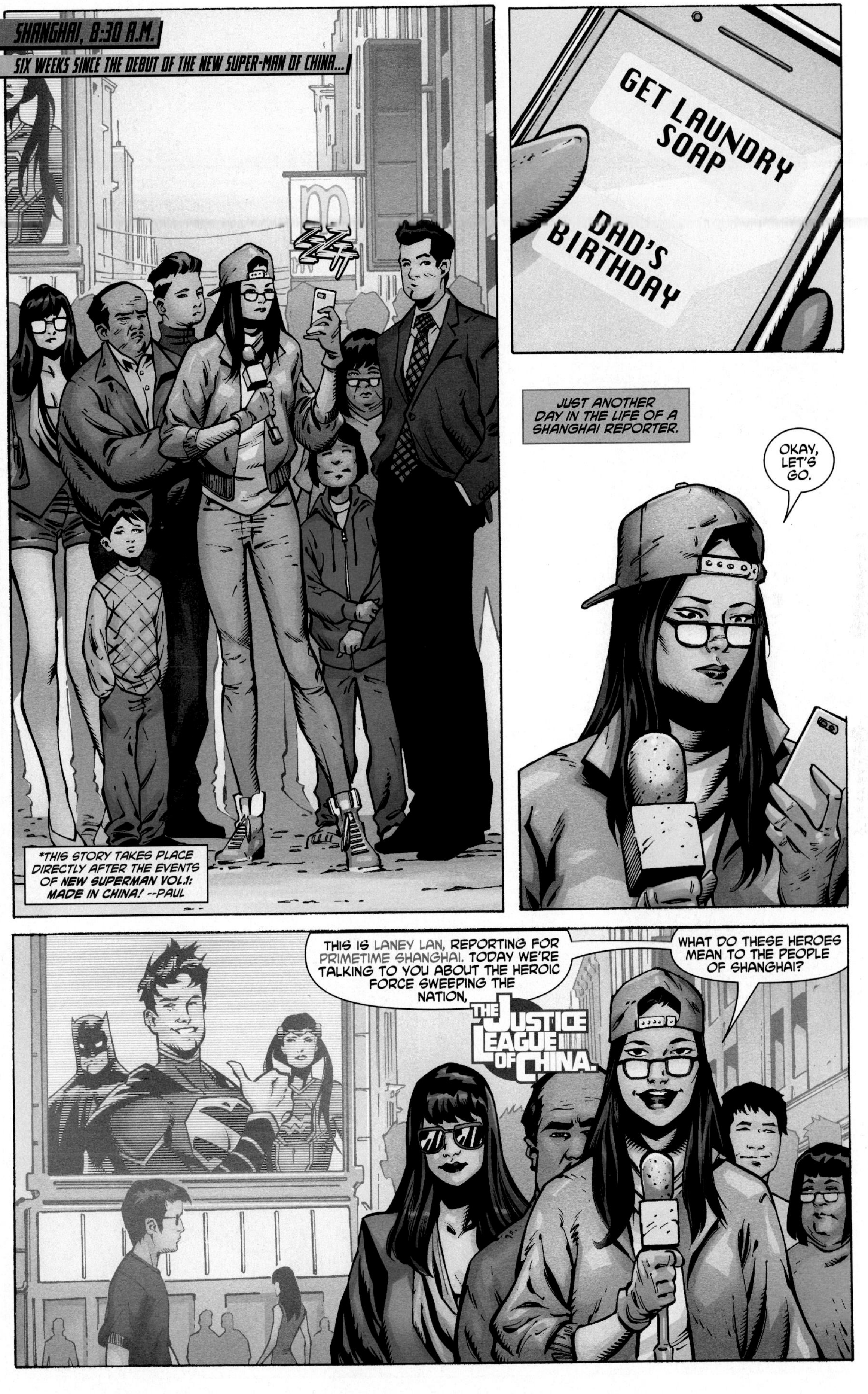
SHANGHAI, 8:30 A.M.
SIX WEEKS SINCE THE DEBUT OF THE NEW SUPER-MAN OF CHINA...
*THIS STORY TAKES PLACE DIRECTLY AFTER THE EVENTS OF NEW SUPERMAN VOL.1: MADE IN CHINA! --PAUL
GET LAUNDRY SOAP
DAD'S BIRTHDAY
JUST ANOTHER DAY IN THE LIFE OF A SHANGHAI REPORTER.
OKAY, LET'S GO.
THIS IS LANEY LAN, REPORTING FOR PRIMETIME SHANGHAI. TODAY WE'RE TALKING TO YOU ABOUT THE HEROIC FORCE SWEEPING THE NATION,
THE JUSTICE LEAGUE OF CHINA.
WHAT DO THESE HEROES MEAN TO THE PEOPLE OF SHANGHAI?

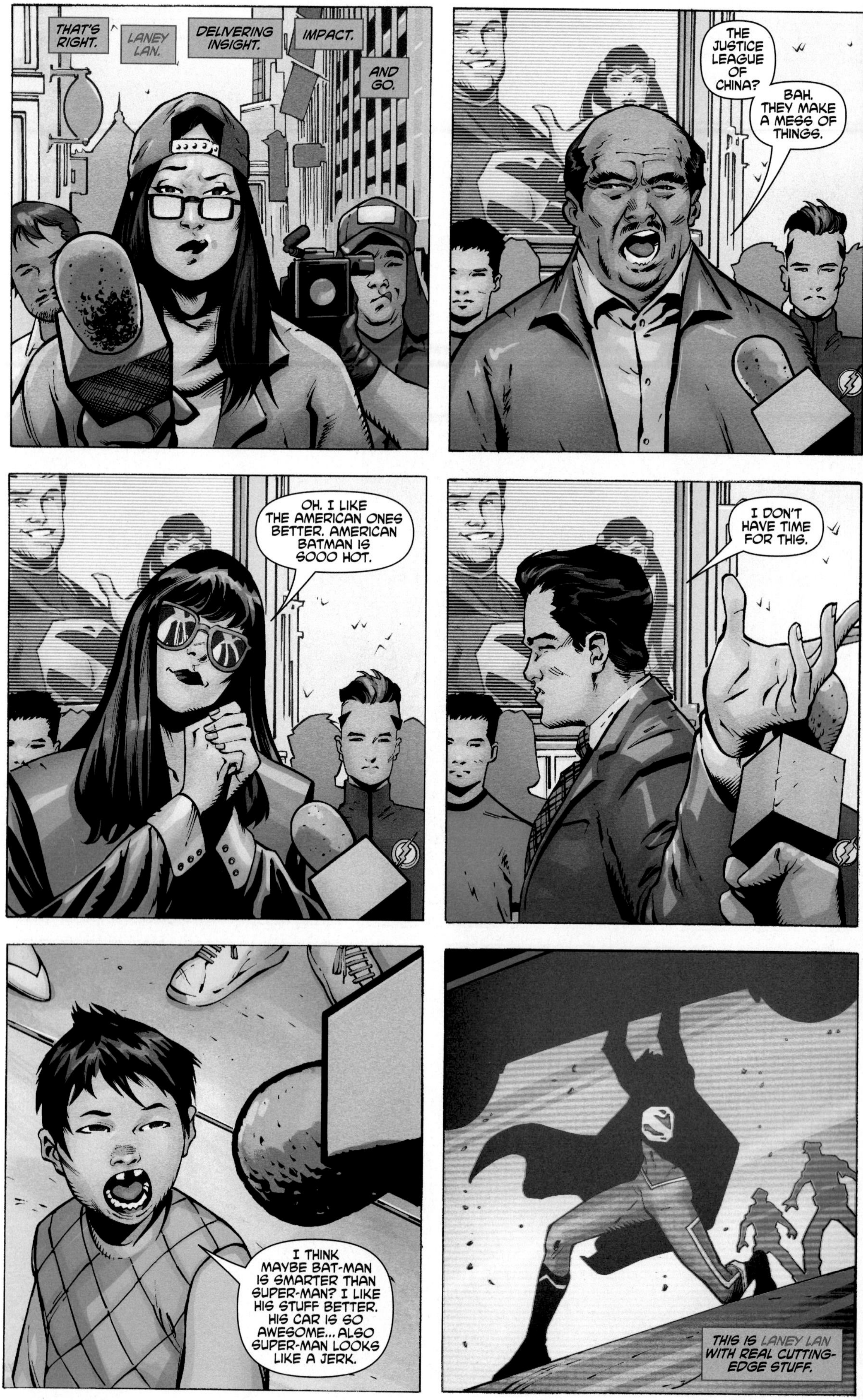
THAT'S RIGHT.
LANEY LAN.
DELIVERING INSIGHT.
IMPACT.
AND GO.
THE JUSTICE LEAGUE OF CHINA?
BAH. THEY MAKE A MESS OF THINGS.
OH. I LIKE THE AMERICAN ONES BETTER. AMERICAN BATMAN IS SOOO HOT.
I DON'T HAVE TIME FOR THIS.
I THINK MAYBE BAT-MAN IS SMARTER THAN SUPER-MAN? I LIKE HIS STUFF BETTER. HIS CAR IS SO AWESOME... ALSO SUPER-MAN LOOKS LIKE A JERK.
THIS IS LANEY LAN WITH REAL CUTTING-EDGE STUFF.

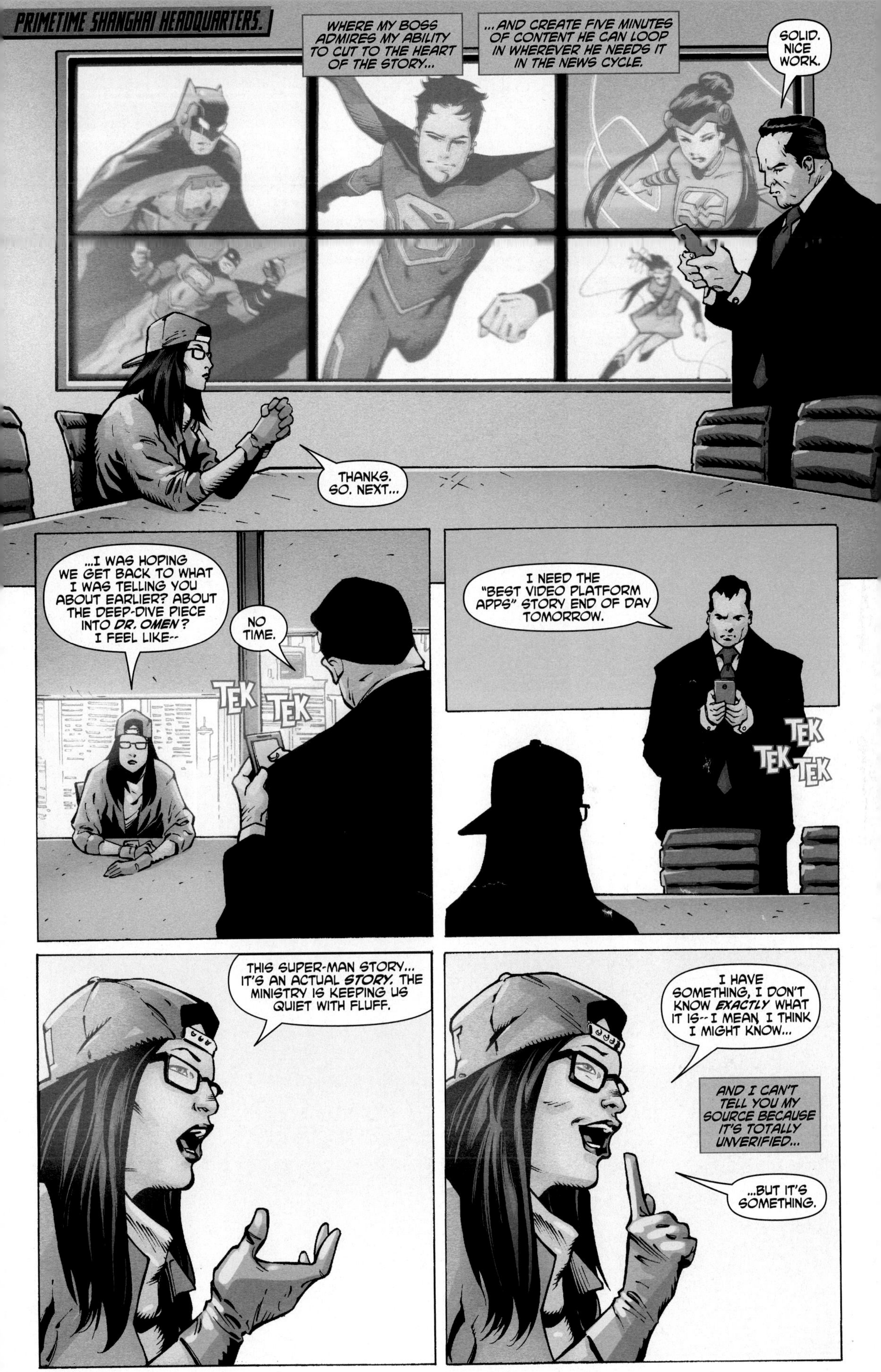
PRIMETIME SHANGHAI HEADQUARTERS.
WHERE MY BOSS ADMIRES MY ABILITY TO CUT TO THE HEART OF THE STORY...
...AND CREATE FIVE MINUTES OF CONTENT HE CAN LOOP IN WHEREVER HE NEEDS IT IN THE NEWS CYCLE.
SOLID. NICE WORK.
THANKS. SO. NEXT...
...I WAS HOPING WE GET BACK TO WHAT I WAS TELLING YOU ABOUT EARLIER? ABOUT THE DEEP-DIVE PIECE INTO DR. OMEN? I FEEL LIKE--
NO TIME.
TEK TEK
I NEED THE "BEST VIDEO PLATFORM APPS" STORY END OF DAY TOMORROW.
TEK TEK TEK
THIS SUPER-MAN STORY... IT'S AN ACTUAL STORY. THE MINISTRY IS KEEPING US QUIET WITH FLUFF.
I HAVE SOMETHING, I DON'T KNOW EXACTLY WHAT IT IS--I MEAN, I THINK I MIGHT KNOW...
AND I CAN'T TELL YOU MY SOURCE BECAUSE IT'S TOTALLY UNVERIFIED...
...BUT IT'S SOMETHING.

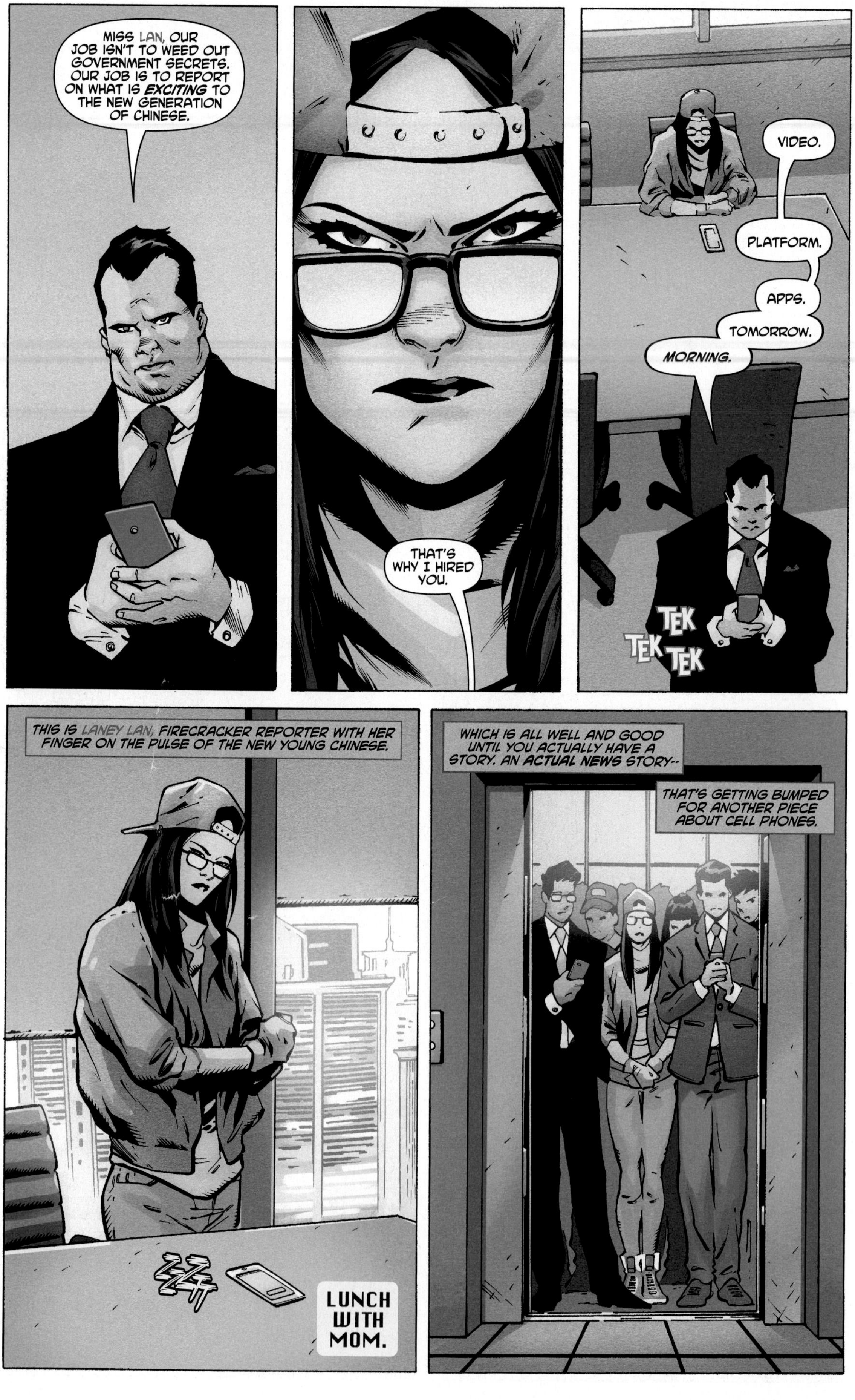
MISS LAN, OUR JOB ISN'T TO WEED OUT GOVERNMENT SECRETS. OUR JOB IS TO REPORT ON WHAT IS EXCITING TO THE NEW GENERATION OF CHINESE.
THAT'S WHY I HIRED YOU.
VIDEO.
PLATFORM.
APPS.
TOMORROW.
MORNING.
TEK
TEK
TEK
THIS IS LANEY LAN, FIRECRACKER REPORTER WITH HER FINGER ON THE PULSE OF THE NEW YOUNG CHINESE.
LUNCH WITH MOM.
WHICH IS ALL WELL AND GOOD UNTIL YOU ACTUALLY HAVE A STORY. AN ACTUAL NEWS STORY--
THAT'S GETTING BUMPED FOR ANOTHER PIECE ABOUT CELL PHONES.

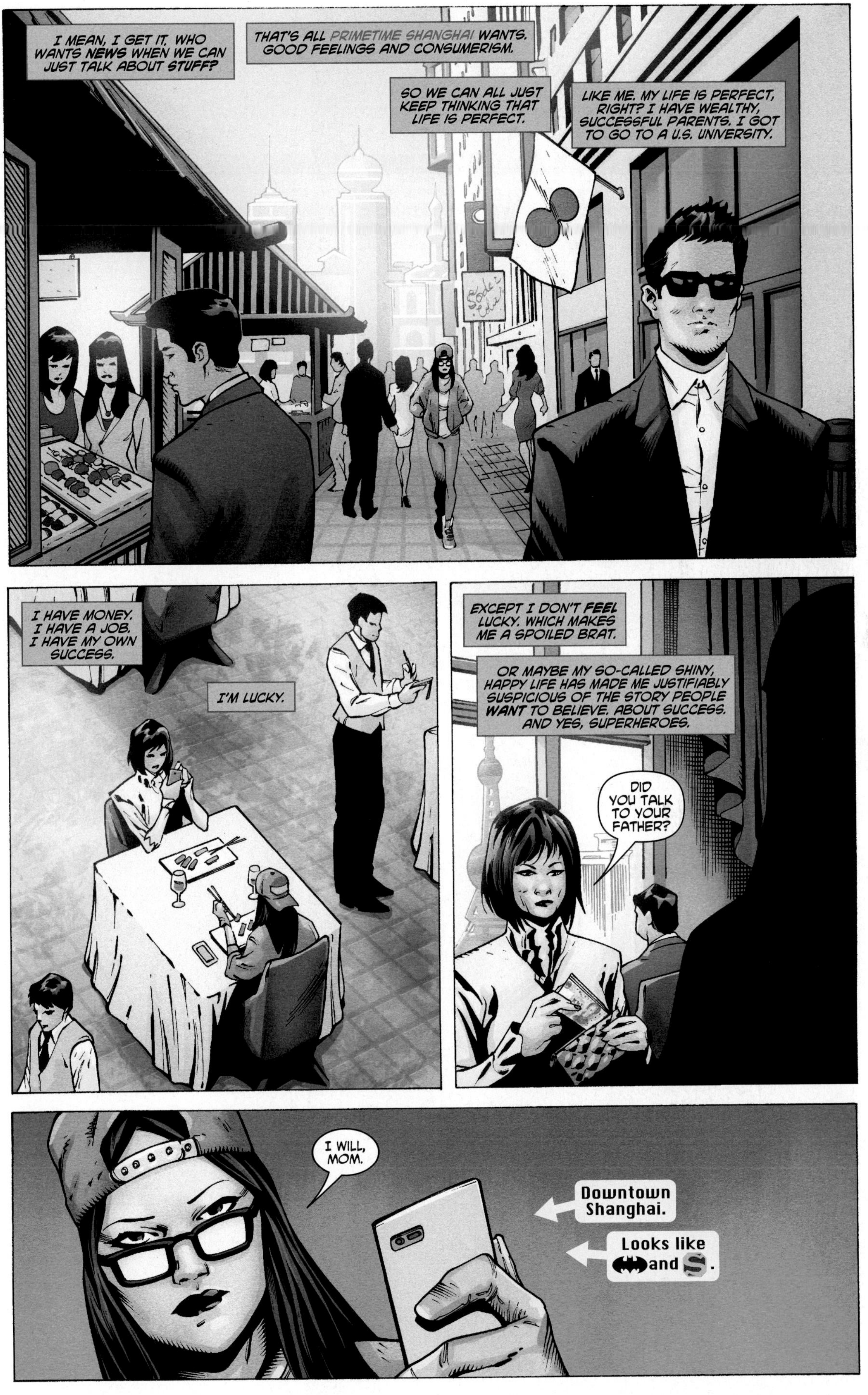

I MEAN, I GET IT. WHO WANTS NEWS WHEN WE CAN JUST TALK ABOUT STUFF?
THAT'S ALL PRIMETIME SHANGHAI WANTS. GOOD FEELINGS AND CONSUMERISM.
SO WE CAN ALL JUST KEEP THINKING THAT LIFE IS PERFECT.
LIKE ME. MY LIFE IS PERFECT, RIGHT? I HAVE WEALTHY, SUCCESSFUL PARENTS. I GOT TO GO TO A U.S. UNIVERSITY.
I HAVE MONEY. I HAVE A JOB. I HAVE MY OWN SUCCESS.
I'M LUCKY.
EXCEPT I DON'T FEEL LUCKY. WHICH MAKES ME A SPOILED BRAT.
OR MAYBE MY SO-CALLED SHINY, HAPPY LIFE HAS MADE ME JUSTIFIABLY SUSPICIOUS OF THE STORY PEOPLE WANT TO BELIEVE. ABOUT SUCCESS. AND YES, SUPERHEROES.
DID YOU TALK TO YOUR FATHER?
I WILL, MOM.
Downtown Shanghai.
Looks like and .

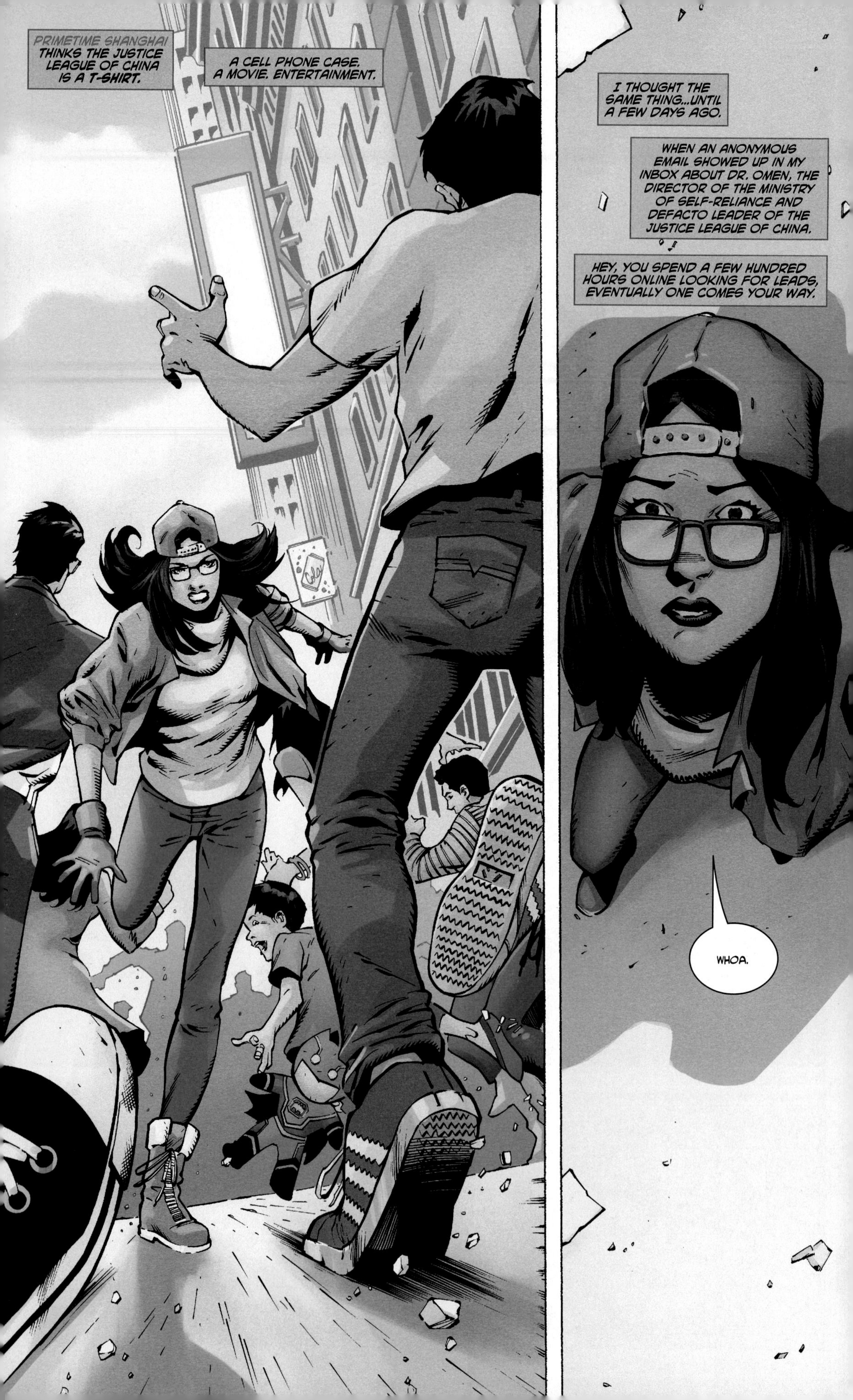
PRIMETIME SHANGHAI THINKS THE JUSTICE LEAGUE OF CHINA IS A T-SHIRT.
A CELL PHONE CASE. A MOVIE. ENTERTAINMENT.
I THOUGHT THE SAME THING...UNTIL A FEW DAYS AGO.
WHEN AN ANONYMOUS EMAIL SHOWED UP IN MY INBOX ABOUT DR. OMEN, THE DIRECTOR OF THE MINISTRY OF SELF-RELIANCE AND DEFACTO LEADER OF THE JUSTICE LEAGUE OF CHINA.
HEY, YOU SPEND A FEW HUNDRED HOURS ONLINE LOOKING FOR LEADS, EVENTUALLY ONE COMES YOUR WAY.
WHOA.

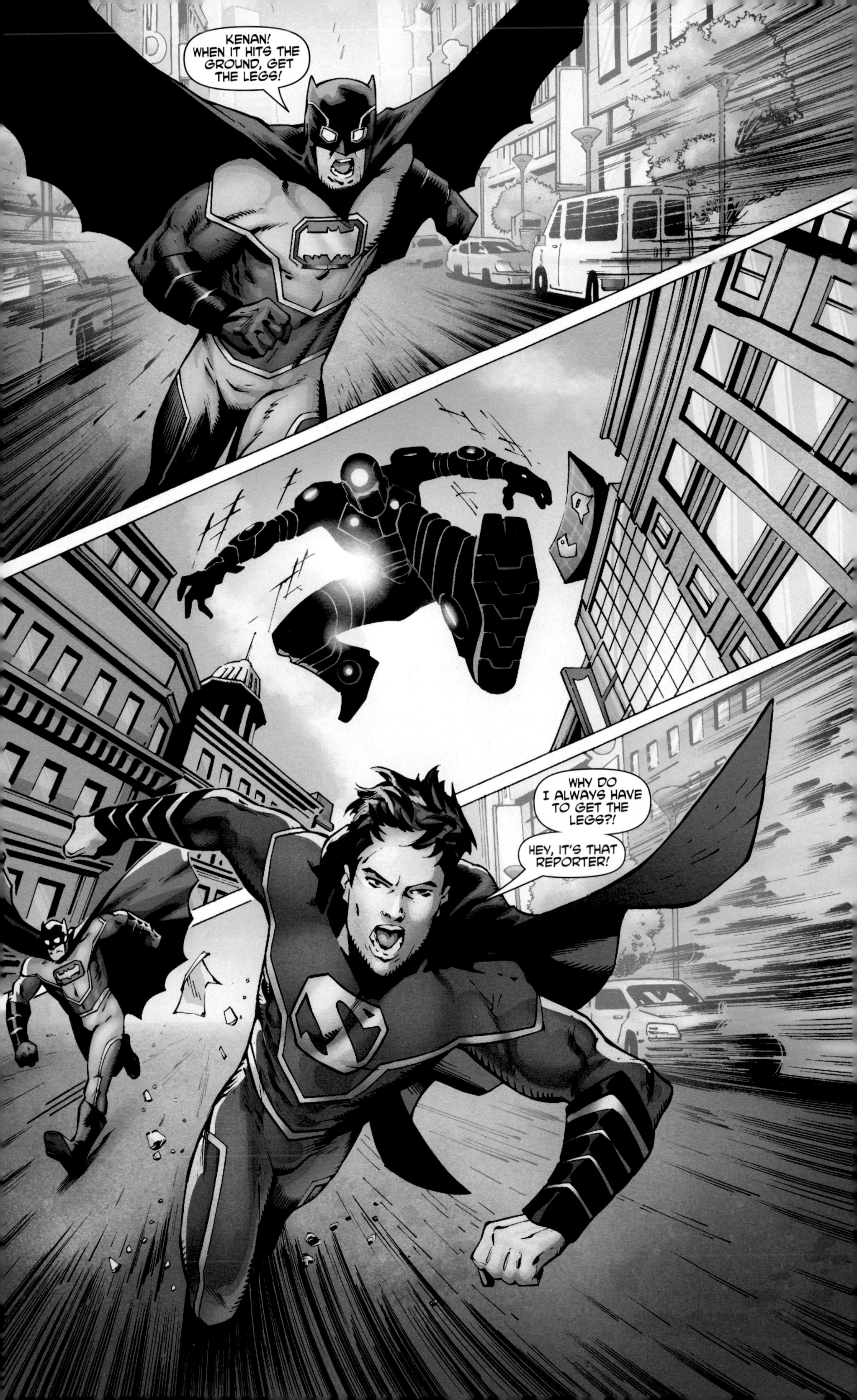
KENAN! WHEN IT HITS THE GROUND, GET THE LEGS!
WHY DO I ALWAYS HAVE TO GET THE LEGS?!
HEY, IT'S THAT REPORTER!

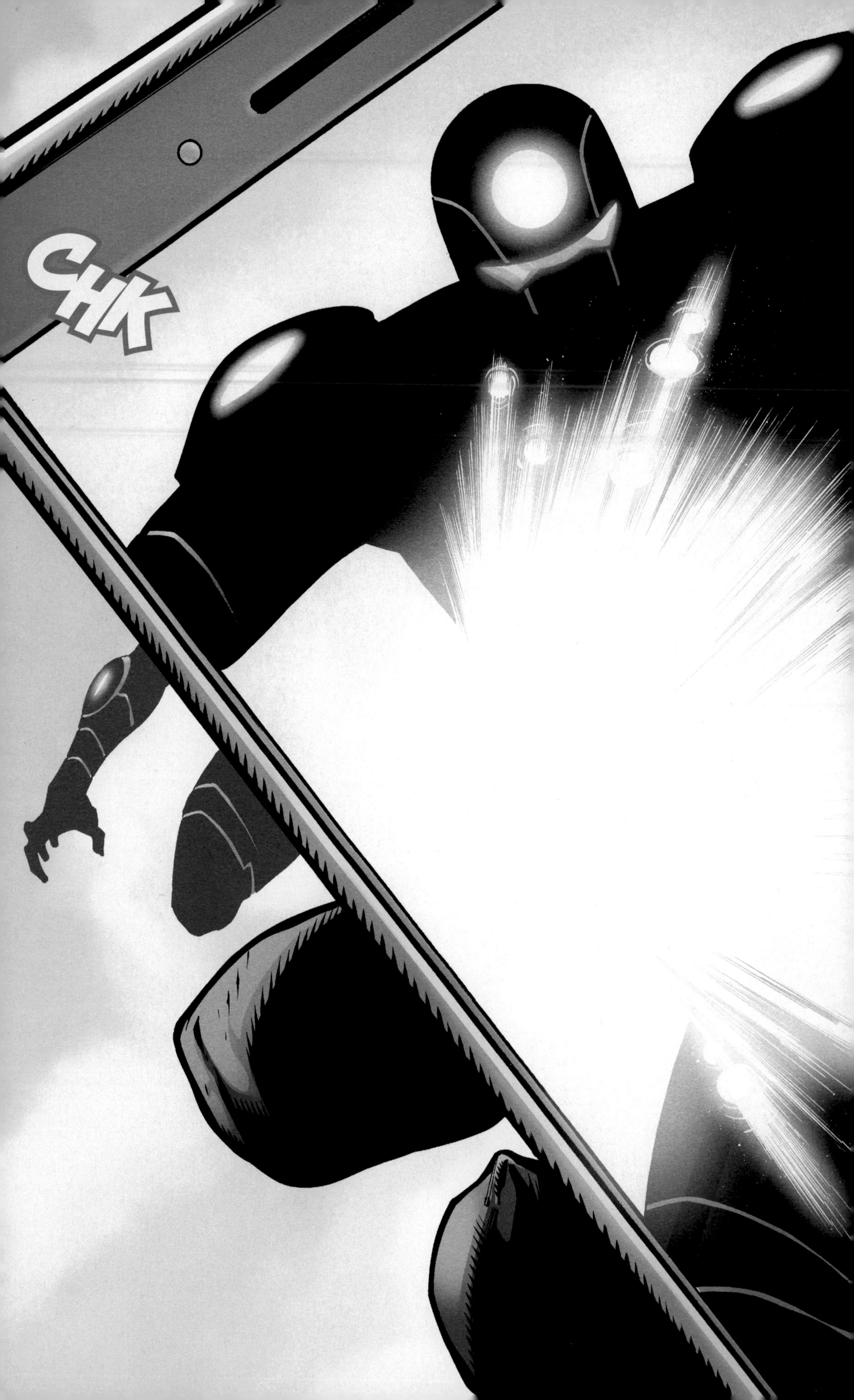
CHK

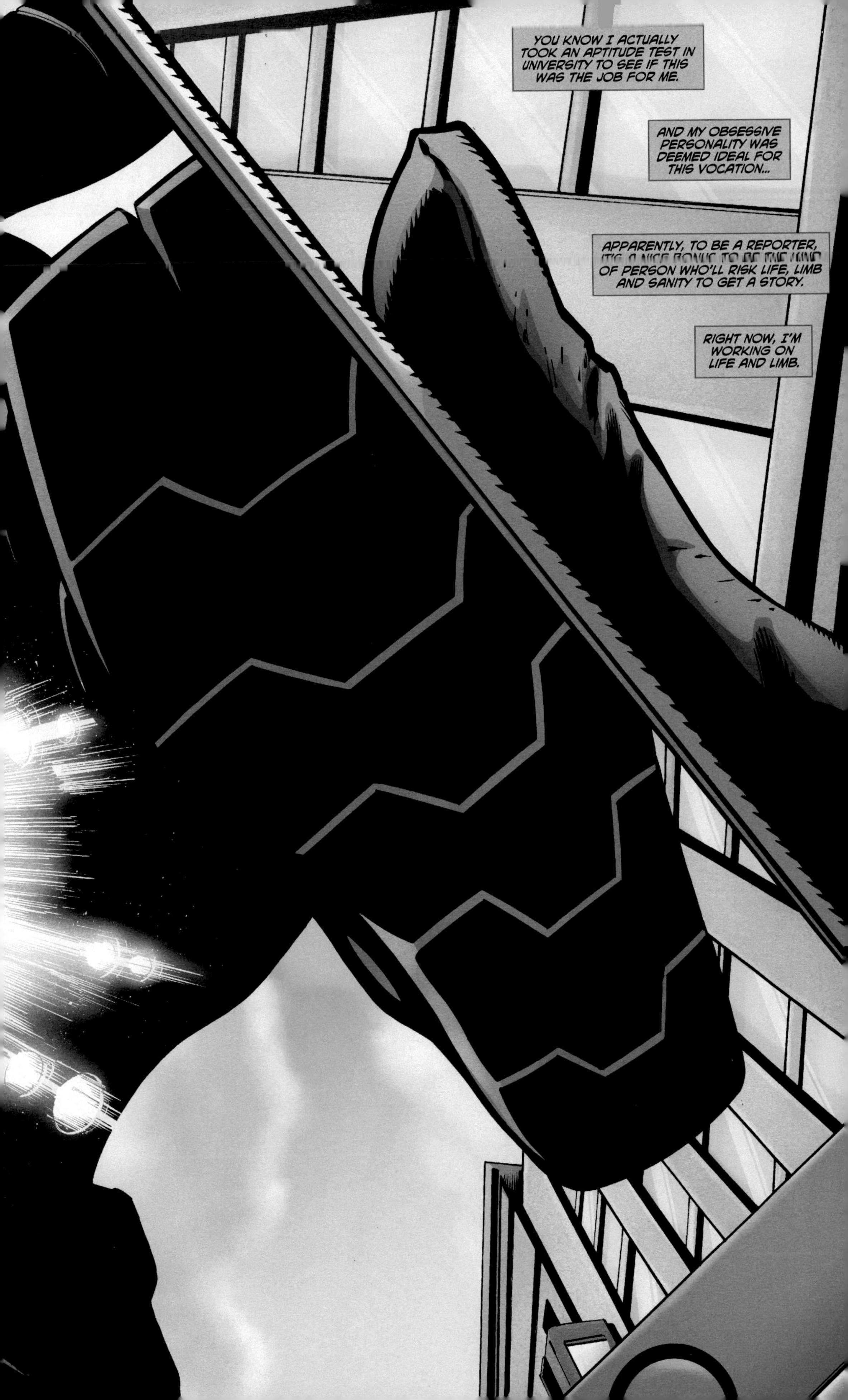
YOU KNOW I ACTUALLY TOOK AN APTITUDE TEST IN UNIVERSITY TO SEE IF THIS WAS THE JOB FOR ME.
AND MY OBSESSIVE PERSONALITY WAS DEEMED IDEAL FOR THIS VOCATION...
APPARENTLY, TO BE A REPORTER, IT'S A NICE BONUS TO BE THE KIND OF PERSON WHO'LL RISK LIFE, LIMB AND SANITY TO GET A STORY.
RIGHT NOW, I'M WORKING ON LIFE AND LIMB.

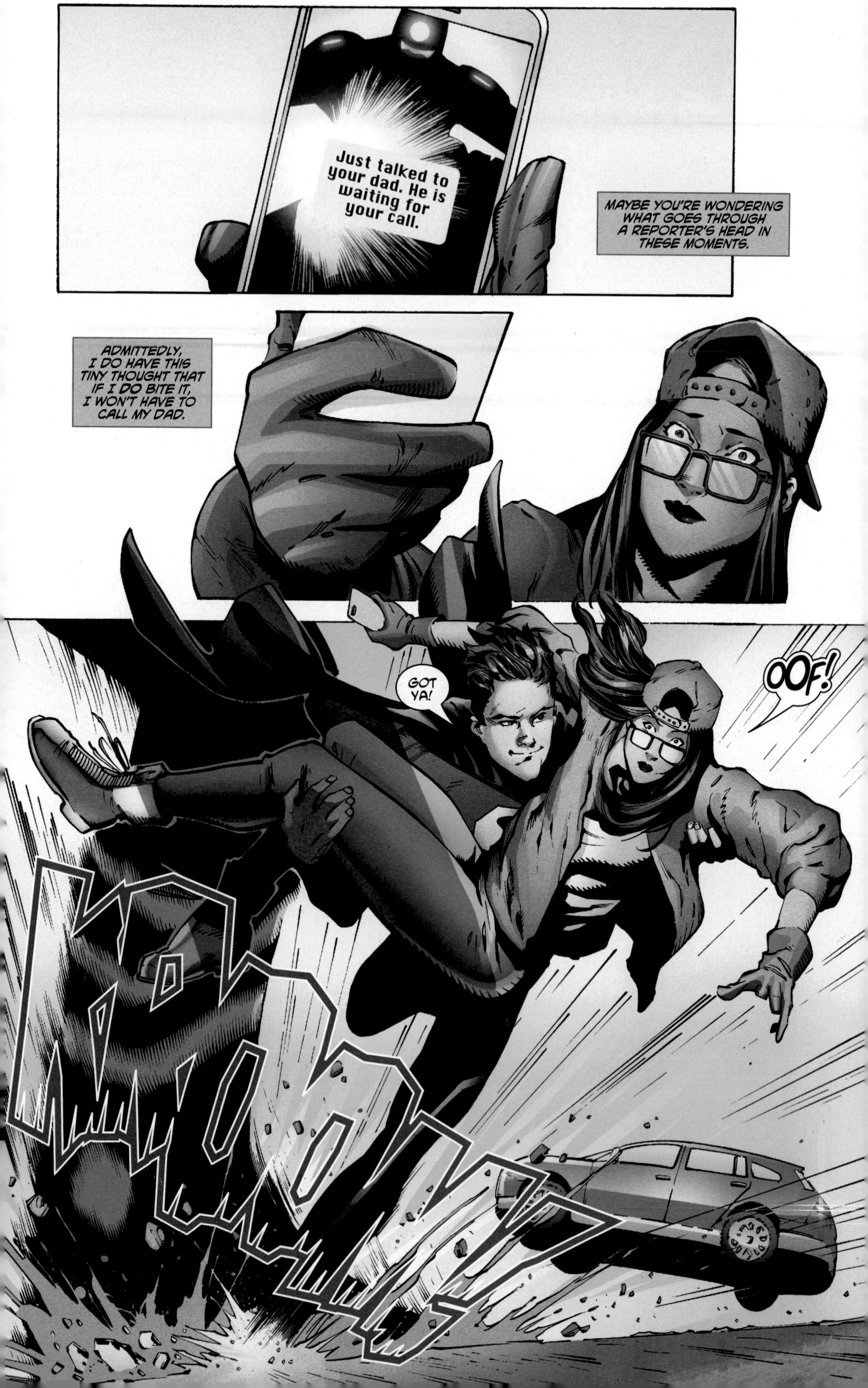
Just talked to your dad. He is waiting for your call.
MAYBE YOU'RE WONDERING WHAT GOES THROUGH A REPORTER'S HEAD IN THESE MOMENTS.
ADMITTEDLY, I DO HAVE THIS TINY THOUGHT THAT IF I DO BITE IT, I WON'T HAVE TO CALL MY DAD.
GOT YA!
OOF!

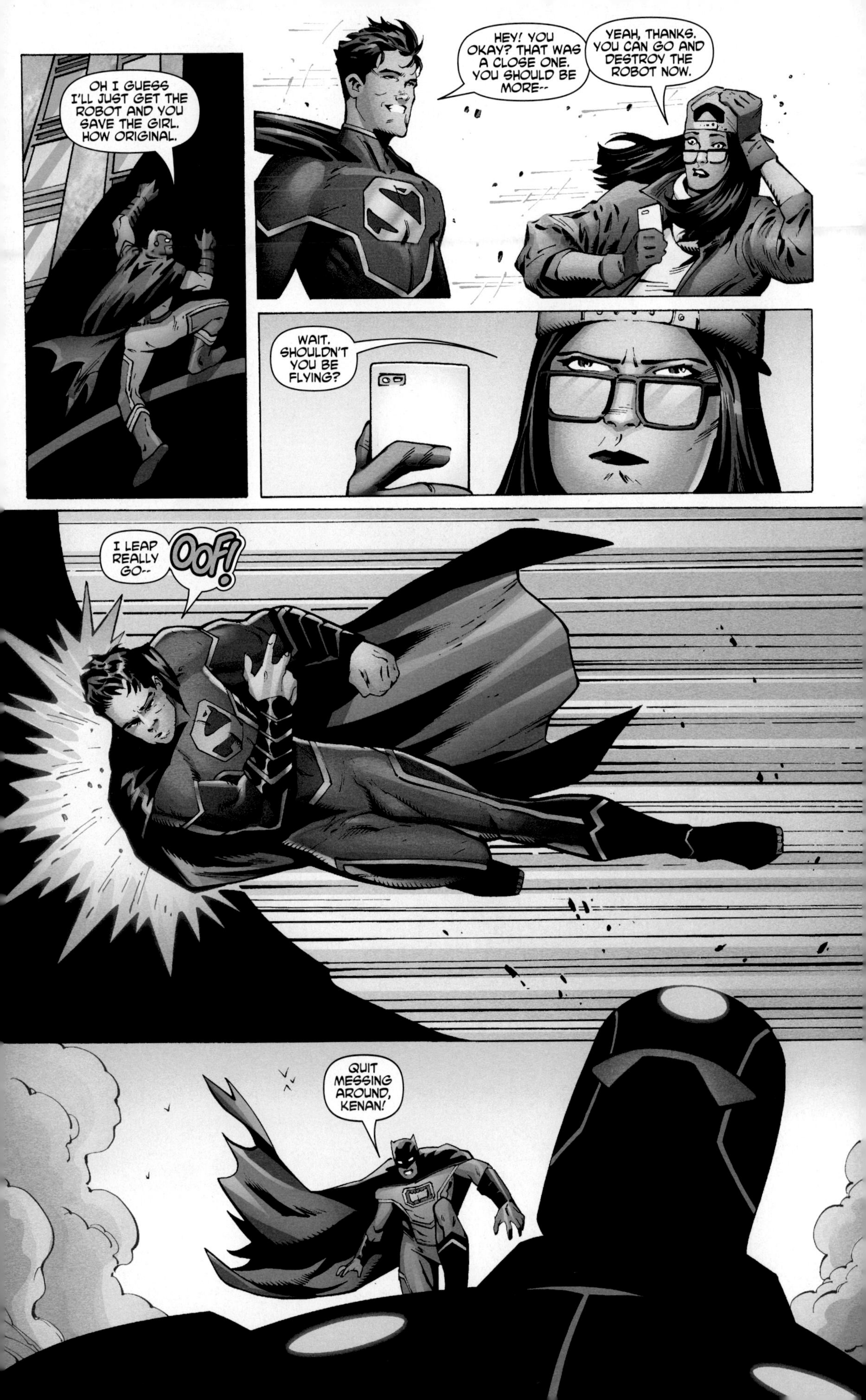
OH I GUESS I'LL JUST GET THE ROBOT AND YOU SAVE THE GIRL. HOW ORIGINAL.
HEY! YOU OKAY? THAT WAS A CLOSE ONE. YOU SHOULD BE MORE--
YEAH, THANKS. YOU CAN GO AND DESTROY THE ROBOT NOW.
WAIT. SHOULDN'T YOU BE FLYING?
I LEAP REALLY GO--
OOF!
QUIT MESSING AROUND, KENAN!

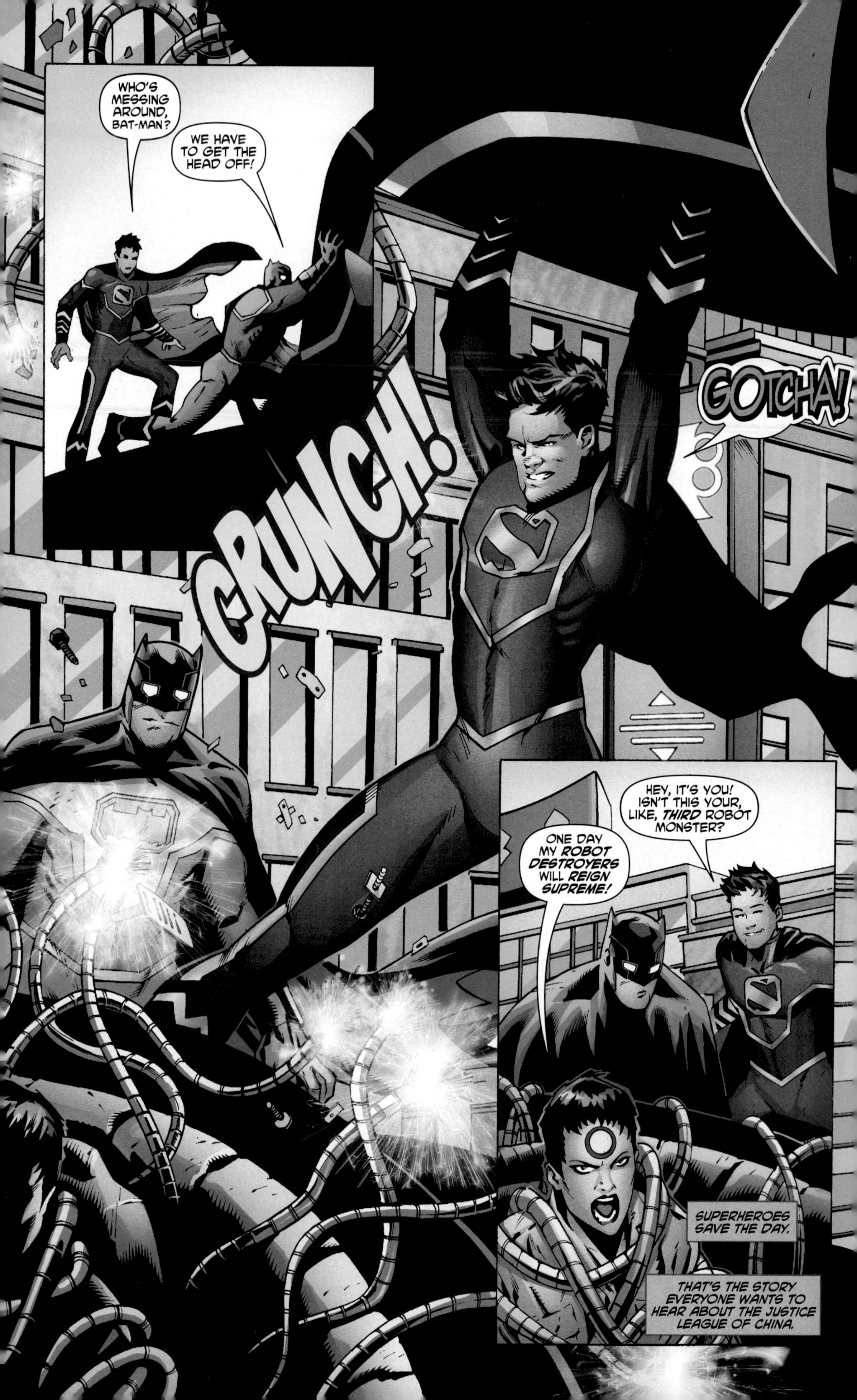
WHO'S MESSING AROUND, BAT-MAN?
WE HAVE TO GET THE HEAD OFF!
CRUNCH!
GOTCHA!
HEY, IT'S YOU! ISN'T THIS YOUR, LIKE, THIRD ROBOT MONSTER?
ONE DAY MY ROBOT DESTROYERS WILL REIGN SUPREME!
SUPERHEROES SAVE THE DAY.
THAT'S THE STORY EVERYONE WANTS TO HEAR ABOUT THE JUSTICE LEAGUE OF CHINA.

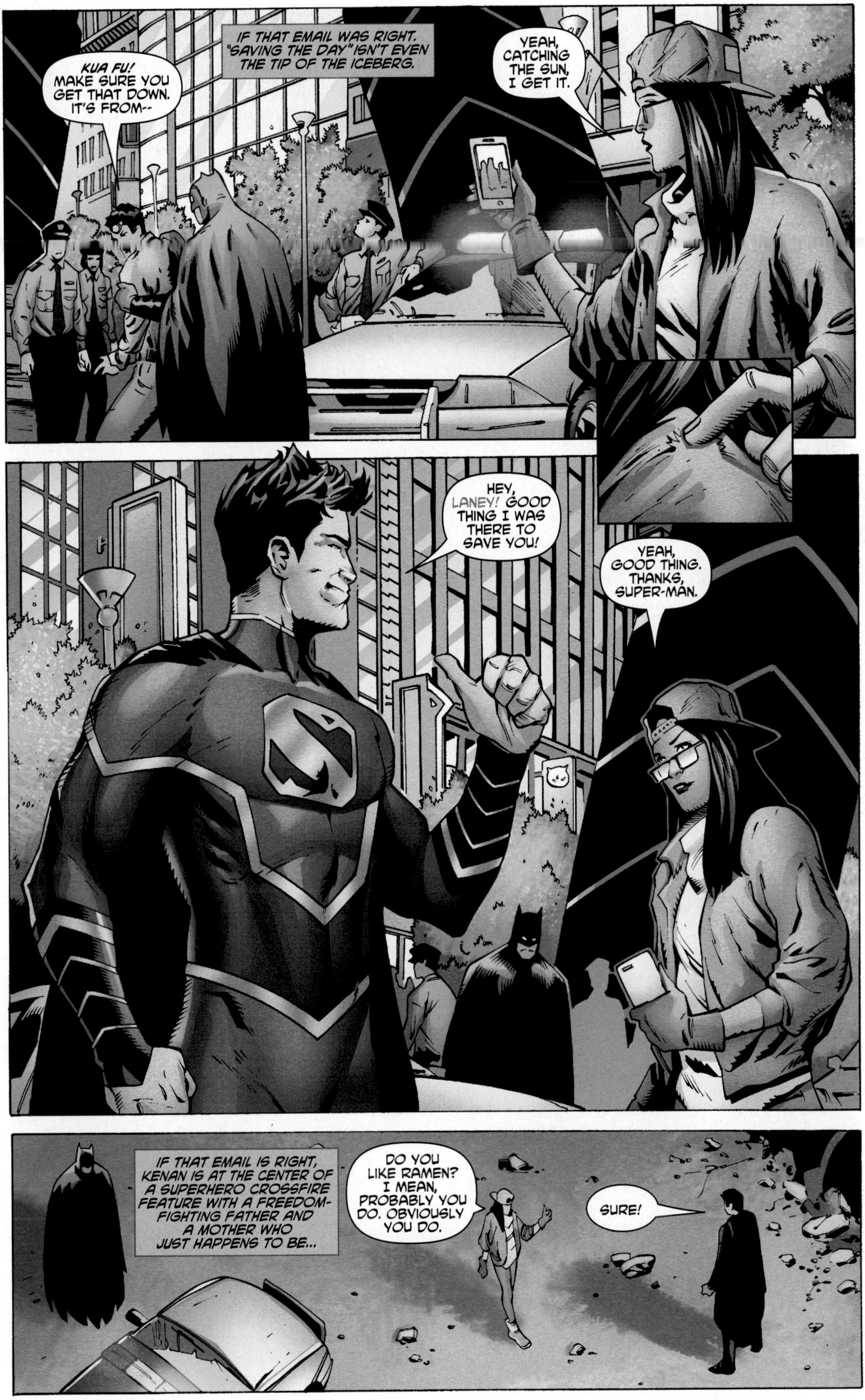

KUA FU! MAKE SURE YOU GET THAT DOWN. IT'S FROM--
IF THAT EMAIL WAS RIGHT. "SAVING THE DAY" ISN'T EVEN THE TIP OF THE ICEBERG.
YEAH, CATCHING THE SUN, I GET IT.
HEY, LANEY! GOOD THING I WAS THERE TO SAVE YOU!
YEAH, GOOD THING. THANKS, SUPER-MAN.
IF THAT EMAIL IS RIGHT, KENAN IS AT THE CENTER OF A SUPERHERO CROSSFIRE FEATURE WITH A FREEDOM-FIGHTING FATHER AND A MOTHER WHO JUST HAPPENS TO BE...
DO YOU LIKE RAMEN? I MEAN, PROBABLY YOU DO. OBVIOUSLY YOU DO.
SURE!

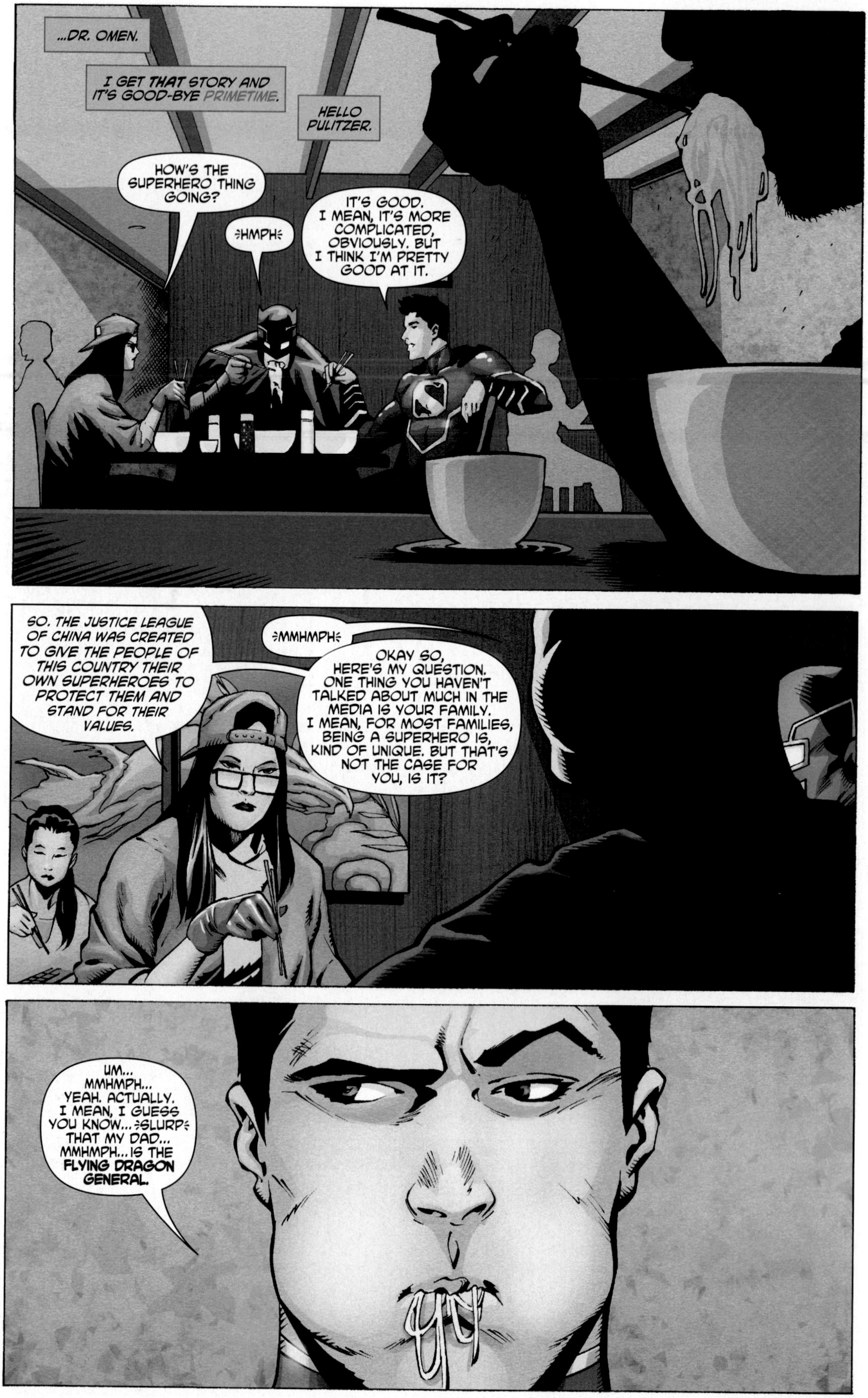
...DR. OMEN.
I GET THAT STORY AND IT'S GOOD-BYE PRIMETIME.
HELLO PULITZER.
HOW'S THE SUPERHERO THING GOING?
HMPH
IT'S GOOD. I MEAN, IT'S MORE COMPLICATED, OBVIOUSLY. BUT I THINK I'M PRETTY GOOD AT IT.
SO. THE JUSTICE LEAGUE OF CHINA WAS CREATED TO GIVE THE PEOPLE OF THIS COUNTRY THEIR OWN SUPERHEROES TO PROTECT THEM AND STAND FOR THEIR VALUES.
MMHMPH
OKAY SO, HERE'S MY QUESTION. ONE THING YOU HAVEN'T TALKED ABOUT MUCH IN THE MEDIA IS YOUR FAMILY. I MEAN, FOR MOST FAMILIES, BEING A SUPERHERO IS, KIND OF UNIQUE. BUT THAT'S NOT THE CASE FOR YOU, IS IT?
UM... MMHMPH... YEAH. ACTUALLY. I MEAN, I GUESS YOU KNOW... SLURP THAT MY DAD... MMHMPH... IS THE FLYING DRAGON GENERAL.

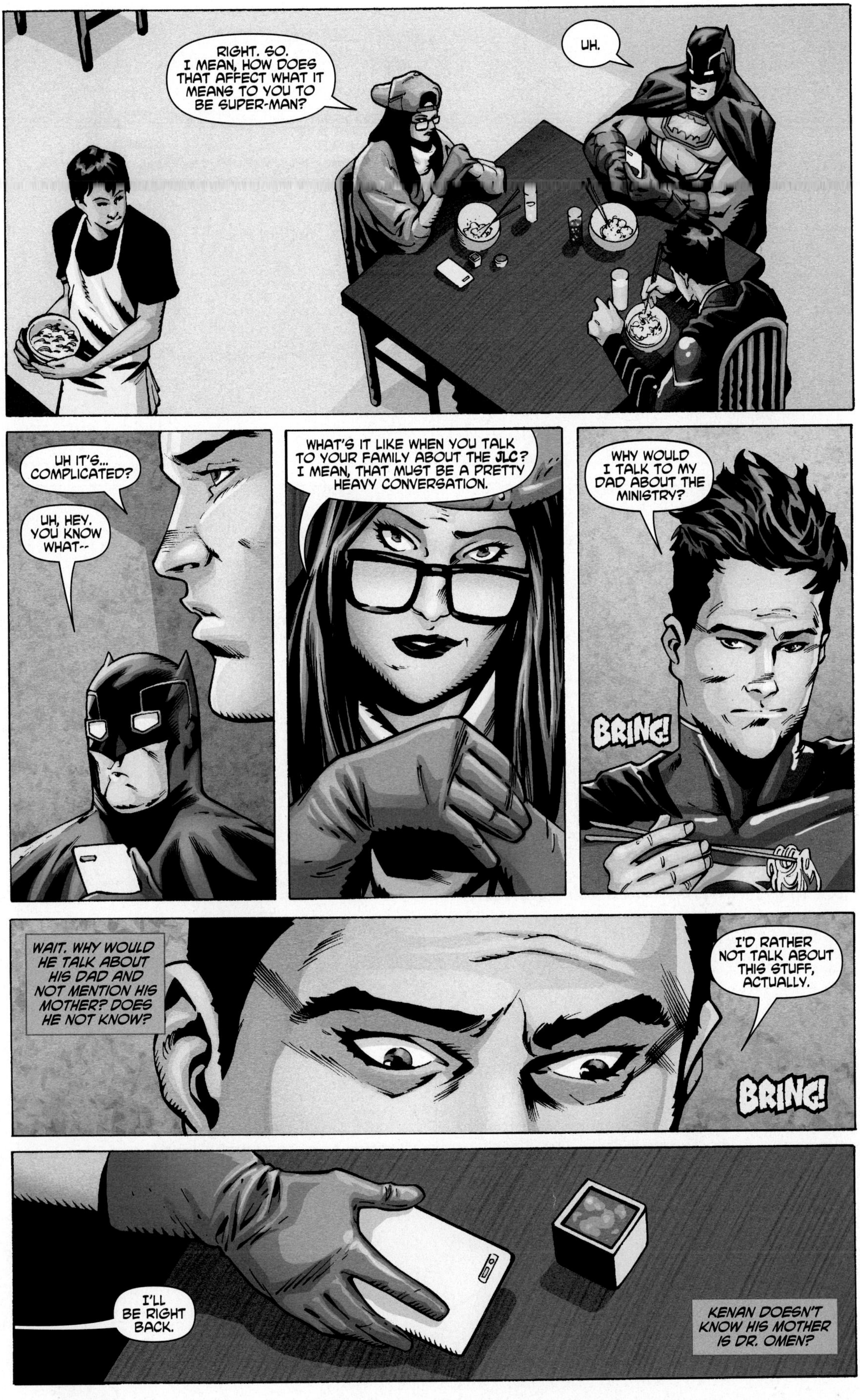
RIGHT. SO. I MEAN, HOW DOES THAT AFFECT WHAT IT MEANS TO YOU TO BE SUPER-MAN?
UH.
UH IT'S... COMPLICATED?
UH, HEY. YOU KNOW WHAT--
WHAT'S IT LIKE WHEN YOU TALK TO YOUR FAMILY ABOUT THE JLC? I MEAN, THAT MUST BE A PRETTY HEAVY CONVERSATION.
WHY WOULD I TALK TO MY DAD ABOUT THE MINISTRY?
BRING!
WAIT. WHY WOULD HE TALK ABOUT HIS DAD AND NOT MENTION HIS MOTHER? DOES HE NOT KNOW?
I'D RATHER NOT TALK ABOUT THIS STUFF, ACTUALLY.
BRING!
I'LL BE RIGHT BACK.
KENAN DOESN'T KNOW HIS MOTHER IS DR. OMEN?

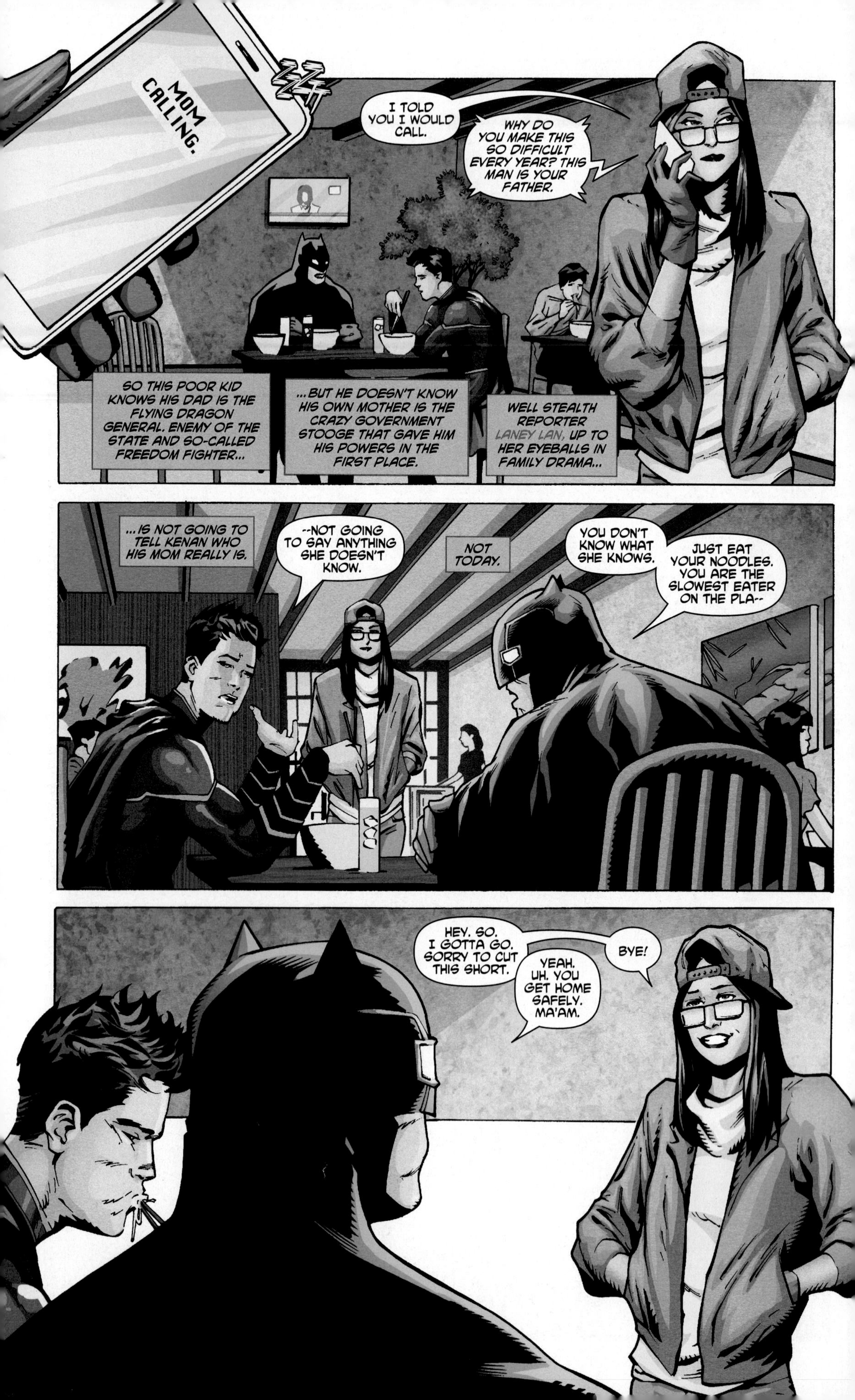
MOM CALLING.
I TOLD YOU I WOULD CALL.
WHY DO YOU MAKE THIS SO DIFFICULT EVERY YEAR? THIS MAN IS YOUR FATHER.
SO THIS POOR KID KNOWS HIS DAD IS THE FLYING DRAGON GENERAL. ENEMY OF THE STATE AND SO-CALLED FREEDOM FIGHTER...
...BUT HE DOESN'T KNOW HIS OWN MOTHER IS THE CRAZY GOVERNMENT STOOGE THAT GAVE HIM HIS POWERS IN THE FIRST PLACE.
WELL STEALTH REPORTER LANEY LAN, UP TO HER EYEBALLS IN FAMILY DRAMA...
...IS NOT GOING TO TELL KENAN WHO HIS MOM REALLY IS.
--NOT GOING TO SAY ANYTHING SHE DOESN'T KNOW.
NOT TODAY.
YOU DON'T KNOW WHAT SHE KNOWS.
JUST EAT YOUR NOODLES. YOU ARE THE SLOWEST EATER ON THE PLA--
HEY. SO. I GOTTA GO. SORRY TO CUT THIS SHORT.
BYE!
YEAH. UH. YOU GET HOME SAFELY. MA'AM.

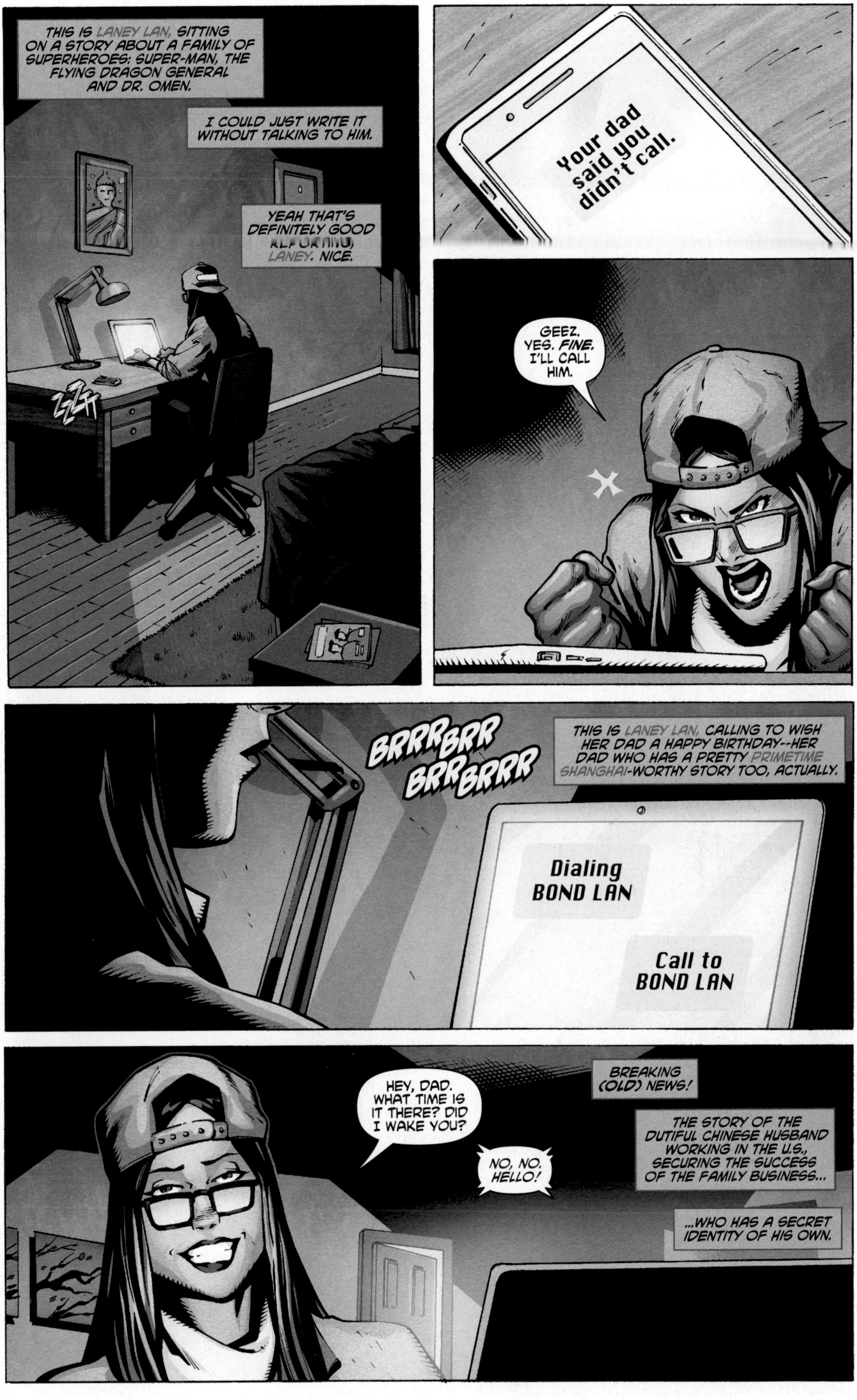
THIS IS LANEY LAN, SITTING ON A STORY ABOUT A FAMILY OF SUPERHEROES: SUPER-MAN, THE FLYING DRAGON GENERAL AND DR. OMEN.
I COULD JUST WRITE IT WITHOUT TALKING TO HIM.
YEAH THAT'S DEFINITELY GOOD
LANEY. NICE.
ZZZT
Your dad said you didn't call.
GEEZ. YES. FINE. I'LL CALL HIM.
BRRRBRR BRRBRRR
THIS IS LANEY LAN, CALLING TO WISH HER DAD A HAPPY BIRTHDAY--HER DAD WHO HAS A PRETTY PRIMETIME SHANGHAI-WORTHY STORY TOO, ACTUALLY.
Dialing BOND LAN
Call to BOND LAN
HEY, DAD. WHAT TIME IS IT THERE? DID I WAKE YOU?
NO, NO. HELLO!
BREAKING (OLD) NEWS!
THE STORY OF THE DUTIFUL CHINESE HUSBAND WORKING IN THE U.S., SECURING THE SUCCESS OF THE FAMILY BUSINESS...
...WHO HAS A SECRET IDENTITY OF HIS OWN.

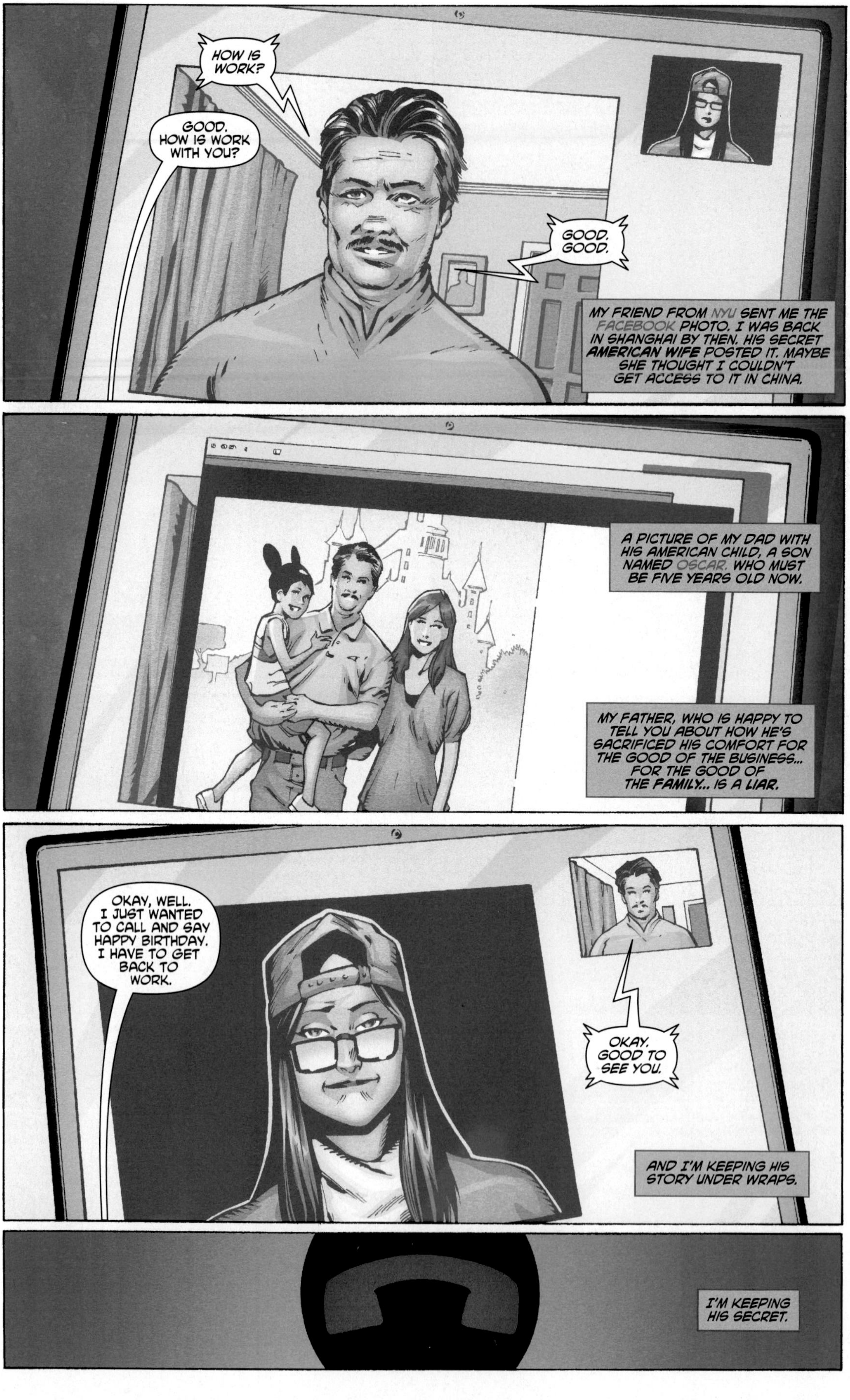
HOW IS WORK?
GOOD. HOW IS WORK WITH YOU?
GOOD. GOOD.
MY FRIEND FROM NYU SENT ME THE FACEBOOK PHOTO. I WAS BACK IN SHANGHAI BY THEN. HIS SECRET AMERICAN WIFE POSTED IT. MAYBE SHE THOUGHT I COULDN'T GET ACCESS TO IT IN CHINA.
A PICTURE OF MY DAD WITH HIS AMERICAN CHILD, A SON NAMED OSCAR, WHO MUST BE FIVE YEARS OLD NOW.
MY FATHER, WHO IS HAPPY TO TELL YOU ABOUT HOW HE'S SACRIFICED HIS COMFORT FOR THE GOOD OF THE BUSINESS... FOR THE GOOD OF THE FAMILY... IS A LIAR.
OKAY, WELL. I JUST WANTED TO CALL AND SAY HAPPY BIRTHDAY. I HAVE TO GET BACK TO WORK.
OKAY. GOOD TO SEE YOU.
AND I'M KEEPING HIS STORY UNDER WRAPS.
I'M KEEPING HIS SECRET.

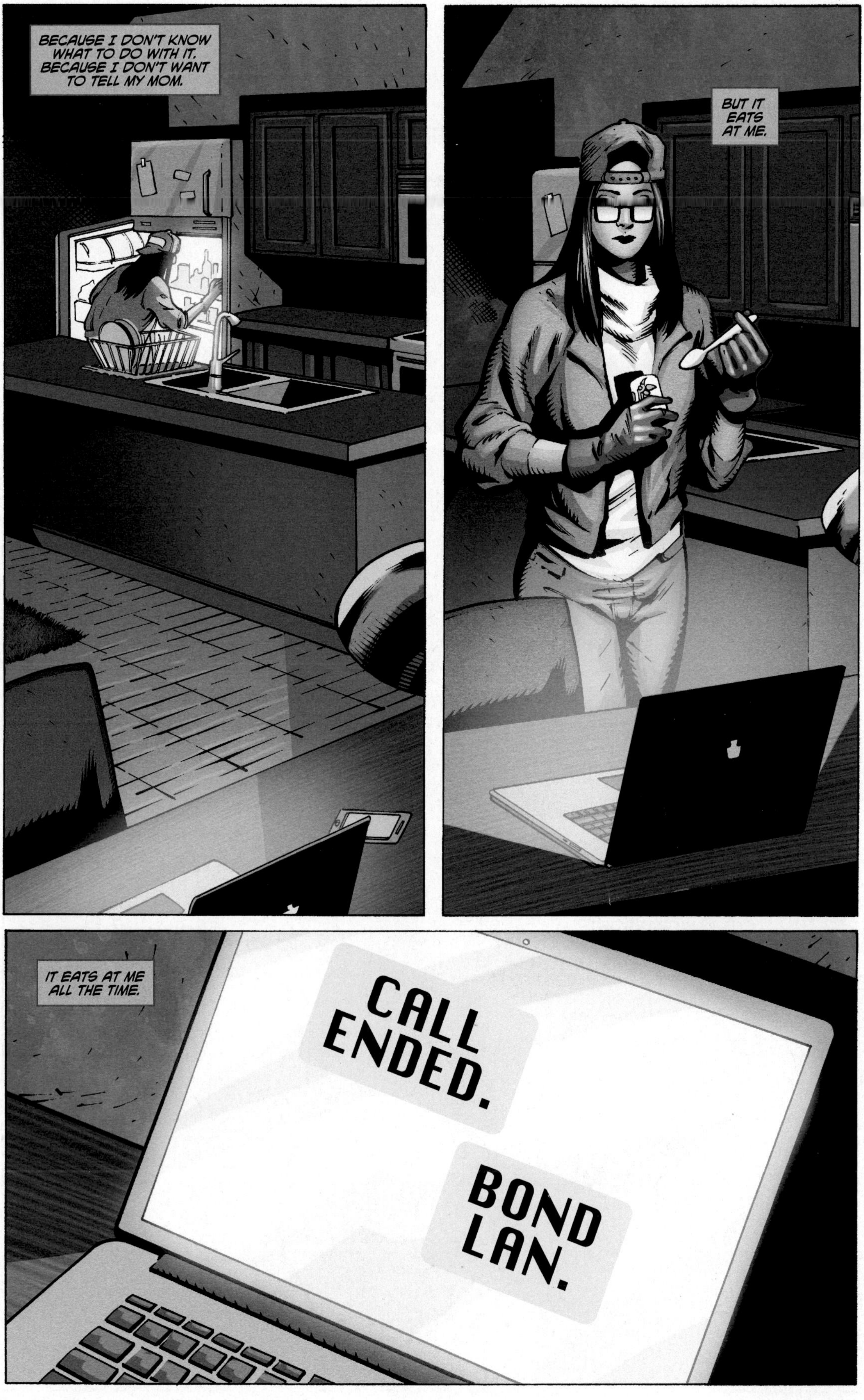
BECAUSE I DON'T KNOW WHAT TO DO WITH IT. BECAUSE I DON'T WANT TO TELL MY MOM.
BUT IT EATS AT ME.
IT EATS AT ME ALL THE TIME.
CALL ENDED.
BOND LAN.

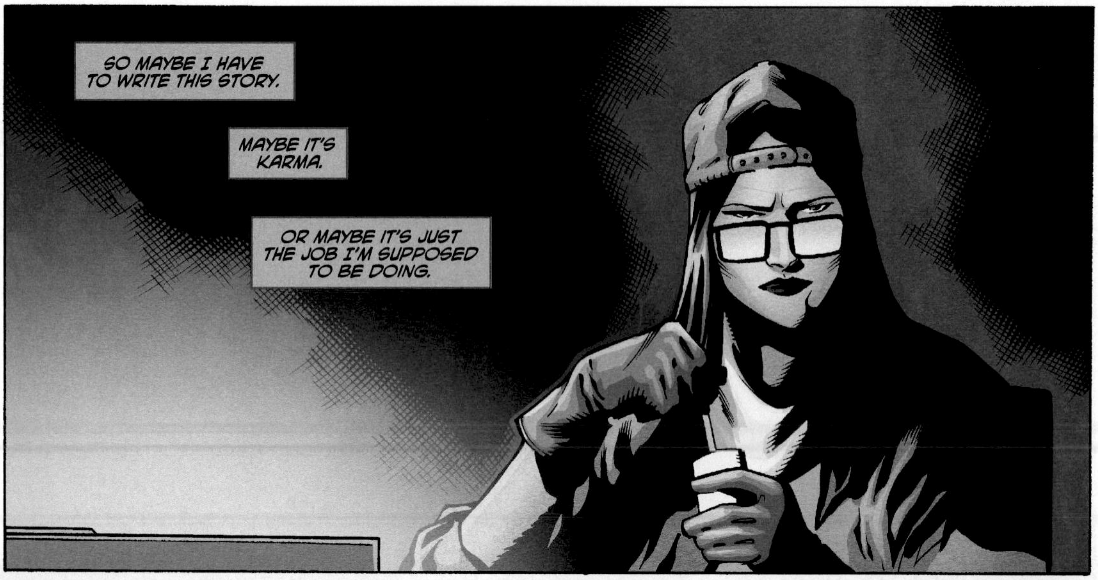
SO MAYBE I HAVE TO WRITE THIS STORY.
MAYBE IT'S KARMA.
OR MAYBE IT'S JUST THE JOB I'M SUPPOSED TO BE DOING.

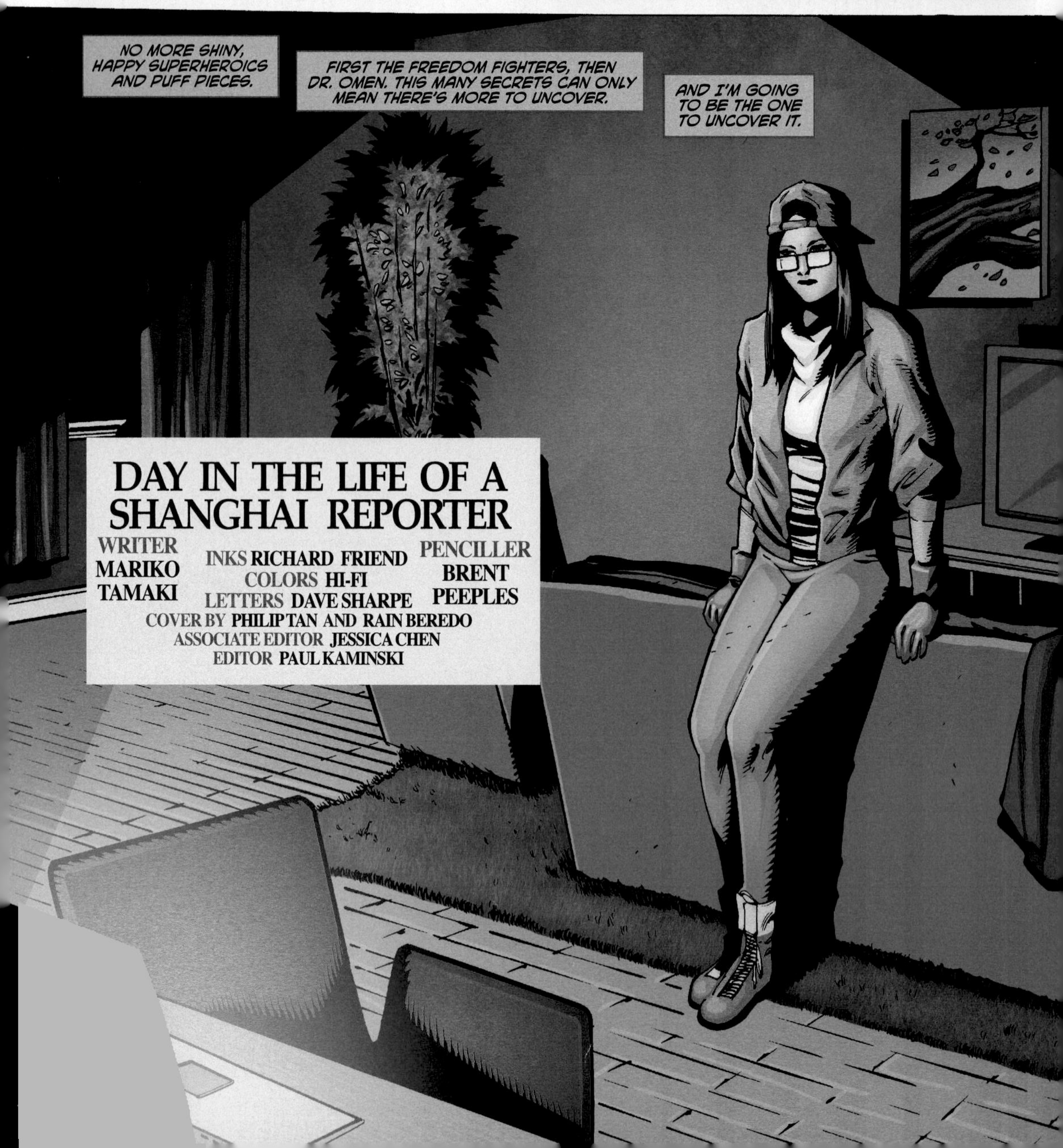
NO MORE SHINY, HAPPY SUPERHEROICS AND PUFF PIECES.
FIRST THE FREEDOM FIGHTERS, THEN DR. OMEN. THIS MANY SECRETS CAN ONLY MEAN THERE'S MORE TO UNCOVER.
AND I'M GOING TO BE THE ONE TO UNCOVER IT.
DAY IN THE LIFE OF A SHANGHAI REPORTER
WRITER MARIKO TAMAKI
INKS RICHARD FRIEND
COLORS HI-FI
LETTERS DAVE SHARPE
PENCILLER BRENT PEEPLES
COVER BY PHILIP TAN AND RAIN BEREDO
ASSOCIATE EDITOR JESSICA CHEN
EDITOR PAUL KAMINSKI

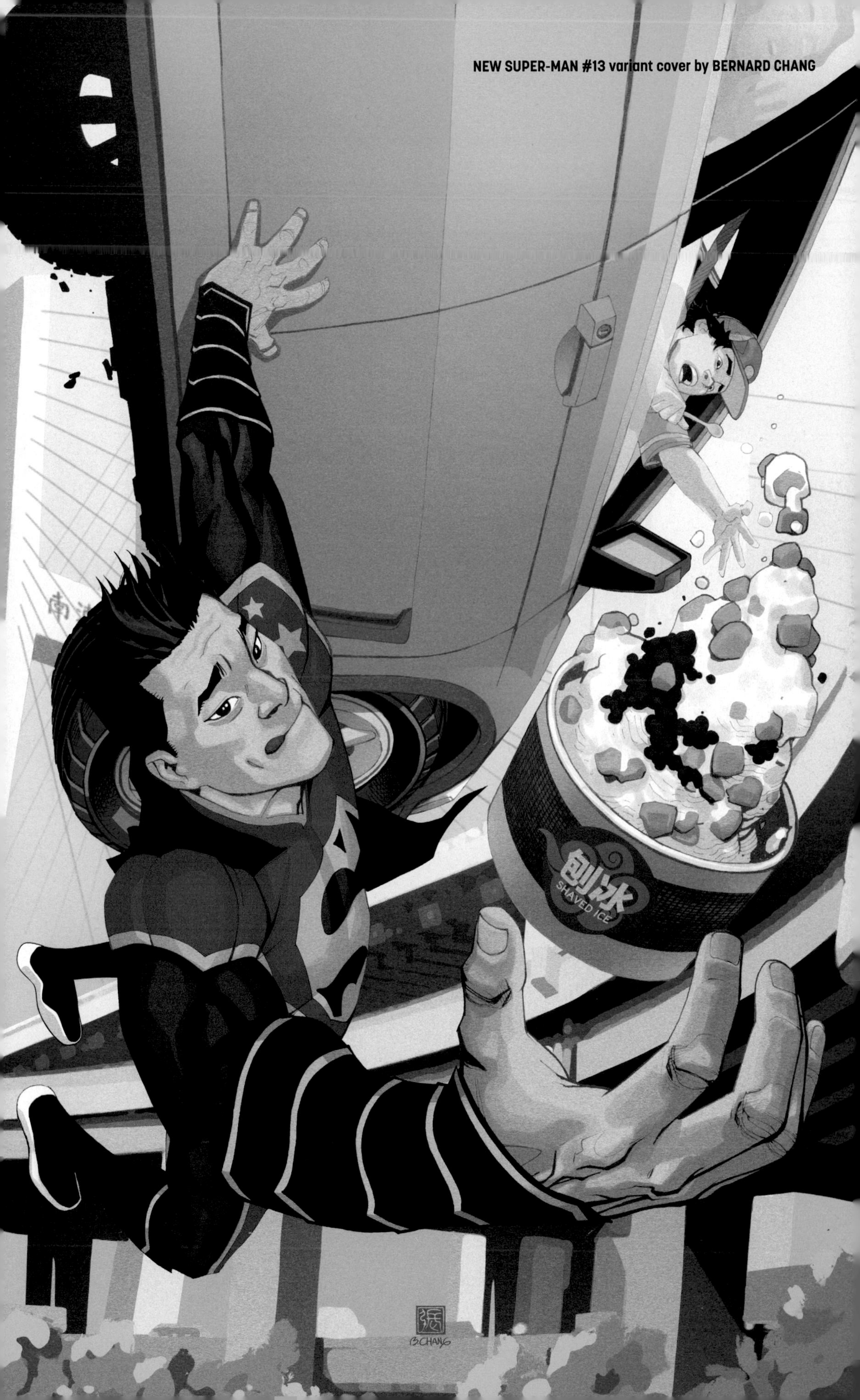
刨冰
SHAVED ICE
B.CHANG
NEW SUPER-MAN #13 variant cover by BERNARD CHANG

NEW SUPER-MAN #14 variant cover by BERNARD CHANG

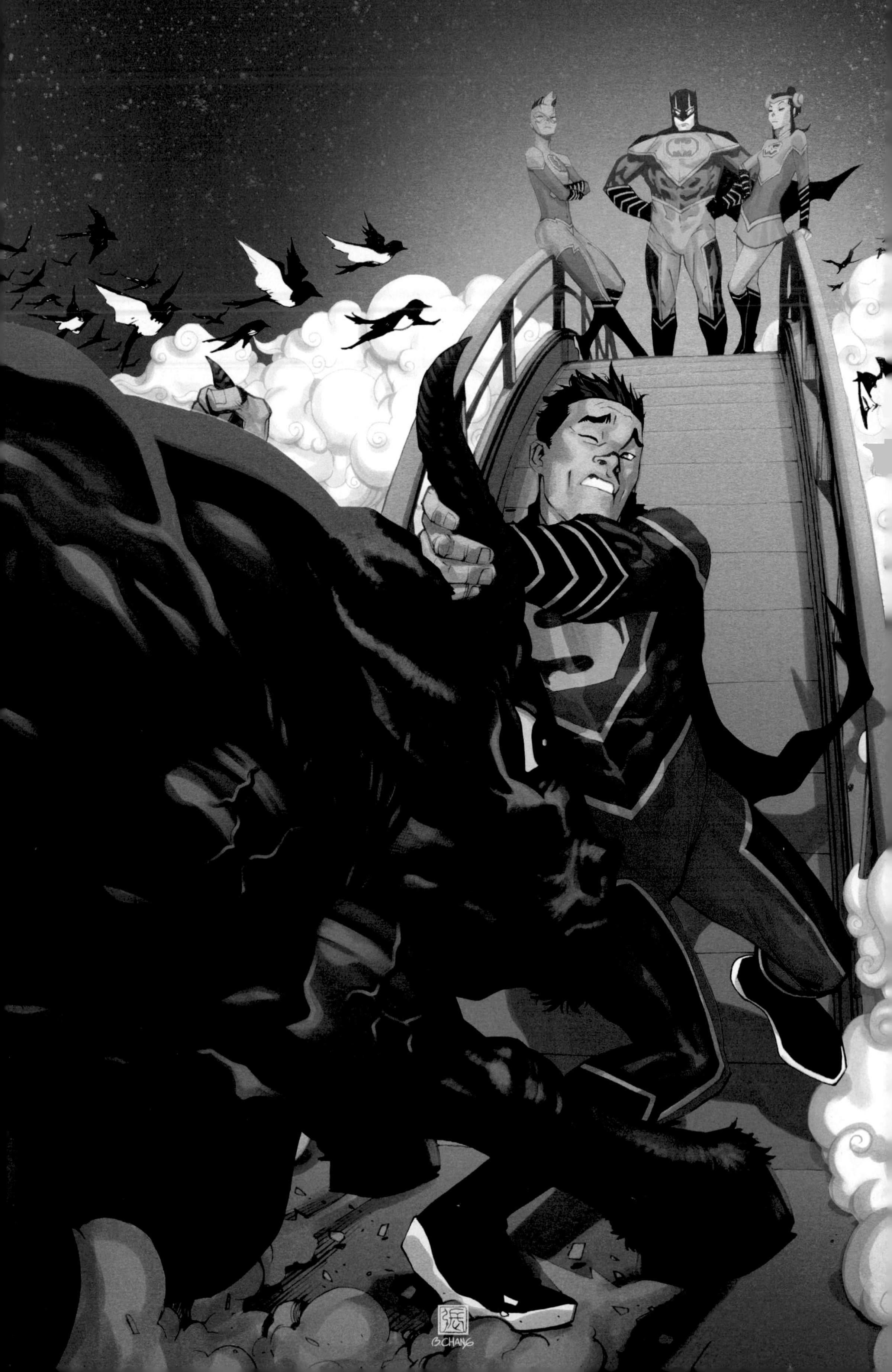

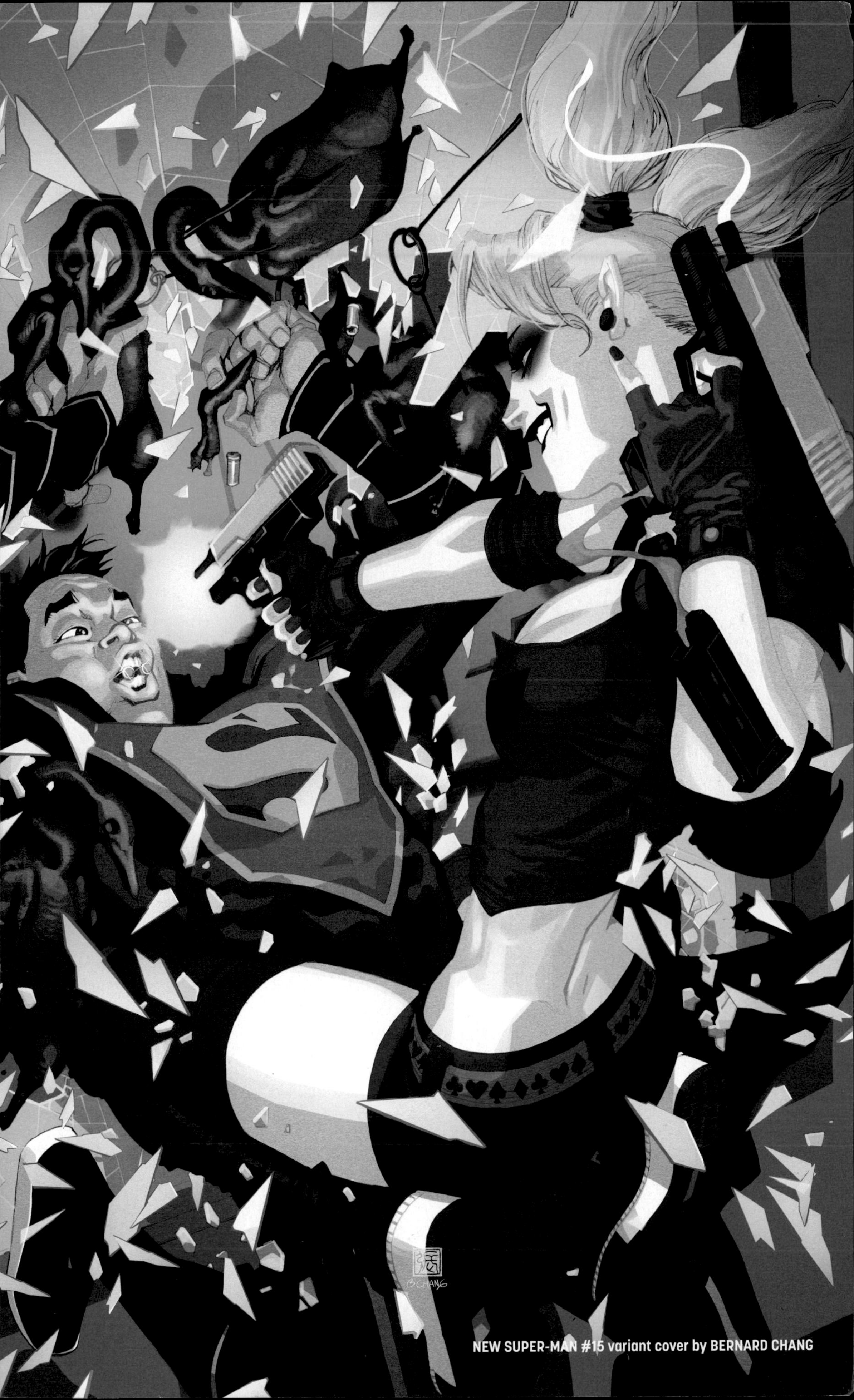

NEW SUPER-MAN #15 variant cover by BERNARD CHANG

NEW SUPER-MAN #16 variant cover by BERNARD CHANG

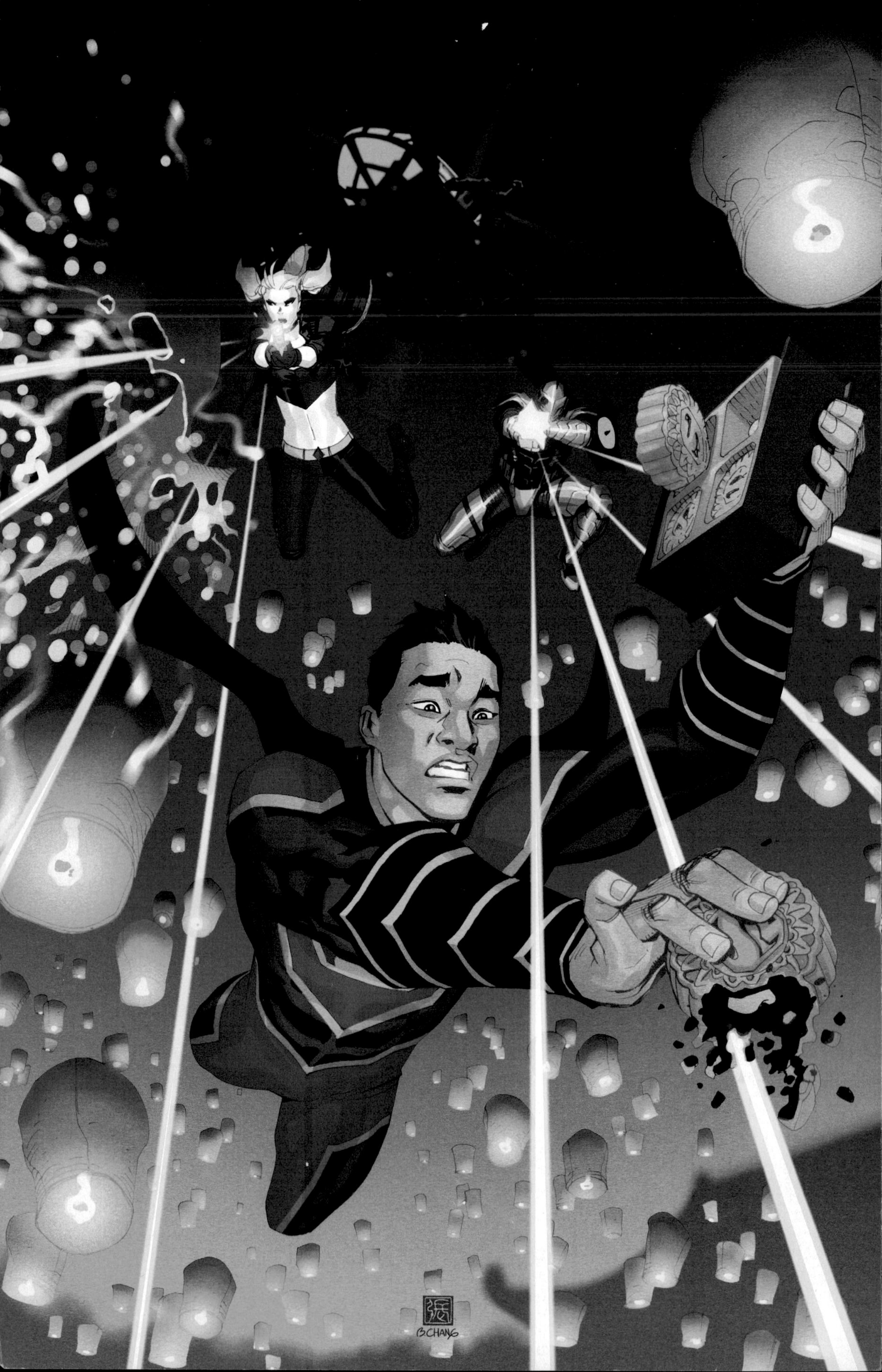

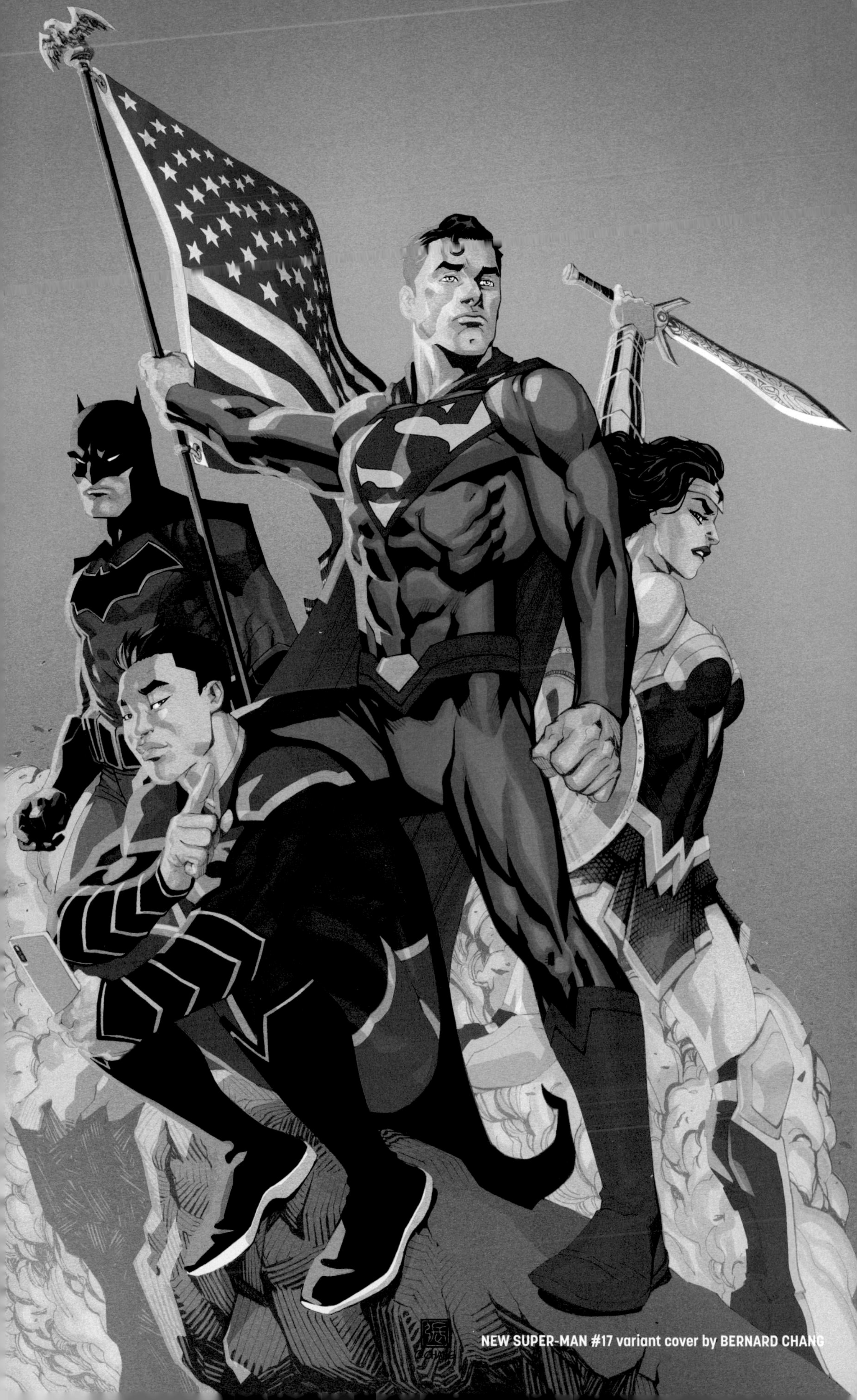

NEW SUPER-MAN #17 variant cover by BERNARD CHANG

NEW SUPER-MAN #18 variant cover by BERNARD CHANG

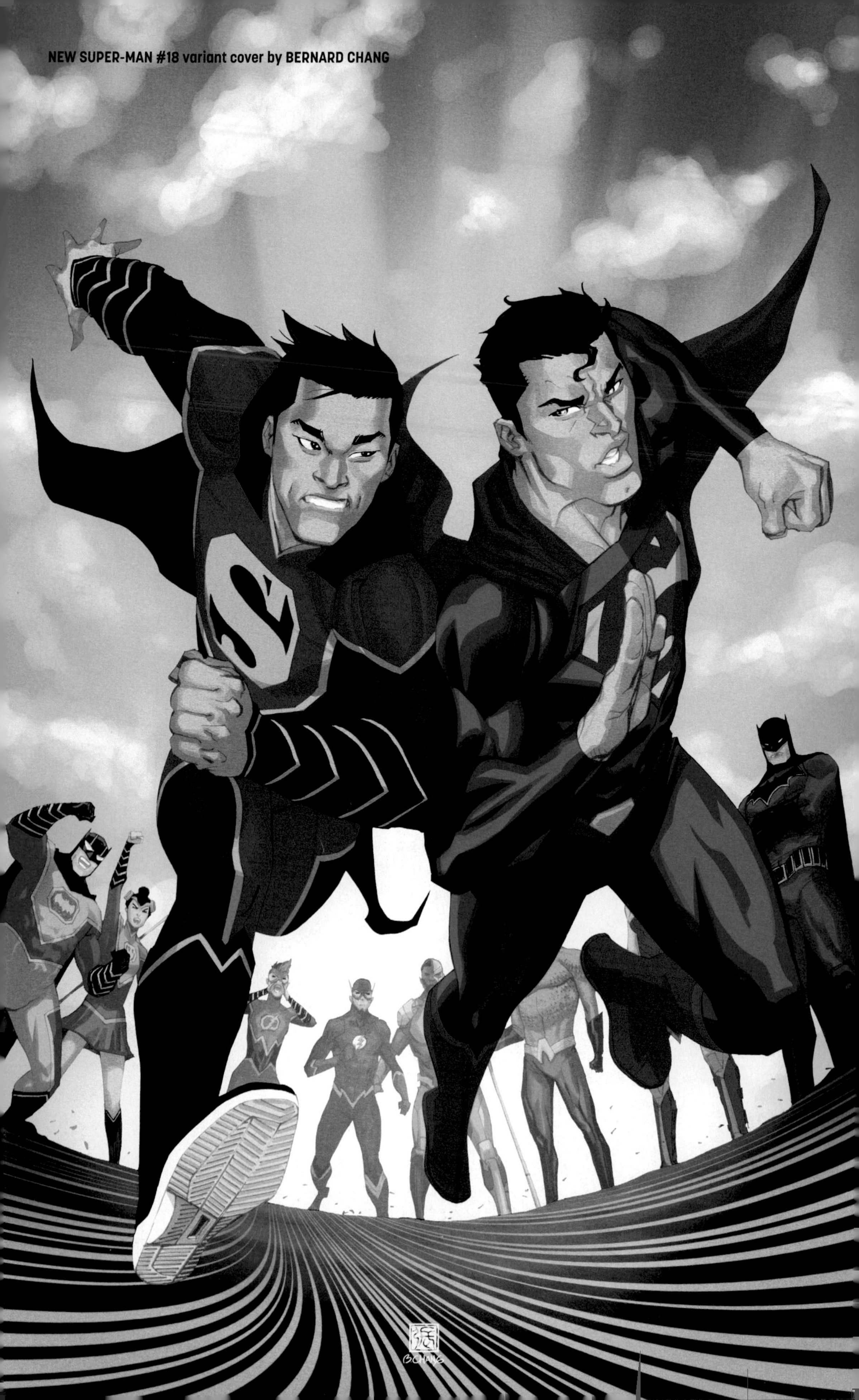

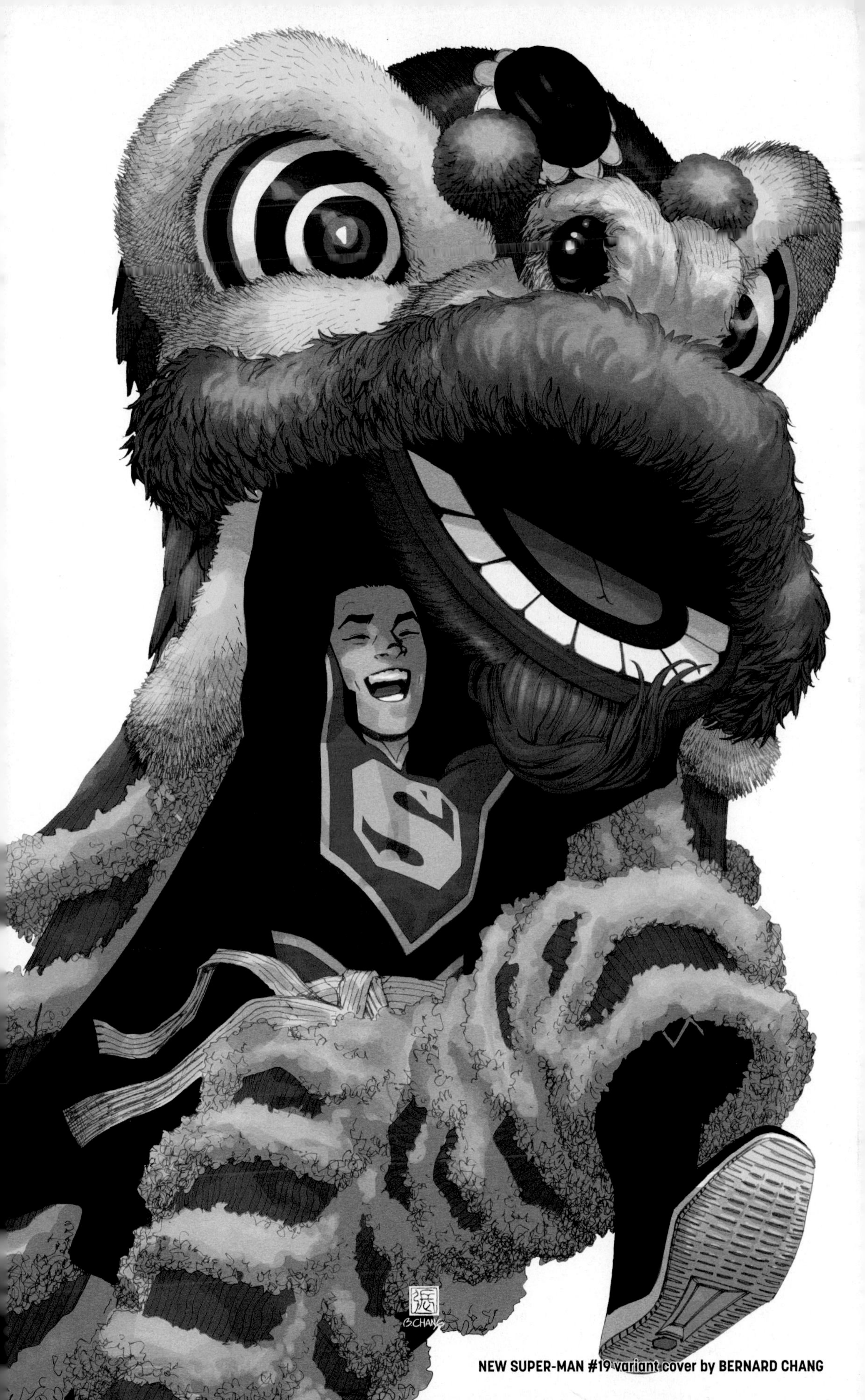
B CHANG

NEW SUPER-MAN #19 variant cover by BERNARD CHANG

EMPEROR DOOMSDAY SUPER-MAN CHARACTER DESIGNS
by BRENT PEEPLES

SHARP TEETH
WHITE HAIR
NORMAL COLOR WAY FOR COSTUME
GRAY SCALEY/ROCKY body SKIN
SPIKES
RIPPED BODY SUIT
RIPPED CAPE
CRACKED ARMOR

SHARP TEETH
CRACKED HELMET ALLOWS SOME HAIR THROUGH
NORMAL COLOR WAY FOR COSTUME
GRAY SCALEY/ROCKY body SKIN
SPIKES
RIPPED BODY SUIT
RIPPED CAPE
CRACKED ARMOR

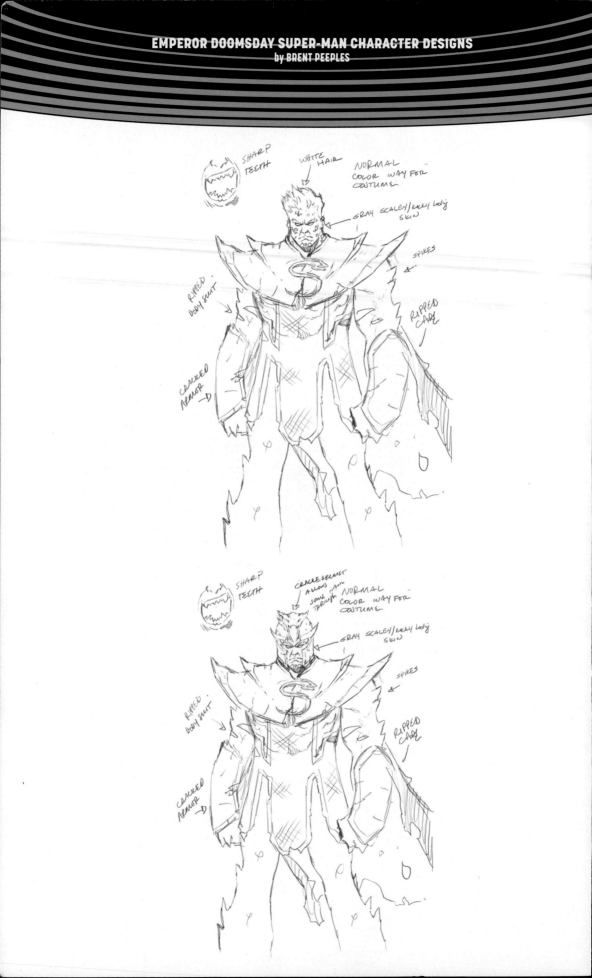

LANTERN CORPS OF CHINA CHARACTER DESIGN
by BRENT PEEPLES

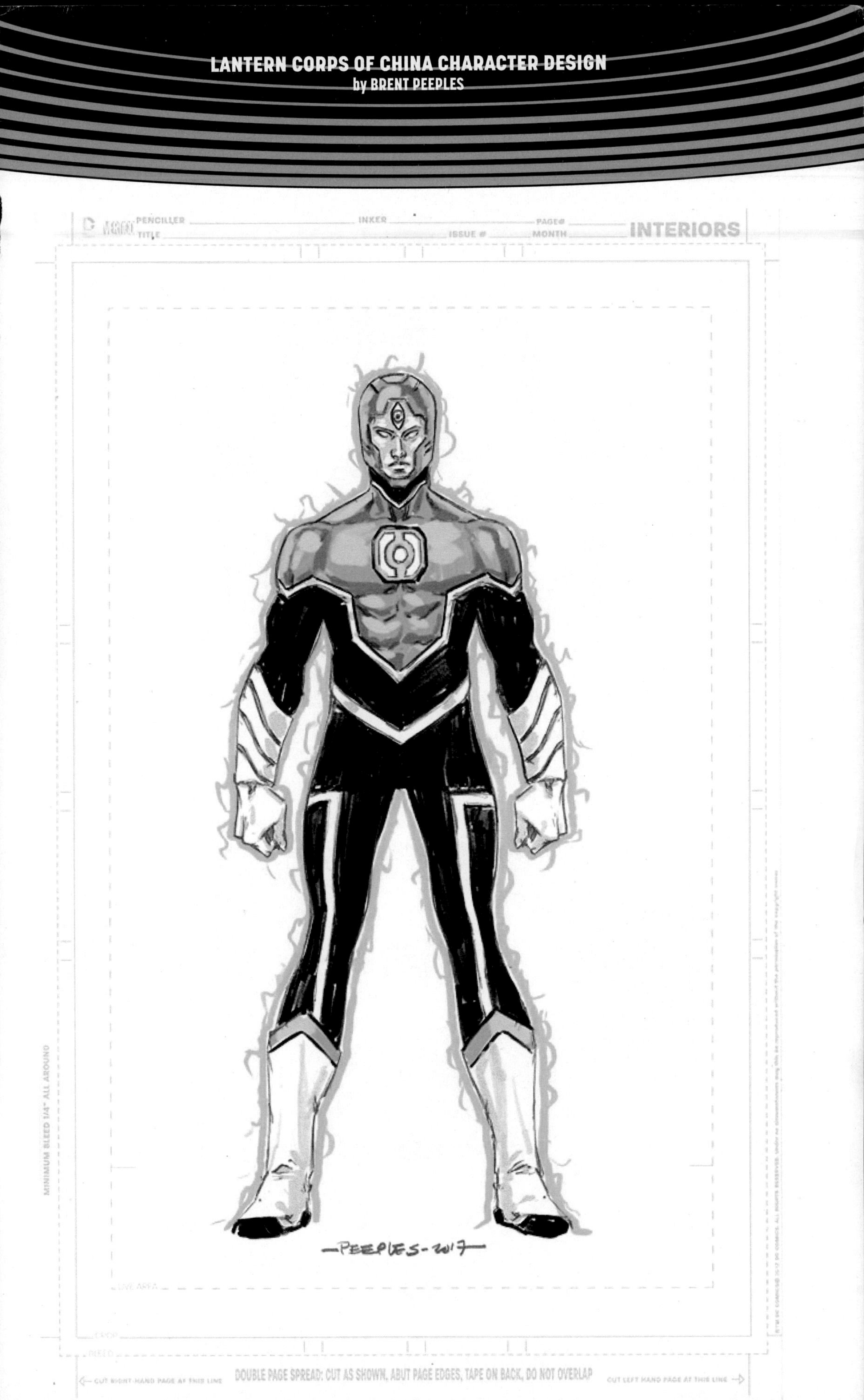
PENCILLER
INKER
PAGE#
TITLE
ISSUE #
MONTH
INTERIORS
-PEEPLES-2017
DOUBLE PAGE SPREAD: CUT AS SHOWN, ABUT PAGE EDGES, TAPE ON BACK, DO NOT OVERLAP

LANTERN CORPS OF CHINA SYMBOL DESIGN
by GENE LUEN YANG

KONG KENAN'S NEW SHIELD DESIGN
by GENE LUEN YANG

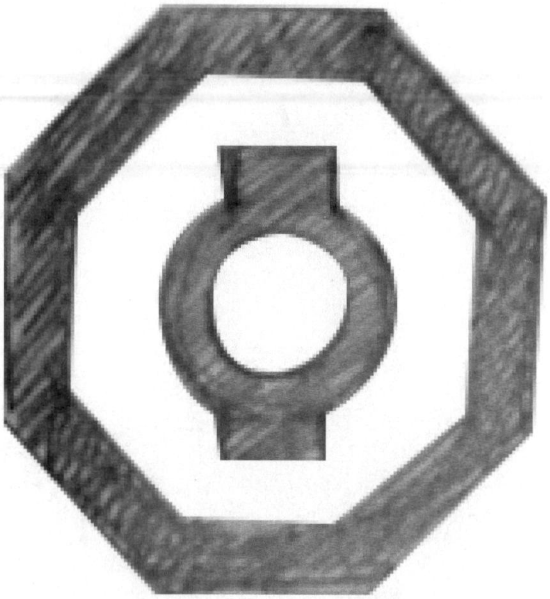

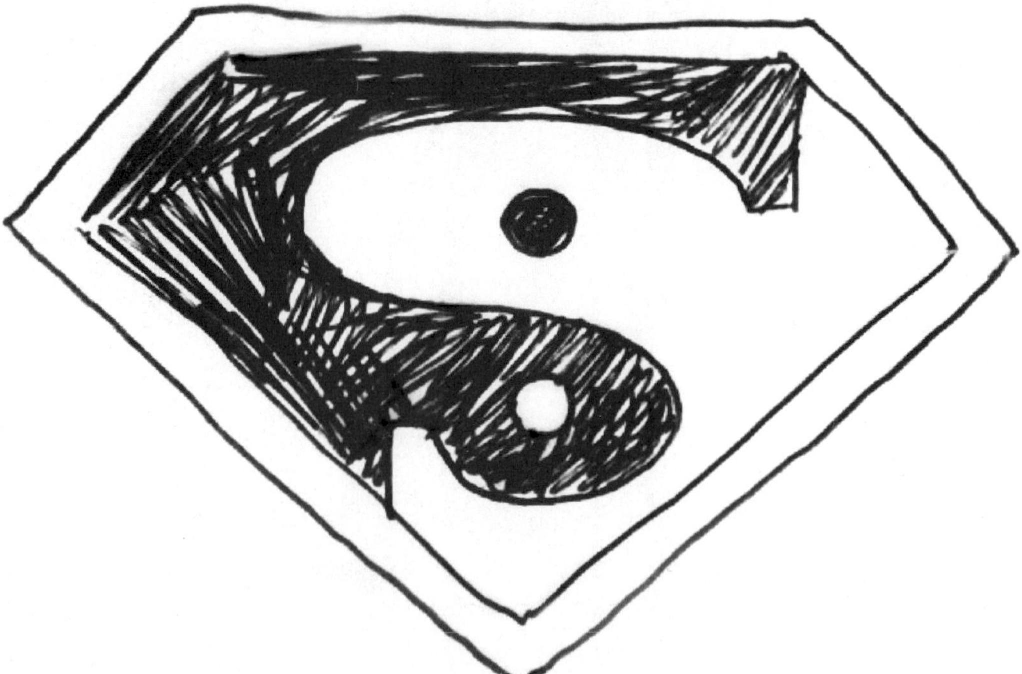